SAPIENTIA

OPEN READINGS IN PHILOSOPHY

COLLECTED & EDITED BY HENRY IMLER

An Aperion Press OER

Columbia, MO

SAPIENTIA

This work was built from a variety of sources including
- Reading for Philosophical Inquiry edited by Lee Archie and John G. Archie
- Introduction to Philosophy Reader, edited by Noah Levin
- The Originals: Classic Readings in Western Philosophy edited by Jeff McLaughlin
- primary texts from a variety of authors; and
- original content and editing by Henry Imler.

THE ORIGINALS USE

INTRODUCTION TO PHILOSOPHY READER USE

PRIMARY TEXTS USE

The inclusion of primary texts are governed by
- the Public Domain,
- the Fair Use Doctrine, or
- by permission of the author.

At the end of each reading we provide which of these uses applies to the best of our judgement.

COVER IMAGE

Blake, William. *Nebuchadnezzar* (between c. 1795 and 1805)
The painting is in the public domain.

COMPLAINT MECHANISM

If you believe yourself to be the copyright holder of any of the primary texts and believe that our use of the work is not governed by the Public Domain, Fair Use, or you wish to rescind the permission given, please contact the editor by means of the following:

Email henryi@macc.edu with the subject "Sapientia Copyright Complaint".

Upon receiving your communication, we will dialog with you concerning the use and go from there, possibly removing the work from the primary texts portion.

CONTENTS

INTRODUCTION

Henry Imler

> Information is power. But like all power, there are those who want to keep it for themselves. The world's entire scientific and cultural heritage, published over centuries in books and journals, is increasingly being digitized and locked up by a handful of private corporations. Want to read the papers featuring the most famous results of the sciences? You'll need to send enormous amounts to publishers...

> — Aaron Swartz

Working from the premises that information is not a commodity and that access to it is a human right, we have assembled the following open educational resource OER). It is built from a multitude of sources, the most significant including:

- Bertrand Russell's *The Problems of Philosophy*
- *Reading for Philosophical Inquiry* edited by Lee Archie and John G. Archie
- *Introduction to Philosophy Reader*, edited by Noah Levin
- *The Originals: Classic Readings in Western Philosophy* edited by Jeff McLaughlin

The book is organized into five parts, each for major branches of philosophical inquiry:

- **epistemology** – the study of knowledge and interpretation;
- **metaphysics** — the study of reality, identity, and being beyond the questions and methods of physics;
- **ethics** — the study of applied value; and
- **political philosophy** — they study of organizing societies and resources.

The text is designed for use in an introductory course on philosophy in a community college classroom. As the base level, this text is covered by the Creative Commons Attribution-NonCommercial-ShareAlike 4.0 International license.

This is the second edition of the text.

PHILOSOPHY IN AND OF ITSELF

THE ALLEGORY OF THE CAVE

Plato

Socrates: AND NOW, I SAID, let me show in a figure how far our nature is enlightened or unenlightened:–Behold! human beings living in an underground den, which has a mouth open towards the light and reaching all along the den; here they have been from their childhood, and have their legs and necks chained so that they cannot move, and can only see before them, being prevented by the chains from turning round their heads. Above and behind them a fire is blazing at a distance, and between the fire and the prisoners there is a raised way; and you will see, if you look, a low wall built along the way, like the screen which marionette players have in front of them, over which they show the puppets.

Glaucon: I see.

Soctates: And do you see, I said, men passing along the wall carrying all sorts of vessels, and statues and figures of animals made of wood and stone and various materials, which appear over the wall? Some of them are talking, others silent.

Glaucon: You have shown me a strange image, and they are strange prisoners.

Socrates: Like ourselves and they see only their own shadows, or the shadows of one another, which the fire throws on the opposite wall of the cave?

Glaucon: True how could they see anything but the shadows if they were never allowed to move their heads?

Socrates: And of the objects which are being carried in like manner they would only see the shadows?

Glaucon: Yes.

Socrates: And if they were able to converse with one another, would they not suppose that they were naming what was actually before them?

Glaucon: Very true.

Socrates: And suppose further that the prison had an echo which came from the other side, would they not be sure to fancy when one of the passersby spoke that the voice which they heard came from the passing shadow?

Glaucon: No question.

Socrates: To them, the truth would be literally nothing but the shadows of the images.

Glaucon: That is certain.

Socrates: And now look again, and see what will naturally follow if the prisoners are released and disabused of their error. At first, when any of them is liberated and compelled suddenly to stand up and turn his neck round and walk and look towards the light, he will suffer sharp pains; the glare will distress him, and he will be unable to see the realities of which in his former state he had seen the shadows; and then conceive some one saying to him, that what he saw before was an illusion, but that now, when he is approaching nearer to being and his eye is turned towards more real existence, he has a clearer vision, what will be his reply?

And you may further imagine that his instructor is pointing to the objects as they pass and requiring him to name them, will he not be perplexed? Will he not fancy that the shadows which he formerly saw are truer than the objects which are now shown to him?

Glaucon: Far truer.

Socrates: And if he is compelled to look straight at the light, will he not have a pain in his eyes which will make him turn away to take and take in the objects of vision which he can see, and which he will conceive to be in reality clearer than the things which are now being shown to him?

Glaucon: True.

Socrates: And suppose once more, that he is reluctantly dragged up a steep and rugged ascent, and held fast until he's forced into the presence of the sun himself, is he not likely to be pained and irritated? When he approaches the light his eyes will be dazzled, and he will not be able to see anything at all of what are now called realities.

Glaucon: Not all in a moment.

Socrates: He will require to grow accustomed to the sight of the upper world. And first he will see the shadows best, next the reflections of men and other objects in the water, and then the objects themselves; then he will gaze upon the light of the moon and the stars and the spangled heaven; and he will see the sky and the stars by night better than the sun or the light of the sun by day?

Glaucon: Certainly.

Socrates: Last of he will be able to see the sun, and not mere reflections of him in the water, but he will see him in his own proper place, and not in another; and he will contemplate him as he is.

Glaucon: Certainly.

Socrates: He will then proceed to argue that this is he who gives the season and the years, and is the guardian of all that is in the visible world, and in a certain way the cause of all things which he and his fellows have been accustomed to behold?

Glaucon: Clearly he would first see the sun and then reason about him.

Socrates: And when he remembered his old habitation, and the wisdom of the den and his fellow prisoners, do you not suppose that he would felicitate himself on the change, and pity them?

Glaucon: Certainly, he would.

Socrates: And if they were in the habit of conferring honors among themselves on those who were quickest to observe the passing shadows and to remark which of them went before, and which followed after, and which were together; and who were therefore best able to draw conclusions as to the future, do you think that he would care for such honors and glories, or envy the possessors of them? Would he not say with Homer,

to be the poor servant of a poor master,

And to endure anything, rather than think as they do and live after their manner?

Glaucon: Yes, I think that he would rather suffer anything than entertain these false notions and live in this miserable manner.

Socrates: Imagine once more, such an one coming suddenly out of the sun to be replaced in his old situation;

would he not be certain to have his eyes full of darkness?

Glaucon: To be sure.

Socrates: And if there were a contest, and he had to compete in measuring the shadows with the prisoners who had never moved out of the den, while his sight was still weak, and before his eyes had become steady (and the time which would be needed to acquire this new habit of sight might be very considerable) would he not be ridiculous? Men would say of him that up he went and down he came without his eyes; and that it was better not even to think of ascending; and if any one tried to loose another and lead him up to the light, let them only catch the offender, and they would put him to death.

Glaucon: No question.

Socrates: This entire allegory, you may now append, dear Glaucon, to the previous argument; the prison house is the world of sight, the light of the fire is the sun, and you will not misapprehend me if you interpret the journey upwards to be the ascent of the soul into the intellectual world according to my poor belief, which, at your desire, I have expressed whether rightly or wrongly God knows. But, whether true or false, my opinion is that in the world of knowledge the idea of good appears last of all, and is seen only with an effort; and, when seen, is also inferred to be the universal author of all things beautiful and right, parent of light and of the lord of light in this visible world, and the immediate source of reason and truth in the intellectual; and that this is the power upon which he who would act rationally, either in public or private life must have his eye fixed.

Glaucon: I agree, as far as I am able to understand you.

Socrates: Moreover, you must not wonder that those who attain to this beatific vision are unwilling to descend to human affairs; for their souls are ever hastening into the upper world where they desire to dwell; which desire of theirs is very natural, if our allegory may be trusted.

Glaucon: Yes, very natural.

Socrates: And is there anything surprising in one who passes from divine contemplations to the evil state of man, misbehaving himself in a ridiculous manner; if, while his eyes are blinking and before he has become accustomed to the surrounding darkness, he is compelled to fight in courts of law, or in other places, about the images or the shadows of images of justice, and is endeavoring to meet the conceptions of those who have never yet seen absolute justice?

Glaucon: Anything but surprising, he replied.

Socrates: Anyone who has common sense will remember

that the bewilderments of the eyes are of two kinds, and arise from two causes, either from coming out of the light or from going into the light, which is true of the mind's eye, quite as much as of the bodily eye; and he who remembers this when he sees any one whose vision is perplexed and weak, will not be too ready to laugh; he will first ask whether that soul of man has come out of the brighter light, and is unable to see because unaccustomed to the dark, or having turned from darkness to the day is dazzled by excess of light. And he will count the one happy in his condition and state of being, and he will pity the other; or, if he have a mind to laugh at the soul which comes from below into the light, there will be more reason in this than in the laugh which greets him who returns from above out of the light into the den.

Glaucon: That, is a very just distinction.

Socrates: But then, if I am right, certain professors of education must be wrong when they say that they can put a knowledge into the soul which was not there before, like sight into blind eyes.

Glaucon: They undoubtedly say this.

Socrates: Whereas, our argument shows that the power and capacity of learning exists in the soul already; and that just as the eye was unable to turn from darkness to light without the whole body, so too the instrument of knowledge can only by the movement of the whole soul be turned from the world of becoming into that of being, and learn by degrees to endure the sight of being, and of the brightest and best of being, or in other words, of the good.

Glaucon: Very true.

Socrates: And must there not be some art which will effect conversion in the easiest and quickest manner; not implanting the faculty of sight, for that exists already, but has been turned in the wrong direction, and is looking away from the truth?

Glaucon: Yes, such an art may be presumed.

Socrates: And whereas the other socalled virtues of the soul seem to be akin to bodily qualities, for even when they are not originally innate they can be implanted later by habit and exercise, the virtue of wisdom more than anything else contains a divine element which always remains, and by this conversion is rendered useful and profitable; or, on the other hand, hurtful and useless. Did you never observe the narrow intelligence flashing from the keen eye of a clever rogue–how eager he is, how clearly his paltry soul sees the way to his end; he is the reverse of blind, but his keen eyesight is forced into the service of evil, and he is mischievous in proportion to his cleverness.

Glaucon: Very true.

Socrates: But what if there had been a circumcision of such natures in the days of their youth; and they had been severed from those sensual pleasures, such as eating and drinking, which, like leaden weights, were attached to them at their birth, and which drag them down and turn the vision of their souls upon the things that are below–if, I say, they had been released from these impediments and turned in the opposite direction, the very same faculty in them would have seen the truth as keenly as they see what their eyes are turned to now.

Glaucon: Very likely.

Socrates: Yes, and there is another thing which is likely. or rather a necessary inference from what has preceded, that neither the uneducated and uninformed of the truth, nor yet those who never make an end of their education, will be able ministers of State; not the former, because they have no single aim of duty which is the rule of all their actions, private as well as public; nor the latter, because they will not act at all except upon compulsion, fancying that they are already dwelling apart in the islands of the blest.

Glaucon: Very true.

Socrates: Then, the business of us who are the founders of the State will be to compel the best minds to attain that knowledge which we have already shown to be the greatest of allthey must continue to ascend until they arrive at the good; but when they have ascended and seen enough we must not allow them to do as they do now.

Glaucon: What do you mean?

Socrates: I mean that they remain in the upper world: but this must not be allowed; they must be made to descend again among the prisoners in the den, and partake of their labours and honors, whether they are worth having or not.

Glaucon: But is not this unjust? Ought we to give them a worse life, when they might have a better?

Socrates: You have again forgotten, my friend, the intention of the legislator, who did not aim at making any one class in the State happy above the rest; the happiness was to be in the whole State, and he held the citizens together by persuasion and necessity, making them benefactors of the State, and therefore benefactors of one another; to this end he created them, not to please themselves, but to be his instruments in binding up the State.

Citation and Use

The text was taken from the following work.

Plato, "Republic, Book 7," in PLATO IN TWELVE VOLUMES, trans. Paul Shorey, vol. 5 and 6, 12 vols. (Cambridge, MA: Harvard University Press, 1969), http://data.perseus.org/citations/urn:cts:greek-Lit:tlg0059.tlg030.perseus-eng1:1.

THE APOLOGY

Plato

Socrates Requests a Just Listening

How you, O Athenians, have been affected by my accusers, I cannot tell; but I know that they almost made me forget who I was—so persuasively did they speak; and yet they have hardly uttered a word of truth. But of the many falsehoods told by them, there was one which quite amazed me;—I mean when they said that you should be upon your guard and not allow yourselves to be deceived by the force of my eloquence. To say this, when they were certain to be detected as soon as I opened my lips and proved myself to be anything but a great speaker, did indeed appear to me most shameless—unless by the force of eloquence they mean the force of truth; for is such is their meaning, I admit that I am eloquent. But in how different a way from theirs! Well, as I was saying, they have scarcely spoken the truth at all; but from me you shall hear the whole truth: not, however, delivered after their manner in a set oration duly ornamented with words and phrases. No, by heaven! but I shall use the words and arguments which occur to me at the moment; for I am confident in the justice of my cause (Or, I am certain that I am right in taking this course.): at my time of life I ought not to be appearing before you, O men of Athens, in the character of a juvenile orator—let no one expect it of me. And I must beg of you to grant me a favor:—If I defend myself in my accustomed manner, and you hear me using the words which I have been in the habit of using in the agora, at the tables of the money changers, or anywhere else, I would ask you not to be surprised, and not to interrupt me on this account. For I am more than seventy years of age, and appearing now for the first time in a court of law, I am quite a stranger to the language of the place; and therefore I would have you regard me as if I were really a stranger, whom you would excuse if he spoke in his native tongue, and after the fashion of his country:—Am I making an unfair request of you? Never mind the manner, which may or may not be good; but think only of the truth of my words, and give heed to that: let the speaker speak truly and the judge decide justly.

Charges of the Older Accusers

And first, I have to reply to the older charges and to my first accusers, and then I will go on to the later ones. For of old I have had many accusers, who have accused me falsely to you during many years; and I am more afraid of them than of Anytus and his associates, who are dangerous, too, in their own way. But far more dangerous are the others, who began when you were children, and took possession of your minds with their falsehoods, telling of one Socrates, a wise man, who speculated about the heaven above, and searched into the earth beneath, and made the worse appear the better cause. The disseminators of this tale are the accusers whom I dread; for their hearers are apt to fancy that such enquirers do not believe in the existence of the gods. And they are many, and their charges against me are of ancient date, and they were made by them in the days when you were more impressible than you are now—in childhood, or it may have been in youth—and the cause when heard went by default, for there was none to answer. And hardest of all, I do not know and cannot tell the names of my accusers; unless in the chance case of a Comic poet.

All who from envy and malice have persuaded you—some of them having first convinced themselves—all this class of men are most difficult to deal with; for I cannot have them up here, and cross-examine them, and therefore I must simply fight with shadows in my own defense, and argue when there is no one who answers. I will ask you then to assume with me, as I was saying, that my opponents are of two kinds; one recent, the other ancient: and I hope that you will see the propriety of my answering the latter first, for these accusations you heard long before the others, and much oftener.

Well, then, I must make my defense, and endeavor to clear away in a short time, a slander which has lasted a long time. May I succeed, if to succeed be for my good and yours, or likely to avail me in my cause! The task is not an easy one; I quite understand the nature of it. And so leaving the event with God, in obedience to the law I will now make my defense.

Defense Against Older Accusations

I will begin at the beginning, and ask what is the accusation which has given rise to the slander of me, and in fact has encouraged Meletus to proof this charge against me. Well, what do the slanderers say? They shall be my prosecutors, and I will sum up their words in an affidavit: "Socrates is an evildoer, and a curious person, who searches into things under the earth and in heaven, and he makes the worse appear the better cause; and he teaches the aforesaid doctrines to others."

Such is the nature of the accusation: it is just what you have yourselves seen in the comedy of Aristophanes, who has introduced a man whom he calls Socrates, going about and saying that he walks in air, and talking a deal of nonsense concerning matters of which I do not pretend to know either much or little—not that I mean to speak disparagingly of any one who is a student of natural philosophy.

I should be very sorry if Meletus could bring so grave a charge against me. But the simple truth is, O Athenians, that I have nothing to do with physical speculations. Very many of those here present are witnesses to the truth of this, and to them I appeal. Speak then, you who have heard me, and tell your neighbours whether any of you have ever known me hold forth in few words or in many upon such matters. . .You hear their answer. And from what they say of this part of the charge you will be able to judge of the truth of the rest.

As little foundation is there for the report that I am a teacher, and take money; this accusation has no more truth in it than the other. Although, if a man were really able to instruct mankind, to receive money for giving instruction would, in my opinion, be an honor to him. There is Gorgias of Leontium, and Prodicus of Ceos, and Hippias of Elis, who go the round of the cities, and are able to persuade the young men to leave their own citizens by whom they might be taught for nothing, and come to them whom they not only pay, but are thankful if they may be allowed to pay them. There is at this time a Parian philosopher residing in Athens, of whom I have heard; and I came to hear of him in this way:—I came across a man who has spent a world of money on the Sophists, Callias, the son of Hipponicus, and knowing that he had sons, I asked him: "Callias," I said, "if your two sons were foals or calves, there would be no difficulty in finding some one to put over them; we should hire a trainer of horses, or a farmer probably, who would improve and perfect them in their own proper virtue and excellence; but as they are human beings, whom are you thinking of placing over them? Is there any one who understands human and political virtue? You must have thought about the matter, for you have sons; is there any one?" "There is," he said. "Who is he?" said I; "and of what country? and what does he charge?" "Evenus the Parian," he replied; "he is the man, and his charge is five minae." Happy is Evenus, I said to myself, if he really has this wisdom, and teaches at such a moderate charge. Had I the same, I should have been very proud and conceited; but the truth is that I have no knowledge of the kind.

Delphic Oracle

I dare say, Athenians, that some one among you will reply, "Yes, Socrates, but what is the origin of these accusations which are brought against you; there must have been something strange which you have been doing? All these rumours and this talk about you would never have arisen if you had been like other men: tell us, then, what is the cause of them, for we should be sorry to judge hastily of you." Now I regard this as a fair challenge, and I will endeavour to explain to you the reason why I am called wise and have such an evil fame. Please to attend then. And although some of you may think that I am joking, I declare that I will tell you the entire truth. Men of Athens, this reputation of mine has come of a certain sort of wisdom which I possess. If you ask me what kind of wisdom, I reply, wisdom such as may perhaps be attained by man, for to that extent I am inclined to believe that I am wise; whereas the persons of whom I was speaking have a superhuman wisdom which I may fail to describe, because I have it not myself; and he who says that I have, speaks falsely, and is taking away my character. And here, O men of Athens, I must beg you not to interrupt me, even if I seem to say something extravagant. For the word which I will speak is not mine. I will refer you to a witness who is worthy of credit; that witness shall be the God of Delphi—he will tell you about my wisdom, if I have any, and of what sort it is. You must have known Chaerephon; he was early a friend of mine, and also a friend of yours, for he shared in the recent exile of the people, and returned with you. Well, Chaerephon, as you know, was very impetuous in all his doings, and he went to Delphi and boldly asked the oracle to tell him whether—as I was saying, I must beg you not to interrupt—he asked the oracle to tell him whether anyone was wiser than I was, and the Pythian prophetess answered, that there was no man wiser. Chaerephon is dead himself; but his brother, who is in court, will confirm the truth of what I am saying.

Socrates Cross-examines Others

Why do I mention this? Because I am going to explain to you why I have such an evil name. When I heard the answer, I said to myself, What can the god mean? and what is the interpretation of his riddle? for I know that I have no wisdom, small or great. What then can he mean when he says that I am the wisest of men? And yet he is a god, and cannot lie; that would be against his nature. After long consideration, I thought of a method of trying the question. I reflected that if I could only find a man wiser than myself, then I might go to the god with a refutation in my hand. I should say to him, "Here is a man who is wiser than I am; but you said that I was the wisest." Accordingly I went to one who had the reputation of wisdom, and observed him—his name I need not mention; he was a politician whom I selected for examination—and the result was as follows: When I began to talk with him, I could not help thinking that he was not really wise, although he was thought wise by many, and still wiser by himself; and thereupon I tried to explain to him that he thought himself wise, but was not really wise; and the consequence was that he hated me, and his enmity was shared by several who were present and heard me. So, I left him, saying to myself, as I went away: Well, although I do not suppose that either of us knows anything really beautiful and good, I am better off than he is, — for he knows nothing, and thinks that he knows; I neither know nor think that I know. In this latter particular, then, I seem to have slightly the advantage of him. Then I went to another who had still higher pretensions to wisdom, and my conclusion was exactly the same. Whereupon I made another enemy of him, and of many others besides him. Then I went to one man after another, being not unconscious of the enmity which I provoked, and I lamented and feared this: but necessity was laid upon me, —the word of God, I thought, ought to be considered first. And I said to myself, Go I must to all who appear to know, and find out the meaning of the oracle. And I swear to you, Athenians, by the dog I swear! —for I must tell you the truth—the result of my mission was just this: I found that the men most in repute were all but the most foolish; and that others less esteemed were really wiser and better. I will tell you the tale of my wanderings and of the "Herculean" labors, as I may call them, which I endured only to find at last the oracle irrefutable. After the politicians, I went to the poets; tragic, dithyrambic, and all sorts. And there, I said to myself, you will be instantly detected; now you will find out that you are more ignorant than they are. Accordingly, I took them some of the most elaborate passages in their own writings, and asked what was the meaning of them—thinking that they would teach me something. Will you believe me? I am almost ashamed to confess the truth, but I must say that there is hardly a person present who would not have talked better about their poetry than they did themselves. Then I knew that not by wisdom do poets write poetry, but by a sort of genius and inspiration; they are like diviners or soothsayers who also say many fine things, but do not understand the meaning of them. The poets appeared to me to be much in the same case; and I further observed that upon the strength of their poetry they believed themselves to be the wisest of men in other things in which they were not wise. So, I departed, conceiving myself to be superior to them for the same reason that I was superior to the politicians.

At last I went to the artisans. I was conscious that I knew nothing at all, as I may say, and I was sure that they knew many fine things; and here I was not mistaken, for they did know many things of which I was ignorant, and in this they certainly were wiser than I was. But I observed that even the good artisans fell into the same error as the poets;—because they were good workmen they thought that they also knew all sorts of high matters, and this defect in them overshadowed their wisdom; and therefore I asked myself on behalf of the oracle, whether I would like to be as I was, neither having their knowledge nor their ignorance, or like them in both; and I made answer to myself and to the oracle that I was better off as I was.

Why Socrates is Wise

This inquisition has led to my having many enemies of the worst and most dangerous kind, and has given occasion also to many calumnies. And I am called wise, for my hearers always imagine that I myself possess the wisdom which I find wanting in others: but the truth is, O men of Athens, that God only is wise; and by his answer he intends to show that the wisdom of men is worth little or nothing; he is not speaking of Socrates, he is only using my name by way of illustration, as if he said, He, O men, is the wisest, who, like Socrates, knows that his wisdom is in truth worth nothing. And so I go about the world, obedient to the god, and search and make inquiry into the wisdom of any one, whether citizen or stranger, who appears to be wise; and if he is not wise, then in vindication of the oracle I show him that he is not wise; and my occupation quite absorbs me, and I have no time to give either to any public matter of interest or to any concern of my own, but I am in utter poverty by reason of my devotion to the god.

Prejudice Against Socrates

There is another thing:—young men of the richer classes, who have not much to do, come about me of their own accord; they like to hear the pretenders examined, and they often imitate me, and proceed to examine others; there are plenty of persons, as they quickly discover, who think that they know something, but really know little or nothing; and then those who are examined by them instead of being angry with themselves are angry with me: This confounded Socrates, they say; this villainous misleader of youth!— and then if somebody asks them, Why, what evil does he practice or teach? they do not know, and cannot tell; but in order that they may not appear to be at a loss, they repeat the ready made charges which are used against all philosophers about teaching things up in the clouds and under the earth, and having no gods, and making the worse appear the better cause; for they do not like to confess that their pretense of knowledge has been detected— which is the truth; and as they are numerous and ambitious and energetic, and are drawn up in battle array and have persuasive tongues, they have filled your ears with their loud and inveterate calumnies. And this is the reason why my three accusers, Meletus and Anytus and Lycon, have set upon me; Meletus, who has a quarrel with me on behalf of the poets; Anytus, on behalf of the craftsmen and politicians; Lycon, on behalf of the rhetoricians: and as I said at the beginning, I cannot expect to get rid of such a mass of calumny all in a moment. And this, O men of Athens, is the truth and the whole truth; I have concealed nothing, I have dissembled nothing. And yet, I know that my plainness of speech makes them hate me, and what is their hatred but a proof that I am speaking the truth? —Hence has arisen the prejudice against me; and this is the reason of it, as you will find out either in this or in any future inquiry.

Defence Against Corruption of the Youth

Editor's Note: For this part of the Apology, we have added in who is speaking at any particular point as Socrates asks questions and others answer.

Socrates: I have said enough in my defense against the first class of my accusers; I turn to the second class. They are headed by Meletus, that good man and true lover of his country, as he calls himself. Against these, too, I must try to make a defense: —Let their affidavit be read: it contains something of this kind: It says that Socrates is a doer of evil, who corrupts the youth; and who does not believe in the gods of the state, but has other new divinities of his own. Such is the charge; and now let us examine the particular counts. He says that I am a doer of evil, and corrupt the youth; but I say, O men of Athens, that Meletus is a doer of evil, in that he pretends to be in earnest when he is only in jest, and is so eager to bring men to trial from a pretended zeal and interest about matters in which he really never had the smallest interest. And the truth of this I will endeavor to prove to you. Come hither, Meletus, and let me ask a question of you. You think a great deal about the improvement of youth?

Meletus: Yes, I do.

Socrates: Tell the judges, then, who is their improver; for you must know, as you have taken the pains to discover their corrupter, and are citing and accusing me before them. Speak, then, and tell the judges who their improver is—observe, Meletus, that you are silent, and have nothing to say. But is not this rather disgraceful, and a very considerable proof of what I was saying, that you have no interest in the matter? Speak up, friend, and tell us who their improver is.

Meletus: The laws.

Socrates: But that, my good sir, is not my meaning. I want to know who the person is, who, in the first place, knows the laws.

Meletus: The judges, Socrates, who are present in court.

Socrates: What, do you mean to say, Meletus, that they are able to instruct and improve youth?

Meletus: Certainly, they are.

What, all of them, or some only and not others?

Meletus: All of them.

Socrates: By the goddess Here, that is good news! There are plenty of improvers, then. And what do you say of the audience—do they improve them?

Meletus: Yes, they do.

And the senators?

Meletus: Yes, the senators improve them.

Socrates: But perhaps the members of the assembly corrupt them? —or do they too improve them?

Meletus: They improve them.

Socrates: Then every Athenian improves and elevates them; all with the exception of myself; and I alone am their corrupter? Is that what you affirm?

Meletus: That is what I stoutly affirm.

Socrates: I am very unfortunate if you are right. But suppose I ask you a question: How about horses? Does one man do them harm and all the world good? Is not the exact opposite the truth? One man is able to do them good, or at least not many; —the trainer of horses, that is to say, does them good, and others who have to do with them rather injure them? Is not that true, Meletus, of horses, or of any other animals? Most assuredly it is; whether you and Anytus say yes or no. Happy indeed would be the condition of youth if they had one corrupter only, and all the rest of the world were their improvers. But you, Meletus, have sufficiently shown that you never had a thought about the young: your carelessness is seen in your not caring about the very things which you bring against me.

And now, Meletus, I will ask you another question—by Zeus I will: Which is better, to live among bad citizens, or among good ones? Answer, friend, I say; the question is one which may be easily answered. Do not the good do their neighbors good, and the bad do them evil?

Meletus: Certainly.

Socrates: And is there anyone who would rather be injured than benefited by those who live with him? Answer, my good friend, the law requires you to answer—does any one like to be injured?

Meletus: Certainly not.

Socrates: And when you accuse me of corrupting and deteriorating the youth, do you allege that I corrupt them intentionally or unintentionally?

Meletus: Intentionally, I say.

Socrates: But you have just admitted that the good do their neighbors good, and the evil do them evil. Now, is that a truth which your superior wisdom has recognized thus early in life, and am I, at my age, in such darkness and ignorance as not to know that if a man with whom I have to live is corrupted by me, I am very likely to be harmed by him; and yet I corrupt him, and intentionally, too—so you say, although neither I nor any other human being is ever likely to be convinced by you. But either I do not corrupt them, or I corrupt them unintentionally; and on either view of the case you lie. If my offence is unintentional, the law has no cognizance of unintentional offences: you ought to have taken me privately, and warned and admonished me; for if I had been better advised, I should have left off doing what I only did unintentionally—no doubt I should; but you would have nothing to say to me and refused to teach me. And now you bring me up in this court, which is a place not of instruction, but of punishment.

Defense Against Atheism

Editor's Note: For this part of the Apology, we have added in who is speaking at any particular point as Socrates asks questions and others answer.

Socrates: It will be very clear to you, Athenians, as I was saying, that Meletus has no care at all, great or small, about the matter. But still I should like to know, Meletus, in what I am affirmed to corrupt the young. I suppose you mean, as I infer from your indictment, that I teach them not to acknowledge the gods which the state acknowledges, but some other new divinities or spiritual agencies in their stead. These are the lessons by which I corrupt the youth, as you say.

Meletus: Yes, that I say emphatically.

Socrates: Then, by the gods, Meletus, of whom we are speaking, tell me and the court, in somewhat plainer terms, what you mean! for I do not as yet understand whether you affirm that I teach other men to acknowledge some gods, and therefore that I do believe in gods, and am not an entire atheist— this you do not lay to my charge,—but only you say that they are not the same gods which the city recognizes—the charge is that they are different gods. Or, do you mean that I am an atheist simply, and a teacher of atheism?

Meletus: I mean the latter—that you are a complete atheist.

Socrates: What an extraordinary statement! Why do you think so, Meletus? Do you mean that I do not believe in the godhead of the sun or moon, like other men?

Meletus: I assure you, judges, that he does not: for he says that the sun is stone, and the moon earth.

Socrates: Friend Meletus, you think that you are accusing Anaxagoras: and you have but a bad opinion of the judges, if you fancy them illiterate to such a degree as not to know that these doctrines are found in the books of Anaxagoras the Clazomenian, which are full of them. And so, forsooth, the youth are said to be taught them by Socrates, when there are not unfrequently exhibitions of them at the theatre (Probably in allusion to Aristophanes who caricatured, and to Euripides who borrowed the notions of Anaxagoras, as well as to other dramatic poets.) (price of admission one drachma at the most); and they might pay their money, and laugh at Socrates if he pretends to father these extraordi-

nary views. And so, Meletus, you really think that I do not believe in any god?

Meletus: I swear by Zeus that you believe absolutely in none at all.

Socrates: Nobody will believe you, Meletus, and I am pretty sure that you do not believe yourself. I cannot help thinking, men of Athens, that Meletus is reckless and impudent, and that he has written this indictment in a spirit of mere wantonness and youthful bravado. Has he not compounded a riddle, thinking to try me? He said to himself: —I shall see whether the wise Socrates will discover my facetious contradiction, or whether I shall be able to deceive him and the rest of them. For he certainly does appear to me to contradict himself in the indictment as much as if he said that Socrates is guilty of not believing in the gods, and yet of believing in them—but this is not like a person who is in earnest.

I should like you, O men of Athens, to join me in examining what I conceive to be his inconsistency; and do you, Meletus, answer. And I must remind the audience of my request that they would not make a disturbance if I speak in my accustomed manner: Did ever man, Meletus, believe in the existence of human things, and not of human beings? . . . I wish, men of Athens, that he would answer, and not be always trying to get up an interruption. Did ever any man believe in horsemanship, and not in horses? or in flute playing, and not in fluteplayers? No, my friend; I will answer to you and to the court, as you refuse to answer for yourself. There is no man who ever did. But now please to answer the next question: Can a man believe in spiritual and divine agencies, and not in spirits or demigods?

Meletus: He cannot.

Socrates: How lucky I am to have extracted that answer, by the assistance of the court! But then you swear in the indictment that I teach and believe in divine or spiritual agencies (new or old, no matter for that); at any rate, I believe in spiritual agencies, —so you say and swear in the affidavit; and yet if I believe in divine beings, how can I help believing in spirits or demigods; —must I not? To be sure I must; and therefore, I may assume that your silence gives consent. Now what are spirits or demigods? Are they not either gods or the sons of gods?

Meletus: Certainly, they are.

Socrates: But this is what I call the facetious riddle invented by you: the demigods or spirits are gods, and you say first that I do not believe in gods, and then again that I do believe in gods; that is, if I believe in demigods. For if the demigods are the illegitimate sons of gods, whether by the nymphs or by any other mothers, of whom they are said to be the sons—what human being will ever believe that there are no gods if they are the sons of gods? You might as well affirm the existence of mules, and deny that of horses and asses. Such nonsense, Meletus, could only have been intended by you to make trial of me. You have put this into the indictment because you had nothing real of which to accuse me. But no one who has a particle of understanding will ever be convinced by you that the same men can believe in divine and superhuman things, and yet not believe that there are gods and demigods and heroes.

Socrates: I have said enough in answer to the charge of Meletus: any elaborate defense is unnecessary, but I know only too well how many are the enmities which I have incurred, and this is what will be my destruction if I am destroyed;— not Meletus, nor yet Anytus, but the envy and detraction of the world, which has been the death of many good men, and will probably be the death of many more; there is no danger of my being the last of them.

Do What's Right, Regardless

Someone will say: And are you not ashamed, Socrates, of a course of life which is likely to bring you to an untimely end? To him I may fairly answer: There you are mistaken: a man who is good for anything ought not to calculate the chance of living or dying; he ought only to consider whether in doing anything he is doing right or wrong—acting the part of a good man or of a bad. Whereas, upon your view, the heroes who fell at Troy were not good for much, and the son of Thetis above all, who altogether despised danger in comparison with disgrace; and when he was so eager to slay Hector, his goddess mother said to him, that if he avenged his companion Patroclus, and slew Hector, he would die himself—"Fate," she said, in these or the like words, "waits for you next after Hector;" he, receiving this warning, utterly despised danger and death, and instead of fearing them, feared rather to live in dishonor, and not to avenge his friend. "Let me die forthwith," he replies, "and be avenged of my enemy, rather than abide here by the beaked ships, a laughingstock and a burden of the earth." Had Achilles any thought of death and danger? For wherever a man's place is, whether the place which he has chosen or that in which he has been placed by a commander, there he ought to remain in the hour of danger; he should not think of death or of anything but of disgrace. And this, O men of Athens, is a true saying. Strange, indeed, would be my conduct, O men of Athens, if I who, when I was ordered by the generals whom you chose to command me at Potidaea and Amphipolis and Delium, remained where they placed me, like any other man, facing death—if now, when, as I conceive and imagine, God orders me to fulfil the philosopher's mission of searching into myself and other men, I were to desert my post through fear of death, or any other fear; that would indeed be strange, and I might justly be arraigned in court for denying the existence of the gods, if I disobeyed the oracle because I was afraid of death, fancying that I was wise when I was not wise. For the fear of death is indeed the pretense of wisdom, and not real wisdom, being a pretense of knowing the unknown; and no one knows whether death, which men in their fear apprehend to be the greatest evil, may not be the greatest good. Is not this ignorance of a disgraceful sort, the ignorance which is the conceit that a man knows what he does not know? And in this respect only I believe myself to differ from between us that you should hear me to the end: I have something more to say, at which you may be inclined to cry out; but

I believe that to hear me will be good for you, and therefore I beg that you will not cry out. I would have you know, that if you kill such a one as I am, you will injure yourselves more than you will injure me. Nothing will injure me, not Meletus nor yet Anytus—they cannot, for a bad man is not permitted to injure a better than himself. I do not deny that Anytus may, perhaps, kill him, or drive him into exile, or deprive him of civil rights; and he may imagine, and others may imagine, that he is inflicting a great injury upon him: but there I do not agree. For the evil of doing as he is doing—the evil of unjustly taking away the life of another—is greater far.

Socrates, a Gadfly

And now, Athenians, I am not going to argue for my own sake, as you may think, but for yours, that you may not sin against the God by condemning me, who am his gift to you. For if you kill me you will not easily find a successor to me, who, if I may use such a ludicrous figure of speech, am a sort of gadfly, given to the state by God; and the state is a great and noble steed who is tardy in his motions owing to his very size, and requires to be stirred into life. I am that gadfly which God has attached to the state, and all day long and in all places am always fastening upon you, arousing, and persuading and reproaching you. You will not easily find another like me, and therefore I would advise you to spare me. I dare say that you may feel out of temper (like a person who is suddenly awakened from sleep), and you think that you might easily strike me dead as Anytus advises, and then you would sleep on for the remainder of your lives, unless God in is care of you sent you another gadfly. When I say that I am given to you by God, the proof of my mission is this: —if I had been like other men, I should not have neglected all my own concerns or patiently seen the neglect of them during all these years, and have been doing yours, coming to you individually like a father or elder brother, exhorting you to regard virtue; such conduct, I say, would be unlike human nature. If I had gained anything, or if my exhortations had been paid, there would have been some sense in my doing so; but now, as you will perceive, not even the impudence of my accusers dares to say that I have ever exacted or sought pay of any one; of that they have no witness. And I have a sufficient witness to the truth of what I say—my poverty.

Socrates' Divine Sign

Someone may wonder why I go about in private giving advice and busying myself with the concerns of others, but do not venture to come forward in public and advise the state. I will tell you why. You have heard me speak at sundry times and in divers places of an oracle or sign which comes to me, and is the divinity which Meletus ridicules in the indictment. This sign, which is a kind of voice, first began to come to me when I was a child; it always forbids but never commands me to do anything which I am going to do. This is what deters me from being a politician. And rightly, as I think. For I am certain, O men of Athens, that if I had engaged in politics, I should have perished long ago, and done no good either to you or to myself. And do not be offended at my telling you the truth: for the truth is, that no man who goes to war with you or any other multitude, honestly striving against the many lawless and unrighteous deeds which are done in a state, will save his life; he who will fight for the right, if he would live even for a brief space, must have a private station and not a public one.

Doing What's Right, Regardless of Threat

I can give you convincing evidence of what I say, not words only, but what you value far more—actions. Let me relate to you a passage of my own life which will prove to you that I should never have yielded to injustice from any fear of death, and that "as I should have refused to yield" I must have died at once. I will tell you a tale of the courts, not very interesting perhaps, but nevertheless true. The only office of state which I ever held, O men of Athens, was that of senator: the tribe Antiochis, which is my tribe, had the presidency at the trial of the generals who had not taken up the bodies of the slain after the battle of Arginusae; and you proposed to try them in a body, contrary to law, as you all thought afterwards; but at the time I was the only one of the Prytanes who was opposed to the illegality, and I gave my vote against you; and when the orators threatened to impeach and arrest me, and you called and shouted, I made up my mind that I would run the risk, having law and justice with me, rather than take part in your injustice because I feared imprisonment and death. This happened in the days of the democracy. But when the oligarchy of the Thirty was in power, they sent for me and four others into the rotunda, and bade us bring Leon the Salaminian from Salamis, as they wanted to put him to death. This was a specimen of the sort of commands which they were always giving with the view of implicating as many as possible in their crimes; and then I showed, not in word only but in deed, that, if I may be allowed to use such an expression, I cared not a straw for death, and that my great and only care was lest I should do an unrighteous or unholy thing. For the strong arm of that oppressive power did not frighten me into doing wrong; and when we came out of the rotunda the other four went to Salamis and fetched Leon, but I went quietly home. For which I might have lost my life, had not the power of the Thirty shortly afterwards come to an end. And many will witness to my words. Now do you really imagine that I could have survived all these years, if I had led a public life, supposing that like a good man I had always maintained the right and had made justice, as I ought, the first thing? No indeed, men of Athens, neither I nor any other man. But I have been always the same in all my actions, public as well as private, and never have I yielded any base compliance to those who are slanderously termed my disciples, or to any other. Not that I have any regular disciples. But if any one likes to come and hear me while I am pursuing my mission, whether he be young or old, he is not excluded. Nor do I converse only with those who pay; but any one, whether he be rich or poor, may ask and answer me and listen to my words; and whether he turns out to be a bad man or a good one, neither result can be justly imputed to me; for I never taught or professed to teach him anything. And if any one

says that he has ever learned or heard anything from me in private which all the world has not heard, let me tell you that he is lying.

But I shall be asked, Why do people delight in continually conversing with to his mind, and he may be set against me, and vote in anger because he is displeased at me on this account. Now if there be such a person among you,—mind, I do not say that there is,—to him I may fairly reply: My friend, I am a man, and like other men, a creature of flesh and blood, and not "of wood or stone," as Homer says; and I have a family, yes, and sons, O Athenians, three in number, one almost a man, and two others who are still young; and yet I will not bring any of them hither in order to petition you for an acquittal. And why not? Not from any self-assertion or want of respect for you. Whether I am or am not afraid of death is another question, of which I will not now speak. But, having regard to public opinion, I feel that such conduct would be discreditable to myself, and to you, and to the whole state. One who has reached my years, and who has a name for wisdom, ought not to demean himself. Whether this opinion of me be deserved or not, at any rate the world has decided that Socrates is in some way superior to other men. And if those among you who are said to be superior in wisdom and courage, and any other virtue, demean themselves in this way, how shameful is their conduct! I have seen men of reputation, when they have been condemned, behaving in the strangest manner: they seemed to fancy that they were going to suffer something dreadful if they died, and that they could be immortal if you only allowed them to live; and I think that such are a dishonor to the state, and that any stranger coming in would have said of them that the most eminent men of Athens, to whom the Athenians themselves give honor and command, are no better than women. And I say that these things ought not to be done by those of us who have a reputation; and if they are done, you ought not to permit them; you ought rather to show that you are far more disposed to condemn the man who gets up a doleful scene and makes the city ridiculous, than him who holds his peace.

The Defense Concluded

But, setting aside the question of public opinion, there seems to be something wrong in asking a favor of a judge, and thus procuring an acquittal, instead of informing and convincing him. For his duty is, not to make a present of justice, but to give judgment; and he has sworn that he will judge according to the laws, and not according to his own good pleasure; and we ought not to encourage you, nor should you allow yourselves to be encouraged, in this habit of perjury—there can be no piety in that. Do not then require me to do what I consider dishonorable and impious and wrong, especially now, when I am being tried for impiety on the indictment of Meletus. For if, O men of Athens, by force of persuasion and entreaty I could overpower your oaths, then I should be teaching you to believe that there are no gods, and in defending should simply convict myself of the charge of not believing in them. But that is not so—far otherwise. For I do believe that there are gods, and in a sense higher than that in which any of my accusers

believe in them. And to you and to God I commit my cause,
to be determined by you as is best for you and me.

Citation and Use

The text was taken from the following work.

Plato, "The Apology," in *Plato in Twelve Volumes*, trans. Paul Shorey, vol. 1, 12 vols. (Cambridge, MA:
   Harvard University Press, 1969), http://www.perseus.tufts.edu/hopper/
   text?doc=Perseus:text:1999.01.0170:text=Apol.

THE VALUE OF PHILOSOPHY

Bertrand Russell

We need to consider what is the value of philosophy and why it ought to be studied. It is the more necessary to consider this question, in view of the fact that many people, under the influence of science or of practical affairs, are inclined to doubt whether philosophy is anything better than innocent but useless trifling, hairsplitting distinctions, and controversies on matters concerning which knowledge is impossible.

This view of philosophy appears to result, partly from a wrong conception of the ends of life, partly from a wrong conception of the kind of goods which philosophy strives to achieve. Physical science, through the medium of inventions, is useful to innumerable people who are wholly ignorant of it; thus the study of physical science is to be recommended, not only, or primarily, because of the effect on the student, but rather because of the effect on mankind in general. This utility does not belong to philosophy. If the study of philosophy has any value at all for others than students of philosophy, it must be only indirectly, through its effects upon the lives of those who study it. It is in these effects, therefore, if anywhere, that the value of philosophy must be primarily sought.

But further, if we are not to fail in our endeavor to determine the value of philosophy, we must first free our minds from the prejudices of what are wrongly called "practical" people. The "practical" person, as this word is often used, is one who recognizes only material needs, who realizes that people must have food for the body, but is oblivious of the necessity of providing food for the mind. If all people were well off, if poverty and disease had been reduced to their lowest possible point, there would still remain much to be done to produce a valuable society; and even in the existing world the goods of the mind are at least as important as the goods of the body. It is exclusively among the goods of the mind that the value of philosophy is to be found; and only those who are not indifferent to these goods can be persuaded that the study of philosophy is not a waste of time.

Philosophy, like all other studies, aims primarily at knowledge. The knowledge it aims it is the kind of knowledge which gives unity and system to the body of the sciences, and the kind which results from a critical examination of the grounds of our convictions, prejudices, and beliefs. But it cannot be maintained that philosophy has had any very great measure of success in its attempts to provide definite answers to its questions. If you ask a mathematician, a mineralogist, a historian, or any other person of learning, what definite body of truths has been ascertained by his science, his answer will last as long as you are willing to listen. But if you put the same question to a philosopher, he will, if he is candid, have to confess that his study has not achieved positive results such as have been achieved by other sciences. It is true that this is partly accounted for by the fact that, as soon as definite knowledge concerning any subject becomes possible, this subject ceases to be called philosophy, and becomes a separate science. The whole study of the heavens, which now belongs to astronomy, was once included in philosophy; Newton's great work was called "the mathematical principles of natural philosophy." Similarly, the study of the human mind, which was, until very lately, a part of philosophy, has now been separated from philosophy and has become the science of psychology. Thus, to a great extent, the uncertainty of philosophy is more apparent than real: those questions which are already capable of definite answers are placed in the sciences, while those only to which, at present, no definite answer can be given, remain to form the residue which is called philosophy.

This is, however, only a part of the truth concerning the uncertainty of philosophy. There are many questions—and among them those that are of the profoundest interest to our spiritual life—which, so far as we can see, must remain insoluble to the human intellect unless its powers become of quite a different order from what they are now. Has the universe any unity of plan or purpose, or is it a fortuitous concourse of atoms? Is consciousness a permanent part of the universe, giving hope of indefinite growth in wisdom, or is it a transitory accident on a small planet on which life must ultimately become impossible? Are good and evil of importance to the universe or only to humanity? Such questions are asked by philosophy, and variously answered by various philosophers. But it would seem that, whether answers be otherwise discoverable or not, the answers suggested by philosophy are none of them demonstrably true. Yet, however slight may be the hope of discovering an answer, it is part of the business of philosophy to continue the consideration of such questions, to make us aware of their importance, to examine all the approaches to them, and to keep alive that speculative interest in the universe which is apt to be killed by confining ourselves to definitely ascertainable knowledge.

Many philosophers, it is true, have held that philosophy could establish the truth of certain answers to such fundamental questions. They have supposed that what is of most importance in religious beliefs could be proved by strict demonstration to be true. In order to judge of such attempts, it is necessary to take a survey of human knowledge, and to form an opinion as to its methods and its limitations. On such a subject it would be unwise to pronounce dogmatically; but if the investigations of our previous chapters have not led us astray, we shall be compelled to renounce the hope of finding philosophical proofs of religious beliefs. We cannot, therefore, include as part of the value of philosophy any definite set of answers to such questions. Hence, once more, the value of philosophy must not depend upon any supposed body of definitely ascertainable knowledge to be acquired by those who study it.

The value of philosophy is, in fact, to be sought largely in its very uncertainty. The person who has no tincture of philosophy goes through life imprisoned in the prejudices derived from common sense, from the habitual beliefs of his age or his nation, and from convictions which have grown up in his mind without the cooperation or consent of his deliberate reason. To such a person the world tends to become definite, finite, obvious; common objects rouse no questions, and unfamiliar possibilities are contemptuously rejected. As soon as we begin to philosophize, on the contrary, we find, as we saw in our opening chapters, that even the most everyday things lead to problems to which only very incomplete answers can be given. Philosophy, though unable to tell us with certainty what is the true answer to the doubts which it raises, is able to suggest many possibilities which enlarge our thoughts and free them from the tyranny of custom. Thus, while diminishing our feeling of certainty as to what things are, it greatly increases our knowledge as to what they may be; it removes the somewhat arrogant dogmatism of those who have never traveled into the region of liberating doubt, and it keeps alive our sense of wonder by showing familiar things in an unfamiliar aspect.

Apart from its utility in showing unsuspected possibilities, philosophy has a value—perhaps its chief value—through the greatness of the objects which it contemplates, and the freedom from narrow and personal aims resulting from this contemplation. The life of the instinctive person is shut up within the circle of his private interests: family and friends may be included, but the outer world is not regarded except as it may help or hinder what comes within the circle of instinctive wishes. In such a life there is something feverish and confined, in comparison with which the philosophic life is calm and free. The private world of instinctive interests is a small one, set in the midst of a great and powerful world which must, sooner or later, lay our private world in ruins. Unless we can so enlarge our interests as to include the whole outer world, we remain like a garrison in a beleaguered fortress, knowing that the enemy prevents escape and that ultimate surrender is inevitable. In such a life there is no peace, but a constant strife between the insistence of desire and the powerlessness of will. In one way or another, if our life is to be great and free, we must escape this prison and this strife.

One way of escape is by philosophic contemplation. Philosophic contemplation does not, in its widest survey, divide the universe into two hostile camps—friends and foes, helpful and hostile, good and bad—it views the whole impartially. Philosophic contemplation, when it is unalloyed, does not aim at proving that the rest of the universe is akin to humanity. All acquisition of knowledge is an enlargement of the Self, but this enlargement is best attained when it is not directly sought. It is obtained when the desire for knowledge is alone operative, by a study which does not wish in advance that its objects should have this or that character, but adapts the Self to the characters which it finds in its objects. This enlargement of Self is not obtained when, taking the Self as it is, we try to show that the world is so similar to this Self that knowledge of it is possible without any admission of what seems alien. The desire to prove this is a form of self-assertion, and like all self-assertion, it is an obstacle to the growth of Self which it desires, and of which the Self knows that it is capable. Self-assertion, in philosophic speculation as elsewhere, views the world as a means to its own ends; thus it makes the world of less account than Self, and the Self sets bounds to the greatness of its goods. In contemplation, on the contrary, we start from the not-Self, and through its greatness the boundaries of Self are enlarged; through the infinity of the universe the mind which contemplates it achieves some share in infinity.

For this reason greatness of soul is not fostered by those philosophies which assimilate the universe to Humanity. Knowledge is a form of union of Self and not-Self; like all union, it is impaired by dominion, and therefore by any attempt to force the universe into conformity with what we find in ourselves. There is a widespread philosophical tendency towards the view which tells us that humanity is the measure of all things, that truth is person-made, that space and time and the world of universals are properties of the mind, and that, if there be anything not created by the mind, it is unknowable and of no account for us. This view, if our previous discussions were correct, is untrue; but in addition to being untrue, it has the effect of robbing philosophic contemplation of all that gives it value, since it fetters contemplation to Self. What it calls knowledge is not a union with the not-Self, but a set of prejudices, habits, and desires, making an impenetrable veil between us and the world beyond. The person who finds pleasure in such a theory of knowledge is like the person who never leaves the domestic circle for fear his word might not be law.

The true philosophic contemplation, on the contrary, finds

its satisfaction in every enlargement of the not-Self, in everything that magnifies the objects contemplated, and thereby the subject contemplating. Everything, in contemplation, that is personal or private, everything that depends upon habit, self-interest, or desire, distorts the object, and hence impairs the union which the intellect seeks. By thus making a barrier between subject and object, such personal and private things become a prison to the intellect. The free intellect will see as God might see, without a *here* and *now*, without hopes and fears, without the trammels of customary beliefs and traditional prejudices, calmly, dispassionately, in the sole and exclusive desire of knowledge—knowledge as impersonal, as purely contemplative, as it is possible for humanity to attain. Hence also the free intellect will value more the abstract and universal knowledge into which the accidents of private history do not enter, than the knowledge brought by the senses, and dependent, as such knowledge must be, upon an exclusive and personal point of view and a body whose sense-organs distort as much as they reveal.

The mind which has become accustomed to the freedom and impartiality of philosophic contemplation will preserve something of the same freedom and impartiality in the world of action and emotion. It will view its purposes and desires as parts of the whole, with the absence of insistence that results from seeing them as infinitesimal fragments in a world of which all the rest is unaffected by any one person's deeds. The impartiality which, in contemplation, is the unalloyed desire for truth, is the very same quality of mind which, in action, is justice, and in emotion is that universal love which can be given to all, and not only to those who are judged useful or admirable. Thus, contemplation enlarges not only the objects of our thoughts, but also the objects of our actions and our affections: it makes us citizens of the universe, not only of one walled city at war with all the rest. In this citizenship of the universe consists humanity's true freedom, and his liberation from the thralldom of narrow hopes and fears.

Thus, to sum up our discussion of the value of philosophy: Philosophy is to be studied, not for the sake of any definite answers to its questions, since no definite answers can, as a rule, be known to be true, but rather for the sake of the questions themselves; because these questions enlarge our conception of what is possible, enrich our intellectual imagination, and diminish the dogmatic assurance which closes the mind against speculation; but above all because, through the greatness of the universe which philosophy contemplates, the mind also is rendered great, and becomes capable of that union with the universe which constitutes its highest good.

Citation and Use

The text was taken from the following work.

Bertrand Russell, *The Problems of Philosophy* (Urbana, IL: Project Gutenberg, 2004), http://www.gutenberg.org/ebooks/5827.

EPISTEMOLOGY

HATÄTA

Zera Yacob

The following is a short selection of passages from *Hatata*, written in 1662 CE by Zera Yacob (1599-1692 CE). A recollection of his philosophical investigations into the nature of knowledge and the nature of God, it was written decades after his self-imposed exile from Aksum, the then-capital of Ethiopia. Notice the parallels with the contemporary *Meditations* (1641 CE) from Descartes in France.

Chapter Two

While I was teaching in my district, many of my friends came to dislike me. During this period there was no real friendship and as a result men became jealous of one another. I surpassed the others in knowledge and in love of one's neighbor and I was on good terms with all, even with the Frang [foreigners; i.e. the Portuguese] and the Copts. And while I was teaching and interpreting the Books, I used to say: "The Frang say this and this" or "The Copts say that and that," and I did not say: "This is good, that is bad," but I said:

"All these things are good if we ourselves are good." Hence I was disliked by all; the Copts took me for a Frang, the Frang for a Copt. They brought a charge against me many times to the king; but God saved me.

At that time, a certain enemy of mine, Walda Yohannes, a priest from Aksum and a friend of the king, went [to bring a charge against me:] since the love of kings could be won by perfidious tongue. This betrayer went to the king and said this about me: "Truly this man misleads the people and tells them we should rise for the sake of our faith, kill the king and expel the Frang." He also said many other similar words against me.

But being aware of all this and frightened by it, I took three measures of gold which I possessed and the Psalms of David, with which I prayed, and fled at night. I did not tell anyone where was going. I reached a place close to the Takkaze River, and the next day, as I felt hungry I went out in fear to beg the farmers for some bread. I ate what they gave me and ran away. I lived in this manner for many days. On my way to Shoa, I found an uninhabited location. There was a beautiful cave at the foot of a deep valley, and I said [to myself:]

"I shall live here unnoticed." I lived there for two years until [King] Susenyos died. "At times I would leave [the cave] and go to the market or to the country of the Ahmara as they took me for a hermit who goes about begging and gave me enough to appease my hunger. People however, did not know where I dwelt. Alone in my cave, I felt I was living in heaven. Knowing the boundless badness of men, I disliked contact with them. I built a fence of stone and thorny bush so that wild animals would not endanger my life at night, and I made an exit through which I could escape if ever people searched for me; there I lived peacefully praying with all my heart on the Psalms of David and trusting that God was hearing me.

Chapter Four

Later on I thought, saying to myself: "Is everything is written in the Holy Scriptures true?" Although I thought much [about these things] I understood nothing, so I said to myself: "I shall go and consult scholars and thinkers; they will tell me the truth."

But afterwards I thought, saying to myself: "What will men tell me other than what is in their heart?" Indeed each one says: "My faith is right, and those who believe in another faith believe in falsehood, and are the enemies of God." These days the Frang tell us: "Our faith is right, yours is false." We on the other hand tell them: "It is not so; your faith is wrong, ours right." "If we also ask the Mohammedans and the Jews, they will claim the same thing, and who would be the judge for such a kind of argument? "No single human being [can judge:] for all men are plaintiffs and defendants between themselves. Once I asked a Frang scholar many things concerning our faith; he interpreted them all according to his own faith. Afterwards I asked a well-known Ethiopian scholar and he also interpreted all things according to his own faith. If I had asked the Mohammedans and the Jews, they also would have interpreted according to their own faith; then, where could I obtain a judge that tells the truth? As my own faith appears true to me, so does another one find his own faith true; but truth is one. While thinking over this matter, I said: "O my creator, wise among the wise and just among the just, who created me with an intelligence, help me to understand, for men lack wisdom and truthfulness; as David said, no man can be relied upon."

I thought further and said: "Why do men lie over problems of such great importance, even to the point of destroying themselves?" And they seemed to do so because although they pretend to know all, they know nothing. Convinced they know all, they do not attempt to investigate the truth. "As David said: "Their hearts are curdled like milk." Their heart is curdled because they assume what they have heard from their predecessors and they do not inquire whether it is true or false.

But I said: "O Lord! who strike me down with such torment, it is fitting that I know your judgement. You chastise me with truth and admonish me with mercy. But never let my head be anointed with the oil of sinners and of masters in lying: make me understand, for you created me with intelligence." I asked myself: "If I am intelligent, what is it I understand?" And I said: "I understand there is a creator, greater than all creatures; since from his overabundant greatness, he created things that are so great. He is intelligent who understands all, for he created us as intelligent from the abundance of his intelligence; and we ought to worship him, for he is the master of all things. If we pray to him, he will listen to us; for he is almighty."

I went on saying in my thought: "God did not create me intelligent without a purpose, that is to look for him and to grasp him and his wisdom in the path he has opened for me and to worship him as long as l live." And still thinking on the same subject, I said to myself: "Why is it that all men do not adhere to truth, instead of [believing] falsehood?" [The cause] seemed to be the nature of man which is weak and sluggish. Man aspires to know truth and the hidden things of nature, but this endeavor is difficult and can only be attained with great labor and patience, as Solomon said: "With the help of wisdom I have been at pains to study all that is done under heaven; oh, what a weary task God has given mankind to labor at!"

Hence people hastily accept what they have heard from their fathers and shy from any [critical] examination. But God created man to be the master of his own actions, so that he will be what he wills to be, good or bad. If a man chooses to be wicked he can continue in this way until he receives the punishment he deserves for his wickedness. But being carnal, man likes what is of the flesh; whether they are good or bad, he finds ways and means through which he can satisfy his carnal desire. God did not create man to be evil, but to choose what he would like to be, so that he may receive his reward if he is good or his condemnation if he is bad. If a liar, who desires to achieve wealth or honors among men, needs to use foul means to obtain them, he will say he is convinced this falsehood was for him a just thing. To those people who do not want to search, this action seems to be true, and they believe in the liar's strong faith.

I ask [you,] how many falsehoods do our people believe in? They believe wholeheartedly in astrology and other calculations, in the mumbling of secret words, in omens, in the conjuration of devils, and in all kinds of magical art and in the utterances of soothsayers. They believe in all these because they did not investigate the truth but listened to their predecessors. Why did these predecessors lie unless it was for obtaining wealth and honors? Similarly those who wanted to rule the people said: "We were sent by God to proclaim the truth to you;" and the people believed them. Those who came after them accepted their fathers' faith without question; rather, as a proof of their faith, they added to it by including stories of signs and omens. Indeed they said: "God did those things;" and so they made God a witness of falsehood and a party to liars.

Chapter Six

There is a further great inquiry, [namely:] all men are equal in the presence of God; and all are intelligent, since they are his creatures; he did not assign one people for life, another for death, one for mercy, another for judgement. Our reason teaches us that this sort of discrimination cannot exist in the sight of God, who is perfect in all his works. But Moses was sent to teach only the Jews, and David himself said: "He never does this for other nations, he never reveals his rulings to them." Why did God reveal his law to one nation, withhold it from another? At this very time Christians say: "God's doctrine is only found with us;" similarly with the Jews, the Mohammedans, the Indians and the others. Moreover the Christians do not agree among themselves: the Frang tell us: "God's doctrine is not with you, but with us;" we hold the same thing, and if we would listen to men, God's doctrine has reached only a very few people. We cannot even ascertain to which of these few it goes.

Is it not possible for God to entrust his word to men whenever it pleases him? God in his wisdom has not allowed them to agree on what is false, lest it appears to them as the truth. When all people agree on one thing, that thing appears to be true; but it is not possible that all men agree on falsehood, just as by no means do they agree on their faith. I pray [you,] let us think why all men agree that there is a God, creator of all things? Because reason in all men knows that all we see was created, that no creature can be found without a creator and that the existence of a creator is the pure truth. Hence all men agree on this.

When we examine the beliefs taught by men, we do not agree with them, because we find in them falsehood mixed with truth. Men quarrel among themselves; one says: "This is the truth;" another says: "No, that is false." All of them lie when they claim to attribute to the Word of God the word of men. I kept on reflecting and said to myself: "Even if the faith of men does not come from God, it is however necessary for them and produces good effects, since it deters the wicked from doing evil and comforts the good in their patience."

To me such a faith is like a wife who gives birth to an illegitimate child, without the knowledge of the husband; the husband rejoices taking the child for his son, and loves the mother; were he to discover that she bore him an illegitimate child, he would be sad and would send her out with her child. Likewise, when I found out that my faith was adulterous or false, I became sad on account of it and of the children that were born from this adultery, namely: hatred, persecution, torture, bondage, death, seeing that these had forced me to take refuge in this cave.

However, to say the truth, the Christian faith as it was founded in the days of the Gospel was not evil, since it invites all men to love one another and to practice mercy towards all. But today my countrymen have set aside the love recommended by the Gospel and turned away towards hatred, violence, the poison of snakes; they have pulled their faith to pieces down to its very foundation; they teach things that are vain; they do things that are evil, so that they are falsely called Christians.

Citation and Use

The reading was taken from the following work:

Sumner, Claude, ed. *Ethiopian Philosophy: Volume II*. Addis Ababa, 1976.

Use of this reading is governed by the Fair Use doctrine.

Further Readings

The African Enlightenment by Dag Herbjørnsrud

COGITO

Rene Descartes

Below are Meditations I and II from Rene Descartes' *Meditations on First Philosophy* (1641 CE), where Descartes (1596-1650 CE) employs radical doubt to inquiry what we may know for certain. Notice the parelells with Yacob's Hatäta.

Meditation I

OF THE THINGS OF WHICH WE MAY DOUBT.

SEVERAL years have now elapsed since I first became aware that I had accepted, even from my youth, many false opinions for true, and that consequently what I afterward based on such principles was highly doubtful; and from that time I was convinced of the necessity of undertaking once in my life to rid myself of all the opinions I had adopted, and of commencing anew the work of building from the foundation, if I desired to establish a firm and abiding superstructure in the sciences. But as this enterprise appeared to me to be one of great magnitude, I waited until I had attained an age so mature as to leave me no hope that at any stage of life more advanced I should be better able to execute my design. On this account, I have delayed so long that I should henceforth consider I was doing wrong were I still to consume in deliberation any of the time that now remains for action. To-day, then, since I have opportunely freed my mind from all cares [and am happily disturbed by no passions], and since I am in the secure possession of leisure in a peaceable retirement, I will at length apply myself earnestly and freely to the general overthrow of all my former opinions.

But, to this end, it will not be necessary for me to show that the whole of these are false—a point, perhaps, which I shall never reach; but as even now my reason convinces me that I ought not the less carefully to withhold belief from what is not entirely certain and indubitable, than from what is manifestly false, it will be sufficient to justify the rejection of the whole if I shall find in each some ground for doubt.

Nor for this purpose will it be necessary even to deal with each belief individually, which would be truly an endless labor; but, as the removal from below of the foundation necessarily involves the downfall of the whole edifice, I will at once approach the criticism of the principles on which all my former beliefs rested.

All that I have, up to this moment, accepted as possessed of the highest truth and certainty, I received either from or through the senses. I observed, however, that these sometimes misled us; and it is the part of prudence not to place absolute confidence in that by which we have even once been deceived.

But it may be said, perhaps, that, although the senses occasionally mislead us respecting minute objects, and such as are so far removed from us as to be beyond the reach of close observation, there are yet many other of their informations (presentations), of the truth of which it is manifestly impossible to doubt; as for example, that I am in this place, seated by the fire, clothed in a winter dressing gown, that I hold in my hands this piece of paper, with other intimations of the same nature. But how could I deny that I possess these hands and this body, and withal escape being classed with persons in a state of insanity, whose brains are so disordered and clouded by dark bilious vapors as to cause them pertinaciously to assert that they are monarchs when they are in the greatest poverty; or clothed [in gold] and purple when destitute of any covering; or that their head is made of clay, their body of glass, or that they are gourds? I should certainly be not less insane than they, were I to regulate my procedure according to examples so extravagant.

Though this be true, I must nevertheless here consider that I am a man, and that, consequently, I am in the habit of sleeping, and representing to myself in dreams those same things, or even sometimes others less probable, which the insane think are presented to them in their waking moments. How often have I dreamt that I was in these familiar circumstances, that I was dressed, and occupied this place by the fire, when I was lying undressed in bed? At the present moment, however, I certainly look upon this paper with eyes wide awake; the head which I now move is not asleep; I extend this hand consciously and with express purpose, and I perceive it; the occurrences in sleep are not so distinct as all this. But I cannot forget that, at other times I have been deceived in sleep by similar illusions; and, attentively considering those cases, I perceive so clearly that there exist no certain marks by which the state of waking can ever be distinguished from sleep, that I feel greatly astonished; and in amazement I almost persuade myself that I am now dreaming.

Let us suppose, then, that we are dreaming, and that all these particulars—namely, the opening of the eyes, the motion of the head, the forth-putting of the hands—are merely illusions; and even that we really possess neither an entire body nor hands such as we see. Nevertheless it must be admitted at least that the objects which appear to us in sleep are, as it were, painted representations which could not have been formed unless in the likeness of realities; and, therefore, that those general objects, at all events, namely, eyes, a head, hands, and an entire body, are not simply imaginary, but really existent. For, in truth, painters themselves, even when they study to represent sirens and satyrs by forms the most fantastic and extraordinary, cannot bestow upon them natures absolutely new, but can only make a certain medley of the members of different animals; or if they chance to imagine something so novel that nothing at all similar has ever been seen before, and such as is, therefore, purely fictitious and absolutely false, it is at least certain that the colors of which this is composed are real. And on the same principle, although these general objects, viz. [a body], eyes, a head, hands, and the like, be imaginary, we are nevertheless absolutely necessitated to admit the reality at least of some other objects still more simple and universal than these, of which, just as of certain real colors, all those images of things, whether true and real, or false and fantastic, that are found in our consciousness (cogitatio), are formed.

To this class of objects seem to belong corporeal nature in general and its extension; the figure of extended things, their quantity or magnitude, and their number, as also the place in, and the time during, which they exist, and other things of the same sort.

We will not, therefore, perhaps reason illegitimately if we conclude from this that Physics, Astronomy, Medicine, and all the other sciences that have for their end the consideration of composite objects, are indeed of a doubtful character; but that Arithmetic, Geometry, and the other sciences of the same class, which regard merely the simplest and most general objects, and scarcely inquire whether or not these are really existent, contain somewhat that is certain and indubitable: for whether I am awake or dreaming, it remains true that two and three make five, and that a square has but four sides; nor does it seem possible that truths so apparent can ever fall under a suspicion of falsity [or incertitude].

Nevertheless, the belief that there is a God who is all powerful, and who created me, such as I am, has, for a long time, obtained steady possession of my mind. How, then, do I know that he has not arranged that there should be neither earth, nor sky, nor any extended thing, nor figure, nor magnitude, nor place, providing at the same time, however, for [the rise in me of the perceptions of all these objects, and] the persuasion that these do not exist otherwise than as I perceive them ? And further, as I sometimes think that others are in error respecting matters of which they believe themselves to possess a perfect knowledge, how do I know that I am not also deceived each time I add together two and three, or number the sides of a square, or form some judgment still more simple, if more simple indeed can be imagined? But perhaps Deity has not been willing that I should be thus deceived, for he is said to be supremely good. If, however, it were repugnant to the goodness of Deity to have created me subject to constant deception, it would seem likewise to be contrary to his goodness to allow me to be occasionally deceived; and yet it is clear that this is permitted.

Some, indeed, might perhaps be found who would be disposed rather to deny the existence of a Being so powerful than to believe that there is nothing certain. But let us for the present refrain from opposing this opinion, and grant that all which is here said of a Deity is fabulous: nevertheless, in whatever way it be supposed that I reach the state in which I exist, whether by fate, or chance, or by an endless series of antecedents and consequents, or by any other means, it is clear (since to be deceived and to err is a certain defect) that the probability of my being so imperfect as to be the constant victim of deception, will be increased exactly in proportion as the power possessed by the cause, to which they assign my origin, is lessened. To these reasonings I have assuredly nothing to reply, but am constrained at last to avow that there is nothing of all that I formerly believed to be true of which it is impossible to doubt, and that not through thoughtlessness or levity, but from cogent and maturely considered reasons; so that henceforward, if I desire to discover anything certain, I ought not the less carefully to refrain from assenting to those same opinions than to what might be shown to be manifestly false.

But it is not sufficient to have made these observations; care must be taken likewise to keep them in remembrance. For those old and customary opinions perpetually recur—long and familiar usage giving them the right of occupying my mind, even almost against my will, and subduing my belief; nor will I lose the habit of deferring to them and confiding in them so long as I shall consider them to be what in truth they are, viz, opinions to some extent doubtful, as I have already shown, but still highly probable, and such as it is much more reasonable to believe than deny. It is for this reason I am persuaded that I shall not be doing wrong, if, taking an opposite judgment of deliberate design, I become my own deceiver, by supposing, for a time, that all those opinions are entirely false and imaginary, until at length, having thus balanced my old by my new prejudices, my judgment shall no longer be turned aside by perverted usage from the path that may conduct to the perception of truth. For I am assured that, meanwhile, there will arise neither peril nor error from this course, and that I cannot for the present yield too much to distrust, since the end I now seek is not action but knowledge.

I will suppose, then, not that Deity, who is sovereignly good and the fountain of truth, but that some malignant demon, who is at once exceedingly potent and deceitful, has employed all his artifice to deceive me; I will suppose that the sky, the air, the earth, colors, figures, sounds, and all external things, are nothing better than the illusions of dreams, by means of which this being has laid snares for my credulity; I will consider myself as without hands, eyes, flesh, blood, or any of the senses, and as falsely believing that I am possessed of these; I will continue resolutely fixed in this belief, and if indeed by this means it be not in my power to arrive at the knowledge of truth, I shall at least do what is in my power, viz., [suspend my judgment], and guard with settled purpose against giving my assent to what is false, and being imposed upon by this deceiver, whatever be his power and artifice. But this undertaking is arduous, and a certain indolence insensibly leads me back to my ordinary course of life; and just as the captive, who, perchance, was enjoying in his dreams an imaginary liberty, when he begins to suspect that it is but a vision, dreads awakening, and conspires with the agreeable illusions that the deception may be prolonged; so I, of my own accord, fall back into the train of my former beliefs, and fear to arouse myself from my slumber, lest the time of laborious wakefulness that would succeed this quiet rest, in place of bringing any light of day, should prove inadequate to dispel the darkness that will arise from the difficulties that have now been raised.

Meditation II

OF THE NATURE OF THE HUMAN MIND; AND THAT IT IS MORE EASILY KNOWN THAN THE BODY.

The Meditation of yesterday has filled my mind with so many doubts, that it is no longer in my power to forget them. Nor do I see, meanwhile, any principle on which they can be resolved; and, just as if I had fallen all of a sudden into very deep water, I am so greatly disconcerted as to be unable either to plant my feet firmly on the bottom or sustain myself by swimming on the surface. I will, nevertheless, make an effort, and try anew the same path on which I had entered yesterday, that is, proceed by casting aside all that admits of the slightest doubt, not less than if I had discovered it to be absolutely false; and I will continue always in this track until I shall find something that is certain, or at least, if I can do nothing more, until I shall know

with certainty that there is nothing certain. Archimedes, that he might transport the entire globe from the place it occupied to another, demanded only a point that was firm and immovable; so, also, I shall be entitled to entertain the highest expectations, if I am fortunate enough to discover only one thing that is certain and indubitable.

I suppose, accordingly, that all the things which I see are false (fictitious); I believe that none of those objects which my fallacious memory represents ever existed; I suppose that I possess no senses; I believe that body, figure, extension, motion, and place are merely fictions of my mind. What is there, then, that can be esteemed true ? Perhaps this only, that there is absolutely nothing certain.

But how do I know that there is not something different altogether from the objects I have now enumerated, of which it is impossible to entertain the slightest doubt? Is there not a God, or some being, by whatever name I may designate him, who causes these thoughts to arise in my mind ? But why suppose such a being, for it may be I myself am capable of producing them? Am I, then, at least not something? But I before denied that I possessed senses or a body; I hesitate, however, for what follows from that? Am I so dependent on the body and the senses that without these I cannot exist? But I had the persuasion that there was absolutely nothing in the world, that there was no sky and no earth, neither minds nor bodies; was I not, therefore, at the same time, persuaded that I did not exist? Far from it; I assuredly existed, since I was persuaded. But there is I know not what being, who is possessed at once of the highest power and the deepest cunning, who is constantly employing all his ingenuity in deceiving me. Doubtless, then, I exist, since I am deceived; and, let him deceive me as he may, he can never bring it about that I am nothing, so long as I shall be conscious that I am something. So that it must, in fine, be maintained, all things being maturely and carefully considered, that this proposition (pronunciatum) I am, I exist, is necessarily true each time it is expressed by me, or conceived in my mind.

But I do not yet know with sufficient clearness what I am, though assured that I am; and hence, in the next place, I must take care, lest perchance I inconsiderately substitute some other object in room of what is properly myself, and thus wander from truth, even in that knowledge (cognition) which I hold to be of all others the most certain and evident. For this reason, I will now consider anew what I formerly believed myself to be, before I entered on the present train of thought; and of my previous opinion I will retrench all that can in the least be invalidated by the grounds of doubt I have adduced, in order that there may at length remain nothing but what is certain and indubitable.

What then did I formerly think I was ? Undoubtedly I judged that I was a man. But what is a man ? Shall I say a rational animal ? Assuredly not; for it would be necessary forthwith to inquire into what is meant by animal, and what by rational, and thus, from a single question, I should insensibly glide into others, and these more difficult than the first; nor do I now possess enough of leisure to warrant me in wasting my time amid subtleties of this sort. I prefer here to attend to the thoughts that sprung up of themselves in my mind, and were inspired by my own nature alone, when I applied myself to the consideration of what I was. In the first place, then, I thought that I possessed a countenance, hands, arms, and all the fabric of members that appears in a corpse, and which I called by the name of body. It further occurred to me that I was nourished, that I walked, perceived, and thought, and all those actions I referred to the soul; but what the soul itself was I either did not stay to consider, or, if I did, I imagined that it was something extremely rare and subtile, like wind, or flame, or ether, spread through my grosser parts. As regarded the body, I did not even doubt of its nature, but thought I distinctly knew it, and if I had wished to describe it according to the notions I then entertained, I should have explained myself in this manner: By body I understand all that can be terminated by a certain figure; that can be comprised in a certain place, and so fill a certain space as therefrom to exclude every other body; that can be perceived either by touch, sight, hearing, taste, or smell; that can be moved in different ways, not indeed of itself, but by something foreign to it by which it is touched [and from which it receives the impression]; for the power of self-motion, as likewise that of perceiving and thinking, I held as by no means pertaining to the nature of body; on the contrary, I was somewhat astonished to find such faculties existing in some bodies.

But [as to myself, what can I now say that I am], since I suppose there exists an extremely powerful, and, if I may so speak, malignant being, whose whole endeavors are directed toward deceiving me ? Can I affirm that I possess any one of all those attributes of which I have lately spoken as belonging to the nature of body ? After attentively considering them in my own mind, I find none of them that can properly be said to belong to myself. To recount them were idle and tedious. Let us pass, then, to the attributes of the soul. The first mentioned were the powers of nutrition and walking; but, if it be true that I have no body, it is true likewise that I am capable neither of walking nor of being nourished. Perception is another attribute of the soul; but perception too is impossible without the body; besides, I have frequently, during sleep, believed that I perceived objects which I afterward observed I did not in reality perceive. Thinking is another attribute of the soul; and here I discover what properly belongs to myself. This alone is inseparable from me. I am—I exist: this is certain; but how often? As often as I think; for perhaps it would even happen, if I should wholly cease to think, that I should at the same time altogether cease to be. I now admit nothing that is not necessarily true. I am therefore, precisely speaking, only a thinking thing, that is, a mind (mens sive animus), understanding, or reason, terms whose signification was before unknown to me. I am, however, a real thing, and really existent; but what thing? The answer was, a thinking thing.

The question now arises, am I aught besides ? I will stimulate my imagination with a view to discover whether I am not still something more than a thinking being. Now it is plain I am not the assemblage of members called the human body; I am not a thin and penetrating air diffused through all these members, or wind, or flame, or vapor, or breath, or any of all the things I can imagine; for I supposed that all these were not, and, without changing the supposition, I find that I still feel assured of my existence. But it is true, perhaps, that those very things which I suppose to be non-existent, because they are unknown to me, are not in truth different from myself whom I know. This is a point I cannot determine, and do not now enter into any dispute regarding it. I can only judge of things that are known to me: I am conscious that I exist, and I who know that I exist inquire into what I am. It is, however, perfectly certain that the knowledge of my existence, thus precisely taken, is not dependent on things, the existence of which is as yet unknown to me: and consequently it is not dependent on any of the things I can feign in imagination. Moreover, the phrase itself, I frame an image (effingo), reminds me of my error; for I should in truth frame one if I were to imagine myself to be anything, since to imagine is nothing more than to contemplate the figure or image of a corporeal thing; but I already know that I exist, and that it is possible at the same time that all those images, and in general all that relates to the nature of body, are merely dreams [or chimeras]. From this I discover that it is not more reasonable to say, I will excite my imagination that I may know more distinctly what I am, than to express myself as follows: I am now awake, and perceive something real; but because my perception is not sufficiently clear, I will of express purpose go to sleep that my dreams may represent to me the object of my perception with more truth and clearness. And, therefore, I know that nothing of all that I can embrace in imagination belongs to the knowledge which I have of myself, and that there is need to recall with the utmost care the mind from this mode of thinking, that it may be able to know its own nature with perfect distinctness.

But what, then, am I ? A thinking thing, it has been said. But what is a thinking thing? It is a thing that doubts, understands, [conceives], affirms, denies, wills, refuses; that imagines also, and perceives.

Assuredly it is not little, if all these properties belong to my nature. But why should they not belong to it ? Am I not that very being who now doubts of almost everything; who, for all that, understands and conceives certain things; who affirms one alone as true, and denies the others; who desires to know more of them, and does not wish to be deceived; who imagines many things, sometimes even despite his will; and is likewise percipient of many, as if through the medium of the senses. Is there nothing of all this as true as that I am, even although I should be always dreaming, and although he who gave me being employed all his ingenuity to deceive me ? Is there also any one of these attributes that can be properly distinguished from my thought, or that can be said to be separate from myself ? For it is of itself so evident that it is I who doubt, I who understand, and I who desire, that it is here unnecessary to add anything by way of rendering it more clear. And I am as certainly the same being who imagines; for although it may be (as I before supposed) that nothing I imagine is true, still the power of imagination does not cease really to exist in me and to form part of my thought. In fine, I am the same being who perceives, that is, who apprehends certain objects as by the organs of sense, since, in truth, I see light, hear a noise, and feel heat. But it will be said that these presentations are false, and that I am dreaming. Let it be so. At all events it is certain that I seem to see light, hear a noise, and feel heat; this cannot be false, and this is what in me is properly called perceiving (sentire), which is nothing else than thinking.

From this I begin to know what I am with somewhat greater clearness and distinctness than heretofore. But, nevertheless, it still seems to me, and I cannot help believing, that corporeal things, whose images are formed by thought [which fall under the senses], and are examined by the same, are known with much greater distinctness than that I know not what part of myself which is not imaginable; although, in truth, it may seem strange to say that I know and comprehend with greater distinctness things whose existence appears to me doubtful, that are unknown, and do not belong to me, than others of whose reality I am persuaded, that are known to me, and appertain to my proper nature; in a word, than myself. But I see clearly what is the state of the case. My mind is apt to wander, and will not yet submit to be restrained within the limits of truth. Let us therefore leave the mind to itself once more, and, according to it every kind of liberty [permit it to consider the objects that appear to it from without], in order that, having afterward withdrawn it from these gently and opportunely [and fixed it on the consideration of its being and the properties it finds in itself], it may then be the more easily controlled.

Let us now accordingly consider the objects that are commonly thought to be [the most easily, and likewise] the most distinctly known, viz, the bodies we touch and see; not, indeed, bodies in general, for these general notions are usually somewhat more confused, but one body in particular. Take, for example, this piece of wax; it is quite fresh, having been but recently taken from the beehive; it has not yet lost the sweetness of the honey it contained; it still retains somewhat of the odor of the flowers from which it was gathered; its color, figure, size, are apparent (to the sight); it is hard, cold, easily handled; and sounds when struck upon with the finger. In fine, all that contributes to make a body as distinctly known as possible, is found in the one before us. But, while I am speaking, let it be placed near the fire—what remained of the taste exhales, the smell evaporates, the color changes, its figure is destroyed, its size increases, it becomes liquid, it grows hot, it can hardly be handled, and, although struck upon, it emits no sound. Does the same wax still remain after this change? It must be admitted that it does remain; no one doubts it, or judges otherwise. What, then, was it I knew with so much distinctness in the piece of wax? Assuredly, it could be nothing of all that I observed by means of the senses, since all the things that fell under taste, smell, sight, touch, and hearing are changed, and yet the same wax remains.

It was perhaps what I now think, viz, that this wax was neither the sweetness of honey, the pleasant odor of flowers,

the whiteness, the figure, nor the sound, but only a body that a little before appeared to me conspicuous under these forms, and which is now perceived under others. But, to speak precisely, what is it that I imagine when I think of it in this way? Let it be attentively considered, and, retrenching all that does not belong to the wax, let us see what remains. There certainly remains nothing, except something extended, flexible, and movable. But what is meant by flexible and movable? Is it not that I imagine that the piece of wax, being round, is capable of becoming square, or of passing from a square into a triangular figure? Assuredly such is not the case, because I conceive that it admits of an infinity of similar changes; and I am, moreover, unable to compass this infinity by imagination, and consequently this conception which I have of the wax is not the product of the faculty of imagination. But what now is this extension? Is it not also unknown? for it becomes greater when the wax is melted, greater when it is boiled, and greater still when the heat increases; and I should not conceive [clearly and] according to truth, the wax as it is, if I did not suppose that the piece we are considering admitted even of a wider variety of extension than I ever imagined, I must, therefore, admit that I cannot even comprehend by imagination what the piece of wax is, and that it is the mind alone (mens, Lat., entendement, F.) which perceives it. I speak of one piece in particular; for as to wax in general, this is still more evident. But what is the piece of wax that can be perceived only by the [understanding or] mind? It is certainly the same which I see, touch, imagine; and, in fine, it is the same which, from the beginning, I believed it to be. But (and this it is of moment to observe) the perception of it is neither an act of sight, of touch, nor of imagination, and never was either of these, though it might formerly seem so, but is simply an intuition (inspectio) of the mind, which may be imperfect and confused, as it formerly was, or very clear and distinct, as it is at present, according as the attention is more or less directed to the elements which it contains, and of which it is composed.

But, meanwhile, I feel greatly astonished when I observe [the weakness of my mind, and] its proneness to error. For although, without at all giving expression to what I think, I consider all this in my own mind, words yet occasionally impede my progress, and I am almost led into error by the terms of ordinary language. We say, for example, that we see the same wax when it is before us, and not that we judge it to be the same from its retaining the same color and figure: whence I should forthwith be disposed to conclude that the wax is known by the act of sight, and not by the intuition of the mind alone, were it not for the analogous instance of human beings passing on in the street below, as observed from a window. In this case I do not fail to say that I see the men themselves, just as I say that I see the wax; and yet what do I see from the window beyond hats and cloaks that might cover artificial machines, whose motions might be determined by springs? But I judge that there are human beings from these appearances, and thus I comprehend, by the faculty of judgment alone which is in the mind, what I believed I saw with my eyes.

The man who makes it his aim to rise to knowledge superior

to the common, ought to be ashamed to seek occasions of doubting from the vulgar forms of speech: instead, therefore, of doing this, I shall proceed with the matter in hand, and inquire whether I had a clearer and more perfect perception of the piece of wax when I first saw it, and when I thought I knew it by means of the external sense itself, or, at all events, by the common sense (sensus communis), as it is called, that is, by the imaginative faculty; or whether I rather apprehend it more clearly at present, after having examined with greater care, both what it is, and in what way it can be known. It would certainly be ridiculous to entertain any doubt on this point. For what, in that first perception, was there distinct ? What did I perceive which any animal might not have perceived ? But when I distinguish the wax from its exterior forms, and when, as if I had stripped it of its vestments, I consider it quite naked, it is certain, although some error may still be found in my judgment, that I cannot, nevertheless, thus apprehend it without possessing a human mind.

But finally, what shall I say of the mind itself, that is, of myself ? for as yet I do not admit that I am anything but mind. What, then! I who seem to possess so distinct an apprehension of the piece of wax, do I not know myself, both with greater truth and certitude, and also much more distinctly and clearly? For if I judge that the wax exists because I see it, it assuredly follows, much more evidently, that I myself am or exist, for the same reason: for it is possible that what I see may not in truth be wax, and that I do not even possess eyes with which to see anything; but it cannot be that when I see, or, which comes to the same thing, when I think I see, I myself who think am nothing.

So likewise, if I judge that the wax exists because I touch it, it will still also follow that I am; and if I determine that my imagination, or any other cause, whatever it be, persuades me of the existence of the wax, I will still draw the same conclusion. And what is here remarked of the piece of wax, is applicable to all the other things that are external to me. And further, if the [notion or] perception of wax appeared to me more precise and distinct, after that not only sight and touch, but many other causes besides, rendered it manifest to my apprehension, with how much greater distinctness must I now know myself, since all the reasons that contribute to the knowledge of the nature of wax, or of any body whatever, manifest still better the nature of my mind ? And there are besides so many other things in the mind itself that contribute to the illustration of its nature, that those dependent on the body, to which I have here referred, scarcely merit to be taken into account.

But, in conclusion, I find I have insensibly reverted to the point I desired; for, since it is now manifest to me that bodies themselves are not properly perceived by the senses nor by the faculty of imagination, but by the intellect alone; and since they are not perceived because they are seen and touched, but only because they are understood [or rightly comprehended by thought], I readily discover that there is nothing more easily or clearly apprehended than my own mind. But because it is difficult to rid one's self so promptly of an opinion to which one has been long accustomed, it will be desirable to tarry for some time at this stage, that, by long continued meditation, I may more deeply impress upon my memory this new knowledge.

Citation and Use

The text was taken from the following work.

René Descartes, THE METHOD, MEDITATIONS AND PHILOSOPHY OF DESCARTES, trans. John Veitch (Washington and London: M. Walter Dunne, 1901).

The use of this work is governed by the Public Domain.

EMPIRICISM

John Locke

BOOK I —Neither Principles nor Ideas are Innate

CHAPTER I —No Innate Speculative Principles

1. The way shown how we come by any Knowledge, sufficient to prove it not innate.

It is an established opinion amongst some men, that there are in the understanding certain INNATE PRINCIPLES; some primary notions, KOIVAI EVVOIAI, characters, as it were stamped upon the mind of man; which the soul receives in its very first being, and brings into the world with it. It would be sufficient to convince unprejudiced readers of the falseness of this supposition, if I should only show (as I hope I shall in the following parts of this Discourse) how men, barely by the use of their natural faculties may attain to all the knowledge they have, without the help of any innate impressions; and may arrive at certainty, without any such original notions or principles. For I imagine any one will easily grant that it would be impertinent to suppose the ideas of colours innate in a creature to whom God hath given sight, and a power to receive them by the eyes from external objects: and no less unreasonable would it be to attribute several truths to the impressions of nature, and innate characters, when we may observe in ourselves faculties fit to attain as easy and certain knowledge of them as if they were originally imprinted on the mind.

But because a man is not permitted without censure to follow his own thoughts in the search of truth, when they lead him ever so little out of the common road, I shall set down the reasons that made me doubt of the truth of that opinion, as an excuse for my mistake, if I be in one; which I leave to be considered by those who, with me, dispose themselves to embrace truth wherever they find it.

2. General Assent the great Argument.

There is nothing more commonly taken for granted than that there are certain PRINCIPLES, both SPECULATIVE and PRACTICAL, (for they speak of both), universally agreed upon by all mankind: which therefore, they argue, must needs be the constant impressions which the souls of men receive in their first beings, and which they bring into the world with them, as necessarily and really as they do any of their inherent faculties.

3. Universal Consent proves nothing innate.

This argument, drawn from universal consent, has this misfortune in it, that if it were true in matter of fact, that there were certain truths wherein all mankind agreed, it would not prove them innate, if there can be any other way shown how men may come to that universal agreement, in the things they do consent in, which I presume may be done.

4. "What is is," and "It is possible for the same Thing to be and not to be," not universally assented to.

But, which is worse, this argument of universal consent, which is made use of to prove innate principles, seems to me a demonstration that there are none such: because there are none to which all mankind give an universal assent. I shall begin with the speculative, and instance in those magnified principles of demonstration, "Whatsoever is, is," and "It is impossible for the same thing to be and not to be"; which, of all others, I think have the most allowed title to innate. These have so settled a reputation of maxims universally received, that it will no doubt be thought strange if any one should seem to question it. But yet I take liberty to say, that these propositions are so far from having an universal assent, that there are a great part of mankind to whom they are not so much as known . . .

BOOK II—OF IDEAS

CHAPTER I.—OF IDEAS IN GENERAL, AND THEIR ORIGINAL.

1. Idea is the Object of Thinking.

Every man being conscious to himself that he thinks; and that which his mind is applied about whilst thinking being the IDEAS that are there, it is past doubt that men have in their minds several ideas,—such as are those expressed by the words whiteness, hardness, sweetness, thinking, motion, man, elephant, army, drunkenness, and others: it is in the first place then to be inquired, HOW HE COMES BY THEM?

I know it is a received doctrine, that men have native ideas, and original characters, stamped upon their minds in their very first being. This opinion I have at large examined already; and, I suppose what I have said in the foregoing Book will be much more easily admitted, when I have shown whence the understanding may get all the ideas it has; and by what ways and degrees they may come into the mind;—for which I shall appeal to every one's own observation and experience.

2. All Ideas come from Sensation or Reflection.

Let us then suppose the mind to be, as we say, white paper, void of all characters, without any ideas:—How comes it to be furnished? Whence comes it by that vast store which the busy and boundless fancy of man has painted on it with an almost endless variety? Whence has it all the MATERIALS of reason and knowledge? To this I answer, in one word, from EXPERIENCE. In that all our knowledge is founded; and from that it ultimately derives itself. Our observation employed either, about external sensible objects, or about the internal operations of our minds perceived and reflected on by ourselves, is that which supplies our understandings with all the MATERIALS of thinking. These two are the fountains of knowledge, from whence all the ideas we have, or can naturally have, do spring.

3. The Objects of Sensation one Source of Ideas

First, our Senses, conversant about particular sensible objects, do convey into the mind several distinct perceptions of things, according to those various ways wherein those objects do affect them. And thus we come by those IDEAS we have of yellow, white, heat, cold, soft, hard, bitter, sweet, and all those which we call sensible qualities; which when I say the senses convey into the mind, I mean, they from external objects convey into the mind what produces there those perceptions. This great source of most of the ideas we have, depending wholly upon our senses, and derived by them to the understanding, I call SENSATION.

4. The Operations of our Minds, the other Source of them.

Secondly, the other fountain from which experience furnisheth the understanding with ideas is,—the perception of the operations of our own mind within us, as it is employed about the ideas it has got;—which operations, when the soul comes to reflect on and consider, do furnish the understanding with another set of ideas, which could not be had from things without. And such are perception, thinking, doubting, believing, reasoning, knowing, willing, and all the different actings of our own minds;—which we being conscious of, and observing in ourselves, do from these receive into our understandings as distinct ideas as we do from bodies affecting our senses. This source of ideas every man has wholly in himself; and though it be not sense, as having nothing to do with external objects, yet it is very like

it, and might properly enough be called INTERNAL SENSE. But as I call the other Sensation, so I call this REFLECTION, the ideas it affords being such only as the mind gets by reflecting on its own operations within itself. By reflection then, in the following part of this discourse, I would be understood to mean, that notice which the mind takes of its own operations, and the manner of them, by reason whereof there come to be ideas of these operations in the understanding. These two, I say, viz. external material things, as the objects of SENSATION, and the operations of our own minds within, as the objects of REFLECTION, are to me the only originals from whence all our ideas take their beginnings. The term OPERATIONS here I use in a large sense, as comprehending not barely the actions of the mind about its ideas, but some sort of passions arising sometimes from them, such as is the satisfaction or uneasiness arising from any thought.

5. All our Ideas are of the one or of the other of these.

The understanding seems to me not to have the least glimmering of any ideas which it doth not receive from one of these two. EXTERNAL OBJECTS furnish the mind with the ideas of sensible qualities, which are all those different perceptions they produce in us; and THE MIND furnishes the understanding with ideas of its own operations.

These, when we have taken a full survey of them, and their several modes, and the compositions made out of them we shall find to contain all our whole stock of ideas; and that we have nothing in our minds which did not come in one of these two ways. Let any one examine his own thoughts, and thoroughly search into his understanding; and then let him tell me, whether all the original ideas he has there, are any other than of the objects of his senses, or of the operations of his mind, considered as objects of his reflection. And how great a mass of knowledge soever he imagines to be lodged there, he will, upon taking a strict view, see that he has not any idea in his mind but what one of these two have imprinted;—though perhaps, with infinite variety compounded and enlarged by the understanding, as we shall see hereafter.

6. Observable in Children.

He that attentively considers the state of a child, at his first coming into the world, will have little reason to think him stored with plenty of ideas, that are to be the matter of his future knowledge. It is BY DEGREES he comes to be furnished with them. And though the ideas of obvious and familiar qualities imprint themselves before the memory begins to keep a register of time or order, yet it is often so late before some unusual qualities come in the way, that there are few men that cannot recollect the beginning of their acquaintance with them. And if it were worth while, no doubt a child might be so ordered as to have but a very few, even of the ordinary ideas, till he were grown up to a man. But all that are born into the world, being surrounded with bodies that perpetually and diversely affect them, variety of ideas, whether care be taken of it or not, are imprinted on the minds of children. Light and colours are busy at hand everywhere, when the eye is but open; sounds and some tangible qualities fail not to solicit their proper senses, and force an entrance to the mind;—but yet, I think, it will be granted easily, that if a child were kept in a place where he never saw any other but black and white till he were a man, he would have no more ideas of scarlet or green, than he that from his childhood never tasted an oyster, or a pine-apple, has of those particular relishes.

7. Men are differently furnished with these, according to the different Objects they converse with.

Men then come to be furnished with fewer or more simple ideas from without, according as the objects they converse with afford greater or less variety; and from the operations of their minds within, according as they more or less reflect on them. For, though he that contemplates the operations of his mind, cannot but have plain and clear ideas of them; yet, unless he turn his thoughts that way, and considers them ATTENTIVELY, he will no more have clear and distinct ideas of all the operations of his mind, and all that may be observed therein, than he will have all the particular ideas of any landscape, or of the parts and motions of a clock, who will not turn his eyes to it, and with attention heed all the parts of it. The picture, or clock may be so placed, that they may come in his way every day; but yet he will have but a confused idea of all the parts they are made up of, till he applies himself with attention, to consider them each in particular.

8. Ideas of Reflection later, because they need Attention.

And hence we see the reason why it is pretty late before most children get ideas of the operations of their own minds; and some have not any very clear or perfect ideas of the greatest part of them all their lives. Because, though they pass there continually, yet, like floating visions, they make not deep impressions enough to leave in their mind clear, distinct, lasting ideas, till the understanding turns inward upon itself, reflects on its own operations, and makes them the objects of its own contemplation. Children when they come first into it, are surrounded with a world of new things which, by a constant solicitation of their senses, draw the mind constantly to them; forward to take notice of new, and apt to be delighted with the variety of changing objects. Thus the first years are usually employed and diverted in looking abroad. Men's business in them is to acquaint themselves with what is to be found without; and so growing up in a constant attention to outward sensations, seldom make any considerable reflection on what passes within them, till they come to be of riper years; and some scarce ever at all.

9. The Soul begins to have Ideas when it begins to perceive.

To ask, at what TIME a man has first any ideas, is to ask, when he begins to perceive;—HAVING IDEAS, and PERCEPTION, being the same thing. I know it is an opinion, that the soul always thinks, and that it has the actual perception of ideas in itself constantly, as long as it exists;

and that actual thinking is as inseparable from the soul as actual extension is from the body; which if true, to inquire after the beginning of a man's ideas is the same as to inquire after the beginning of his soul. For, by this account, soul and its ideas, as body and its extension, will begin to exist both at the same time.

10. The Soul thinks not always; for this wants Proofs.

But whether the soul be supposed to exist antecedent to, or coeval with, or some time after the first rudiments of organization, or the beginnings of life in the body, I leave to be disputed by those who have better thought of that matter. I confess myself to have one of those dull souls, that doth not perceive itself always to contemplate ideas; nor can conceive it any more necessary for the soul always to think, than for the body always to move: the perception of ideas being (as I conceive) to the soul, what motion is to the body; not its essence, but one of its operations. And therefore, though thinking be supposed never so much the proper action of the soul, yet it is not necessary to suppose that it should be always thinking, always in action. That, perhaps, is the privilege of the infinite Author and Preserver of all things, who "never slumbers nor sleeps"; but is not competent to any finite being, at least not to the soul of man. We know certainly, by experience, that we SOMETIMES think; and thence draw this infallible consequence,—that there is something in us that has a power to think. But whether that substance PERPETUALLY thinks or no, we can be no further assured than experience informs us. For, to say that actual thinking is essential to the soul, and inseparable from it, is to beg what is in question, and not to prove it by reason;—which is necessary to be done, if it be not a self-evident proposition. But whether this, "That the soul always thinks," be a self-evident proposition, that everybody assents to at first hearing, I appeal to mankind. It is doubted whether I thought at all last night or no. The question being about a matter of fact, it is begging it to bring, as a proof for it, an hypothesis, which is the very thing in dispute: by which way one may prove anything, and it is but supposing that all watches, whilst the balance beats, think, and it is sufficiently proved, and past doubt, that my watch thought all last night. But he that would not deceive himself, ought to build his hypothesis on matter of fact, and make it out by sensible experience, and not presume on matter of fact, because of his hypothesis, that is, because he supposes it to be so; which way of proving amounts to this, that I must necessarily think all last night, because another supposes I always think, though I myself cannot perceive that I always do so.

But men in love with their opinions may not only suppose what is in question, but allege wrong matter of fact. How else could any one make it an inference of mine, that a thing is not, because we are not sensible of it in our sleep? I do not say there is no SOUL in a man, because he is not sensible of it in his sleep; but I do say, he cannot THINK at any time, waking or sleeping, without being sensible of it. Our being sensible of it is not necessary to anything but to our thoughts; and to them it is; and to them it always will be necessary, till we can think without being conscious of it.

11. It is not always conscious of it.

I grant that the soul, in a waking man, is never without thought, because it is the condition of being awake. But whether sleeping without dreaming be not an affection of the whole man, mind as well as body, may be worth a waking man's consideration; it being hard to conceive that anything should think and not be conscious of it. If the soul doth think in a sleeping man without being conscious of it, I ask whether, during such thinking, it has any pleasure or pain, or be capable of happiness or misery? I am sure the man is not; no more than the bed or earth he lies on. For to be happy or miserable without being conscious of it, seems to me utterly inconsistent and impossible. Or if it be possible that the SOUL can, whilst the body is sleeping, have its thinking, enjoyments, and concerns, its pleasures or pain, apart, which the MAN is not conscious of nor partakes in,—it is certain that Socrates asleep and Socrates awake is not the same person; but his soul when he sleeps, and Socrates the man, consisting of body and soul, when he is waking, are two persons: since waking Socrates has no knowledge of, or concernment for that happiness or misery of his soul, which it enjoys alone by itself whilst he sleeps, without perceiving anything of it; no more than he has for the happiness or misery of a man in the Indies, whom he knows not. For, if we take wholly away all consciousness of our actions and sensations, especially of pleasure and pain, and the concernment that accompanies it, it will be hard to know wherein to place personal identity.

12. If a sleeping Man thinks without knowing it, the sleeping and waking Man are two Persons.

The soul, during sound sleep, thinks, say these men. Whilst it thinks and perceives, it is capable certainly of those of delight or trouble, as well as any other perceptions; and IT must necessarily be CONSCIOUS of its own perceptions. But it has all this apart: the sleeping MAN, it is plain, is conscious of nothing of all this. Let us suppose, then, the soul of Castor, while he is sleeping, retired from his body; which is no impossible supposition for the men I have here to do with, who so liberally allow life, without a thinking soul, to all other animals. These men cannot then judge it impossible, or a contradiction, that the body should live without the soul; nor that the soul should subsist and think, or have perception, even perception of happiness or misery, without the body. Let us then, I say, suppose the soul of Castor separated during his sleep from his body, to think apart. Let us suppose, too, that it chooses for its scene of thinking the body of another man, v. g. Pollux, who is sleeping without a soul. For, if Castor's soul can think, whilst Castor is asleep, what Castor is never conscious of, it is no matter what PLACE it chooses to think in. We have here, then, the bodies of two men with only one soul between them, which we will suppose to sleep and wake by turns; and the soul still thinking in the waking man, whereof the sleeping man is never conscious, has never the least perception. I ask, then, whether Castor and Pollux, thus with only one soul between them, which thinks and perceives in one what the other is never conscious of, nor is concerned for, are not two as distinct PERSONS as Castor and Hercules, or as Socrates and Plato were? And whether one of them might not be very happy, and the other very miserable? Just by the same reason, they make the soul and the man two persons, who make the soul think apart what the man is not conscious of. For, I suppose nobody will make identity of persons to consist in the soul's being united to the very same numerical particles of matter. For if that be necessary to identity, it will be impossible, in that constant flux of the particles of our bodies, that any man should be the same person two days, or two moments, together.

13. Impossible to convince those that sleep without dreaming, that they think.

Thus, methinks, every drowsy nod shakes their doctrine, who teach that the soul is always thinking. Those, at least, who do at any time SLEEP WITHOUT DREAMING, can never be convinced that their thoughts are sometimes for four hours busy without their knowing of it; and if they are taken in the very act, waked in the middle of that sleeping contemplation, can give no manner of account of it.

14. That men dream without remembering it, in vain urged.

It will perhaps be said,—That the soul thinks even in the soundest sleep, but the MEMORY retains it not. That the soul in a sleeping man should be this moment busy a thinking, and the next moment in a waking man not remember nor be able to recollect one jot of all those thoughts, is very hard to be conceived, and would need some better proof than bare assertion to make it be believed. For who can without any more ado, but being barely told so, imagine that the greatest part of men do, during all their lives, for several hours every day, think of something, which if they were asked, even in the middle of these thoughts, they could remember nothing at all of? Most men, I think, pass a great part of their sleep without dreaming. I once knew a man that was bred a scholar, and had no bad memory, who told me he had never dreamed in his life, till he had that fever he was then newly recovered of, which was about the five or six and twentieth year of his age. I suppose the world affords more such instances: at least every one's acquaintance will furnish him with examples enough of such as pass most of their nights without dreaming.

15. Upon this Hypothesis, the Thoughts of a sleeping Man ought to be most rational.

To think often, and never to retain it so much as one moment, is a very useless sort of thinking; and the soul, in such a state of thinking, does very little, if at all, excel that of a looking-glass, which constantly receives variety of images, or ideas, but retains none; they disappear and vanish, and there remain no footsteps of them; the looking-glass is never the better for such ideas, nor the soul for, such thoughts. Perhaps it will be said, that in a waking MAN the materials of the body are employed, and made use of, in thinking; and that the memory of thoughts is retained by the impressions that are made on the brain, and the traces there left after such thinking; but that in the thinking of the SOUL, which is not perceived in a sleeping man, there the soul thinks apart, and making no use of the organs of the body, leaves no impressions on it, and consequently no memory of such thoughts. Not to mention again the absurdity of two distinct persons, which follows from this supposition, I answer, further,—That whatever ideas the mind can receive and contemplate without the help of the body, it is reasonable to conclude it can retain without the help of the body too; or else the soul, or any separate spirit, will have but little advantage by thinking. If it has no memory of its own thoughts; if it cannot lay them up for its own use, and be able to recall them upon occasion; if it cannot reflect upon what is past, and make use of its former experiences, reasonings, and contemplations, to what, purpose does it think? They who make the soul a thinking thing, at this rate, will not make it a much more noble being than those do whom they condemn, for allowing it to be nothing but the subtilist parts of matter. Characters drawn on dust, that the first breath of wind effaces; or impressions made on a heap of atoms, or animal spirits, are altogether as useful, and render the subject as noble, as the thoughts of a soul that perish in thinking; that, once out of sight, are gone for ever, and leave no memory of themselves behind them. Nature never makes excellent things for mean or no uses: and it is hardly to be conceived that our infinitely wise Creator should make so admirable a faculty as the power of thinking, that faculty which comes nearest the excellency of his own incomprehensible being, to be so idly and uselessly employed, at least a fourth part of its time here, as to think constantly, without remembering any of those thoughts, without doing any good to itself or others, or being any way useful to any other part of the creation. If we will examine it, we shall not find, I suppose, the motion of dull and senseless matter, any where in the universe, made so little use of and so wholly thrown away.

16. On this Hypothesis, the Soul must have Ideas not derived from Sensation or Reflection, of which there is no Appearance.

It is true, we have sometimes instances of perception whilst we are asleep, and retain the memory of those thoughts: but how extravagant and incoherent for the most part they are; how little conformable to the perfection and order of a rational being, those who are acquainted with dreams need not be told. This I would willingly be satisfied in,—whether the soul, when it thinks thus apart, and as it were separate from the body, acts less rationally than when conjointly with it, or no. If its separate thoughts be less rational, then these men must say, that the soul owes the perfection of rational thinking to the body: if it does not, it is a wonder that our dreams should be, for the most part, so frivolous and irrational; and that the soul should retain none of its more rational soliloquies and meditations.

17. If I think when I know it not, nobody else can know it.

Those who so confidently tell us that the soul always actually thinks, I would they would also tell us, what those ideas are that are in the soul of a child, before or just at the union with the body, before it hath received any by sensation. The dreams of sleeping men are, as I take it, all made up of the waking man's ideas; though for the most part oddly put together. It is strange, if the soul has ideas of its own that it derived not from sensation or reflection, (as it must have, if it thought before it received any impressions from the body,) that it should never, in its private thinking, (so private, that the man himself perceives it not,) retain any of them the very moment it wakes out of them, and then make the man glad with new discoveries. Who can find it reason that the soul should, in its retirement during sleep, have so many hours' thoughts, and yet never light on any of those ideas it borrowed not from sensation or reflection; or at least preserve the memory of none but such, which, being occasioned from the body, must needs be less natural to a spirit? It is strange the soul should never once in a man's whole life recall over any of its pure native thoughts, and those ideas it had before it borrowed anything from the body; never bring into the waking man's view any other ideas but what have a tang of the cask, and manifestly derive their original from that union. If it always thinks, and so had ideas before it was united, or before it received any from the body, it is not to be supposed but that during sleep it recollects its native ideas; and during that retirement from communicating with the body, whilst it thinks by itself, the ideas it is busied about should be, sometimes at least, those more natural and congenial ones which it had in itself, underived from the body, or its own operations about them: which, since the waking man never remembers, we must from this hypothesis conclude either that the soul remembers something that the man does not; or else that memory belongs only to such ideas as are derived from the body, or the mind's operations about them.

18. How knows any one that the Soul always thinks? For if it be not a self-evident Proposition, it needs Proof.

I would be glad also to learn from these men who so confidently pronounce that the human soul, or, which is all one, that a man always thinks, how they come to know it; nay, how they come to know that they themselves think, when they themselves do not perceive it. This, I am afraid, is to be sure without proofs, and to know without perceiving. It is, I suspect, a confused notion, taken up to serve an hypothesis; and none of those clear truths, that either their own evidence forces us to admit, or common experience makes it impudence to deny. For the most that can be said of it is, that it is possible the soul may always think, but not always retain it in memory. And I say, it is as possible that the soul may not always think; and much more probable that it should sometimes not think, than that it should often think, and that a long while together, and not be conscious to itself, the next moment after, that it had thought.

19. That a Man should be busy in Thinking, and yet not retain it the next moment, very improbable.

To suppose the soul to think, and the man not to perceive it, is, as has been said, to make two persons in one man. And if one considers well these men's way of speaking, one should be led into a suspicion that they do so. For those who tell us that the SOUL always thinks, do never, that I remember, say that a MAN always thinks. Can the soul think, and not the man? Or a man think, and not be conscious of it? This, perhaps, would be suspected of jargon in others. If they say the man thinks always, but is not always conscious of it, they may as well say his body is extended without having parts. For it is altogether as intelligible to say that a body is extended without parts, as that anything thinks without being conscious of it, or perceiving that it does so. They who talk thus may, with as much reason, if it be necessary to their hypothesis, say that a man is always hungry, but that he does not always feel it; whereas hunger consists in that very sensation, as thinking consists in being conscious that one thinks. If they say that a man is always conscious to himself of thinking, I ask, How they know it? Consciousness is the perception of what passes in a man's own mind. Can another man perceive that I am conscious of anything, when I perceive it not myself? No man's knowledge here can go beyond his experience. Wake a man out of a sound sleep, and ask him what he was that moment thinking of. If he himself be conscious of nothing he then thought on, he must be a notable diviner of thoughts that can assure him that he was thinking. May he not, with more reason, assure him he was not asleep? This is something beyond philosophy; and it cannot be less than revelation, that discovers to another thoughts in my mind, when I can find none there myself. And they must needs have a penetrating sight who can certainly see that I think, when I cannot perceive it myself, and when I declare that I do not; and yet can see that dogs or elephants do not think, when they give all the demonstration of it imaginable, except only telling us that they do so. This some may suspect to be a step beyond the Rosicrucians; it seeming easier to make one's self invisible to others, than to make another's thoughts visible to me, which are not visible to himself. But it is but defining the soul to be "a substance that always thinks," and the business is done. If such definition be of any authority, I know not what it can serve for but to make many men suspect that they have no souls at all; since they find a good part of their lives pass away without thinking. For no definitions that I know, no suppositions of any sect, are of force enough to destroy constant experience; and perhaps it is the affectation of knowing beyond what we perceive, that makes so much useless dispute and noise in the world.

20. No ideas but from Sensation and Reflection, evident, if we observe Children.

I see no reason, therefore, to believe that the soul thinks before the senses have furnished it with ideas to think on; and as those are increased and retained, so it comes, by exercise, to improve its faculty of thinking in the several parts of it; as well as, afterwards, by compounding those ideas, and reflecting on its own operations, it increases its stock, as well as facility in remembering, imagining, reasoning, and other modes of thinking.

21. State of a child on the mother's womb.

He that will suffer himself to be informed by observation and experience, and not make his own hypothesis the rule of nature, will find few signs of a soul accustomed to much thinking in a new-born child, and much fewer of any reasoning at all. And yet it is hard to imagine that the rational soul should think so much, and not reason at all, And he that will consider that infants newly come into the world spend the greatest part of their time in sleep, and are seldom awake but when either hunger calls for the teat, or some pain (the most importunate of all sensations), or some other violent impression on the body, forces the mind to perceive and attend to it;—he, I say, who considers this, will perhaps find reason to imagine that a FOETUS in the mother's womb differs not much from the state of a vegetable, but passes the greatest part of its time without perception or thought; doing very little but sleep in a place where it needs not seek for food, and is surrounded with liquor, always equally soft, and near of the same temper; where the eyes have no light, and the ears so shut up are not very susceptible of sounds; and where there is little or no variety, or change of objects, to move the senses.

22. The mind thinks in proportion to the matter it gets from experience to think about.

Follow a child from its birth, and observe the alterations that time makes, and you shall find, as the mind by the senses comes more and more to be furnished with ideas, it comes to be more and more awake; thinks more, the more it has matter to think on. After some time it begins to know the objects which, being most familiar with it, have made lasting impressions. Thus it comes by degrees to know the persons it daily converses with, and distinguishes them from strangers; which are instances and effects of its coming to retain and distinguish the ideas the senses convey to it. And so we may observe how the mind, BY DEGREES, improves in these; and ADVANCES to the exercise of those other faculties of enlarging, compounding, and abstracting its ideas, and of reasoning about them, and reflecting upon all these; of which I shall have occasion to speak more hereafter.

23. A man begins to have ideas when he first has sensation. What sensation is.

If it shall be demanded then, WHEN a man BEGINS to have any ideas, I think the true answer is,—WHEN HE FIRST HAS ANY SENSATION. For, since there appear not to be any ideas in the mind before the senses have conveyed any in, I conceive that ideas in the understanding are coeval with SENSATION; WHICH IS SUCH AN IMPRESSION OR MOTION MADE IN SOME PART OF THE BODY, AS MAKES IT BE TAKEN NOTICE OF IN THE UNDERSTANDING.

24. The Original of all our Knowledge.

The impressions then that are made on our sense by outward objects that are extrinsical to the mind; and its own operations about these impressions, reflected on by itself, as proper objects to be contemplated by it, are, I conceive, the original of all knowledge. Thus the first capacity of human intellect is,—that the mind is fitted to receive the impressions made on it; either through the senses by outward objects, or by its own operations when it reflects on them. This is the first step a man makes towards the discovery of anything, and the groundwork whereon to build all those notions which ever he shall have naturally in this world. All those sublime thoughts which tower above the clouds, and reach as high as heaven itself, take their rise and footing here: in all that great extent wherein the mind wanders, in those remote speculations it may seem to be elevated with, it stirs not one jot beyond those ideas which SENSE or REFLECTION have offered for its contemplation.

25. In the Reception of simple Ideas, the Understanding is for the most part passive.

In this part the understanding is merely passive; and

whether or no it will have these beginnings, and as it were materials of knowledge, is not in its own power. For the objects of our senses do, many of them, obtrude their particular ideas upon our minds whether we will or not; and the operations of our minds will not let us be without, at least, some obscure notions of them. No man can be wholly ignorant of what he does when he thinks. These simple ideas, when offered to the mind, the understanding can no more refuse to have, nor alter when they are imprinted, nor blot them out and make new ones itself, than a mirror can refuse, alter, or obliterate the images or ideas which the objects set before it do therein produce. As the bodies that surround us do diversely affect our organs, the mind is forced to receive the impressions; and cannot avoid the perception of those ideas that are annexed to them.

Citation and Use

The text was taken from the following work.

John Locke, *An Essay Concerning Humane Understanding*, vol. 1, 2 vols. (Urbana, IL: Project Gutenberg, 2004), http://www.gutenberg.org/ebooks/10615.

ESSE EST PERCIPI

George Berkeley

The First Dialogue

Philonous Good morrow, Hylas: I did not expect to find you abroad so early.

Hylas It is indeed something unusual; but my thoughts were so taken up with a subject I was discoursing of last night, that finding I could not sleep, I resolved to rise and take a turn in the garden.

Philonous It happened well, to let you see what innocent and agreeable pleasures you lose every morning. Can there be a pleasanter time of the day, or a more delightful season of the year? That purple sky, those wild but sweet notes of birds, the fragrant bloom upon the trees and flowers, the gentle influence of the rising sun, these and a thousand nameless beauties of nature inspire the soul with secret transports; its faculties too being at this time fresh and lively, are fit for those meditations, which the solitude of a garden and tranquillity of the morning naturally dispose us to. But I am afraid I interrupt your thoughts: for you seemed very intent on something.

Hylas It is true, I was, and shall be obliged to you if you will permit me to go on in the same vein; not that I would by any means deprive myself of your company, for my thoughts always flow more easily in conversation with a friend, than when I am alone: but my request is, that you would suffer me to impart my reflexions to you.

Philonous With all my heart, it is what I should have requested myself if you had not prevented me.

Hylas I was considering the odd fate of those men who have in all ages, through an affectation of being distinguished from the vulgar, or some unaccountable turn of thought, pretended either to believe nothing at all, or to believe the most extravagant things in the world. This however might be borne, if their paradoxes and scepticism did not draw after them some consequences of general disadvantage to mankind. But the mischief lieth here; that when men of less leisure see them who are supposed to have spent their whole time in the pursuits of knowledge professing an entire ignorance of all things, or advancing such notions as are repugnant to plain and commonly received principles, they will be tempted to entertain suspicions concerning the most important truths, which they had hitherto held sacred and unquestionable.

Philonous I entirely agree with you, as to the ill tendency of the affected doubts of some philosophers, and fantastical conceits of others. I am even so far gone of late in this way of thinking, that I have quitted several of the sublime notions I had got in their schools for vulgar opinions. And I give it you on my word; since this revolt from metaphysical notions to the plain dictates of nature and common sense, I find my understanding strangely enlightened, so that I can now easily comprehend a great many things which before were all mystery and riddle.

Hylas I am glad to find there was nothing in the accounts I heard of you.

Philonous Pray, what were those?

Hylas You were represented, in last night's conversation, as one who maintained the most extravagant opinion that ever entered into the mind of man, to wit, that there is no such thing as MATERIAL SUBSTANCE in the world.

Philonous That there is no such thing as what PHILOSOPHERS CALL MATERIAL SUBSTANCE, I am seriously persuaded: but, if I were made to see anything absurd or sceptical in this, I should then have the same reason to renounce this that I imagine I have now to reject the contrary opinion.

Hylas What I can anything be more fantastical, more repugnant to Common Sense, or a more manifest piece of Scepticism, than to believe there is no such thing as MATTER?

Philonous Softly, good Hylas. What if it should prove that you, who hold there is, are, by virtue of that opinion, a greater sceptic, and maintain more paradoxes and repugnances to Common Sense, than I who believe no such thing?

Hylas You may as soon persuade me, the part is greater than the whole, as that, in order to avoid absurdity and Scepticism, I should ever be obliged to give up my opinion in this point.

Philonous Well then, are you content to admit that opinion for true, which upon examination shall appear most agreeable to Common Sense, and remote from Scepticism?

Hylas With all my heart. Since you are for raising disputes about the plainest things in nature, I am content for once to hear what you have to say.

Philonous Pray, Hylas, what do you mean by a SCEPTIC?

Hylas I mean what all men mean–one that doubts of everything.

Philonous He then who entertains no doubts concerning some particular point, with regard to that point cannot be thought a sceptic.

Hylas I agree with you.

Philonous Whether doth doubting consist in embracing the affirmative or negative side of a question?

Hylas In neither; for whoever understands English cannot but know that DOUBTING signifies a suspense between both.

Philonous He then that denies any point, can no more be said to doubt of it, than he who affirmeth it with the same degree of assurance.

Hylas True.

Philonous And, consequently, for such his denial is no more to be esteemed a sceptic than the other.

Hylas I acknowledge it.

Philonous How cometh it to pass then, Hylas, that you pronounce me A SCEPTIC, because I deny what you affirm, to wit, the existence of Matter? Since, for aught you can tell, I am as peremptory in my denial, as you in your affirmation.

Hylas Hold, Philonous, I have been a little out in my definition; but every false step a man makes in discourse is not to be insisted on. I said indeed that a SCEPTIC was one who doubted of everything; but I should have added, or who denies the reality and truth of things.

Philonous What things? Do you mean the principles and theorems of sciences? But these you know are universal intellectual notions, and consequently independent of Matter. The denial therefore of this doth not imply the denying them.

Hylas I grant it. But are there no other things? What think you of distrusting the senses, of denying the real existence of sensible things, or pretending to know nothing of them. Is not this sufficient to denominate a man a SCEPTIC?

Philonous Shall we therefore examine which of us it is that denies the reality of sensible things, or professes the greatest ignorance of them; since, if I take you rightly, he is to be esteemed the greatest SCEPTIC?

Hylas That is what I desire.

Philonous What mean you by Sensible Things?

Hylas Those things which are perceived by the senses. Can you imagine that I mean anything else?

Philonous Pardon me, Hylas, if I am desirous clearly to apprehend your notions, since this may much shorten our inquiry. Suffer me then to ask you this farther question. Are those things only perceived by the senses which are perceived immediately? Or, may those things properly be said to be SENSIBLE which are perceived mediately, or not without the intervention of others?

Hylas I do not sufficiently understand you.

Philonous In reading a book, what I immediately perceive are the letters; but mediately, or by means of these, are suggested to my mind the notions of God, virtue, truth, &c. Now, that the letters are truly sensible things, or perceived by sense, there is no doubt: but I would know whether you take the things suggested by them to be so too.

Hylas No, certainly: it were absurd to think GOD or VIRTUE sensible things; though they may be signified and suggested to the mind by sensible marks, with which they have an arbitrary connexion.

Philonous It seems then, that by SENSIBLE THINGS you mean those only which can be perceived IMMEDIATELY by sense?

Hylas Right.

Philonous Doth it not follow from this, that though I see one part of the sky red, and another blue, and that my reason doth thence evidently conclude there must be some cause of that diversity of colors, yet that cause cannot be said to be a sensible thing, or perceived by the sense of seeing?

Hylas It doth.

Philonous In like manner, though I hear variety of sounds, yet I cannot be said to hear the causes of those sounds?

Hylas You cannot.

Philonous And when by my touch I perceive a thing to be

hot and heavy, I cannot say, with any truth or propriety, that I feel the cause of its heat or weight?

Hylas To prevent any more questions of this kind, I tell you once for all, that by SENSIBLE THINGS I mean those only which are perceived by sense; and that in truth the senses perceive nothing which they do not perceive IMMEDIATELY: for they make no inferences. The deducing therefore of causes or occasions from effects and appearances, which alone are perceived by sense, entirely relates to reason.

Philonous This point then is agreed between us–That SENSIBLE THINGS ARE THOSE ONLY WHICH ARE IMMEDIATELY PERCEIVED BY SENSE. You will farther inform me, whether we immediately perceive by sight anything beside light, and colors, and figures; or by hearing, anything but sounds; by the palate, anything beside tastes; by the smell, beside odours; or by the touch, more than tangible qualities.

Hylas We do not.

Philonous It seems, therefore, that if you take away all sensible qualities, there remains nothing sensible?

Hylas I grant it.

Philonous Sensible things therefore are nothing else but so many sensible qualities, or combinations of sensible qualities?

Hylas Nothing else.

Philonous HEAT then is a sensible thing?

Hylas Certainly.

Philonous Doth the REALITY of sensible things consist in being perceived? or, is it something distinct from their being perceived, and that bears no relation to the mind?

Hylas To EXIST is one thing, and to be PERCEIVED is another.

Philonous I speak with regard to sensible things only. And of these I ask, whether by their real existence you mean a subsistence exterior to the mind, and distinct from their being perceived?

Hylas I mean a real absolute being, distinct from, and without any relation to, their being perceived.

Philonous Heat therefore, if it be allowed a real being, must exist without the mind?

Hylas It must.

Philonous Tell me, Hylas, is this real existence equally compatible to all degrees of heat, which we perceive; or is there any reason why we should attribute it to some,

and deny it to others? And if there be, pray let me know that reason.

Hylas Whatever degree of heat we perceive by sense, we may be sure the same exists in the object that occasions it.

Philonous What! the greatest as well as the least?

Hylas _I_ tell you, the reason is plainly the same in respect of both. They are both perceived by sense; nay, the greater degree of heat is more sensibly perceived; and consequently, if there is any difference, we are more certain of its real existence than we can be of the reality of a lesser degree.

Philonous But is not the most vehement and intense degree of heat a very great pain?

Hylas No one can deny it.

Philonous And is any unperceiving thing capable of pain or pleasure?

Hylas No, certainly.

Philonous Is your material substance a senseless being, or a being endowed with sense and perception?

Hylas It is senseless without doubt.

Philonous It cannot therefore be the subject of pain?

Hylas By no means.

Philonous Nor consequently of the greatest heat perceived by sense, since you acknowledge this to be no small pain?

Hylas I grant it.

Philonous What shall we say then of your external object; is it a material Substance, or no?

Hylas It is a material substance with the sensible qualities inhering in it.

Philonous How then can a great heat exist in it, since you own it cannot in a material substance? I desire you would clear this point.

Hylas Hold, Philonous, I fear I was out in yielding intense heat to be a pain. It should seem rather, that pain is something distinct from heat, and the consequence or effect of it.

Philonous Upon putting your hand near the fire, do you perceive one simple uniform sensation, or two distinct sensations?

Hylas But one simple sensation.

Philonous Is not the heat immediately perceived?

Hylas It is.

Philonous And the pain?

Hylas True.

Philonous Seeing therefore they are both immediately perceived at the same time, and the fire affects you only with one simple or uncompounded idea, it follows that this same simple idea is both the intense heat immediately perceived, and the pain; and, consequently, that the intense heat immediately perceived is nothing distinct from a particular sort of pain.

Hylas It seems so.

Philonous Again, try in your thoughts, Hylas, if you can conceive a vehement sensation to be without pain or pleasure.

Hylas I cannot.

Philonous Or can you frame to yourself an idea of sensible pain or pleasure in general, abstracted from every particular idea of heat, cold, tastes, smells? &c.

Hylas I do not find that I can.

Philonous Doth it not therefore follow, that sensible pain is nothing distinct from those sensations or ideas, in an intense degree?

Hylas It is undeniable; and, to speak the truth, I begin to suspect a very great heat cannot exist but in a mind perceiving it.

Philonous What! are you then in that sceptical state of suspense, between affirming and denying?

Hylas I think I may be positive in the point. A very violent and painful heat cannot exist without the mind.

Philonous It hath not therefore according to you, any REAL being?

Hylas I own it.

Philonous Is it therefore certain, that there is no body in nature really hot?

Hylas I have not denied there is any real heat in bodies. I only say, there is no such thing as an intense real heat.

Philonous But, did you not say before that all degrees of heat were equally real; or, if there was any difference, that the greater were more undoubtedly real than the lesser?

Hylas True: but it was because I did not then consider the ground there is for distinguishing between them, which I now plainly see. And it is this: because intense heat is nothing else but a particular kind of painful sensation; and pain cannot exist but in a perceiving

being; it follows that no intense heat can really exist in an unperceiving corporeal substance. But this is no reason why we should deny heat in an inferior degree to exist in such a substance.

Philonous But how shall we be able to discern those degrees of heat which exist only in the mind from those which exist without it?

Hylas That is no difficult matter. You know the least pain cannot exist unperceived; whatever, therefore, degree of heat is a pain exists only in the mind. But, as for all other degrees of heat, nothing obliges us to think the same of them.

Philonous I think you granted before that no unperceiving being was capable of pleasure, any more than of pain.

Hylas I did.

Philonous And is not warmth, or a more gentle degree of heat than what causes uneasiness, a pleasure?

Hylas What then?

Philonous Consequently, it cannot exist without the mind in an unperceiving substance, or body.

Hylas So it seems.

Philonous Since, therefore, as well those degrees of heat that are not painful, as those that are, can exist only in a thinking substance; may we not conclude that external bodies are absolutely incapable of any degree of heat whatsoever?

Hylas On second thoughts, I do not think it so evident that warmth is a pleasure as that a great degree of heat is a pain.

Philonous _I_ do not pretend that warmth is as great a pleasure as heat is a pain. But, if you grant it to be even a small pleasure, it serves to make good my conclusion.

Hylas I could rather call it an INDOLENCE. It seems to be nothing more than a privation of both pain and pleasure. And that such a quality or state as this may agree to an unthinking substance, I hope you will not deny.

Philonous If you are resolved to maintain that warmth, or a gentle degree of heat, is no pleasure, I know not how to convince you otherwise than by appealing to your own sense. But what think you of cold?

Hylas The same that I do of heat. An intense degree of cold is a pain; for to feel a very great cold, is to perceive a great uneasiness: it cannot therefore exist without the mind; but a lesser degree of cold may, as well as a lesser degree of heat.

Philonous Those bodies, therefore, upon whose application to our own, we perceive a moderate degree of heat, must be concluded to have a moderate degree of heat or warmth in them; and those, upon whose application we feel a like degree of cold, must be thought to have cold in them.

Hylas They must.

Philonous Can any doctrine be true that necessarily leads a man into an absurdity?

Hylas Without doubt it cannot.

Philonous Is it not an absurdity to think that the same thing should be at the same time both cold and warm?

Hylas It is.

Philonous Suppose now one of your hands hot, and the other cold, and that they are both at once put into the same vessel of water, in an intermediate state; will not the water seem cold to one hand, and warm to the other?

Hylas It will.

Philonous Ought we not therefore, by your principles, to conclude it is really both cold and warm at the same time, that is, according to your own concession, to believe an absurdity?

Hylas I confess it seems so.

Philonous Consequently, the principles themselves are false, since you have granted that no true principle leads to an absurdity.

Hylas But, after all, can anything be more absurd than to say, THERE IS NO HEAT IN THE FIRE?

Philonous To make the point still clearer; tell me whether, in two cases exactly alike, we ought not to make the same judgment?

Hylas We ought.

Philonous When a pin pricks your finger, doth it not rend and divide the fibres of your flesh?

Hylas It doth.

Philonous And when a coal burns your finger, doth it any more?

Hylas It doth not.

Philonous Since, therefore, you neither judge the sensation itself occasioned by the pin, nor anything like it to be in the pin; you should not, conformably to what you have now granted, judge the sensation occasioned by the fire, or anything like it, to be in the fire.

Hylas Well, since it must be so, I am content to yield this point, and acknowledge that heat and cold are only sensations existing in our minds. But there still remain qualities enough to secure the reality of external things.

Philonous But what will you say, Hylas, if it shall appear that the case is the same with regard to all other sensible qualities, and that they can no more be supposed to exist without the mind, than heat and cold?

Hylas Then indeed you will have done something to the purpose; but that is what I despair of seeing proved.

Philonous Let us examine them in order. What think you of TASTES, do they exist without the mind, or no?

Hylas Can any man in his senses doubt whether sugar is sweet, or wormwood bitter?

Philonous Inform me, Hylas. Is a sweet taste a particular kind of pleasure or pleasant sensation, or is it not?

Hylas It is.

Philonous And is not bitterness some kind of uneasiness or pain?

Hylas I grant it.

Philonous If therefore sugar and wormwood are unthinking corporeal substances existing without the mind, how can sweetness and bitterness, that is, Pleasure and pain, agree to them?

Hylas Hold, Philonous, I now see what it was delude time. You asked whether heat and cold, sweetness at were not particular sorts of pleasure and pain; to which simply, that they were. Whereas I should have thus distinguished: those qualities, as perceived by us, are pleasures or pair existing in the external objects. We must not therefore conclude absolutely, that there is no heat in the fire, or sweetness in the sugar, but only that heat or sweetness, as perceived by us, are not in the fire or sugar. What say you to this?

Philonous I say it is nothing to the purpose. Our discourse proceeded altogether concerning sensible things, which you defined to be, THE THINGS WE IMMEDIATELY PERCEIVE BY OUR SENSES. Whatever other qualities, therefore, you speak of as distinct from these, I know nothing of them, neither do they at all belong to the point in dispute. You may, indeed, pretend to have discovered certain qualities which you do not perceive, and assert those insensible qualities exist in fire and sugar. But what use can be made of this to your present purpose, I am at a loss to conceive. Tell me then once more, do you acknowledge that heat and cold, sweetness and bitterness (meaning those qualities which are perceived by the senses), do not exist without the mind?

Hylas I see it is to no purpose to hold out, so I give up the cause as to those mentioned qualities. Though I profess it sounds oddly, to say that sugar is not sweet.

Philonous But, for your farther satisfaction, take this along with you: that which at other times seems sweet, shall, to a distempered palate, appear bitter. And, nothing can be plainer than that divers persons perceive different tastes in the same food; since that which one man delights in, another abhors. And how could this be, if the taste was something really inherent in the food?

Hylas I acknowledge I know not how.

Philonous In the next place, ODOURS are to be considered. And, with regard to these, I would fain know whether what hath been said of tastes doth not exactly agree to them? Are they not so many pleasing or displeasing sensations?

Hylas They are.

Philonous Can you then conceive it possible that they should exist in an unperceiving thing?

Hylas I cannot.

Philonous Or, can you imagine that filth and ordure affect those brute animals that feed on them out of choice, with the same smells which we perceive in them?

Hylas By no means.

Philonous May we not therefore conclude of smells, as of the other forementioned qualities, that they cannot exist in any but a perceiving substance or mind?

Hylas I think so.

Philonous Then as to SOUNDS, what must we think of them: are they accidents really inherent in external bodies, or not?

Hylas That they inhere not in the sonorous bodies is plain from hence: because a bell struck in the exhausted receiver of an air-pump sends forth no sound. The air, therefore, must be thought the subject of sound.

Philonous What reason is there for that, Hylas?

Hylas Because, when any motion is raised in the air, we perceive a sound greater or lesser, according to the air's motion; but without some motion in the air, we never hear any sound at all.

Philonous And granting that we never hear a sound but when some motion is produced in the air, yet I do not see how you can infer from thence, that the sound itself is in the air.

Hylas It is this very motion in the external air that produces in the mind the sensation of SOUND..For, striking on the drum of the ear, it causeth a vibration, which by the auditory nerves being communicated to the brain, the soul is thereupon affected with the sensation called SOUND.

Philonous What! is sound then a sensation?

Hylas I tell you, as perceived by us, it is a particular sensation in the mind.

Philonous And can any sensation exist without the mind?

Hylas No, certainly.

Philonous How then can sound, being a sensation, exist in the air, if by the AIR you mean a senseless substance existing without the mind?

Hylas You must distinguish, Philonous, between sound as it is perceived by us, and as it is in itself; or (which is the same thing) between the sound we immediately perceive, and that which exists without us. The former, indeed, is a particular kind of sensation, but the latter is merely a vibrative or undulatory motion the air.

Philonous I thought I had already obviated that distinction, by answer I gave when you were applying it in a like case before. But, to say no more of that, are you sure then that sound is really nothing but motion?

Hylas I am.

Philonous Whatever therefore agrees to real sound, may with truth be attributed to motion?

Hylas It may.

Philonous It is then good sense to speak of MOTION as of a thing that is LOUD, SWEET, ACUTE, or GRAVE.

Hylas _I_ see you are resolved not to understand me. Is it not evident those accidents or modes belong only to sensible sound, or SOUND in the common acceptation of the word, but not to sound in the real and philosophic sense; which, as I just now told you, is nothing but a certain motion of the air?

Philonous It seems then there are two sorts of sound–the one vulgar, or that which is heard, the other philosophical and real?

Hylas Even so.

Philonous And the latter consists in motion?

Hylas I told you so before.

Philonous Tell me, Hylas, to which of the senses, think you, the idea of motion belongs? to the hearing?

Hylas No, certainly; but to the sight and touch.

Philonous It should follow then, that, according to you, real sounds may possibly be SEEN OR FELT, but never HEARD.

Hylas Look you, Philonous, you may, if you please, make a jest of my opinion, but that will not alter the truth of things. I own, indeed, the inferences you draw me into sound something oddly; but common language, you know, is framed by, and for the use of the vulgar: we must not therefore wonder if expressions adapted to exact philosophic notions seem uncouth and out of the way.

Philonous Is it come to that? I assure you, I imagine myself to have gained no small point, since you make so light of departing from common phrases and opinions; it being a main part of our inquiry, to examine whose notions are widest of the common road, and most repugnant to the general sense of the world. But, can you think it no more than a philosophical paradox, to say that REAL SOUNDS ARE NEVER HEARD, and that the idea of them is obtained by some other sense? And is there nothing in this contrary to nature and the truth of things?

Hylas To deal ingenuously, I do not like it. And, after the concessions already made, I had as well grant that sounds too have no real being without the mind.

Philonous And I hope you will make no difficulty to acknowledge the same of colorS.

Hylas Pardon me: the case of colors is very different. Can anything be plainer than that we see them on the objects?

Philonous The objects you speak of are, I suppose, corporeal Substances existing without the mind?

Hylas They are.

Philonous And have true and real colors inhering in them?

Hylas Each visible object hath that color which we see in it.

Philonous How! is there anything visible but what we perceive by sight?

Hylas There is not.

Philonous And, do we perceive anything by sense which we do not perceive immediately?

Hylas How often must I be obliged to repeat the same thing? I tell you, we do not.

Philonous Have patience, good Hylas; and tell me once more, whether there is anything immediately perceived by the senses, except sensible qualities. I know you asserted there was not; but I would now be informed, whether you still persist in the same opinion.

Hylas I do.

Philonous Pray, is your corporeal substance either a sensible quality, or made up of sensible qualities?

Hylas What a question that is! who ever thought it was?

Philonous My reason for asking was, because in saying, EACH VISIBLE OBJECT HATH THAT color WHICH WE SEE IN IT, you make visible objects to be corporeal substances; which implies either that corporeal substances are sensible qualities, or else that there is something besides sensible qualities perceived by sight: but, as this point was formerly agreed between us, and is still maintained by you, it is a clear consequence, that your CORPOREAL SUBSTANCE is nothing distinct from SENSIBLE QUALITIES.

Hylas You may draw as many absurd consequences as you please, and endeavour to perplex the plainest things; but you shall never persuade me out of my senses. I clearly understand my own meaning.

Philonous I wish you would make me understand it too. But, since you are unwilling to have your notion of corporeal substance examined, I shall urge that point no farther. Only be pleased to let me know, whether the same colors which we see exist in external bodies, or some other.

Hylas The very same.

Philonous What! are then the beautiful red and purple we see on yonder clouds really in them? Or do you imagine they have in themselves any other form than that of a dark mist or vapour?

Hylas I must own, Philonous, those colors are not really in the clouds as they seem to be at this distance. They are only apparent colors.

Philonous APPARENT call you them? how shall we distinguish these apparent colors from real?

Hylas Very easily. Those are to be thought apparent which, appearing only at a distance, vanish upon a nearer approach.

Philonous And those, I suppose, are to be thought real which are discovered by the most near and exact survey.

Hylas Right.

Philonous Is the nearest and exactest survey made by the help of a microscope, or by the naked eye?

Hylas By a microscope, doubtless.

Philonous But a microscope often discovers colors in an object different from those perceived by the unassisted sight. And, in case we had microscopes magnifying to any assigned degree, it is certain that no object whatsoever, viewed through them, would appear in the same color which it exhibits to the naked eye.

Hylas And what will you conclude from all this? You cannot argue that there are really and naturally no colors on objects: because by artificial managements they may be altered, or made to vanish.

Philonous I think it may evidently be concluded from your own concessions, that all the colors we see with our naked eyes are only apparent as those on the clouds, since they vanish upon a more close and accurate inspection which is afforded us by a microscope. Then' as to what you say by way of prevention: I ask you whether the real and natural state of an object is better discovered by a very sharp and piercing sight, or by one which is less sharp?

Hylas By the former without doubt.

Philonous Is it not plain from DIOPTRICS that microscopes make the sight more penetrating, and represent objects as they would appear to the eye in case it were naturally endowed with a most exquisite sharpness?

Hylas It is.

Philonous Consequently the microscopical representation is to be thought that which best sets forth the real nature of the thing, or what it is in itself. The colors, therefore, by it perceived are more genuine and real than those perceived otherwise.

Hylas I confess there is something in what you say.

Philonous Besides, it is not only possible but manifest, that there actually are animals whose eyes are by nature framed to perceive those things which by reason of their minuteness escape our sight. What think you of those inconceivably small animals perceived by glasses? must we suppose they are all stark blind? Or, in case they see, can it be imagined their sight hath not the same use in preserving their bodies from injuries, which appears in that of all other animals? And if it hath, is it not evident they must see particles less than their own bodies; which will present them with a far different view in each object from that which strikes our senses? Even our own eyes do not always represent objects to us after the same manner. In the jaundice every one knows that all things seem yellow. Is it not therefore highly probable those animals in whose eyes we discern a very different texture from that of ours, and whose bodies abound with different humours, do not see the same colors in every object that we do? From all which, should it not seem to follow that all colors are equally apparent, and that none of those which we perceive are really inherent in any outward object?

Hylas It should.

Philonous The point will be past all doubt, if you consider that, in case colors were real properties or affections inherent in external bodies, they could admit of no alteration without some change wrought in the very bodies themselves: but, is it not evident from what hath been said that, upon the use of microscopes, upon a change happening in the burnouts of the eye, or a variation of distance, without any manner of real alteration in the thing itself, the colors of any object are either changed, or totally disappear? Nay, all other circumstances remaining the same, change but the situation of some objects, and they shall present different colors to the eye. The same thing happens upon viewing an object in various degrees of light. And what is more known than that the same bodies appear differently colored by candle-light from what they do in the open day? Add to these the experiment of a prism which, separating the heterogeneous rays of light, alters the color of any object, and will cause the whitest to appear of a deep blue or red to the naked eye. And now tell me whether you are still of opinion that every body hath its true real color inhering in it; and, if you think it hath, I would fain know farther from you, what certain distance and position of the object, what peculiar texture and formation of the eye, what degree or kind of light is necessary for ascertaining that true color, and distinguishing it from apparent ones.

Hylas I own myself entirely satisfied, that they are all equally apparent, and that there is no such thing as color really inhering in external bodies, but that it is altogether in the light. And what confirms me in this opinion is, that in proportion to the light colors are still more or less vivid; and if there be no light, then are there no colors perceived. Besides, allowing there are colors on external objects, yet, how is it possible for us to perceive them? For no external body affects the mind, unless it acts first on our organs of sense. But the only action of bodies is motion; and motion cannot be communicated otherwise than by impulse. A distant object therefore cannot act on the eye; nor consequently make itself or its properties perceivable to the soul. Whence it plainly follows that it is immediately some contiguous substance, which, operating on the eye, occasions a perception of colors: and such is light.

Philonous Howl is light then a substance?

Hylas . I tell you, Philonous, external light is nothing but a thin fluid substance, whose minute particles being agitated with a brisk motion, and in various manners reflected from the different surfaces of outward objects to the eyes, communicate different motions to the optic nerves; which, being propagated to the brain, cause therein various impressions; and these are attended with the sensations of red, blue, yellow, &c.

Philonous It seems then the light doth no more than shake the optic nerves.

Hylas Nothing else.

Philonous And consequent to each particular motion of the nerves, the mind is affected with a sensation, which is some particular color.

Hylas Right.

Philonous And these sensations have no existence without the mind.

Hylas They have not.

Philonous How then do you affirm that colors are in the light; since by LIGHT you understand a corporeal substance external to the mind?

Hylas Light and colors, as immediately perceived by us, I grant cannot exist without the mind. But in themselves they are only the motions and configurations of certain insensible particles of matter.

Philonous colors then, in the vulgar sense, or taken for the immediate objects of sight, cannot agree to any but a perceiving substance.

Hylas That is what I say.

Philonous Well then, since you give up the point as to those sensible qualities which are alone thought colors by all mankind beside, you may hold what you please with regard to those invisible ones of the philosophers. It is not my business to dispute about THEM; only I would advise you to bethink yourself, whether, considering the inquiry we are upon, it be prudent for you to affirm—THE RED AND BLUE WHICH WE SEE ARE NOT REAL colorS, BUT CERTAIN UNKNOWN MOTIONS AND FIGURES WHICH NO MAN EVER DID OR CAN SEE ARE TRULY SO. Are not these shocking notions, and are not they subject to as many ridiculous inferences, as those you were obliged to renounce before in the case of sounds?

Hylas I frankly own, Philonous, that it is in vain to longer. colors, sounds, tastes, in a word all those termed SECONDARY QUALITIES, have certainly no existence without the mind. But by this acknowledgment I must not be supposed to derogate, the reality of Matter, or external objects; seeing it is no more than several philosophers maintain, who nevertheless are the farthest imaginable from denying Matter. For the clearer understanding of this, you must know sensible qualities are by philosophers divided into PRIMARY and SECONDARY. The former are Extension, Figure, Solidity, Gravity, Motion, and Rest; and these they hold exist really in bodies. The latter are those above enumerated; or, briefly, ALL SENSIBLE QUALITIES BESIDE THE PRIMARY; which they assert are only so many sensations or ideas existing nowhere but in the mind. But all this, I doubt not, you are apprised of. For my part, I have been a long time sensible there was such an opinion current among philosophers, but was never thoroughly convinced of its truth until now.

Philonous You are still then of opinion that EXTENSION and FIGURES are inherent in external unthinking substances?

Hylas I am.

Philonous But what if the same arguments which are brought against Secondary Qualities will hold good against these also?

Hylas Why then I shall be obliged to think, they too exist only in the mind.

Philonous Is it your opinion the very figure and extension which you perceive by sense exist in the outward object or material substance?

Hylas It is.

Philonous Have all other animals as good grounds to think the same of the figure and extension which they see and feel?

Hylas Without doubt, if they have any thought at all.

Philonous Answer me, Hylas. Think you the senses were bestowed upon all animals for their preservation and well-being in life? or were they given to men alone for this end?

Hylas I make no question but they have the same use in all other animals.

Philonous If so, is it not necessary they should be enabled by them to perceive their own limbs, and those bodies which are capable of harming them?

Hylas Certainly.

Philonous A mite therefore must be supposed to see his own foot, and things equal or even less than it, as bodies of some considerable dimension; though at the same time they appear to you scarce discernible, or at best as so many visible points?

Hylas I cannot deny it.

Philonous And to creatures less than the mite they will seem yet larger?

Hylas They will.

Philonous Insomuch that what you can hardly discern will to another extremely minute animal appear as some huge mountain?

Hylas All this I grant.

Philonous Can one and the same thing be at the same time in itself of different dimensions?

Hylas That were absurd to imagine.

Philonous But, from what you have laid down it follows that both the extension by you perceived, and that perceived by the mite itself, as likewise all those perceived by lesser animals, are each of them the true extension of the mite's foot; that is to say, by your own principles you are led into an absurdity.

Hylas There seems to be some difficulty in the point.

Philonous Again, have you not acknowledged that no real

inherent property of any object can be changed without some change in the thing itself?

Hylas I have.

Philonous But, as we approach to or recede from an object, the visible extension varies, being at one distance ten or a hundred times greater than another. Doth it not therefore follow from hence likewise that it is not really inherent in the object?

Hylas I own I am at a loss what to think.

Philonous Your judgment will soon be determined, if you will venture to think as freely concerning this quality as you have done concerning the rest. Was it not admitted as a good argument, that neither heat nor cold was in the water, because it seemed warm to one hand and cold to the other?

Hylas It was.

Philonous Is it not the very same reasoning to conclude, there is no extension or figure in an object, because to one eye it shall seem little, smooth, and round, when at the same time it appears to the other, great, uneven, and regular?

Hylas The very same. But does this latter fact ever happen?

Philonous You may at any time make the experiment, by looking with one eye bare, and with the other through a microscope.

Hylas I know not how to maintain it; and yet I am loath to give up EXTENSION, I see so many odd consequences following upon such a concession.

Philonous Odd, say you? After the concessions already made, I hope you will stick at nothing for its oddness. But, on the other hand, should it not seem very odd, if the general reasoning which includes all other sensible qualities did not also include extension? If it be allowed that no idea, nor anything like an idea, can exist in an unperceiving substance, then surely it follows that no figure, or mode of extension, which we can either perceive, or imagine, or have any idea of, can be really inherent in Matter; not to mention the peculiar difficulty there must be in conceiving a material substance, prior to and distinct from extension to be the SUBSTRATUM of extension. Be the sensible quality what it will–figure, or sound, or color, it seems alike impossible it should subsist in that which doth not perceive it.

Hylas I give up the point for the present, reserving still a right to retract my opinion, in case I shall hereafter discover any false step in my progress to it.

Philonous That is a right you cannot be denied. Figures and extension being despatched, we proceed next to

MOTION. Can a real motion in any external body be at the same time very swift and very slow?

Hylas It cannot.

Philonous Is not the motion of a body swift in a reciprocal proportion to the time it takes up in describing any given space? Thus a body that describes a mile in an hour moves three times faster than it would in case it described only a mile in three hours.

Hylas I agree with you.

Philonous And is not time measured by the succession of ideas in our minds?

Hylas It is.

Philonous And is it not possible ideas should succeed one another twice as fast in your mind as they do in mine, or in that of some spirit of another kind?

Hylas I own it.

Philonous Consequently the same body may to another seem to perform its motion over any space in half the time that it doth to you. And the same reasoning will hold as to any other proportion: that is to say, according to your principles (since the motions perceived are both really in the object) it is possible one and the same body shall be really moved the same way at once, both very swift and very slow. How is this consistent either with common sense, or with what you just now granted?

Hylas I have nothing to say to it.

Philonous Then as for SOLIDITY; either you do not mean any sensible quality by that word, and so it is beside our inquiry: or if you do, it must be either hardness or resistance. But both the one and the other are plainly relative to our senses: it being evident that what seems hard to one animal may appear soft to another, who hath greater force and firmness of limbs. Nor is it less plain that the resistance I feel is not in the body.

Hylas I own the very SENSATION of resistance, which is all you immediately perceive, is not in the body; but the CAUSE of that sensation is.

Philonous But the causes of our sensations are not things immediately perceived, and therefore are not sensible. This point I thought had been already determined.

Hylas I own it was; but you will pardon me if I seem a little embarrassed: I know not how to quit my old notions.

Philonous To help you out, do but consider that if EXTENSION be once acknowledged to have no existence without the mind, the same must necessarily be granted of motion, solidity, and gravity; since they all evidently suppose extension. It is therefore superfluous to inquire particularly concerning each of them. In denying extension, you have denied them all to have any real existence.

Hylas I wonder, Philonous, if what you say be true, why those philosophers who deny the Secondary Qualities any real existence should yet attribute it to the Primary. If there is no difference between them, how can this be accounted for?

Philonous It is not my business to account for every opinion of the philosophers. But, among other reasons which may be assigned for this, it seems probable that pleasure and pain being rather annexed to the former than the latter may be one. Heat and cold, tastes and smells, have something more vividly pleasing or disagreeable than the ideas of extension, figure, and motion affect us with. And, it being too visibly absurd to hold that pain or pleasure can be in an unperceiving substance, men are more easily weaned from believing the external existence of the Secondary than the Primary Qualities. You will be satisfied there is something in this, if you recollect the difference you made between an intense and more moderate degree of heat; allowing the one a real existence, while you denied it to the other. But, after all, there is no rational ground for that distinction; for, surely an indifferent sensation is as truly a SENSATION as one more pleasing or painful; and consequently should not any more than they be supposed to exist in an unthinking subject.

Hylas It is just come into my head, Philonous, that I have somewhere heard of a distinction between absolute and sensible extension. Now, though it be acknowledged that GREAT and SMALL, consisting merely in the relation which other extended beings have to the parts of our own bodies, do not really inhere in the substances themselves; yet nothing obliges us to hold the same with regard to ABSOLUTE EXTENSION, which is something abstracted from GREAT and SMALL, from this or that particular magnitude or figure. So likewise as to motion; SWIFT and SLOW are altogether relative to the succession of ideas in our own minds. But, it doth not follow, because those modifications of motion exist not without the mind, that therefore absolute motion abstracted from them doth not.

Philonous Pray what is it that distinguishes one motion, or one part of extension, from another? Is it not something sensible, as some degree of swiftness or slowness, some certain magnitude or figure peculiar to each?

Hylas I think so.

Philonous These qualities, therefore, stripped of all sensible properties, are without all specific and numerical differences, as the schools call them.

Hylas They are.

Philonous That is to say, they are extension in general, and motion in general.

Hylas Let it be so.

Philonous But it is a universally received maxim that EVERYTHING WHICH EXISTS IS PARTICULAR. How then can motion in general, or extension in general, exist in any corporeal substance?

Hylas I will take time to solve your difficulty.

Philonous But I think the point may be speedily decided. Without doubt you can tell whether you are able to frame this or that idea. Now I am content to put our dispute on this issue. If you can frame in your thoughts a distinct ABSTRACT IDEA of motion or extension, divested of all those sensible modes, as swift and slow, great and small, round and square, and the like, which are acknowledged to exist only in the mind, I will then yield the point you contend for. But if you cannot, it will be unreasonable on your side to insist any longer upon what you have no notion of.

Hylas To confess ingenuously, I cannot.

Philonous Can you even separate the ideas of extension and motion from the ideas of all those qualities which they who make the distinction term SECONDARY?

Hylas What! is it not an easy matter to consider extension and motion by themselves, abstracted from all other sensible qualities? Pray how do the mathematicians treat of them?

Philonous I acknowledge, Hylas, it is not difficult to form general propositions and reasonings about those qualities, without mentioning any other; and, in this sense, to consider or treat of them abstractedly. But, how doth it follow that, because I can pronounce the word MOTION by itself, I can form the idea of it in my mind exclusive of body? or, because theorems may be made of extension and figures, without any mention of GREAT or SMALL, or any other sensible mode or quality, that therefore it is possible such an abstract idea of extension, without any particular size or figure, or sensible quality, should be distinctly formed, and apprehended by the mind? Mathematicians treat of quantity, without regarding what other sensible. qualities it is attended with, as being altogether indifferent to their demonstrations. But, when laying aside the words, they contemplate the bare ideas, I believe you will find, they are not the pure abstracted ideas of extension.

Hylas But what say you to PURE INTELLECT? May not abstracted ideas be framed by that faculty?

Philonous Since I cannot frame abstract ideas at all, it is plain I cannot frame them by the help of PURE INTELLECT; whatsoever faculty you understand by those words. Besides, not to inquire into the nature of pure intellect and its spiritual objects, as VIRTUE, REASON, GOD, or the like, thus much seems manifest—that sensible things are only to be perceived by sense, or represented by the imagination. Figures, therefore, and extension, being originally perceived by sense, do not belong to pure intellect: but, for your farther satisfaction, try if you can frame the idea of any figure, abstracted from all particularities of size, or even from other sensible qualities.

Hylas Let me think a little–I do not find that I can.

Philonous And can you think it possible that should really exist in nature which implies a repugnancy in its conception?

Hylas By no means.

Philonous Since therefore it is impossible even for the mind to disunite the ideas of extension and motion from all other sensible qualities, doth it not follow, that where the one exist there necessarily the other exist likewise?

Hylas It should seem so.

Philonous Consequently, the very same arguments which you admitted as conclusive against the Secondary Qualities are, without any farther application of force, against the Primary too. Besides, if you will trust your senses, is it not plain all sensible qualities coexist, or to them appear as being in the same place? Do they ever represent a motion, or figure, as being divested of all other visible and tangible qualities?

Hylas You need say no more on this head. I am free to own, if there be no secret error or oversight in our proceedings hitherto, that all sensible qualities are alike to be denied existence without the mind. But, my fear is that I have been too liberal in my former concessions, or overlooked some fallacy or other. In short, I did not take time to think.

Philonous For that matter, Hylas, you may take what time you please in reviewing the progress of our inquiry. You are at liberty to recover any slips you might have made, or offer whatever you have omitted which makes for your first opinion.

Hylas One great oversight I take to be this–that I did not sufficiently distinguish the OBJECT from the SENSATION. Now, though this latter may not exist without the mind, yet it will not thence follow that the former cannot.

Philonous What object do you mean? the object of the senses?

Hylas The same.

Philonous It is then immediately perceived?

Hylas Right.

Philonous Make me to understand the difference between what is immediately perceived and a sensation.

Hylas The sensation I take to be an act of the mind perceiving; besides which, there is something perceived; and this I call the OBJECT. For example, there is red and yellow on that tulip. But then the act of perceiving those colors is in me only, and not in the tulip.

Philonous What tulip do you speak of? Is it that which you see?

Hylas The same.

Philonous And what do you see beside color, figure, and extension?

Hylas Nothing.

Philonous What you would say then is that the red and yellow are coexistent with the extension; is it not?

Hylas That is not all; I would say they have a real existence without the mind, in some unthinking substance.

Philonous That the colors are really in the tulip which I see is manifest. Neither can it be denied that this tulip may exist independent of your mind or mine; but, that any immediate object of the senses,–that is, any idea, or combination of ideas– should exist in an unthinking substance, or exterior to ALL minds, is in itself an evident contradiction. Nor can I imagine how this follows from what you said just now, to wit, that the red and yellow were on the tulip you SAW, since you do not pretend to SEE that unthinking substance.

Hylas You have an artful way, Philonous, of diverting our inquiry from the subject.

Philonous I see you have no mind to be pressed that way. To return then to your distinction between SENSATION and OBJECT; if I take you right, you distinguish in every perception two things, the one an action of the mind, the other not.

Hylas True.

Philonous And this action cannot exist in, or belong to, any unthinking thing; but, whatever beside is implied in a perception may?

Hylas That is my meaning.

Philonous So that if there was a perception without any act of the mind, it were possible such a perception should exist in an unthinking substance?

Hylas I grant it. But it is impossible there should be such a perception.

Philonous When is the mind said to be active?

Hylas When it produces, puts an end to, or changes, anything.

Philonous Can the mind produce, discontinue, or change anything, but by an act of the will?

Hylas It cannot.

Philonous The mind therefore is to be accounted ACTIVE in its perceptions so far forth as VOLITION is included in them?

Hylas It is.

Philonous In plucking this flower I am active; because I do it by the motion of my hand, which was consequent upon my volition; so likewise in applying it to my nose. But is either of these smelling?

Hylas NO.

Philonous I act too in drawing the air through my nose; because my breathing so rather than otherwise is the effect of my volition. But neither can this be called SMELLING: for, if it were, I should smell every time I breathed in that manner?

Hylas True.

Philonous Smelling then is somewhat consequent to all this?

Hylas It is.

Philonous But I do not find my will concerned any farther. Whatever more there is—as that I perceive such a particular smell, or any smell at all—this is independent of my will, and therein I am altogether passive. Do you find it otherwise with you, Hylas?

Hylas No, the very same.

Philonous Then, as to seeing, is it not in your power to open your eyes, or keep them shut; to turn them this or that way?

Hylas Without doubt.

Philonous But, doth it in like manner depend on YOUR will that in looking on this flower you perceive WHITE rather than any other color? Or, directing your open eyes towards yonder part of the heaven, can you avoid seeing the sun? Or is light or darkness the effect of your volition?

Hylas No, certainly.

Philonous You are then in these respects altogether passive?

Hylas I am.

Philonous Tell me now, whether SEEING consists in perceiving light and colors, or in opening and turning the eyes?

Hylas Without doubt, in the former.

Philonous Since therefore you are in the very perception of light and colors altogether passive, what is become of that action you were speaking of as an ingredient in every sensation? And, doth it not follow from your own concessions, that the perception of light and colors, including no action in it, may exist in an unperceiving substance? And is not this a plain contradiction?

Hylas I know not what to think of it.

Philonous Besides, since you distinguish the ACTIVE and PASSIVE in every perception, you must do it in that of pain. But how is it possible that pain, be it as little active as you please, should exist in an unperceiving substance? In short, do but consider the point, and then confess ingenuously, whether light and colors, tastes, sounds, &c. are not all equally passions or sensations in the soul. You may indeed call them EXTERNAL OBJECTS, and give them in words what subsistence you please. But, examine your own thoughts, and then tell me whether it be not as I say?

Hylas I acknowledge, Philonous, that, upon a fair observation of what passes in my mind, I can discover nothing else but that I am a thinking being, affected with variety of sensations; neither is it possible to conceive how a sensation should exist in an unperceiving substance. But then, on the other hand, when I look on sensible things in a different view, considering them as so many modes and qualities, I find it necessary to suppose a MATERIAL SUBSTRATUM, without which they cannot be conceived to exist.

Philonous MATERIAL SUBSTRATUM call you it? Pray, by which of your senses came you acquainted with that being?

Hylas It is not itself sensible; its modes and qualities only being perceived by the senses.

Philonous I presume then it was by reflexion and reason you obtained the idea of it?

Hylas I do not pretend to any proper positive IDEA of it. However, I conclude it exists, because qualities cannot be conceived to exist without a support.

Philonous It seems then you have only a relative NOTION of it, or that you conceive it not otherwise than by conceiving the relation it bears to sensible qualities?

Hylas Right.

Philonous Be pleased therefore to let me know wherein that relation consists.

Hylas Is it not sufficiently expressed in the term SUBSTRATUM, or SUBSTANCE?

Philonous If so, the word SUBSTRATUM should import that it is spread under the sensible qualities or accidents?

Hylas True.

Philonous And consequently under extension?

Hylas I own it.

Philonous It is therefore somewhat in its own nature entirely distinct from extension?

Hylas I tell you, extension is only a mode, and Matter is something that supports modes. And is it not evident the thing supported is different from the thing supporting?

Philonous So that something distinct from, and exclusive of, extension is supposed to be the SUBSTRATUM of extension?

Hylas Just so.

Philonous Answer me, Hylas. Can a thing be spread without extension? or is not the idea of extension necessarily included in SPREADING?

Hylas It is.

Philonous Whatsoever therefore you suppose spread under anything must have in itself an extension distinct from the extension of that thing under which it is spread?

Hylas It must.

Philonous Consequently, every corporeal substance, being the SUBSTRATUM of extension, must have in itself another extension, by which it is qualified to be a SUBSTRATUM: and so on to infinity. And I ask whether this be not absurd in itself, and repugnant to what you granted just now, to wit, that the SUBSTRATUM was something distinct from and exclusive of extension?

Hylas Aye but, Philonous, you take me wrong. I do not mean that Matter is SPREAD in a gross literal sense under extension. The word SUBSTRATUM is used only to express in general the same thing with SUBSTANCE.

Philonous Well then, let us examine the relation implied in the term SUBSTANCE. Is it not that it stands under accidents?

Hylas The very same.

Philonous But, that one thing may stand under or support another, must it not be extended?

Hylas It must.

Philonous Is not therefore this supposition liable to the same absurdity with the former?

Hylas You still take things in a strict literal sense. That is not fair, Philonous.

Philonous I am not for imposing any sense on your words:

you are at liberty to explain them as you please. Only, I beseech you, make me understand something by them. You tell me Matter supports or stands under accidents. How! is it as your legs support your body?

Hylas No; that is the literal sense.

Philonous Pray let me know any sense, literal or not literal, that you understand it in.–How long must I wait for an answer, Hylas?

Hylas I declare I know not what to say. I once thought I understood well enough what was meant by Matter's supporting accidents. But now, the more I think on it the less can I comprehend it: in short I find that I know nothing of it.

Philonous It seems then you have no idea at all, neither relative nor positive, of Matter; you know neither what it is in itself, nor what relation it bears to accidents?

Hylas I acknowledge it.

Philonous And yet you asserted that you could not conceive how qualities or accidents should really exist, without conceiving at the same time a material support of them?

Hylas I did.

Philonous That is to say, when you conceive the real existence of qualities, you do withal conceive Something which you cannot conceive?

Hylas It was wrong, I own. But still I fear there is some fallacy or other. Pray what think you of this? It is just come into my head that the ground of all our mistake lies in your treating of each quality by itself. Now, I grant that each quality cannot singly subsist without the mind. color cannot without extension, neither can figure without some other sensible quality. But, as the several qualities united or blended together form entire sensible things, nothing hinders why such things may not be supposed to exist without the mind.

Philonous Either, Hylas, you are jesting, or have a very bad memory. Though indeed we went through all the qualities by name one after another, yet my arguments or rather your concessions, nowhere tended to prove that the Secondary Qualities did not subsist each alone by itself; but, that they were not AT ALL without the mind. Indeed, in treating of figure and motion we concluded they could not exist without the mind, because it was impossible even in thought to separate them from all secondary qualities, so as to conceive them existing by themselves. But then this was not the only argument made use of upon that occasion. But (to pass by all that hath been hitherto said, and reckon it for nothing, if you will have it so) I am content to put the whole upon this issue. If you can conceive it possible for any mixture or combination of qualities, or any sensible object whatever, to exist without the mind, then I will grant it actually to be so.

Hylas If it comes to that the point will soon be decided. What more easy than to conceive a tree or house existing by itself, independent of, and unperceived by, any mind whatsoever? I do at this present time conceive them existing after that manner.

Philonous How say you, Hylas, can you see a thing which is at the same time unseen?

Hylas No, that were a contradiction.

Philonous Is it not as great a contradiction to talk of CONCEIVING a thing which is UNCONCEIVED?

Hylas It is.

Philonous The, tree or house therefore which you think of is conceived by you?

Hylas How should it be otherwise?

Philonous And what is conceived is surely in the mind?

Hylas Without question, that which is conceived is in the mind.

Philonous How then came you to say, you conceived a house or tree existing independent and out of all minds whatsoever?

Hylas That was I own an oversight; but stay, let me consider what led me into it.–It is a pleasant mistake enough. As I was thinking of a tree in a solitary place, where no one was present to see it, methought that was to conceive a tree as existing unperceived or unthought of; not considering that I myself conceived it all the while. But now I plainly see that all I can do is to frame ideas in my own mind. I may indeed conceive in my own thoughts the idea of a tree, or a house, or a mountain, but that is all. And this is far from proving that I can conceive them EXISTING OUT OF THE MINDS OF ALL SPIRITS.

Philonous You acknowledge then that you cannot possibly conceive how any one corporeal sensible thing should exist otherwise than in the mind?

Hylas I do.

Philonous And yet you will earnestly contend for the truth of that which you cannot so much as conceive?

Hylas I profess I know not what to think; but still there are some scruples remain with me. Is it not certain I SEE THINGS at a distance? Do we not perceive the stars and moon, for example, to be a great way off? Is not this, I say, manifest to the senses?

Philonous Do you not in a dream too perceive those or the like objects?

Hylas I do.

Philonous And have they not then the same appearance of being distant?

Hylas They have.

Philonous But you do not thence conclude the apparitions in a dream to be without the mind?

Hylas By no means.

Philonous You ought not therefore to conclude that sensible objects are without the mind, from their appearance, or manner wherein they are perceived.

Hylas I acknowledge it. But doth not my sense deceive me in those cases?

Philonous By no means. The idea or thing which you immediately perceive, neither sense nor reason informs you that it actually exists without the mind. By sense you only know that you are affected with such certain sensations of light and colors, &c. And these you will not say are without the mind.

Hylas True: but, beside all that, do you not think the sight suggests something of OUTNESS OR DISTANCE?

Philonous Upon approaching a distant object, do the visible size and figure change perpetually, or do they appear the same at all distances?

Hylas They are in a continual change.

Philonous Sight therefore doth not suggest, or any way inform you, that the visible object you immediately perceive exists at a distance, or will be perceived when you advance farther onward; there being a continued series of visible objects succeeding each other during the whole time of your approach.

Hylas It doth not; but still I know, upon seeing an object, what object I shall perceive after having passed over a certain distance: no matter whether it be exactly the same or no: there is still something of distance suggested in the case.

Philonous Good Hylas, do but reflect a little on the point, and then tell me whether there be any more in it than this: from the ideas you actually perceive by sight, you have by experience learned to collect what other ideas you will (according to the standing order of nature) be affected with, after such a certain succession of time and motion.

Hylas Upon the whole, I take it to be nothing else.

Philonous Now, is it not plain that if we suppose a man born blind was on a sudden made to see, he could at first have no experience of what may be SUGGESTED by sight?

Hylas It is.

Philonous He would not then, according to you, have any notion of distance annexed to the things he saw; but would take them for a new set of sensations, existing only in his mind?

Hylas It is undeniable.

Philonous But, to make it still more plain: is not DISTANCE a line turned endwise to the eye?

Hylas It is.

Philonous And can a line so situated be perceived by sight?

Hylas It cannot.

Philonous Doth it not therefore follow that distance is not properly and immediately perceived by sight?

Hylas It should seem so.

Philonous Again, is it your opinion that colors are at a distance?

Hylas It must be acknowledged they are only in the mind.

Philonous But do not colors appear to the eye as coexisting in the same place with extension and figures?

Hylas They do.

Philonous How can you then conclude from sight that figures exist without, when you acknowledge colors do not; the sensible appearance being the very same with regard to both?

Hylas I know not what to answer.

Philonous But, allowing that distance was truly and immediately perceived by the mind, yet it would not thence follow it existed out of the mind. For, whatever is immediately perceived is an idea: and can any idea exist out of the mind?

Hylas To suppose that were absurd: but, inform me, Philonous, can we perceive or know nothing beside our ideas?

Philonous As for the rational deducing of causes from effects, that is beside our inquiry. And, by the senses you can best tell whether you perceive anything which is not immediately perceived. And I ask you, whether the things immediately perceived are other than your own sensations or ideas? You have indeed more than once, in the course of this conversation, declared yourself on those points; but you seem, by this last question, to have departed from what you then thought.

Hylas To speak the truth, Philonous, I think there are two kinds of objects:–the one perceived immediately, which are likewise called IDEAS; the other are real things or external objects, perceived by the mediation of ideas, which are their images and representations. Now, I own ideas do not exist without the mind; but the latter sort of objects do. I am sorry I did not think of this distinction sooner; it would probably have cut short your discourse.

Philonous Are those external objects perceived by sense or by some other faculty?

Hylas They are perceived by sense.

Philonous Howl Is there any thing perceived by sense which is not immediately perceived?

Hylas Yes, Philonous, in some sort there is. For example, when I look on a picture or statue of Julius Caesar, I may be said after a manner to perceive him (though not immediately) by my senses.

Philonous It seems then you will have our ideas, which alone are immediately perceived, to be pictures of external things: and that these also are perceived by sense, inasmuch as they have a conformity or resemblance to our ideas?

Hylas That is my meaning.

Philonous And, in the same way that Julius Caesar, in himself invisible, is nevertheless perceived by sight; real things, in themselves imperceptible, are perceived by sense.

Hylas In the very same.

Philonous Tell me, Hylas, when you behold the picture of Julius Caesar, do you see with your eyes any more than some colors and figures, with a certain symmetry and composition of the whole?

Hylas Nothing else.

Philonous And would not a man who had never known anything of Julius Caesar see as much?

Hylas He would.

Philonous Consequently he hath his sight, and the use of it, in as perfect a degree as you?

Hylas I agree with you.

Philonous Whence comes it then that your thoughts are directed to the Roman emperor, and his are not? This cannot proceed from the sensations or ideas of sense by you then perceived; since you acknowledge you have no advantage over him in that respect. It should seem therefore to proceed from reason and memory: should it not?

Hylas It should.

Philonous Consequently, it will not follow from that

instance that anything is perceived by sense which is not, immediately perceived. Though I grant we may, in one acceptation, be said to perceive sensible things mediately by sense: that is, when, from a frequently perceived connexion, the immediate perception of ideas by one sense SUGGESTS to the mind others, perhaps belonging to another sense, which are wont to be connected with them. For instance, when I hear a coach drive along the streets, immediately I perceive only the sound; but, from the experience I have had that such a sound is connected with a coach, I am said to hear the coach. It is nevertheless evident that, in truth and strictness, nothing can be HEARD BUT SOUND; and the coach is not then properly perceived by sense, but suggested from experience. So likewise when we are said to see a red-hot bar of iron; the solidity and heat of the iron are not the objects of sight, but suggested to the imagination by the color and figure which are properly perceived by that sense. In short, those things alone are actually and strictly perceived by any sense, which would have been perceived in case that same sense had then been first conferred on us. As for other things, it is plain they are only suggested to the mind by experience, grounded on former perceptions. But, to return to your comparison of Caesar's picture, it is plain, if you keep to that, you must hold the real things, or archetypes of our ideas, are not perceived by sense, but by some internal faculty of the soul, as reason or memory. I would therefore fain know what arguments you can draw from reason for the existence of what you call REAL THINGS OR MATERIAL OBJECTS. Or, whether you remember to have seen them formerly as they are in themselves; or, if you have heard or read of any one that did.

Hylas I see, Philonous, you are disposed to raillery; but that will never convince me.

Philonous My aim is only to learn from you the way to come at the knowledge of MATERIAL BEINGS. Whatever we perceive is perceived immediately or mediately: by sense, or by reason and reflexion. But, as you have excluded sense, pray shew me what reason you have to believe their existence; or what MEDIUM you can possibly make use of to prove it, either to mine or your own understanding.

Hylas To deal ingenuously, Philonous, now I consider the point, I do not find I can give you any good reason for it. But, thus much seems pretty plain, that it is at least possible such things may really exist. And, as long as there is no absurdity in supposing them, I am resolved to believe as I did, till you bring good reasons to the contrary.

Philonous What! Is it come to this, that you only BELIEVE the existence of material objects, and that your belief is founded barely on the possibility of its being true? Then you will have me bring reasons against it: though another would think it reasonable the proof should lie on him who holds the affirmative. And, after all, this very point which you are now resolved to maintain, without any reason, is in effect what you have more than once during this discourse seen good reason to give up. But, to pass over all this; if I understand you rightly, you say our ideas do not exist without the mind, but that they are copies, images, or representations, of certain originals that do?

Hylas You take me right.

Philonous They are then like external things?

Hylas They are.

Philonous Have those things a stable and permanent nature, independent of our senses; or are they in a perpetual change, upon our producing any motions in our bodies—suspending, exerting, or altering, our faculties or organs of sense?

Hylas Real things, it is plain, have a fixed and real nature, which remains the same notwithstanding any change in our senses, or in the posture and motion of our bodies; which indeed may affect the ideas in our minds, but it were absurd to think they had the same effect on things existing without the mind.

Philonous How then is it possible that things perpetually fleeting and variable as our ideas should be copies or images of anything fixed and constant? Or, in other words, since all sensible qualities, as size, figure, color, &c., that is, our ideas, are continually changing, upon every alteration in the distance, medium, or instruments of sensation; how can any determinate material objects be properly represented or painted forth by several distinct things, each of which is so different from and unlike the rest? Or, if you say it resembles some one only of our ideas, how shall we be able to distinguish the true copy from all the false ones?

Hylas I profess, Philonous, I am at a loss. I know not what to say to this.

Philonous But neither is this all. Which are material objects in themselves—perceptible or imperceptible?

Hylas Properly and immediately nothing can be perceived but ideas. All material things, therefore, are in themselves insensible, and to be perceived only by our ideas.

Philonous Ideas then are sensible, and their archetypes or originals insensible?

Hylas Right.

Philonous But how can that which is sensible be like that which is insensible? Can a real thing, in itself INVISIBLE, be like a color; or a real thing, which is not AUDIBLE, be like a SOUND? In a word, can anything be like a sensation or idea, but another sensation or idea?

Hylas I must own, I think not.

Philonous Is it possible there should be any doubt on the point? Do. you not perfectly know your own ideas?

Hylas I know them perfectly; since what I do not perceive or know can be no part of my idea.

Philonous Consider, therefore, and examine them, and then tell me if there be anything in them which can exist without the mind: or if you can conceive anything like them existing without the mind.

Hylas Upon inquiry, I find it is impossible for me to conceive or understand how anything but an idea can be like an idea. And it is most evident that NO IDEA CAN EXIST WITHOUT THE MIND.

Philonous You are therefore, by your principles, forced to deny the REALITY of sensible things; since you made it to consist in an absolute existence exterior to the mind. That is to say, you are a downright sceptic. So I have gained my point, which was to shew your principles led to Scepticism.

Hylas For the present I am, if not entirely convinced, at least silenced.

Philonous I would fain know what more you would require in order to a perfect conviction. Have you not had the liberty of explaining yourself all manner of ways? Were any little slips in discourse laid hold and insisted on? Or were you not allowed to retract or reinforce anything you had offered, as best served your purpose? Hath not everything you could say been heard and examined with all the fairness imaginable? In a word have you not in every point been convinced out of your own mouth? And, if you can at present discover any flaw in any of your former concessions, or think of any remaining subterfuge, any new distinction, color, or comment whatsoever, why do you not produce it?

Hylas A little patience, Philonous. I am at present so amazed to see myself ensnared, and as it were imprisoned in the labyrinths you have drawn me into, that on the sudden it cannot be expected I should find my way out. You must give me time to look about me and recollect myself.

Philonous Hark; is not this the college bell?

Hylas It rings for prayers.

Philonous We will go in then, if you please, and meet here again tomorrow morning. In the meantime, you may employ your thoughts on this morning's discourse, and try if you can find any fallacy in it, or invent any new means to extricate yourself.

Hylas Agreed.

The Second Dialogue

Hylas I beg your pardon, Philonous, for not meeting you sooner. All this morning my head was so filled with our late conversation that I had not leisure to think of the time of the day, or indeed of anything else.

PHILONOUS. I am glad you were so intent upon it, in hopes if there were any mistakes in your concessions, or fallacies in my reasonings from them, you will now discover them to me.

Hylas I assure you I have done nothing ever since I saw you but search after mistakes and fallacies, and, with that view, have minutely examined the whole series of yesterday's discourse: but all in vain, for the notions it led me into, upon review, appear still more clear and evident; and, the more I consider them, the more irresistibly do they force my assent.

Philonous And is not this, think you, a sign that they are genuine, that they proceed from nature, and are conformable to right reason? Truth and beauty are in this alike, that the strictest survey sets them both off to advantage; while the false lustre of error and disguise cannot endure being reviewed, or too nearly inspected.

Hylas I own there is a great deal in what you say. Nor can any one be more entirely satisfied of the truth of those odd consequences, so long as I have in view the reasonings that lead to them. But, when these are out of my thoughts, there seems, on the other hand, something so satisfactory, so natural and intelligible, in the modern way of explaining things that, I profess, I know not how to reject it.

Philonous I know not what way you mean.

Hylas I mean the way of accounting for our sensations or ideas.

Philonous How is that?

Hylas It is supposed the soul makes her residence in some part of the brain, from which the nerves take their rise, and are thence extended to all parts of the body; and that outward objects, by the different impressions they make on the organs of sense, communicate certain vibrative motions to the nerves; and these being filled with spirits propagate them to the brain or seat of the soul, which, according to the various impressions or traces thereby made in the brain, is variously affected with ideas.

Philonous And call you this an explication of the manner whereby we are affected with ideas?

Hylas Why not, Philonous? Have you anything to object against it?

Philonous I would first know whether I rightly understand your hypothesis. You make certain traces in the brain to be the causes or occasions of our ideas. Pray tell me whether by the BRAIN you mean any sensible thing.

Hylas What else think you I could mean?

Philonous Sensible things are all immediately perceivable; and those things which are immediately perceivable are ideas; and these exist only in the mind. Thus much you have, if I mistake not, long since agreed to.

Hylas I do not deny it.

Philonous The brain therefore you speak of, being a sensible thing, exists only in the mind. Now, I would fain know whether you think it reasonable to suppose that one idea or thing existing in the mind occasions all other ideas. And, if you think so, pray how do you account for the origin of that primary idea or brain itself?

Hylas I do not explain the origin of our ideas by that brain which is perceivable to sense–this being itself only a combination of sensible ideas–but by another which I imagine.

Philonous But are not things imagined as truly IN THE MIND as things perceived?

Hylas I must confess they are.

Philonous It comes, therefore, to the same thing; and you have been all this while accounting for ideas by certain motions or impressions of the brain; that is, by some alterations in an idea, whether sensible or imaginable it matters not.

Hylas I begin to suspect my hypothesis.

Philonous Besides spirits, all that we know or conceive are our own ideas. When, therefore, you say all ideas are occasioned by impressions in the brain, do you conceive this brain or no? If you do, then you talk of ideas imprinted in an idea causing that same idea, which is absurd. If you do not conceive it, you talk unintelligibly, instead of forming a reasonable hypothesis.

Hylas I now clearly see it was a mere dream. There is nothing in it.

Philonous You need not be much concerned at it; for after all, this way of explaining things, as you called it, could never have satisfied any reasonable man. What connexion is there between a motion in the nerves, and the sensations of sound or color in the mind? Or how is it possible these should be the effect of that?

Hylas But I could never think it had so little in it as now it seems to have.

Philonous Well then, are you at length satisfied that no sensible things have a real existence; and that you are in truth an arrant sceptic?

Hylas It is too plain to be denied.

Philonous Look! are not the fields covered with a delightful verdure? Is there not something in the woods and groves, in the rivers and clear springs, that soothes, that delights, that transports the soul? At the prospect of the wide and deep ocean, or some huge mountain whose top is lost in the clouds, or of an old gloomy forest, are not our minds filled with a pleasing horror? Even in rocks and deserts is there not an agreeable wildness? How sincere a pleasure is it to behold the natural beauties of the earth! To preserve and renew our, relish for them, is not the veil of night alternately drawn over her face, and doth she not change her dress with the seasons? How aptly are the elements disposed! What variety and use in the meanest productions of nature! What delicacy, what beauty, what contrivance, in animal and vegetable bodies I How exquisitely are all things suited, as well to their particular ends, as to constitute opposite parts of the whole I And, while they mutually aid and support, do they not also set off and illustrate each other? Raise now your thoughts from this ball of earth to all those glorious luminaries that adorn the high arch of heaven. The motion and situation of the planets, are they not admirable for use and order? Were those (miscalled ERRATIC) globes once known to stray, in their repeated journeys through the pathless void? Do they not measure areas round the sun ever proportioned to the times? So fixed, so immutable are the laws by which the unseen Author of nature actuates the universe. How vivid and radiant is the lustre of the fixed stars! How magnificent and rich that negligent profusion with which they appear to be scattered throughout the whole azure vault! Yet, if you take the telescope, it brings into your sight a new host of stars that escape the naked eye. Here they seem contiguous and minute, but to a nearer view immense orbs of fight at various distances, far sunk in the abyss of space. Now you must call imagination to your aid. The feeble narrow sense cannot descry innumerable worlds revolving round the central fires; and in those worlds the energy of an all-perfect Mind displayed in endless forms. But, neither sense nor imagination are big enough to comprehend the boundless extent, with all its glittering furniture. Though the labouring mind exert and strain each power to its utmost reach, there still stands out ungrasped a surplusage immeasurable. Yet all the vast bodies that compose this mighty frame, how distant and remote soever, are by some secret mechanism, some Divine art and force, linked in a mutual dependence and intercourse with each other; even with this earth, which was almost slipt from my thoughts and lost in the crowd of worlds. Is not the whole system immense, beautiful, glorious beyond expression and beyond thought! What treatment, then, do those philosophers deserve, who would deprive these noble and delightful scenes of all REALITY? How should those Principles be entertained that lead us to think all the visible beauty of the creation a false imaginary glare? To be plain, can you expect this Scepticism of yours will not be thought extravagantly absurd by all men of sense?

Hylas Other men may think as they please; but for your part you have nothing to reproach me with. My comfort is, you are as much a sceptic as I am.

Philonous There, Hylas, I must beg leave to differ from you.

Hylas What! Have you all along agreed to the premises, and do you now deny the conclusion, and leave me to maintain those paradoxes by myself which you led me into? This surely is not fair.

Philonous _I_ deny that I agreed with you in those notions that led to Scepticism. You indeed said the REALITY of sensible things consisted in AN ABSOLUTE EXISTENCE OUT OF THE MINDS OF SPIRITS, or distinct from their being perceived. And pursuant to this notion of reality, YOU are obliged to deny sensible things any real existence: that is, according to your own definition, you profess yourself a sceptic. But I neither said nor thought the reality of sensible things was to be defined after that manner. To me it is evident for the reasons you allow of, that sensible things cannot exist otherwise than in a mind or spirit. Whence I conclude, not that they have no real existence, but that, seeing they depend not on my thought, and have all existence distinct from being perceived by me, THERE MUST BE SOME OTHER MIND WHEREIN THEY EXIST. As sure, therefore, as the sensible world really exists, so sure is there an infinite omnipresent Spirit who contains and supports it.

Hylas What! This is no more than I and all Christians hold; nay, and all others too who believe there is a God, and that He knows and comprehends all things.

Philonous Aye, but here lies the difference. Men commonly believe that all things are known or perceived by God, because they believe the being of a God; whereas I, on the other side, immediately and necessarily conclude the being of a God, because all sensible things must be perceived by Him.

Citation and Use

The text was taken from the following work.

George Berkeley, *Three Dialogues between Hylas and Philonous in Opposition to Sceptics and Atheists* (Urbana, IL: Project Gutenberg, 2009), http://www.gutenberg.org/cache/epub/4724/pg4724.txt.

The use of this work is governed by the Public Domain.

RADICAL EMPIRICISM

David Hume

PART I.

All the objects of human reason or inquiry may naturally be divided into two kinds, to wit, Relations of Ideas, and Matters of Fact. Of the first kind are the sciences of Geometry, Algebra, and Arithmetic; and in short, every affirmation which is either intuitively or demonstratively certain. That the square of the hypotenuse is equal to the square of the two sides, is a proposition which expresses a relation between these figures. That three times five is equal to the half of thirty, expresses a relation between these numbers. Propositions of this kind are discoverable by the mere operation of thought, without dependence on what is anywhere existent in the universe. Though there never were a circle or triangle in nature, the truths demonstrated by Euclid would for ever retain their certainty and evidence.

Matters of fact, which are the second objects of human reason, are not ascertained in the same manner; nor is our evidence of their truth, however great, of a like nature with the foregoing. The contrary of every matter of fact is still possible; because it can never imply a contradiction, and is conceived by the mind with the same facility and distinctness, as if ever so conformable to reality. That the sun will not rise tomorrow is no less intelligible a proposition, and implies no more contradiction than the affirmation, that it will rise. We should in vain, therefore, attempt to demonstrate its falsehood. Were it demonstratively false, it would imply a contradiction, and could never be distinctly conceived by the mind.

It may, therefore, be a subject worthy of curiosity, to inquire what is the nature of that evidence which assures us of any real existence and matter of fact, beyond the present testimony of our senses, or the records of our memory. This part of philosophy, it is observable, has been little cultivated, either by the ancients or moderns; and therefore our doubts and errors, in the prosecution of so important an inquiry, may be the more excusable; while we march through such difficult paths without any guide or direction. They may even prove useful, by exciting curiosity, and destroying that implicit faith and security, which is the bane of all reasoning and free inquiry. The discovery of

defects in the common philosophy, if any such there be, will not, I presume, be a discouragement, but rather an incitement, as is usual, to attempt something more full and satisfactory than has yet been proposed to the public.

All reasonings concerning matter of fact seem to be founded on the relation of Cause and Effect. By means of that relation alone we can go beyond the evidence of our memory and senses. If you were to ask a man, why he believes any matter of fact, which is absent; for instance, that his friend is in the country, or in France; he would give you a reason; and this reason would be some other fact; as a letter received from him, or the knowledge of his former resolutions and promises. A man finding a watch or any other machine in a desert island, would conclude that there had once been men in that island. All our reasonings concerning fact are of the same nature. And here it is constantly supposed that there is a connection between the present fact and that which is inferred from it. Were there nothing to bind them together, the inference would be entirely precarious. The hearing of an articulate voice and rational discourse in the dark assures us of the presence of some person: Why? because these are the effects of the human make and fabric, and closely connected with it. If we anatomize all the other reasonings of this nature, we shall find that they are founded on the relation of cause and effect, and that this relation is either near or remote, direct or collateral. Heat and light are collateral effects of fire, and the one effect may justly be inferred from the other.

If we would satisfy ourselves, therefore, concerning the nature of that evidence, which assures us of matters of fact, we must inquire how we arrive at the knowledge of cause and effect.

I shall venture to affirm, as a general proposition, which admits of no exception, that the knowledge of this relation is not, in any instance, attained by reasonings *a priori*; but arises entirely from experience, when we find that any particular objects are constantly conjoined with each other. Let an object be presented to a man of ever so strong natural reason and abilities; if that object be entirely new to him, he will not be able, by the most accurate examination of its sensible qualities, to discover any of its causes or effects. Adam, though his rational faculties be supposed, at the very first, entirely perfect, could not have inferred from the fluidity and transparency of water that it would suffocate him, or from the light and warmth of fire that it would consume him. No object ever discovers, by the qualities which appear to the senses, either the causes which produced it, or the effects which will arise from it; nor can our reason, unassisted by experience, ever draw any inference concerning real existence and matter of fact.

This proposition, that causes and effects are discoverable, not by reason but by experience, will readily be admitted with regard to such objects, as we remember to have once been altogether unknown to us; since we must be conscious of the utter inability, which we then lay under, of foretelling what would arise from them. Present two smooth pieces of marble to a man who has no tincture of natural philosophy; he will never discover that they will adhere together in such a manner as to require great force to separate them in a direct line, while they make so small a resistance to a lateral pressure. Such events, as bear little analogy to the common course of nature, are also readily confessed to be known only by experience; nor does any man imagine that the explosion of gunpowder, or the attraction of a loadstone, could ever be discovered by arguments *a priori*. In like manner, when an effect is supposed to depend upon an intricate machinery or secret structure of parts, we make no difficulty in attributing all our knowledge of it to experience. Who will assert that he can give the ultimate reason, why milk or bread is proper nourishment for a man, not for a lion or a tiger?

But the same truth may not appear, at first sight, to have the same evidence with regard to events, which have become familiar to us from our first appearance in the world, which bear a close analogy to the whole course of nature, and which are supposed to depend on the simple qualities of objects, without any secret structure of parts. We are apt to imagine that we could discover these effects by the mere operation of our reason, without experience. We fancy, that were we brought on a sudden into this world, we could at first have inferred that one billiard-ball would communicate motion to another upon impulse; and that we needed not to have waited for the event, in order to pronounce with certainty concerning it. Such is the influence of custom, that, where it is strongest, it not only covers our natural ignorance, but even conceals itself, and seems not to take place, merely because it is found in the highest degree.

But to convince us that all the laws of nature, and all the operations of bodies without exception, are known only by experience, the following reflections may, perhaps, suffice. Were any object presented to us, and were we required to pronounce concerning the effect, which will result from it, without consulting past observation; after what manner, I beseech you, must the mind proceed in this operation? It must invent or imagine some event, which it ascribes to the object as its effect; and it is plain that this invention must be entirely arbitrary. The mind can never possibly find the effect in the supposed cause, by the most accurate scrutiny and examination. For the effect is totally different from the cause, and consequently can never be discovered in it. Motion in the second billiard-ball is a quite distinct event from motion in the first; nor is there anything in the one to suggest the smallest hint of the other. A stone or piece of metal raised into the air, and left without any support, immediately falls: but to consider the matter *a priori*, is there anything we discover in this situation which can beget the idea of a downward, rather than an upward, or any other motion, in the stone or metal?

And as the first imagination or invention of a particular effect, in all natural operations, is arbitrary, where we consult not experience; so must we also esteem the supposed tie or connection between the cause and effect, which binds them together, and renders it impossible that any other effect could result from the operation of that cause. When I see, for instance, a billiard-ball moving in a straight line towards another; even suppose motion in the second ball should by accident be suggested to me, as the result of their contact or impulse; may I not conceive, that a hundred different events might as well follow from that cause? May not both these balls remain at absolute rest? May not the first ball return in a straight line, or leap off from the second in any line or direction? All these suppositions are consistent and conceivable. Why then should we give the preference to one, which is no more consistent or conceivable than the rest? All our reasonings *a priori* will never be able to show us any foundation for this preference.

In a word, then, every effect is a distinct event from its cause. It could not, therefore, be discovered in the cause, and the first invention or conception of it, *a priori*, must be entirely arbitrary. And even after it is suggested, the conjunction of it with the cause must appear equally arbitrary; since there are always many other effects, which, to reason, must seem fully as consistent and natural. In vain, therefore, should we pretend to determine any single event, or infer any cause or effect, without the assistance of observation and experience.

Hence we may discover the reason why no philosopher, who is rational and modest, has ever pretended to assign the ultimate cause of any natural operation, or to show distinctly the action of that power, which produces any single effect in the universe. It is confessed, that the utmost effort of human reason is to reduce the principles, productive of natural phenomena, to a greater simplicity, and to resolve the many particular effects into a few general causes, by means of reasonings from analogy, experience, and observation. But as to the causes of these general causes, we should in vain attempt their discovery; nor shall we ever be able to satisfy ourselves, by any particular explication of them. These ultimate springs and principles are totally shut up from human curiosity and inquiry. Elasticity, gravity, cohesion of parts, communication of motion by impulse; these are probably the ultimate causes and principles which we shall ever discover in nature; and we may esteem ourselves sufficiently happy, if, by accurate inquiry and reasoning, we can trace up the particular phenomena to, or near to, these general principles. The most perfect philosophy of the natural kind only staves off our ignorance a little longer: as perhaps the most perfect philosophy of the moral or metaphysical kind serves only to discover larger portions of it. Thus the observation of human blindness and weakness is the result of all philosophy, and meets us at every turn, in spite of our endeavorsto elude or avoid it.

Nor is geometry, when taken into the assistance of natural philosophy, ever able to remedy this defect, or lead us into the knowledge of ultimate causes, by all that accuracy of reasoning for which it is so justly celebrated. Every part of mixed mathematics proceeds upon the supposition that certain laws are established by nature in her operations; and abstract reasonings are employed, either to assist experience in the discovery of these laws, or to determine their influence in particular instances, where it depends upon any precise degree of distance and quantity. Thus, it is a law of motion, discovered by experience, that the moment or force of any body in motion is in the compound ratio or proportion of its solid contents and its velocity; and consequently, that a small force may remove the greatest obstacle or raise the greatest weight, if, by any contrivance or machinery, we can increase the velocity of that force, so as to make it an overmatch for its antagonist. Geometry assists us in the application of this law, by giving us the just dimensions of all the parts and figures which can enter into any species of machine; but still the discovery of the law itself is owing merely to experience, and all the abstract reasonings in the world could never lead us one step towards the knowledge of it. When we reason *a priori*, and consider merely any object or cause, as it appears to the mind, independent of all observation, it never could suggest to us the notion of any distinct object, such as its effect; much less, show us the inseparable and inviolable connection between them. A man must be very sagacious who could discover by reasoning that crystal is the effect of heat, and ice of cold, without being previously acquainted with the operation of these qualities.

PART II.

But we have not yet attained any tolerable satisfaction with regard to the question first proposed. Each solution still gives rise to a new question as difficult as the foregoing, and leads us on to farther enquiries. When it is asked, What is the nature of all our reasonings concerning matter of fact? the proper answer seems to be, that they are founded on the relation of cause and effect. When again it is asked, What is the foundation of all our reasonings and conclusions concerning that relation? it may be replied in one word, Experience. But if we still carry on our sifting humor, and ask, What is the foundation of all conclusions from experience? this implies a new question, which may be of more difficult solution and explication. Philosophers, that give themselves airs of superior wisdom and sufficiency, have a hard task when they encounter persons of inquisitive dispositions, who push them from every corner to which they retreat, and who are sure at last to bring them to some dangerous dilemma. The best expedient to prevent this confusion, is to be modest in our pretensions; and even to discover the difficulty ourselves before it is objected to us. By this means, we may make a kind of merit of our very ignorance.

I shall content myself, in this section, with an easy task, and shall pretend only to give a negative answer to the question here proposed. I say then, that, even after we have experience of the operations of cause and effect, our conclusions from that experience are not founded on reasoning, or any process of the understanding. This answer we must endeavour both to explain and to defend.

It must certainly be allowed, that nature has kept us at a great distance from all her secrets, and has afforded us only the knowledge of a few superficial qualities of objects; while she conceals from us those powers and principles on which the influence of those objects entirely depends. Our senses inform us of the color, weight, and consistence of bread; but neither sense nor reason can ever inform us of those qualities which fit it for the nourishment and support of a human body. Sight or feeling conveys an idea of the actual motion of bodies; but as to that wonderful force or power, which would carry on a moving body for ever in a continued change of place, and which bodies never lose but by communicating it to others; of this we cannot form the most distant conception. But notwithstanding this ignorance of natural powers[6] and principles, we always presume, when we see like sensible qualities, that they have like secret powers, and expect that effects, similar to those which we have experienced, will follow from them. If a body of like color and consistence with that bread, which we have formerly eat, be presented to us, we make no scruple of repeating the experiment, and foresee, with certainty, like nourishment and support. Now this is a process of the mind or thought, of which I would willingly know the foundation. It is allowed on all hands that there is no known connection between the sensible qualities and the secret powers; and consequently, that the mind is not led to form such a conclusion concerning their constant and regular conjunction, by anything which it knows of their nature. As to past Experience, it can be allowed to give direct and certain information of those precise objects only, and that precise period of time, which fell under its cognizance: but why this experience should be extended to future times, and to other objects, which for aught we know, may be only in appearance similar; this is the main question on which I would insist. The bread, which I formerly eat, nourished me; that is, a body of such sensible qualities was, at that time, endued with such secret powers: but does it follow, that other bread must also nourish me at another time, and that like sensible qualities must always be attended with like secret powers? The consequence seems nowise necessary. At least, it must be acknowledged that there is here a consequence drawn by the mind; that there is a certain step taken; a process of thought, and an inference, which wants to be explained. These two propositions are far from being the same, I have found that such an object has always been attended with such an effect, and I foresee, that other objects, which are, in appearance, similar, will be attended with similar effects. I shall allow, if you please, that the one proposition may justly be inferred from the other: I know, in fact, that it always is inferred. But if you insist that the inference is made by a chain of reasoning, I desire you to produce that reasoning. The connection between these propositions is not intuitive. There is required a medium, which may enable the mind to draw such an inference, if indeed it be drawn by reasoning and argument. What that medium is, I must confess, passes my comprehension; and it is incumbent on those to produce it, who assert that it really exists, and is the origin of all our conclusions concerning matter of fact.

This negative argument must certainly, in process of time, become altogether convincing, if many penetrating and able philosophers shall turn their enquiries this way and no one be ever able to discover any connecting proposition or intermediate step, which supports the understanding in this conclusion. But as the question is yet new, every reader may not trust so far to his own penetration, as to conclude, because an argument escapes his inquiry, that therefore it does not really exist. For this reason it may be requisite to venture upon a more difficult task; and enumerating all the branches of human knowledge, endeavour to show that none of them can afford such an argument.

All reasonings may be divided into two kinds, namely, demonstrative reasoning, or that concerning relations of ideas, and moral reasoning, or that concerning matter of fact and existence. That there are no demonstrative arguments in the case seems evident; since it implies no contradiction that the course of nature may change, and that an object, seemingly like those which we have experienced, may be attended with different or contrary effects. May I not clearly and distinctly conceive that a body, falling from the clouds, and which, in all other respects, resembles snow, has yet the taste of salt or feeling of fire? Is there any more intelligible proposition than to affirm, that all the trees will flourish in December and January, and decay in May and June? Now whatever is intelligible, and can be distinctly conceived, implies no contradiction, and can never be proved false by any demonstrative argument or abstract reasoning *a priori*.

If we be, therefore, engaged by arguments to put trust in past experience, and make it the standard of our future judgement, these arguments must be probable only, or such as regard matter of fact and real existence, according to the division above mentioned. But that there is no argument of this kind, must appear, if our explication of that species of reasoning be admitted as solid and satisfactory. We have said that all arguments concerning existence are founded on the relation of cause and effect; that our knowledge of that relation is derived entirely from experience; and that all our experimental conclusions proceed upon the supposition that the future will be conformable to the past. To endeavour, therefore, the proof of this last supposition by probable arguments, or arguments regarding existence, must be evidently going in a circle, and taking that for granted, which is the very point in question.

In reality, all arguments from experience are founded on the similarity which we discover among natural objects, and by which we are induced to expect effects similar to those which we have found to follow from such objects. And though none but a fool or madman will ever pretend to dispute the authority of experience, or to reject that great guide of human life, it may surely be allowed a philosopher to have so much curiosity at least as to examine the principle of human nature, which gives this mighty authority to experience, and makes us draw advantage from that similarity which nature has placed among different objects. From causes which appear similar we expect similar effects. This is the sum of all our experimental conclusions. Now it seems evident that, if this conclusion were formed by reason, it would be as perfect at first, and upon one instance, as after ever so long a course of experience. But the case is far otherwise. Nothing so like as eggs; yet no one, on account of this appearing similarity, expects the same taste and relish in all of them. It is only after a long course of uniform experiments in any kind, that we attain a firm reliance and security with regard to a particular event. Now where is that process of reasoning which, from one instance, draws a conclusion, so different from that which it infers from a hundred instances that are nowise different from that single one? This question I propose as much for the sake of information, as with an intention of raising difficulties. I cannot find, I cannot imagine any such reasoning. But I keep my mind still open to instruction, if any one will vouchsafe to bestow it on me.

Should it be said that, from a number of uniform experiments, we infer a connection between the sensible qualities and the secret powers; this, I must confess, seems the same difficulty, couched in different terms. The question still recurs, on what process of argument this inference is founded? Where is the medium, the interposing ideas, which join propositions so very wide of each other? It is confessed that the color, consistence, and other sensible qualities of bread appear not, of themselves, to have any connection with the secret powers of nourishment and support. For otherwise we could infer these secret powers from the first appearance of these sensible qualities, without the aid of experience; contrary to the sentiment of all philosophers, and contrary to plain matter of fact. Here, then, is our natural state of ignorance with regard to the powers and influence of all objects. How is this remedied by experience? It only shows us a number of uniform effects, resulting from certain objects, and teaches us that those particular objects, at that particular time, were endowed with such powers and forces. When a new object, endowed with similar sensible qualities, is produced, we expect similar powers and forces, and look for a like effect. From a body of like color and consistence with bread we expect like nourishment and support. But this surely is a step or progress of the mind, which wants to be explained. When a man says, I have found, in all past instances, such sensible qualities conjoined with such secret powers; And when he says, Similar sensible qualities will always be conjoined with similar secret powers, he is not guilty of a tautology, nor are these propositions in any respect the same. You say that the one proposition is an inference from the other. But you must confess that the inference is not intuitive; neither is it demonstrative: Of what nature is it, then? To say it is experimental, is begging the question. For all inferences from experience suppose, as their foundation, that the future will resemble the past, and that similar powers will be conjoined with similar sensible qualities. If there be any suspicion that the course of nature may change, and that the past may be no rule for the future, all experience becomes useless, and can give rise to no inference or conclusion. It is impossible, therefore, that any arguments from experience can prove this resemblance of the past to the future; since all these arguments are founded on the supposition of that resemblance. Let the course of things be allowed hitherto ever so regular; that alone, without some new argument or inference, proves not that, for the future, it will continue so. In vain do you pretend to have learned the nature of bodies from your past experience. Their secret nature, and consequently all their effects and influence, may change, without any change in their sensible qualities. This happens sometimes, and with regard to some objects: Why may it not happen always, and with regard to all objects? What logic, what process of argument secures you against this supposition? My practice, you say, refutes my doubts. But you mistake the purport of my question. As an agent, I am quite satisfied in the point; but as a philosopher, who has some share of curiosity, I will not say skepticism, I want to learn the foundation of this inference. No reading, no inquiry has yet been able to remove my difficulty, or give me satisfaction in a matter of such importance. Can I do better than propose the difficulty to the public, even though, perhaps, I have small hopes of obtaining a solution? We shall at least, by this means, be sensible of our ignorance, if we do not augment our knowledge.

I must confess that a man is guilty of unpardonable arrogance who concludes, because an argument has escaped his own investigation, that therefore it does not really exist. I must also confess that, though all the learned, for several ages, should have employed themselves in fruitless search upon any subject, it may still, perhaps, be rash to conclude positively that the subject must, therefore, pass all human comprehension. Even though we examine all the sources of our knowledge, and conclude them unfit for such a subject, there may still remain a suspicion, that the enumeration is not complete, or the examination not accurate. But with regard to the present subject, there are some considerations which seem to remove all this accusation of arrogance or suspicion of mistake.

It is certain that the most ignorant and stupid peasants- nay infants, nay even brute beasts- improve by experience, and learn the qualities of natural objects, by observing the effects which result from them. When a child has felt the sensation of pain from touching the flame of a candle, he will be careful not to put his hand near any candle; but will expect a similar effect from a cause which is similar in its sensible qualities and appearance. If you assert, therefore, that the understanding of the child is led into this conclusion by any process of argument or ratiocination, I may justly require you to produce that argument; nor have you any pretense to refuse so equitable a demand. You cannot say that the argument is abstruse, and may possibly escape your inquiry; since you confess that it is obvious to the capacity of a mere infant. If you hesitate, therefore, a moment, or if, after reflection, you produce any intricate or profound argument, you, in a manner, give up the question, and confess that it is not reasoning which engages us to suppose the past resembling the future, and to expect similar effects from causes which are, to appearance, similar. This is the proposition which I intended to enforce in the present section. If I be right, I pretend not to have made any mighty discovery. And if I be wrong, I must acknowledge myself to be indeed a very backward scholar; since I cannot now discover an argument which, it seems, was perfectly familiar to me long before I was out of my cradle.

Citation and Use

The text was taken from the following work.

David Hume, An inquiry Concerning Human Understanding, ed. Lewis Amherst Selby-Bigge (Project Gutenberg, 2006), http://www.gutenberg.org/ebooks/9662.

The use of this work is governed by the Public Domain.

TRANSCENDENTAL IDEALISM

Immanuel Kant

I. Of the difference between pure and empirical knowledge.

THAT all our knowledge begins with experience there can be no doubt. For how is it possible that the faculty of cognition should be awakened into exercise otherwise than by means of objects which affect our senses, and partly of themselves produce representations, partly rouse our powers of understanding into activity, to compare, to connect, or to separate these, and so to convert the raw material of our sensuous impressions into a knowledge of objects, which is called experience? In respect of time, therefore, no knowledge of ours is antecedent to experience, but begins with it.

But, though all our knowledge begins with experience, it by no means follows that all arises out of experience. For, on the contrary, it is quite possible that our empirical knowledge is a compound of that which we receive through impressions, and that which the faculty of cognition supplies from itself (sensuous impressions giving merely the *occasion*), an addition which we cannot distinguish from the original element given by sense, till long practice has made us attentive to, and skilful in separating it. It is, therefore, a question which requires close investigation, and not to be answered at first sight,—whether there exists a knowledge altogether independent of experience, and even of all sensuous impressions? Knowledge of this kind is called *a priori*, in contradistinction to empirical knowledge, which has its sources *a posteriori*, that is, in experience.

But the expression, "*a priori*," is not as yet definite enough adequately to indicate the whole meaning of the question above started. For, in speaking of knowledge which has its sources in experience, we are wont to say, that this or that may be known *a priori*, because we do not derive this knowledge immediately from experience, but from a general rule, which, however, we have itself borrowed from experience. Thus, if a man undermined his house, we say, "he might know *a priori* that it would have fallen;" that is, he needed not to have waited for the experience that it did actually fall. But still, *a priori*, he could not know even this much. For, that bodies are heavy, and, consequently, that they fall when their supports are taken away, must have been known to him previously, by means of experience.

By the term "knowledge *a priori*," therefore, we shall in the sequel understand, not such as is independent of this or that kind of experience, but such as is absolutely so of *all* experience. Opposed to this is empirical knowledge, or that which is possible only *a posteriori*, that is, through experience. Knowledge *a priori* is either pure or impure. Pure knowledge *a priori* is that with which no empirical element is mixed up. For example, the proposition, "Every change has a cause," is a proposition *a priori*, but impure, because change is a conception which can only be derived from experience.

II. The human intellect, even in an unphilosophical state, is in possession of certain cognitions *a priori*.

THE question now is as to a *criterion*, by which we may securely distinguish a pure from an empirical cognition. Experience no doubt teaches us that this or that object is constituted in such and such a manner, but not that it could not possibly exist otherwise. Now, in the first place, if we have a proposition which contains the idea of necessity in its very conception, it is a judgment *a priori*; if, moreover, it is not derived from any other proposition, unless from one equally involving the idea of necessity, it is absolutely *a priori*. Secondly, an empirical judgment never exhibits strict and absolute, but only assumed and comparative universality (by induction); therefore, the most we can say is,—so far as we have hitherto observed, there is no exception to this or that rule. If, on the other hand, a judgment carries with it strict and absolute universality, that is, admits of no possible exception, it is not derived from experience, but is valid absolutely *a priori*.

Empirical universality is, therefore, only an arbitrary extension of validity, from that which may be predicated of a proposition valid in most cases, to that which is asserted of a proposition which holds good in all; as, for example, in the affirmation, "All bodies are heavy." When, on the contrary, strict universality characterizes a judgment, it necessarily indicates another peculiar source of knowledge, namely, a faculty of cognition *a priori*. Necessity and strict universality, therefore, are infallible tests for distinguishing pure from empirical knowledge, and are inseparably connected with each other. But as in the use of these criteria the empirical limitation is sometimes more easily detected than the contingency of the judgment, or the unlimited universality which we attach to a judgment is often a more convincing proof than its necessity, it may be advisable to use the criteria separately, each being by itself infallible.

Now, that in the sphere of human cognition we have judgments which are necessary, and in the strictest sense universal, consequently pure *a priori*, it will be an easy matter to show. If we desire an example from the sciences, we need only take any proposition in mathematics. If we cast our eyes upon the commonest operations of the understanding, the proposition, "every change must have a cause," will amply serve our purpose. In the latter case, indeed, the conception of a cause so plainly involves the conception of a necessity of connection with an effect, and of a strict universality of the law, that the very notion of a cause would entirely disappear, were we to derive it, like Hume, from a frequent association of what happens with that which precedes; and the habit thence originating of connecting representations—the necessity inherent in the judgment being therefore merely subjective. Besides, without seeking for such examples of principles existing *a priori* in cognition, we might easily show that such principles are the indispensable basis of the possibility of experience itself, and consequently prove their existence *a priori*. For whence could our experience itself acquire certainty, if all the rules on which it depends were themselves empirical, and consequently fortuitous? No one, therefore, can admit the validity of the use of such rules as first principles. But, for the present, we may content ourselves with having established the fact, that we do possess and exercise a faculty of pure *a priori* cognition; and, secondly, with having pointed out the proper tests of such cognition, namely, universality and necessity.

Not only in judgments, however, but even in conceptions, is an *a priori* origin manifest. For example, if we take away by degrees from our conceptions of a body all that can be referred to mere sensuous experience—colour, hardness or softness, weight, even impenetrability— the body will then vanish; but the space which it occupied still remains, and this it is utterly impossible to annihilate in thought. Again, if we take away, in like manner, from our empirical conception of any object, corporeal or incorporeal, all properties which mere experience has taught us to connect with it, still we cannot think away those through which we cogitate it as substance, or adhering to substance, although our conception of substance is more determined than that of an object. Compelled, therefore, by that necessity with which the conception of substance forces itself upon us, we must confess that it has its seat in our faculty of cognition *a priori*.

III. Philosophy stands in need of a science

which shall determine the possibility, principles, and extent of human knowledge *a priori*

OF far more importance than all that has been above said, is the consideration that certain of our cognitions rise completely above the sphere of all possible experience, and by means of conceptions, to which there exists in the whole extent of experience no corresponding object, seem to extend the range of our judgments beyond its bounds. And just in this transcendental or supersensible sphere, where experience affords us neither instruction nor guidance, lie the investigations of *Reason*, which, on account of their importance, we consider far preferable to, and as having a far more elevated aim than, all that the understanding can achieve within the sphere of sensuous phenomena. So high a value do we set upon these investigations, that even at the risk of error, we persist in following them out, and permit neither doubt nor disregard nor indifference to restrain us from the pursuit. These unavoidable problems of mere pure reason are GOD, FREEDOM (of will), and IMMORTALITY. The science which, with all its preliminaries, has for its especial object the solution of these problems is named metaphysics—a science which is at the very outset dogmatical, that is, it confidently takes upon itself the execution of this task without any previous investigation of the ability or inability of reason for such an undertaking.

Now the safe ground of experience being thus abandoned, it seems nevertheless natural that we should hesitate to erect a building with the cognitions we possess, without knowing whence they come, and on the strength of principles, the origin of which is undiscovered. Instead of thus trying to build without a foundation, it is rather to be expected that we should long ago have put the question, how the understanding can arrive at these *a priori* cognitions, and what is the extent, validity, and worth which they may possess? We say, this is natural enough, meaning by the word natural, that which is consistent with a just and reasonable way of thinking; but if we understand by the term, that which usually happens, nothing indeed could be more natural and more comprehensible than that this investigation should be left long unattempted. For one part of our pure knowledge, the science of mathematics, has been long firmly established, and thus leads us to form flattering expectations with regard to others, though these may be of quite a different nature. Besides, when we get beyond the bounds of experience, we are of course safe from opposition in that quarter; and the charm of widening the range of our knowledge is so great that, unless we are brought to a standstill by some evident contradiction, we hurry on undoubtingly in our course. This, however, may be avoided, if we are sufficiently cautious in the construction of our fictions, which are not the less fictions on that account.

Mathematical science affords us a brilliant example, how far, independently of all experience, we may carry our *a priori* knowledge. It is true that the mathematician occupies himself with objects and cognitions only in so far as they can be represented by means of intuition. But this circumstance is easily overlooked, because the said intuition can itself be given *a priori*, and therefore is hardly to be distinguished from a mere pure conception. Deceived by such a proof of the power of reason, we can perceive no limits to the extension of our knowledge. The light dove cleaving in free flight the thin air, whose resistance it feels, might imagine that her movements would be far more free and rapid in airless space. Just in the same way did Plato, abandoning the world of sense because of the narrow limits it sets to the understanding, venture upon the wings of ideas beyond it, into the void space of pure intellect. He did not reflect that he made no real progress by all his efforts; for he met with no resistance which might serve him for a support, as it were, whereon to rest, and on which he might apply his powers, in order to let the intellect acquire momentum for its progress. It is, indeed, the common fate of human reason in speculation, to finish the imposing edifice of thought as rapidly as possible, and then for the first time to begin to examine whether the foundation is a solid one or no. Arrived at this point, all sorts of excuses are sought after, in order to console us for its want of stability, or rather, indeed, to enable us to dispense altogether with so late and dangerous an investigation. But what frees us during the process of building from all apprehension or suspicion, and flatters us into the belief of its solidity, is this. A great part, perhaps the greatest part, of the business of our reason consists in the analysation of the conceptions which we already possess of objects. By this means we gain a multitude of cognitions, which although really nothing more than elucidations or explanations of that which (though in a confused manner) was already thought in our conceptions, are, at least in respect of their form, prized as new introspections; whilst, so far as regards their matter or content, we have really made no addition to our conceptions, but only disinvolved them. But as this process does furnish real *a priori* knowledge, which has a sure progress and useful results, reason, deceived by this, slips in, without being itself aware of it, assertions of a quite different kind; in which, to given conceptions it adds others, *a priori* indeed, but entirely foreign to them, without our knowing how it arrives at these, and, indeed, without such a question ever suggesting itself. I shall therefore at once proceed to examine the difference between these two modes of knowledge.

IV. Of the difference between analytical and synthetical judgments.

IN all judgments wherein the relation of a subject to the predicate is cogitated (I mention affirmative judgments only here; the application to negative will be very easy), this relation is possible in two different ways. Either the predicate B belongs to the subject A, as somewhat which is contained (though covertly) in the conception A; or the predicate B lies completely out of the conception A, although it stands in connection with it. In the first instance, I term the judgment analytical, in the second, synthetical. Analytical judgments (affirmative) are therefore those in which the connection of the predicate with the subject is cogitated through identity; those in which this

connection is cogitated without identity, are called synthetical judgments. The former may be called *explicative*, the latter *augmentative*[1] judgments; because the former add in the predicate nothing to the conception of the subject, but only analyse it into its constituent conceptions, which were thought already in the subject, although in a confused manner; the latter add to our conceptions of the subject a predicate which was not contained in it, and which no analysis could ever have discovered therein. For example, when I say, "all bodies are extended," this is an analytical judgment. For I need not go beyond the conception of *body* in order to find extension connected with it, but merely analyse the conception, that is, become conscious of the manifold properties which I think in that conception, in order to discover this predicate in it: it is therefore an analytical judgment. On the other hand, when I say, "all bodies are heavy," the predicate is something totally different from that which I think in the mere conception of a body. By the addition of such a predicate, therefore, it becomes a synthetical judgment.

Judgments of experience, as such, are always synthetical. For it would be absurd to think of grounding an analytical judgment on experience, because in forming such a judgment I need not go out of the sphere of my conceptions, and therefore recourse to the testimony of experience is quite unnecessary. That "bodies are extended" is not an empirical judgment, but a proposition which stands firm *a priori*. For before addressing myself to experience, I already have in my conception all the requisite conditions for the judgment, and I have only to extract the predicate from the conception, according to the principle of contradiction, and thereby at the same time become conscious of the necessity of the judgment, a necessity which I could never learn from experience. On the other hand, though at first I do not at all include the predicate of weight in my conception of body in general, that conception still indicates an object of experience, a part of the totality of experience, to which I can still add other parts; and this I do when I recognize by observation that bodies are heavy. I can cognize beforehand by analysis the conception of body through the characteristics of extension, impenetrability, shape, etc., all which are cogitated in this conception. But now I extend my knowledge, and looking back on experience from which I had derived this conception of body, I find weight at all times connected with the above characteristics, and therefore I synthetically add to my conceptions this as a predicate, and say, "all bodies are heavy." Thus it is experience upon which rests the possibility of the synthesis of the predicate of weight with the conception of body, because both conceptions, although the one is not contained in the other, still belong to one another (only contingently, however), as parts of a whole, namely, of experience, which is itself a synthesis of intuitions.

But to synthetical judgments *a priori*, such aid is entirely wanting. If I go out of and beyond the conception A, in order to recognize another B as connected with it, what foundation have I to rest on, whereby to render the synthesis possible? I have here no longer the advantage of looking out in the sphere of experience for what I want. Let us take, for example, the proposition, "everything that happens has a cause." In the conception of *something that happens*, I indeed think an existence which a certain time antecedes, and from this I can derive analytical judgments. But the conception of a cause lies quite out of the above conception, and indicates something entirely different from "that which happens," and is consequently not contained in that conception. How then am I able to assert concerning the general conception—"that which happens"—something entirely different from that conception, and to recognize the conception of cause although not contained in it, yet as belonging to it, and even necessarily? what is here the unknown = X, upon which the understanding rests when it believes it has found, out of the conception A a foreign predicate B, which it nevertheless considers to be connected with it? It cannot be experience, because the principle adduced annexes the two representations, cause and effect, to the representation existence, not only with universality, which experience cannot give, but also with the expression of necessity, therefore completely *a priori* and from pure conceptions. Upon such synthetical, that is augmentative propositions, depends the whole aim of our speculative knowledge *a priori;* for although analytical judgments are indeed highly important and necessary, they are so, only to arrive at that clearness of conceptions which is requisite for a sure and extended synthesis, and this alone is a real acquisition.

V. In all theoretical sciences of reason, synthetical judgments; *a priori* are contained as principles.

MATHEMATICAL judgments are always synthetical. Hitherto this fact, though incontestably true and very important in its consequences, seems to have escaped the analysts of the human mind, nay, to be in complete opposition to all their conjectures. For as it was found that mathematical conclusions all proceed according to the principle of contradiction (which the nature of every apodeictic certainty requires), people became persuaded that the fundamental principles of the science also were recognized and admitted in the same way. But the notion is fallacious; for although a synthetical proposition can certainly be discerned by means of the principle of contradiction, this is possible only when another synthetical proposition precedes, from which the latter is deduced, but never of itself.

Before all, be it observed, that proper mathematical propositions are always judgments *a priori*, and not empirical, because they carry along with them the conception of necessity, which cannot be given by experience. If this be demurred to, it matters not; I will then limit my assertion to *pure* mathematics, the very conception of which implies that it consists of knowledge altogether non-empirical and *a priori*.

We might, indeed at first suppose that the proposition 7 + 5 = 12 is a merely analytical proposition, following (according to the principle of contradiction) from the conception of a sum of seven and five. But if we regard it more narrowly, we find that our conception of the sum of seven and five contains nothing more than the uniting of both sums into one, whereby it cannot at all be cogitated what this single number is which embraces both. The conception of twelve is by no means obtained by merely cogitating the union of seven and five; and we may analyse our conception of such a possible sum as long as we will, still we shall never discover in it the notion of twelve. We must go beyond these conceptions, and have recourse to an intuition which corresponds to one of the two,—our five fingers, for example, or like Segner in his "Arithmetic," five points, and so by degrees, add the units contained in the five given in the intuition, to the conception of seven. For I first take the number 7, and, for the conception of 5 calling in the aid of the fingers of my hand as objects of intuition, I add the units, which I before took together to make up the number 5, gradually now by means of the material image my hand, to the number 7, and by this process, I at length see the number 12 arise. That 7 should be added to 5, I have certainly cogitated in my conception of a sum = 7 + 5, but not that this sum was equal to 12. Arithmetical propositions are therefore always synthetical, of which we may become more clearly convinced by trying large numbers. For it will thus become quite evident that, turn and twist our conceptions as we may, it is impossible, without having recourse to intuition, to arrive at the sum total or product by means of the mere analysis of our conceptions. Just as little is any principle of pure geometry analytical. "A straight line between two points is the shortest," is a synthetical proposition. For my conception of *straight*, contains no notion of *quantity*, but is merely *qualitative*. The conception of the *shortest* is therefore fore wholly an addition, and by no analysis can it be extracted from our conception of a straight line. Intuition must therefore here lend its aid, by means of which, and thus only, our synthesis is possible.

Some few principles preposited by geometricians are, indeed, really analytical, and depend on the principle of contradiction. They serve, however, like identical propositions, as links in the chain of method, not as principles,—for example, a = a, the whole is equal to itself, or (a + b); a, the whole is greater than its part. And yet even these principles themselves, though they derive their validity from pure conceptions, are only admitted in mathematics because they can be presented in intuition. What causes us here commonly to believe that the predicate of such apodeictic judgments is already contained in our conception, and that the judgment is therefore analytical, is merely the equivocal nature of the expression. We must join in thought a certain predicate to a given conception, and this necessity cleaves already to the conception. But the question is, not what we must join in thought to the given conception, but what we really think therein, though only obscurely, and then it becomes manifest that the predicate pertains to these conceptions, necessarily indeed, yet not as thought in the conception itself, but by virtue of an intuition, which must be added to the conception.

The science of Natural Philosophy (Physics) contains in itself synthetical judgments a priori, as principles. I shall adduce two propositions. For instance, the proposition, "in all changes of the material world, the quantity of matter remains unchanged;" or, that, "in all communication of motion, action and re-action must always be equal." In both of these, not only is the necessity, and therefore their origin *a priori* clear, but also that they are synthetical propositions. For in the conception of matter, I do not cogitate its permanency, but merely its presence in space, which it fills. I therefore really go out of and beyond the conception of matter, in order to think on to it something *a priori*, which I did not think in it. The proposition is therefore not analytical, but synthetical, and nevertheless conceived *a priori*; and so it is with regard to the other propositions of the pure part of natural philosophy.

As to metaphysics, even if we look upon it merely as an attempted science, yet, from the nature of human reason, an indispensable one, we find that it must contain synthetical propositions *a priori*. It is not merely the duty of metaphysics to dissect, and thereby analytically to illustrate the conceptions which we form *a priori* of things; but we seek to widen the range of our *a priori* knowledge. For this purpose, we must avail ourselves of such principles as add something to the original conception—something not identical with, nor contained in it, and by means of synthetical judgments *a priori*, leave far behind us the limits of experience; for example, in the proposition, "the world must have a beginning," and such like. Thus metaphysics, according to the proper aim of the science, consists merely of synthetical propositions *a priori*.

VI. The universal problem of pure reason.

IT is extremely advantageous to be able to bring a number of investigations under the formula of a single problem. For in this manner, we not only facilitate our own labour, inasmuch as we define it clearly to ourselves, but also render it more easy for others to decide whether we have done justice to our undertaking. The proper problem of pure reason, then, is contained in the question: "How are synthetical judgments *a priori* possible?"

That metaphysical science has hitherto remained in so vacillating a state of uncertainty and contradiction, is only to be attributed to the fact that this great problem, and perhaps even the difference between analytical and synthetical judgments, did not sooner suggest itself to philosophers. Upon the solution of this problem, or upon sufficient proof of the impossibility of synthetical knowledge *a priori*, depends the existence or downfall of the science of metaphysics. Among philosophers, David Hume came the nearest of all to this problem; yet it never acquired in his mind sufficient precision, nor did he regard the question in its universality. On the contrary, he stopped short at the synthetical proposition of the connection of an effect with its cause (*principium causalitatis*), insisting that such proposition *a priori* was impossible. According to his conclusions, then, all that we term metaphysical science is a mere delusion, arising from the fancied insight of reason into that which is in truth borrowed from experience, and to which habit has given the appearance of necessity. Against this assertion, destructive to all pure philosophy, he would have been guarded, had he had our problem before his eyes in

its universality. For he would then have perceived that, according to his own argument, there likewise could not be any pure mathematical science, which assuredly cannot exist without synthetical propositions *a priori*,—an absurdity from which his good understanding must have saved him.

In the solution of the above problem is at the same time comprehended the possibility of the use of pure reason in the foundation and construction of all sciences which contain theoretical knowledge *a priori* of objects, that is to say, the answer to the following questions:
1.   How is pure mathematical science possible?
2.   How is pure natural science possible?

Respecting these sciences, as they do certainly exist, it may with propriety be asked, *how* they are possible?—for that they must be possible is shown by the fact of their really existing.[2] But as to metaphysics, the miserable progress it has hitherto made, and the fact that of no one system yet brought forward, far as regards its true aim, can it be said that this science really exists, leaves any one at liberty to doubt with reason the very possibility of its existence.

Yet, in a certain sense, this kind of knowledge must unquestionably be looked upon as *given;* in other words, metaphysics must be considered as really existing, if not as a science, nevertheless as a natural disposition of the human mind (*metaphysica naturalis*). For human reason, without any instigations imputable to the mere vanity of great knowledge, unceasingly progresses, urged on by its own feeling of need, towards such questions as cannot be answered by any empirical application of reason, or principles derived therefrom; and so there has ever really existed in every man some system of metaphysics. It will always exist, so soon as reason awakes to the exercise of its power of speculation. And now the question arises—How is metaphysics, as a natural disposition, possible? In other words, how, from the nature of universal human reason, do those questions arise which pure reason proposes to itself, and which it is impelled by its own feeling of need to answer as well as it can?

But as in all the attempts hitherto made to answer the questions which reason is prompted by its very nature to propose to itself, for example, whether the world had a beginning, or has existed from eternity, it has always met with unavoidable contradictions, we must not rest satisfied with the mere natural disposition of the mind to metaphysics, that is, with the existence of the faculty of pure reason, whence, indeed, some sort of metaphysical system always arises; but it must be possible to arrive at certainty in regard to the question whether we know or do not know the things of which metaphysics treats. We must be able to arrive at a decision on the subjects of its questions, or on the ability or inability of reason to form any judgment respecting them; and therefore either to extend with confidence the bounds of our pure reason, or to set strictly defined and safe limits to its action. This last question, which arises out of the above universal problem, would properly run thus: How is metaphysics possible as a science?

Thus, the critique of reason leads at last, naturally and necessarily, to science; and, on the other hand, the dogmatical use of reason without criticism leads to groundless assertions, against which others equally specious can always be set, thus ending unavoidably in scepticism.

Besides, this science cannot be of great and formidable prolixity, because it has not to do with objects of reason, the variety of which is inexhaustible, but merely with Reason herself and her problems; problems which arise out of her own bosom, and are not proposed to her by the nature of outward things, but by her own nature. And when once Reason has previously become able completely to understand her own power in regard to objects which she meets with in experience, it will be easy to determine securely the extent and limits of her attempted application to objects beyond the confines of experience.

We may and must, therefore, regard the attempts hitherto made to establish metaphysical science dogmatically as non-existent. For what of analysis, that is, mere dissection of conceptions, is contained in one or other, is not the aim of, but only a preparation for metaphysics proper, which has for its object the extension, by means of synthesis, of our *a priori* knowledge. And for this purpose, mere analysis is of course useless, because it only shows what is contained in these conceptions, but not how we arrive, *a priori*, at them; and this it is her duty to show, in order to be able afterwards to determine their valid use in regard to all objects of experience, to all knowledge in general. But little self-denial, indeed, is needed to give up these pretensions, seeing the undeniable, and in the dogmatic mode of procedure, inevitable contradictions of Reason with herself, have long since ruined the reputation of every system of metaphysics that has appeared up to this time. It will require more firmness to remain undeterred by difficulty from within, and opposition from without, from endeavouring, by a method quite opposed to all those hitherto followed, to further the growth and fruitfulness of a science indispensable to human reason—a science from which every branch it has borne may be cut away, but whose roots remain indestructible.

VII. Idea and division of a particular science, under the name of a Critique of Pure Reason.

FROM all that has been said, there results the idea of a particular science, which may be called the *Critique of Pure Reason*. For reason is the faculty which furnishes us with the principles of knowledge *a priori*. Hence, pure reason is the faculty which contains the principles of cognizing anything absolutely *a priori*. An Organon of pure reason would be a compendium of those principles according to which alone all pure cognitions *a priori* can be obtained. The completely extended application of such an organon would afford us a system of pure reason. As this, however, is demanding a great deal, and it is yet doubtful whether any extension of our knowledge be here possible, or, if so, in what cases; we can regard a science of the mere criticism of pure reason, its sources and limits, as the *propaedeutic* to a system of pure reason. Such a science must not be called a doctrine, but only a critique of pure reason; and its use, in regard to speculation, would be only negative, not to enlarge the bounds of, but to purify, our reason, and to shield it against error,—which alone is no little gain. I apply the term *transcendental* to all knowledge which is not so much occupied with objects as with the mode of our cognition of these objects, so far as this mode of cognition is possible *a priori*. A system of such conceptions would be called *Transcendental Philosophy*. But this, again, is still beyond the bounds of our present essay. For as such a science must contain a complete exposition not only of our synthetical *a priori*, but of our analytical *a priori* knowledge, it is of too wide a range for our present purpose, because we do not require to carry our analysis any farther than is necessary to understand, in their full extent, the principles of synthesis *a priori*, with which alone we have to do. This investigation, which we cannot properly call a doctrine, but only a transcendental critique, because it aims not at the enlargement, but at the correction and guidance, of our knowledge, and is to serve as a touchstone of the worth or worthlessness of all knowledge *a priori*, is the sole object of our present essay. Such a critique is consequently, as far as possible, a preparation for an organon; and if this new organon should be found to fail, at least for a canon of pure reason, according to which the complete system of the philosophy of pure reason, whether it extend or limit the bounds of that reason, might one day be set forth both analytically and synthetically. For that this is possible, nay, that such a system is not of so great extent as to preclude the hope of its ever being completed, is evident. For we have not here to do with the nature of outward objects, which is infinite, but solely with the mind, which judges of the nature of objects, and, again, with the mind only in respect of its cognition *a priori*. And the object of our investigations, as it is not to be sought without, but, altogether within, ourselves, cannot remain concealed, and in all probability is limited enough to be completely surveyed and fairly estimated, according to its worth or worthlessness. Still less let the reader here expect a critique of books and systems of pure reason; our present object is exclusively a critique of the faculty of pure reason itself. Only when we make this critique our foundation, do we possess a pure touchstone for estimating the philosophical value of ancient and modern writings on this subject; and without this criterion, the incompetent historian or judge decides upon and corrects the groundless assertions of others with his own, which have themselves just as little foundation.

Transcendental philosophy is the idea of a science, for which the Critique of Pure Reason must sketch the whole plan architectonically, that is, from principles, with a full guarantee for the validity and stability of all the parts which enter into the building. It is the system of all the principles of pure reason. If this Critique itself does not assume the title of transcendental philosophy, it is only because, to be a complete system, it ought to contain a full analysis of all human knowledge *a priori*. Our critique must, indeed, lay before us a complete enumeration of all the radical conceptions which constitute the said pure knowledge. But from the complete analysis of these conceptions themselves, as also from a complete investigation of those derived from them, it abstains with reason; partly because it would be deviating from the end in view to occupy itself with this analysis, since this process is not attended with the difficulty and insecurity to be found in the synthesis, to which our critique is entirely devoted, and partly because it would be inconsistent with the unity of our plan to burden this essay with the vindication of the completeness of such an analysis and deduction, with which, after all, we have at present nothing to do. This completeness of the analysis of these radical conceptions, as well as of the deduction from the conceptions *a priori* which may be given by the analysis, we can, however, easily attain, provided only that we are in possession of all these radical conceptions, which are to serve as principles of the synthesis, and that in respect of this main purpose nothing is wanting.

To the Critique of Pure Reason, therefore, belongs all that constitutes transcendental philosophy; and it is the complete idea of transcendental philosophy, but still not the science itself; because it only proceeds so far with the analysis as is necessary to the power of judging completely of our synthetical knowledge *a priori*.

The principal thing we must attend to, in the division of the parts of a science like this, is: that no conceptions must enter it which contain aught empirical; in other words, that the knowledge *a priori* must be completely pure. Hence, although the highest principles and fundamental conceptions of morality are certainly cognitions *a priori*, yet they do not belong to transcendental philosophy; because though they certainly do not lay the conceptions of pain, pleasure, desires, inclinations, (which are all of empirical origin), at the foundation of its precepts, yet still into the conception of duty,—as an obstacle to be overcome, or as an incitement which should not be made into a motive,—these empirical conceptions must necessarily enter, in the construction of a system of pure morality. Transcendental philosophy is consequently a philosophy of the pure and merely speculative reason. For all that is practical, so far as it contains motives, relates to feelings, and these belong to empirical sources of cognition.

If we wish to divide this science from the universal point of view of a science in general, it ought to comprehend, first, a *Doctrine of the Elements*, and, secondly, a *Doctrine of the Method* of pure reason. Each of these main divisions will have its subdivisions, the separate reasons for which we cannot here particularize. Only so much seems necessary, by way of introduction of premonition, that there are two sources of human knowledge (which probably spring from a common, but to us unknown root), namely, sense and understanding. By the former, objects are *given* to us; by the latter, *thought*. So far as the faculty of sense may contain representations *a priori*, which form the conditions under which objects are given, in so far it belongs to transcendental philosophy. The transcendental doctrine of sense must form the first part of our science of elements, because the conditions under which alone the objects of human knowledge are given must precede those under which they are thought.

Citation and Use

The text was taken from the following work.

Immanuel Kant, *The Critique of Pure Reason* (Project Gutenberg, 2003), http://www.gutenberg.org/ebooks/4280.

The use of this work is governed by the Public Domain

TRUTH IS A HABIT

Richard Rorty

About two hundred years ago, the idea that truth was made rather than found began to take hold of the imagination of Europe. The French Revolution had shown that the whole vocabulary of social relations, and the whole spectrum of social institutions, could be replaced almost overnight. This precedent made utopian politics the rule rather than the exception among intellectuals. Utopian politics sets aside questions about both the will of God and the nature of man and dreams of creating a hitherto unknown form of society.

At about the same time, the Romantic poets were showing what happens when art is thought of no longer as imitation but, rather, as the artist's self creation. The poets claimed for art the place in culture traditionally held by religion and philosophy, the place which the Enlightenment had claimed for science. The precedent the Romantics set lent initial plausibility to their claim. The actual role of novels, poems, plays, paintings, statues, and buildings in the social movements of the last century and a half has given it still greater plausibility.

By now these two tendencies have joined forces and have achieved cultural hegemony. For most contemporary intellectuals, questions of ends as opposed to means questions about how to give a sense to one's own life or that of one's community are questions for art or politics, or both, rather than for religion, philosophy, or science. This development has led to a split within philosophy. Some philosophers have remained faithful to the Enlightenment and have continued to identify themselves with the cause of science. They see the old struggle between science and religion, reason and unreason, as still going on, having now taken the form of a struggle between reason and all those forces within culture which think of truth as made rather than found. These philosophers take science as the paradigmatic human activity, and they insist that natural science discovers truth rather than makes it. They regard "making truth" as a merely metaphorical, and thoroughly misleading, phrase. They think of politics and art as spheres in which the notion of "truth" is out of place. Other philosophers, realizing that the world as it is described by the physical sciences teaches no moral lesson, offers no spiri-

tual comfort, have concluded that science is no more than the handmaiden of technology. These philosophers have ranged themselves alongside the political utopian and the innovative artist.

Whereas the first kind of philosopher contrasts "hard scientific fact" with the "subjective" or with "metaphor," the second kind sees science as one more human activity, rather as the place at which human beings encounter a "hard," nonhuman reality. On this view, great scientists invent descriptions of the world which are useful for purposes of predicting and controlling what happens, just as poets and political thinkers invent other descriptions of it for other purposes. But there is no sense in which any of these descriptions is an accurate representation of the way the world is in itself. These philosophers regard the very idea of such a representation as pointless.

Had the first sort of philosopher, the sort whose hero is the natural scientist, always been the only sort, we should probably never have had an autonomous discipline called "philosophy" a discipline as distinct from the sciences as it is from theology or from the arts. As such a discipline, philosophy is no more than two hundred years old. It owes its existence to attempts by the German idealists to put the sciences in their place and to give a clear sense to the vague idea that human beings make truth rather than find it. Kant wanted to consign science to the realm of second-rate truth — truth about a phenomenal world. Hegel wanted to think of natural science as a description of spirit not yet fully conscious of its own spiritual nature, and thereby to elevate the sort of truth offered by the poet and the political revolutionary to first-rate status.

German idealism, however, was a short-lived and unsatisfactory compromise. For Kant and Hegel went only halfway in their repudiation of the idea that truth is "out there." They were willing to view the world of empirical science as a made world to see matter as constructed by mind, or as consisting in mind insufficiently conscious of its own mental character. But they persisted in seeing mind, spirit, the depths of the human self, as having an intrinsic nature one which could be known by a kind of non-empirical super science called philosophy. This meant that only half of truth the bottom, scientific half was made. Higher truth, the truth about mind, the province of philosophy, was still a matter of discovery rather than creation.

What was needed, and what the idealists were unable to envisage, was a repudiation of the very idea of anything mind or matter, self or world having an intrinsic nature to be expressed or represented. For the idealists confused the idea that nothing has such a nature with the idea that space and time are unreal, that human beings cause the spatiotemporal world to exist.

We need to make a distinction between the claim that the world is out there and the claim that truth is out there. To say that the world is out there, that it is not our creation, is to say, with common sense, that most things in space and time are the effects of causes which do not include human mental states. To say that truth is not out there is simply to say that where there are no sentences there is no truth, that sentences are elements of human languages, and that human languages are human creations.

Truth cannot be out there cannot exist independently of the human mind because sentences cannot so exist, or be out there. The world is out there, but descriptions of the world are not. Only descriptions of the world can be true or false. The world on its own unaided by the describing activities of human beings cannot.

The suggestion that truth, as well as the world, is out there is a legacy of an age in which the world was seen as the creation of a being who had a language of his own. If we cease to attempt to make sense of the idea of such a nonhuman language, we shall not be tempted to confuse the platitude that the world may cause us to be justified in believing a sentence true with the claim that the world splits itself up, on its own initiative, into sentence shaped chunks called "facts." But if one clings to the notion of self subsistent facts, it is easy to start capitalizing the word "truth" and treating it as something identical either with God or with the world as God's project. Then one will say, for example, that Truth is great, and will prevail.

This conflation is facilitated by confining attention to single sentences as opposed to vocabularies. For we often let the world decide the competition between alternative sentences (e.g., between "Red wins" and "Black wins" or between "The butler did it" and "The doctor did it"). In such cases, it is easy to run together the fact that the world contains the causes of our being justified in holding a belief with the claim that some nonlinguistic state of the world is itself an example of truth, or that some such state "makes a belief true" by "corresponding" to it. But it is not so easy when we turn from individual sentences to vocabularies as wholes. When we consider examples of alternative language games the vocabulary of ancient Athenian politics versus Jefferson's, the moral vocabulary of Saint Paul versus Freud's, the jargon of Newton versus that of Aristotle, the idiom of Blake versus that of Dryden it is difficult to think of the world as making one of these better than

another, of the world as deciding between them. When the notion of "description of the world" is moved from the level of criterion governed sentences within language games to language games as wholes, games which we do not choose between by reference to criteria, the idea that the world decides which descriptions are true can no longer be given a clear sense. It becomes hard to think that that vocabulary is somehow already out there in the world, waiting for us to discover it. Attention (of the sort fostered by intellectual historians like Thomas Kuhn and Quentin Skinner) to the vocabularies in which sentences are formulated, rather than to individual sentences, makes us realize, for example, that the fact that Newton's vocabulary lets us predict the world more easily than Aristotle's does not mean that the world speaks Newtonian.

The world does not speak. Only we do. The world can, once we have programmed ourselves with a language, cause us to hold beliefs. But it cannot propose a language for us to speak. Only other human beings can do that. The realization that the world does not tell us what language games to play should not, however, lead us to say that a decision about which to play is arbitrary, nor to say that it is the expression of something deep within us. The moral is not that objective criteria for choice of vocabulary are to be replaced with subjective criteria, reason with will or feeling. It is rather that the notions of criteria and choice (including that of "arbitrary" choice) are no longer in point when it comes to changes from one language game to another. Europe did not decide to accept the idiom of Romantic poetry, or of socialist politics, or of Galilean mechanics. That sort of shift was no more an act of will than it was a result of argument. Rather, Europe gradually lost the habit of using certain words and gradually acquired the habit of using others.

As Kuhn argues in The Copernican Revolution, we did not decide on the basis of some telescopic observations, or on the basis of anything else, that the earth was not the center of the universe, that macroscopic behavior could be explained on the basis of microstructural motion, and that prediction and control should be the principal aim of scientific theorizing. Rather, after a hundred years of inconclusive muddle, the Europeans found themselves speaking in a way which took these interlocked theses for granted. Cultural change of this magnitude does not result from applying criteria (or from "arbitrary decision") any more than individuals become theists or atheists, or shift from one spouse or circle of friends to another, as a result either of applying criteria or of acts gratuity. We should not look within ourselves for criteria of decision in such matters any more than we should look to the world.

The temptation to look for criteria is a species of the more general temptation to think of the world, or the human self, as possessing an intrinsic nature, an essence. That is, it is the result of the temptation to privilege someone among the many languages in which we habitually describe the world or ourselves. As long as we think that there is some relation called "fitting the world" or "expressing the real nature of the self" which can be possessed or lacked by vocabularies-as-wholes, we shall continue the traditional philosophical search for a criterion to tell us which vocabularies have this desirable feature. But if we could ever become reconciled to the idea that most of reality is indifferent to our descriptions of it, and that the human self is created by the use of a vocabulary rather than being adequately or inadequately expressed in a vocabulary, then we should at last have assimilated what was true in the Romantic idea that truth is made rather than found. What is true about this claim is just that languages are made rather than found, and that truth is a property of linguistic entities, of sentences.

[...]

The difficulty faced by a philosopher who, like myself, is sympathetic to this suggestion one who thinks of himself as auxiliary to the poet rather than to the physicist is to avoid hinting that this suggestion gets something right, that my sort of philosophy corresponds to the way things really are. For this talk of correspondence brings back just the idea my sort of philosopher wants to get rid of, the idea that the world or the self has an intrinsic nature. From our point of view, explaining the success of science, or the desirability of political liberalism, by talk of "fitting the world" or "expressing human nature" is like explaining why opium makes you sleepy by talking about its dormitive power. To say that Freud's vocabulary gets at the truth about human nature, or Newton's at the truth about the heavens, is not an explanation of anything. It is just an empty compliment one traditionally paid to writers whose novel jargon we have found useful. To say that there is no such thing as intrinsic nature is not to say that the intrinsic nature of reality has turned out, surprisingly enough, to be extrinsic. It is to say that the term "intrinsic nature" is one which it would pay us not to use, an expression which has caused more trouble than it has been worth. To say that we should drop the idea of truth as out there waiting to be discovered is not to say that we have discovered that, out there, there is no truth.2 It is to say that our purposes would be served best by ceasing to see truth as a deep matter, as a topic of philosophical interest, or "true" as a term which repays "analysis." "The nature of truth" is an unprofitable topic, resembling in this respect "the nature of man" and "the nature of God," and differing from "the nature of the positron," and "the nature of Oedipal fixation." But this claim about relative profitability, in turn, is just the recommendation that we in fact say little about these topics, and see how we get on.

On the view of philosophy which I am offering, philosophers should not be asked for arguments against, for example, the correspondence theory of truth or the idea of the "intrinsic nature of reality." The trouble with arguments against the use of a familiar and time-honored vocabulary is that they are expected to be phrased in that very vocabulary. They are expected to show that central elements in that vocabulary are "inconsistent in their own terms" or that they "deconstruct themselves." But that can never be shown. Any argument to the effect that our familiar use of a familiar term is incoherent, or empty, or confused,

or vague, or "merely metaphorical" is bound to be inconclusive and question begging. For such use is, after all, the paradigm of coherent, meaningful, literal, speech. Such arguments are always parasitic upon, and abbreviations for, claims that a better vocabulary is available. Interesting philosophy is rarely an examination of the pros and cons of a thesis. Usually it is, implicitly or explicitly, a contest between an entrenched vocabulary which has become a nuisance and a half formed new vocabulary which vaguely promises great things.

The latter "method" of philosophy is the same as the "method" of utopian politics or revolutionary science (as opposed to parliamentary politics, or normal science). The method is to redescribe lots and lots of things in new ways, until you have created a pattern of linguistic behavior which will tempt the rising generation to adopt it, thereby causing them to look for appropriate new forms of nonlinguistic behavior, for example, the adoption of new scientific equipment or new social institutions. This sort of philosophy does not work piece by piece, analyzing concept after concept, or testing thesis after thesis. Rather, it works holistically and pragmatically. It says things like "try thinking of it this way" or more specifically, "try to ignore the apparently futile traditional questions by substituting the following new and possibly interesting questions." It does not pretend to have a better candidate for doing the same old things which we did when we spoke in the old way. Rather, it suggests that we might want to stop doing those things and do something else. But it does not argue for this suggestion on the basis of antecedent criteria common to the old and the new language games. For just insofar as the new language really is new, there will be no such criteria.

[...=

Davidson's account of linguistic communication dispenses with the picture of language as a third thing intervening between self and reality, and of different languages as barriers between persons or cultures. To say that one's previous language was inappropriate for dealing with some segment of the world (for example, the starry heavens above, or the raging passions within) is just to say that one is now, having learned a new language, able to handle that segment more easily. To say that two communities have trouble getting along because the words they use are so hard to translate into each other is just to say that the linguistic behavior of inhabitants of one community may, like the rest of their behavior, be hard for inhabitants of the other community to predict. As Davidson puts it,

> We should realize that we have abandoned not only the ordinary notion of a language, but we have erased the boundary between knowing a language and knowing our way around the world generally. For there are no rules for arriving at passing theories that work.... There is no more chance of regularizing, or teaching, this process than there is of regularizing or teaching the process of creating new theories to cope with new data for that is what this process involves....

There is no such thing as a language, not if a language is anything like what philosophers, at least, have supposed. There is therefore no such thing to be learned or mastered. We must give up the idea of a clearly defined shared structure which language users master and then apply to cases ... We should give up the attempt to illuminate how we communicate by appeal to conventions.

[...]

To see the history of language, and thus of the arts, the sciences, and the moral sense, as the history of metaphor is to drop the picture of the human mind, or human languages, becoming better and better suited to the purposes for which God or Nature designed them, for example, able to express more and more meanings or to represent more and more facts. The idea that language has a purpose goes once the idea of language as medium goes. A culture which renounced both ideas would be the triumph of those tendencies in modern thought which began two hundred years ago, the tendencies common to German idealism, Romantic poetry, and utopian politics.

A nonteleological view of intellectual history, including the history of science, does for the theory of culture what the Mendelian, mechanistic, account of natural selection did for evolutionary theory. Mendel let us see mind as something which just happened rather than as something which was the point of the whole process. Davidson lets us think of the history of language, and thus of culture, as Darwin taught us to think of the history of a coral reef. Old metaphors are constantly dying off into literalness, and then serving as a platform and foil for new metaphors. This analogy lets us think of "our language" that is, of the science and culture of twentieth century Europe as something that took shape as a result of a great number of sheer contingencies. Our language and our culture are as much a contingency, as much a result of thousands of small mutations finding niches (and millions of others finding no niches), as are the orchids and the anthropoids.

To accept this analogy, we must follow Mary Hesse in thinking of scientific revolutions as "metaphoric redescriptions" of nature rather than insights into the intrinsic nature of nature.? Further, we must resist the temptation to think that the redescriptions of reality offered by contemporary physical or biological science are somehow closer to "the things themselves," less "mind dependent," than the redescriptions of history offered by contemporary culture criticism. We need to see the constellations of causal forces which produced talk of DNA or of the Big Bang as of a piece with the causal forces which produced talk of "secularization" or of "late capitalism."$ These various constellations are the random factors which have made some things subjects of conversation for us and others not, have made some projects and not others possible and important.

[...]

This account of intellectual history chimes with Nietzsche's definition of "truth" as "a mobile army of metaphors." It also chimes with the description I offered earlier of people like Galileo and Hegel and Yeats, people in whose minds new vocabularies developed, thereby equipping them with tools for doing things which could not even have been envisaged before these tools were available. But in order to accept this picture, we need to see the distinction between the literal and the metaphorical in the way Davidson sees it: not as a distinction between two sorts of meaning, nor as a distinction between two sorts of interpretation, but as a distinction between familiar and unfamiliar uses of noises and marks. The literal uses of noises and marks are the uses we can handle by our old theories about what people will say under various conditions. Their metaphorical use is the sort which makes us get busy developing a new theory.

Davidson puts this point by saying that one should not think of metaphorical expressions as having meanings distinct from their literal ones. To have a meaning is to have a place in a language game. Metaphors, by definition, do not. Davidson denies, in his words, "the thesis that associated with a metaphor is a cognitive content that its author wishes to convey and that the interpreter must grasp if he is to get the message." In his view, tossing a metaphor into a conversation is like suddenly breaking off the conversation long enough to make a face, or pulling a photograph out of your pocket and displaying it, or pointing at a feature of the surroundings, or slapping your interlocutor's face, or kissing him. Tossing a metaphor into a text is like using italics, or illustrations, or odd punctuation or formats.

All these are ways of producing effects on your interlocutor or your reader, but not ways of conveying a message. To none of these is it appropriate to respond with "What exactly are you trying to say?" If one had wanted to say something if one had wanted to utter a sentence with a meaning one would presumably have done so. But instead one thought that one's aim could be better carried out by other means. That one uses familiar words in unfamiliar ways rather than slaps, kisses, pictures, gestures, or grimaces does not show that what one said must have a meaning. An attempt to state that meaning would be an attempt to find some familiar (that is, literal) use of words some sentence which already had a place in the language game and, to claim that one might just as well have that. But the unparaphrasability of metaphor is just the unsuitability of any such familiar sentence for one's purpose.

Uttering a sentence without a fixed place in a language game is, as the positivists rightly have said, to utter something which is neither true nor false something which is not, in Ian Hacking's terms, a "truth-value candidate." This is because it is a sentence which one cannot confirm or disconfirm, argue for or against. One can only savor it or spit it out. But this is not to say that it may not, in time, become a truth-value candidate. If it is savored rather than spat out, the sentence may be repeated, caught up, bandied about. Then it will gradually require a habitual use, a familiar place in the language game. It will thereby have ceased to be a metaphor or, if you like, it will have become what most sentences of our language are, a dead metaphor. It will be just one more, literally true or literally false, sentence of the language. That is to say, our theories about the linguistic behavior of our fellows will suffice to let us cope with its utterance in the same unthinking way in which we cope with most of their other utterances.

[...]

The Platonist and the positivist share a reductionist view of metaphor: They think metaphors are either paraphrasable or useless for the one serious purpose which language has, namely, representing reality. By contrast, the Romantic has an expansionist view: He thinks metaphor is strange, mystic, wonderful. Romantics attribute metaphor to a mysterious faculty called the "imagination," a faculty they suppose to be at the very center of the self, the deep heart's core. Whereas the metaphorical looks irrelevant to Platonists and positivists, the literal looks irrelevant to Romantics. For the former think that the point of language is to represent a hidden reality which lies outside us, and the latter thinks its purpose is to express a hidden reality which lies within us.

Positivist history of culture thus sees language as gradually shaping itself around the contours of the physical world. Romantic history of culture sees language as gradually bringing Spirit to self-consciousness. Nietzschean history of culture, and Davidsonian philosophy of language, see language as we now see evolution, as new forms of life constantly killing off old forms not to accomplish a higher purpose, but blindly. Whereas the positivist sees Galileo as making a discovery finally coming up with the words which were needed to fit the world properly, words Aristotle missed the Davidsonian sees him as having hit upon a tool which happened to work better for certain purposes than any previous tool. Once we found out what could be done with a Galilean vocabulary, nobody was much interested in doing the things which used to be done (and which Thomists thought should still be done) with an Aristotelian vocabulary.

Similarly, whereas the Romantic sees Yeats as having gotten at something which nobody had previously gotten at, expressed something which had long been yearning for expression, the Davidsonian sees him as having hit upon some tools which enabled him to write poems which were not just variations on the poems of his precursors. Once we had Yeats's later poems in hand, we were less interested in reading Rossetti's. What goes for revolutionary, strong scientists and poets goes also for strong philosophers people like Hegel and Davidson, the sort of philosophers who are interested in dissolving inherited problems rather than in solving them. In this view, substituting dialectic for demonstration as the method of philosophy, or getting rid of the correspondence theory of truth, is not a discovery about the nature of a preexistent entity called "philosophy" or "truth." It is changing the way we talk, and thereby changing what we want to do and what we think we are.

But in a Nietzschean view, one which drops the reality appearance distinction, to change how we talk is to change

what, for our own purposes, we are. To say, with Nietzsche, that God is dead, is to say that we serve no higher purposes. The Nietzschean substitution of self creation for discovery substitutes a picture of the hungry generations treading each other down for a picture of humanity approaching closer and closer to the light. A culture in which Nietzschean metaphors were literalized would be one which took for granted that philosophical problems are as temporary as poetic problems, that there are no problems which bind the generations together into a single natural kind called "humanity." A sense of human history as the history of successive metaphors would let us see the poet, in the generic sense of the maker of new words, the shaper of new languages, as the vanguard of the species.

...[T]he world does not provide us with any criterion of choice between alternative metaphors, that we can only compare languages or metaphors with one another, not with something beyond language called "fact."

The only way to argue for this claim is to do what philosophers like Goodman, Putnam, and Davidson have done: exhibit the sterility of attempts to give a sense to phrases like "the way the world is" or "fitting the facts." Such efforts can be supplemented by the work of philosophers of science such as Kuhn and Hesse. These philosophers explain why there is no way to explain the fact that a Galilean vocabulary enables us to make better predictions than an Aristotelian vocabulary by the claim that the book of nature is written in the language of mathematics.

These sorts of arguments by philosophers of language and of science should be seen against the background of the work of intellectual historians: historians who, like Hans Blumenberg, have tried to trace the similarities and dissimilarities between the Age of Faith and the Age of Reason. These historians have made the point I mentioned earlier: The very idea that the world or the self has an intrinsic nature one which the physicist or the poet may have glimpsed is a remnant of the idea that the world is a divine creation, the work of someone who had something in mind, who Himself spoke some language in which He described His own project. Only if we have some such picture in mind, some picture of the universe as either itself a person or as created by a person, can we make sense of the idea that the world has an "intrinsic nature." For the cash value of that phrase is just that some vocabularies are better representations of the world than others, as opposed to being better tools for dealing with the world for one or another purpose.

To drop the idea of languages as representations, and to be thoroughly Wittgensteinian in our approach to language, would be to de-divinize the world. Only if we do that can we fully accept the argument I offered earlier the argument that since truth is a property of sentences, since sentences are dependent for their existence upon vocabularies, and since vocabularies are made by human beings, so are truths. For as long as we think that "the world" names something we ought to respect as well as cope with, something person-like in that it has a preferred description of itself, we shall insist that any philosophical account of truth save the "intuition" that truth is "out there." This institution amounts to the vague sense that it would be hubris on our part to abandon the traditional language of "respect for fact" and "objectivity" that it would be risky, and blasphemous, not to see the scientist (or the philosopher, or the poet, or somebody) as having a priestly function, as putting us in touch with a realm which transcends the human.

On the view I am suggesting, the claim that an "adequate" philosophical doctrine must make room for our intuitions is a reactionary slogan, one which begs the question at hand. 12 For it is essential to my view that we have no prelinguistic consciousness to which language needs to be adequate, no deep sense of how things are which it is the duty of philosophers to spell out in language. What is described as such a consciousness is simply a disposition to use the language of our ancestors, to worship the corpses of their metaphors. Unless we suffer from what Derrida calls "Heideggerian nostalgia," we shall not think of our "intuitions" as more than platitudes, more than the habitual use of a certain repertoire of terms, more than old tools which as yet have no replacements.

I can crudely sum up the story which historians like Blumenberg tell by saying that once upon a time we felt a need to worship something which lay beyond the visible world. Beginning in the seventeenth century we tried to substitute a love of truth for a love of God, treating the world described by science as a quasi-divinity. Beginning at the end of the eighteenth century we tried to substitute a love of ourselves for a love of scientific truth, a worship of our own deep spiritual or poetic nature, treated as one more quasi divinity.

The line of thought common to Blumenberg, Nietzsche, Freud, and Davidson suggests that we try to get to the point where we no longer worship anything, where we treat nothing as a quasi-divinity, where we treat everything our language, our conscience, our community as a product of time and chance. To reach this point would be, in Freud's words, to "treat chance as worthy of determining our fate." In the next chapter I claim that Freud, Nietzsche, and Bloom do for our conscience what Wittgenstein and Davidson do for our language, namely, exhibit its sheer contingency.

Citation and Use

The text was taken from the following work.

Rorty, Richard. "The Contingency of Language." In CONTINGENCY, IRONY, AND SOLIDARITY, 3–22. Cambridge University Press, 1989.

METAPHYSICS

EXISTENCE IS EMPTY

Nāgārjuna

Examination of Conditions

1. Neither from itself nor from another,
   Nor from both,
   Nor without a cause,
   Does anything whatever, anywhere arise.

2. There are four conditions: efficient condition;
   Percept-object condition; immediate condition;
   Dominant condition, just so. |
   There is no fifth condition.

3. The essence of entities
   Is not present in the conditions, etc. .... .
   If there is no essence,
   There can be no otherness-essence.

4. Power to act does not have conditions.
   There is no power to act without conditions.
   There are no conditions without power to act.
   Nor do any have the power to act.

5. These give rise to those,
   So these are called conditions.
   As long as those do not come from these,
   Why are these not non-conditions?

6. For neither an existent nor a non-existent thing
   Is a condition appropriate.
   If a thing is non-existent, how could it have a condition?
   If a thing is already existent, what would a condition do?

7. When neither existents nor
   Non-existents nor existent non-existents are established,
   How could one propose a "productive cause?"*
   If there were one, it would be pointless.

8. An existent entity (mental episode)
   Has no object.
   Since a mental episode is without an object,
   How could there be any percept-condition?

9. Since things are not arisen,
   Cessation is not acceptable.
   Therefore, an immediate condition is not reasonable.
   If something has ceased, how could it be a condition?

10. If things did not exist
    Without essence,
    The phrase, "When this exists so this will be,"
    Would not be acceptable.

11. In the several or united conditions
    The effect cannot be found.
    How could something not in the conditions
    Come from the conditions?

12. However, if a nonexistent effect
    Arises from these conditions,
    Why does it not arise
    From non-conditions?

13. If the effect's essence is the conditions,
    But the conditions don't have their own essence,
    How could an effect whose essence is the conditions
    Come from something that is essence-less?

14. Therefore, neither with conditions as their essence,
    Nor with non-conditions as their essence are there any effects.
    If there are no such effects,
    How could conditions or non-conditions be evident?

Examination of Motion

1. What has been moved is not moving.
   What has not been moved is not moving.
   Apart from what has been moved and what has not been moved,
   Movement cannot be conceived.

2. Where there is change, there is motion.
   Since there is change in the moving,
   And not in the moved or not-moved,
   Motion is in that which is moving.

3. How would it be acceptable

79

For motion to be in the mover?
When it is not moving, it is not acceptable
To call it a mover.

4. For whomever there is motion in the mover,
There could be non-motion
Evident in the mover.
But having motion follows from being a mover.

5. If motion is in the mover,
There would have to be a twofold motion:
One in virtue of which it is a mover,
And one in virtue of which it moves.

6. If there were a twofold motion,
The subject of that motion would be twofold.
For without a subject of motion,
There cannot be motion.

7. If without a mover
It would not be correct to say that there is motion,
Then if there were no motion,
How could there be a mover?

8. Inasmuch as a real mover does not move,
And a non-mover does not move,
Apart from a mover and a non-mover,
What third thing could move?

9. When without motion,
It is unacceptable to call something a mover,
How will it be acceptable
To say that a mover moves?

10. For him from whose perspective a mover moves,
There would be the consequence that
Without motion there could be a mover.
Because a mover moves.

11. If a mover were to move,
There would be a twofold motion:
One in virtue of which he is a mover,
And one in virtue of which the mover moves.

12. Motion does not begin in what has moved,
Nor does it begin in what has not moved,
Nor does it begin in what is moving.
In what, then, does motion begin?

13. Prior to the beginning of motion,
There is no beginning of motion in
The going or in the gone.
How could there be motion in the not-gone?

14. Since the beginning of motion
Cannot be conceived in any way,
What gone thing, what going thing,
And what non-going thing can be posited?

15. Just as a moving thing is not stationary,
A non-moving thing is not stationary.
Apart from the moving and the non-moving,
What third thing is stationary?

16. If without motion
It is not appropriate to posit a mover,
How could it be appropriate to say
That a moving thing is stationary?

17. One does not halt from moving,
Nor from having moved or not having moved.
Motion and coming to rest
And starting to move are similar.

18. That motion just is the mover itself
Is not correct.
Nor is it correct that
They are completely different.

19. It would follow from
The identity of mover and motion
That agent and action
Are identical.

20. It would follow from
A real distinction between motion and mover
That there could be a mover without motion
And motion without a mover.

21. When neither in identity
Nor in difference
Can they be established,
How can these two be established at all?

22. The motion by means of which a mover is manifest
Cannot be the motion by means of which he moves.
He does not exist before that motion.
So what and where is the thing that moves?

23. A mover does not carry out a different motion
From that by means of which he is manifest as a mover.
Moreover, in one mover
A twofold motion is unacceptable.

24. A really existent mover
Doesn't move in any of the three ways.
A non-existent mover
Doesn't move in any of the three ways.

25. Neither an entity nor a non-entity
Moves in any of the three ways.
So motion, mover and
And route are non-existent.

Examination of Elements

1. Prior to a characteristic of space
There is not the slightest space.
If it arose prior to the characteristic
Then it would, absurdly, arise without a characteristic.

2. A thing without a characteristic
Has never existed.
If nothing lacks a characteristic,
Where do characteristics come to be?

3. Neither in the uncharacterized nor in the characterized
   Does a characteristic arise.
   Nor does it arise
   In something different from these two.

4. If characteristics do not appear,
   Then it is not tenable to posit the characterized object.
   If the characterized object is not posited,
   There will be no characteristic either.

5. From this it follows that there is no characterized
   And no existing characteristic.
   Nor is there any entity
   Other than the characterized and the characteristic.

6. If there is no existent thing.
   Of what will there be nonexistence?
   Apart from existent and nonexistent things
   Who knows existence and nonexistence?

7. Therefore, space is not an entity.
   It is not a nonentity.
   Not characterized, not without character.
   The same is true of the other five elements.

8. Fools and reificationists who perceive
   The existence and nonexistence
   Of objects
   Do not see the pacification of objectification.

Citation and Use

The text was taken from the following work.

Jay L Garfield, "Nagarjuna's Fundamental Verses of the Middle Way," in Buddhist Philosophy: Essential Readings, ed. William Edelglass and Jay Garfield (Oxford University Press, USA, 2009), 26–34.

THE FORMS

Plato

We had come from our home at Clazomenae to Athens, and met Adeimantus and Glaucon in the Agora. Welcome, Cephalus, said Adeimantus, taking me by the hand; is there anything which we can do for you in Athens?

Yes; that is why I am here; I wish to ask a favor of you. What may that be? he said.

I want you to tell me the name of your half brother, which I have forgotten; he was a mere child when I last came hither from Clazomenae, but that was a long time ago; his father's name, if I remember rightly, was Pyrilampes?

Yes, he said, and the name of our brother, Antiphon; but why do you ask?

Let me introduce some countrymen of mine, I said; they are lovers of philosophy, and have heard that Antiphon was intimate with a certain Pythodorus, a friend of Zeno, and remembers a conversation which took place between Socrates, Zeno, and Parmenides many years ago, Pythodorus having often recited it to him.

Quite true.

And could we hear it? I asked.

Nothing easier, he replied; when he was a youth he made a careful study of the piece; at present his thoughts run in another direction; like his grandfather Antiphon he is devoted to horses. But, if that is what you want, let us go and look for him; he dwells at Melita, which is quite near, and he has only just left us to go home.

Accordingly we went to look for him; he was at home, and in the act of giving a bridle to a smith to be fitted. When he had done with the smith, his brothers told him the purpose of our visit; and he saluted me as an acquaintance whom he remembered from my former visit, and we asked him to repeat the dialogue. At first he was not very willing, and complained of the trouble, but at length he consented. He told us that Pythodorus had described to him the appearance of Parmenides and Zeno; they came to Athens, as he said, at the great Panathenaea; the former was, at the time

of his visit, about 65 years old, very white with age, but well favored. Zeno was nearly 40 years of age, tall and fair to look upon; in the days of his youth he was reported to have been beloved by Parmenides. He said that they lodged with Pythodorus in the Ceramicus, outside the wall, whither Socrates, then a very young man, came to see them, and many others with him; they wanted to hear the writings of Zeno, which had been brought to Athens for the first time on the occasion of their visit. These Zeno himself read to them in the absence of Parmenides, and had very nearly finished when Pythodorus entered, and with him Parmenides and Aristoteles who was afterwards one of the Thirty, and heard the little that remained of the dialogue. Pythodorus had heard Zeno repeat them before.

When the recitation was completed, Socrates requested that the first thesis of the first argument might be read over again, and this having been done, he said: What is your meaning, Zeno? Do you maintain that if being is many, it must be both like and unlike, and that this is impossible, for neither can the like be unlike, nor the unlike like–is that your position?

Just so, said Zeno.

And if the unlike cannot be like, or the like unlike, then according to you, being could not be many; for this would involve an impossibility. In all that you say have you any other purpose except to disprove the being of the many? And is not each division of your treatise intended to furnish a separate proof of this, there being in all as many proofs of the not-being of the many as you have composed arguments? Is that your meaning, or have I misunderstood you?

No, said Zeno; you have correctly understood my general purpose.

I see, Parmenides, said Socrates, that Zeno would like to be not only one with you in friendship but your second self in his writings too; he puts what you say in another way, and would fain make believe that he is telling us something which is new. For you, in your poems, say The All is one, and of this you adduce excellent proofs; and he on the other hand says There is no many; and on behalf of this he offers overwhelming evidence. You affirm unity, he denies plurality. And so you deceive the world into believing that you are saying different things when really you are saying much the same. This is a strain of art beyond the reach of most of us.

Yes, Socrates, said Zeno. But although you are as keen as a Spartan hound in pursuing the track, you do not fully apprehend the true motive of the composition, which is not really such an artificial work as you imagine; for what you speak of was an accident; there was no pretence of a great purpose; nor any serious intention of deceiving the world. The truth is, that these writings of mine were meant to protect the arguments of Parmenides against those who make fun of him and seek to show the many ridiculous and contradictory results which they suppose to follow from the affirmation of the one. My answer is addressed to the partisans of the many, whose attack I return with interest by retorting upon them that their hypothesis of the being of many, if carried out, appears to be still more ridiculous than the hypothesis of the being of one. Zeal for my master led me to write the book in the days of my youth, but some one stole the copy; and therefore I had no choice whether it should be published or not; the motive, however, of writing, was not the ambition of an elder man, but the pugnacity of a young one. This you do not seem to see, Socrates; though in other respects, as I was saying, your notion is a very just one.

I understand, said Socrates, and quite accept your account. But tell me, Zeno, do you not further think that there is an idea of likeness in itself, and another idea of unlikeness, which is the opposite of likeness, and that in these two, you and I and all other things to which we apply the term many, participate–things which participate in likeness become in that degree and manner like; and so far as they participate in unlikeness become in that degree unlike, or both like and unlike in the degree in which they participate in both? And may not all things partake of both opposites, and be both like and unlike, by reason of this participation?–Where is the wonder? Now if a person could prove the absolute like to become unlike, or the absolute unlike to become like, that, in my opinion, would indeed be a wonder; but there is nothing extraordinary, Zeno, in showing that the things which only partake of likeness and unlikeness experience both. Nor, again, if a person were to show that all is one by partaking of one, and at the same time many by partaking of many, would that be very astonishing. But if he were to show me that the absolute one was many, or the absolute many one, I should be truly amazed. And so of all the rest: I should be surprised to hear that the natures or ideas themselves had these opposite qualities; but not if a person wanted to prove of me that I was many and also one. When he wanted to show that I was many he would say that I have a right and a left side, and a front and a back, and an upper and a lower half, for I cannot deny that I partake of multitude; when, on the other hand, he wants to prove that I am one, he will say, that we who are here assembled are seven, and that I am one and partake of the one. In both instances he proves his case. So again, if a person shows that such things as wood, stones,

and the like, being many are also one, we admit that he shows the coexistence of the one and many, but he does not show that the many are one or the one many; he is uttering not a paradox but a truism. If however, as I just now suggested, some one were to abstract simple notions of like, unlike, one, many, rest, motion, and similar ideas, and then to show that these admit of admixture and separation in themselves, I should be very much astonished. This part of the argument appears to be treated by you, Zeno, in a very spirited manner; but, as I was saying, I should be far more amazed if any one found in the ideas themselves which are apprehended by reason, the same puzzle and entanglement which you have shown to exist in visible objects.

While Socrates was speaking, Pythodorus thought that Parmenides and Zeno were not altogether pleased at the successive steps of the argument; but still they gave the closest attention, and often looked at one another, and smiled as if in admiration of him. When he had finished, Parmenides expressed their feelings in the following words:

Socrates, he said, I admire the bent of your mind towards philosophy; tell me now, was this your own distinction between ideas in themselves and the things which partake of them? and do you think that there is an idea of likeness apart from the likeness which we possess, and of the one and many, and of the other things which Zeno mentioned?

I think that there are such ideas, said Socrates.

Parmenides proceeded: And would you also make absolute ideas of the just and the beautiful and the good, and of all that class?

Yes, he said, I should.

And would you make an idea of man apart from us and from all other human creatures, or of fire and water?

I am often undecided, Parmenides, as to whether I ought to include them or not.

And would you feel equally undecided, Socrates, about things of which the mention may provoke a smile?–I mean such things as hair, mud, dirt, or anything else which is vile and paltry; would you suppose that each of these has an idea distinct from the actual objects with which we come into contact, or not?

Certainly not, said Socrates; visible things like these are such as they appear to us, and I am afraid that there would be an absurdity in assuming any idea of them, although I sometimes get disturbed, and begin to think that there is nothing without an idea; but then again, when I have taken up this position, I run away, because I am afraid that I may fall into a bottomless pit of nonsense, and perish; and so I return to the ideas of which I was just now speaking, and occupy myself with them.

Yes, Socrates, said Parmenides; that is because you are still young; the time will come, if I am not mistaken, when philosophy will have a firmer grasp of you, and then you will not despise even the meanest things; at your age, you are too much disposed to regard the opinions of men. But I should like to know whether you mean that there are certain ideas of which all other things partake, and from which they derive their names; that similars, for example, become similar, because they partake of similarity; and great things become great, because they partake of greatness; and that just and beautiful things become just and beautiful, because they partake of justice and beauty?

Yes, certainly, said Socrates that is my meaning.

Then each individual partakes either of the whole of the idea or else of a part of the idea? Can there be any other mode of participation?

There cannot be, he said.

Then do you think that the whole idea is one, and yet, being one, is in each one of the many?

Why not, Parmenides? said Socrates.

Because one and the same thing will exist as a whole at the same time in many separate individuals, and will therefore be in a state of separation from itself.

Nay, but the idea may be like the day which is one and the same in many places at once, and yet continuous with itself; in this way each idea may be one and the same in all at the same time.

I like your way, Socrates, of making one in many places at once. You mean to say, that if I were to spread out a sail and cover a number of men, there would be one whole including many—is not that your meaning?

I think so.

And would you say that the whole sail includes each man, or a part of it only, and different parts different men?

The latter.

Then, Socrates, the ideas themselves will be divisible, and things which participate in them will have a part of them only and not the whole idea existing in each of them?

That seems to follow.

Then would you like to say, Socrates, that the one idea is really divisible and yet remains one?

Certainly not, he said.

Suppose that you divide absolute greatness, and that of the many great things, each one is great in virtue of a portion of greatness less than absolute greatness—is that conceivable?

No.

Or will each equal thing, if possessing some small portion of equality less than absolute equality, be equal to some other thing by virtue of that portion only?

Impossible.

Or suppose one of us to have a portion of smallness; this is but a part of the small, and therefore the absolutely small is greater; if the absolutely small be greater, that to which the part of the small is added will be smaller and not greater than before.

How absurd!

Then in what way, Socrates, will all things participate in the ideas, if they are unable to participate in them either as parts or wholes?

Indeed, he said, you have asked a question which is not easily answered.

Well, said Parmenides, and what do you say of another question?

What question?

I imagine that the way in which you are led to assume one idea of each kind is as follows: You see a number of great objects, and when you look at them there seems to you to be one and the same idea (or nature) in them all; hence you conceive of greatness as one.

Very true, said Socrates.

And if you go on and allow your mind in like manner to embrace in one view the idea of greatness and of great things which are not the idea, and to compare them, will not another greatness arise, which will appear to be the source of all these?

It would seem so.

Then another idea of greatness now comes into view over and above absolute greatness, and the individuals which partake of it; and then another, over and above all these, by virtue of which they will all be great, and so each idea instead of being one will be infinitely multiplied.

But may not the ideas, asked Socrates, be thoughts only, and have no proper existence except in our minds, Parmenides? For in that case each idea may still be one, and not experience this infinite multiplication.

And can there be individual thoughts which are thoughts of nothing?

Impossible, he said.

The thought must be of something?

Yes.

Of something which is or which is not?

Of something which is.

Must it not be of a single something, which the thought recognizes as attaching to all, being a single form or nature?

Yes.

And will not the something which is apprehended as one and the same in all, be an idea?

From that, again, there is no escape.

Then, said Parmenides, if you say that everything else participates in the ideas, must you not say either that everything is made up of thoughts, and that all things think; or that they are thoughts but have no thought?

The latter view, Parmenides, is no more rational than the previous one. In my opinion, the ideas are, as it were, patterns fixed in nature, and other things are like them, and resemblances of them—what is meant by the participation of other things in the ideas, is really assimilation to them.

But if, said he, the individual is like the idea, must not the idea also be like the individual, in so far as the individual is a resemblance of the idea? That which is like, cannot be conceived of as other than the like of like.

Impossible.

And when two things are alike, must they not partake of the same idea?

They must.

And will not that of which the two partake, and which makes them alike, be the idea itself?

Certainly.

Then the idea cannot be like the individual, or the individual like the idea; for if they are alike, some further idea of likeness will always be coming to light, and if that be like anything else, another; and new ideas will be always arising, if the idea resembles that which partakes of it?

Quite true.

The theory, then, that other things participate in the ideas by resemblance, has to be given up, and some other mode of participation devised?

It would seem so.

Do you see then, Socrates, how great is the difficulty of affirming the ideas to be absolute?

Yes, indeed.

And, further, let me say that as yet you only understand a small part of the difficulty which is involved if you make of each thing a single idea, parting it off from other things.

What difficulty? he said.

There are many, but the greatest of all is this:—If an opponent argues that these ideas, being such as we say they ought to be, must remain unknown, no one can prove to him that he is wrong, unless he who denies their existence be a man of great ability and knowledge, and is willing to follow a long and laborious demonstration; he will remain unconvinced, and still insist that they cannot be known.

What do you mean, Parmenides? said Socrates.

In the first place, I think, Socrates, that you, or any one who maintains the existence of absolute essences, will admit that they cannot exist in us.

No, said Socrates; for then they would be no longer absolute.

True, he said; and therefore when ideas are what they are in relation to one another, their essence is determined by a relation among themselves, and has nothing to do with the resemblances, or whatever they are to be termed, which are in our sphere, and from which we receive this or that name when we partake of them. And the things which are within our sphere and have the same names with them, are likewise only relative to one another, and not to the ideas which have the same names with them, but belong to themselves and not to them.

What do you mean? said Socrates.

I may illustrate my meaning in this way, said Parmenides:—A master has a slave; now there is nothing absolute in the relation between them, which is simply a relation of one man to another. But there is also an idea of mastership in the abstract, which is relative to the idea of slavery in the abstract. These natures have nothing to do with us, nor we with them; they are concerned with themselves only, and we with ourselves. Do you see my meaning?

Yes, said Socrates, I quite see your meaning.

And will not knowledge—I mean absolute knowledge—answer to absolute truth?

Certainly.

And each kind of absolute knowledge will answer to each kind of absolute being?

Yes.

But the knowledge which we have, will answer to the truth which we have; and again, each kind of knowledge which we have, will be a knowledge of each kind of being which we have?

Certainly.

But the ideas themselves, as you admit, we have not, and cannot have?

No, we cannot.

And the absolute natures or kinds are known severally by the absolute idea of knowledge?

Yes.

And we have not got the idea of knowledge?

No.

Then none of the ideas are known to us, because we have no share in absolute knowledge?

I suppose not.

Then the nature of the beautiful in itself, and of the good in itself, and all other ideas which we suppose to exist absolutely, are unknown to us?

It would seem so.

I think that there is a stranger consequence still.

What is it?

Would you, or would you not say, that absolute knowledge, if there is such a thing, must be a far more exact knowledge than our knowledge; and the same of beauty and of the rest?

Yes.

And if there be such a thing as participation in absolute knowledge, no one is more likely than God to have this most exact knowledge?

Certainly.

But then, will God, having absolute knowledge, have a knowledge of human things?

Why not?

Because, Socrates, said Parmenides, we have admitted that the ideas are not valid in relation to human things; nor human things in relation to them; the relations of either are limited to their respective spheres.

Yes, that has been admitted.

And if God has this perfect authority, and perfect knowledge, his authority cannot rule us, nor his knowledge know us, or any human thing; just as our authority does not extend to the gods, nor our knowledge know anything which is divine, so by parity of reason they, being gods, are not our masters, neither do they know the things of men.

Yet, surely, said Socrates, to deprive God of knowledge is monstrous.

These, Socrates, said Parmenides, are a few, and only a few of the difficulties in which we are involved if ideas really are and we determine each one of them to be an absolute unity. He who hears what may be said against them will deny the very existence of

them—and even if they do exist, he will say that they must of necessity be unknown to man; and he will seem to have reason on his side, and as we were remarking just now, will be very difficult to convince; a man must be gifted with very considerable ability before he can learn that everything has a class and an absolute essence; and still more remarkable will he be who discovers all these things for himself, and having thoroughly investigated them is able to teach them to others.

I agree with you, Parmenides, said Socrates; and what you say is very much to my mind.

And yet, Socrates, said Parmenides, if a man, fixing his attention on these and the like difficulties, does away with ideas of things and will not admit that every individual thing has its own determinate idea which is always one and the same, he will have nothing on which his mind can rest; and so he will utterly destroy the power of reasoning, as you seem to me to have particularly noted.

Very true, he said.

But, then, what is to become of philosophy? Whither shall we turn, if the ideas are unknown?

Citation and Use

The text was taken from the following work.

Plato, "Parmenides Dialogue," in *Plato in 12 Volumes*, trans. Harold North Flower, vol. 9, 12 vols. (London: Harvard University Press, 1966), http://data.perseus.org/citations/urn:cts:greek-Lit:tlg0059.tlg009.perseus-eng1:126.

ATMAN AND SELF

Bhagavad Gita

Chapter 2: Transcendental Knowledge

Sanjaya said: Lord Krishna spoke these words to Arjuna whose eyes were tearful and downcast, and who was overwhelmed with compassion and despair. (2.01)

The Supreme Lord said: How has the dejection come to you at this juncture? This is not fit for an Aryan (or the people of noble mind and deeds). It is disgraceful, and it does not lead one to heaven, O Arjuna. (2.02)

Do not become a coward, O Arjuna, because it does not befit you. Shake off this weakness of your heart and get up (for the battle), O Arjuna. (2.03)

Arjuna said: How shall I strike Bheeshma and Drona, who are worthy of my worship, with arrows in battle, O Krishna? (2.04)

It would be better, indeed, to live on alms in this world than to slay these noble gurus, because, by killing them I would enjoy wealth and pleasures stained with (theirs) blood. (2.05)

Neither do we know which alternative (to beg or to kill) is better for us, nor do we know whether we shall conquer them or they will conquer us. We should not even wish to live after killing the sons of Dhritaraashtra who are standing in front of us. (2.06)

My heart is overcome by the weakness of pity, and my mind is confused about Dharma. I request You to tell me, decisively, what is better for me. I am Your disciple. Teach me who has taken refuge in You. (2.07)[1]Dharma

I do not perceive that gaining an unrivaled and prosperous kingdom on this earth, or even lordship over the gods will remove the sorrow that is drying up my senses. (2.08)

Sanjaya said: O King, after speaking like this to Lord Krishna, the mighty Arjuna said to Krishna: I shall not fight, and became silent. (2.09)

O King, Lord Krishna, as if smiling, spoke these words to the despondent Arjuna in the midst of the two armies. (2.10)

The Supreme Lord said: You grieve for those who are not worthy of grief, and yet speak the words of wisdom. The wise grieve neither for the living nor for the dead. (2.11)

There was never a time when I, you, or these kings did not exist; nor shall we ever cease to exist in the future. (2.12)

Just as the Atman acquires a childhood body, a youth body, and an old age body during this life, similarly Atman acquires another body after death. The wise are not deluded by this. (See also 15.08) (2.13)[2]

The contacts of the senses with the sense objects give rise to the feelings of heat and cold, and pain and pleasure. They are transitory and impermanent. Therefore, (learn to) endure them, O Arjuna. (2.14)

Because the calm person, who is not afflicted by these feelings and is steady in pain and pleasure, becomes fit for immortality, O Arjuna. (2.15)

There is no nonexistence of the Sat (or Atman) and no existence of the Asat. The reality of these two is indeed certainly seen by the seers of truth. (2.16) (*Sat exists at all times — past, present, and future. Atman is called Sat. Asat is a notion that does not exist at all (like the horn of a rabbit, or the water in a mirage). The one that has a beginning and an end is neither Sat nor Asat. The body is neither Sat nor Asat, or both Sat and Asat, because, it has a temporary existence. Mithya is the one that appears Sat at first sight, but is really Asat. Body, like the universe or Jagat, is called Mithya.*)

Know That, by which all this (universe) is pervaded, to be indestructible. No one can destroy the indestructible (Atman) . (2.17)

Bodies of the eternal, imperishable, and incomprehensible soul are said to be perishable. Therefore, fight, O Arjuna. (2.18)

The one who thinks that Atman is a slayer, and the one

who thinks that Atman is slain, both are ignorant, because Atman neither slays nor is slain. (2.19)

The Atman is neither born nor does it die at any time, nor having been it will cease to exist again. It is unborn, eternal, permanent, and primeval. The Atman is not destroyed when the body is destroyed. (2.20)

O Arjuna, how can a person who knows that the Atman is indestructible, eternal, unborn, and imperishable, kill anyone or cause anyone to be killed? (2.21)

Just as a person puts on new garments after discarding the old ones, similarly Atman acquires new bodies after casting away the old bodies. (2.22)

Weapons do not cut this Atman, fire does not burn it, water does not make it wet, and the wind does not make it dry. (2.23)

This Atman cannot be cut, burned, wetted, or dried up. It is eternal, all pervading, unchanging, immovable, and primeval. (2.24)

The Atman is said to be unmanifest, unthinkable, and unchanging. Knowing this Atman as such you should not grieve. (2.25)

If you think that this (body) takes birth and dies perpetually, even then, O Arjuna, you should not grieve like this. (2.26)

Because, death is certain for the one who is born, and birth is certain for the one who dies. Therefore, you should not lament over the inevitable. (2.27)

All beings, O Arjuna, are unmanifest before birth and after death. They are manifest between the birth and the death only. What is there to grieve about? (2.28)

Some look upon this Atman as a wonder, another describes it as wonderful, and others hear of it as a wonder. Even after hearing about it no one actually knows it. (2.29)

O Arjuna, the Atman that dwells in the body of all (beings) is eternally indestructible. Therefore, you should not mourn for any body. (2.30)

Considering also your duty as a warrior you should not waver. Because there is nothing more auspicious for a warrior than a righteous war. (2.31)

Only the fortunate warriors, O Arjuna, get such an opportunity for an unsought war that is like an open door to heaven. (2.32)

If you will not fight this righteous war, then you will fail in your duty, lose your reputation, and incur sin. (2.33)

People will talk about your disgrace forever. To the honored, dishonor is worse than death. (2.34)

The great warriors will think that you have retreated from the battle out of fear. Those who have greatly esteemed you will lose respect for you. (2.35)

Your enemies will speak many unmentionable words and scorn your ability. What could be more painful than this? (2.36)

You will go to heaven if killed, or you will enjoy the earth if victorious. Therefore, get up with a determination to fight, O Arjuna. (2.37)

Treating pleasure and pain, gain and loss, victory and defeat alike, engage yourself in your duty. By doing your duty this way you will not incur sin. (2.38)

The wisdom of Saamkhya (or the knowledge of the Self) has been imparted to you, O Arjuna. Now listen to the wisdom of Karma-yoga endowed with which you will free yourself from the bondage of Karma. (2.39)

In Karma-yoga no effort is ever lost, and there is no harm. Even a little practice of this discipline protects one from great fear (of birth and death). (2.40) (*Karma-yoga is also referred to as Nishkaama Karma-yoga, Seva, selfless service, Buddhi yoga, yoga of work, science of proper action, and yoga of equanimity. A Karma-yogi works for the Lord as a matter of duty without a selfish desire for the fruits of work, or any attachment to results. The word Karma also means duty, action, deeds, work, or the results of past deeds.*)

Those who are resolute have only one thought (of Self-realization), but the thoughts of the irresolute are endless and many-branched, O Arjuna. (2.41)

The unwise who delight in flowery words (or the chanting of the Vedas without understanding the real meaning) stress Karma-Kaanda, the ritualistic aspect of the Vedas, O Arjuna, and say that there is nothing else (except material enjoyment). (2.42)

They prescribe various specific rites for the attainment of pleasure and power to those who are full of desires, and hold the attainment of heaven as the highest goal of life. The rebirth is their fruit of action. (2.43)

The resolute determination (of Self-realization) is not formed in the minds of those who are attached to pleasure and power; and whose discernment is obscured by such (ritualistic) activities. (2.44)

The Vedas deal with the three states or Gunas of mind. Become free from dualities, be ever balanced and unconcerned with the thoughts of acquisition and preservation. Rise above the three Gunas, and be Self-conscious, O Arjuna. (2.45) (*Guna means the quality, state, or the property of mind, matter, and the nature. Refer to Chapter 14 for more details on Gunas.*)

To a Self-realized person the Vedas are as useful as a reservoir of water when there is flood water available everywhere. (2.46)

You have Adhikaara over your respective duty only, but no control or claim over the results. The fruits of work should not be your motive. You should never be inactive. (2.47) (*The word Adhikaara means ability and privilege, prerogative, jurisdiction, discretion, right, preference, choice, rightful claim, authority, control.*)

Do your duty to the best of your ability, O Arjuna, with your mind attached to the Lord, abandoning (worry and) attachment to the results, and remaining calm in both success and failure. The equanimity of mind is called Karma-yoga. (2.48)

Work done with selfish motives is inferior by far to the selfless service or Karma-yoga. Therefore be a Karma-yogi, O Arjuna. Those who seek (to enjoy) the fruits of their work are verily unhappy (because one has no control over the results). (2.49)

A Karma-yogi gets freedom from both vice and virtue in this life itself. Therefore, strive for Karma-yoga. Working to the best of one's abilities without getting attached to the fruits of work is called (Nishkaama) Karma-yoga. (2.50)

Wise Karma-yogis, possessed with mental poise by renouncing the attachment to the fruits of work, are indeed freed from the bondage of rebirth and attain the blissful divine state. (2.51)

When your intellect will completely pierce the veil of delusion, then you will become indifferent to what has been heard and what is to be heard (from the scriptures). (2.52)

When your intellect, that is confused by the conflicting opinions and the ritualistic doctrine of the Vedas, shall stay steady and firm with the Self, then you shall attain Self-realization. (2.53)

Arjuna said: O Krishna, what is the mark of a person whose Prajna is steady and merged in superconscious state? How does a person of steady Prajna speak? How does such a person sit and walk? (2.54) (*Prajna means consciousness, mind, intellect, judgment, discrimination, and wisdom.*)

The Supreme Lord said: When one is completely free from all desires of the mind and is satisfied in the Self by the (joy of) Self, then one is called a person of steady Prajna, O Arjuna. (2.55)

A person whose mind is unperturbed by sorrow, who does not crave pleasures, and who is free from attachment, fear, and anger; such a person is called a sage of steady Prajna. (2.56)

Those who are not attached to anything, who are neither elated by getting desired results nor troubled by undesired results, their Prajna is deemed steady. (2.57)

When one can completely withdraw (or restrain) the senses from the sense objects as a tortoise withdraws its limbs (into the shell), then the Prajna of such a person is considered steady. (2.58)

The desire for sensual pleasures fades away if one abstains from sense enjoyment, but the craving (for sense enjoyment) remains. The craving also disappears from the one who has seen (or known) the Supreme. (2.59)

Restless senses, O Arjuna, forcibly carry away the mind of even a wise person striving for perfection. (2.60)

Having brought the senses under control, one should fix one's mind on the Self. One's Prajna becomes steady whose senses are under control. (2.61)

One develops attachment to sense objects by thinking about sense objects. Desire for sense objects comes from attachment to sense objects, and anger comes from unfulfilled desires. (2.62)

Delusion arises from anger. The mind is bewildered by delusion. Reasoning is destroyed when the mind is bewildered. One falls down (from the right path) when reasoning is destroyed. (2.63)

A disciplined person, enjoying sense objects with senses that are under control and free from likes and dislikes, attains tranquillity. (2.64)

All sorrows are destroyed upon attainment of tranquillity. The intellect of such a tranquil person soon becomes completely steady. (2.65)

There is neither Self-knowledge nor Self-perception to those whose senses are not under control. Without Self-perception there is no peace; and without peace there can be no happiness. (2.66)

The mind, when controlled by the roving senses, steals away the Prajna as a storm takes away a boat on the sea from its destination, the spiritual shore. (2.67)

Therefore, O Arjuna, one's Prajna becomes steady whose senses are completely withdrawn from the sense objects. (2.68)

A yogi is aware of the thing (or Atman) about which others are unaware. A sage who sees is unaware of the experience (of sense objects) about which others are aware. (2.69)

One attains peace in whose mind all desires enter without creating any disturbance, as river waters enter the full ocean without creating a disturbance. One who desires material objects is never peaceful. (2.70)

One who abandons all desires and becomes free from longing and the feeling of 'I' and 'my' attains peace. (2.71)

O Arjuna, this is the Braahmee or superconscious state. Attaining this (state), one is no longer deluded. Gaining this state, even at the end of one's life, a person attains oneness with the Supreme. (2.72)

Chapter 5: Path of Renunciation

Arjuna said: O Krishna, You praise transcendental knowledge (the Saamkhya or Karma-Samnyasa) and also performance of unattached action, Karma-yoga. Tell me, definitely, which one is better of the two. (See also 5.05) (5.01) (*Karma-Samnyasa means renunciation of doership, ownership, and selfish motive behind an action, and not the renunciation of work, or the worldly objects. Karma-Samnyasa comes only after the dawn of Self-knowledge. Therefore, words Jnana, Saamkhya, Samnyasa, and Karma-Samnyasa are used interchangeably throughout the Gita. Renunciation is considered the goal of life, and Karma and Jnana are the necessary means to achieve the goal.*)

The Supreme Lord said: Karma-Samnyasa, and Karma-yoga both lead to the Supreme. But, of the two, Karma-yoga is superior to Karma-Samnyasa. (5.02)

A person should be considered a true Samnyasi or renunciant who neither likes nor dislikes. Because, free from the dualities, O Arjuna, one is easily liberated from bondage. (5.03)

The ignorant, not the wise, consider Karma-Samnyasa and Karma-yoga as different from each other. The person who has truly mastered one, gets the benefits of both. (5.04)

Whatever goal a Samnyasi reaches, a Karma-yogi also reaches the same goal. One who sees the path of renunciation and the path of work as the same, really sees. (See also 6.01 and 6.02) (5.05)

But Samnyasa, O Arjuna, is difficult to attain without Karma-yoga. A Karma-yogi sage quickly attains Brahman. (See also 4.31, and 4.38) (5.06)

A Karma-yogi whose mind is pure, whose mind and senses are under control, and who sees one and the same Self in all beings, is not bound (by Karma) though engaged in work. (5.07)

A Samnyasi who knows the truth thinks: I do nothing at all. For in seeing, hearing, touching, smelling, eating, walking, sleeping, breathing; and (5.08)

Speaking, giving, taking, opening and closing the eyes, a Samnyasi believes that only the senses are operating upon their sense objects. (See also 3.27, 13.29, and 14.19) (5.09)

One who does all work as an offering to the Lord, abandoning attachment to the results, is as untouched by sin (or Karmic reaction) as a lotus leaf is untouched by water. (5.10)

A Karma-yogi performs action by body, mind, intellect, and senses, without attachment (or ego), only for self-purification. (5.11)

A Karma-yogi, abandoning the fruit of work, attains Supreme Bliss while others, who are attached to the fruits of work, become bound by selfish work. (5.12)

A person who has subdued the senses and completely renounced (the fruits of) all works, dwells happily in the City of Nine Gates, neither performing nor directing action. (5.13)

The Lord neither creates the urge for action nor the feeling of doership nor the attachment to the results of action in people. All these are done by the (Gunas of) nature. (5.14)

The Lord does not take the (responsibility for) good or evil deeds of anybody. The knowledge is covered by (the veil of) ignorance, thereby people are deluded. (5.15)

But their knowledge, whose ignorance is destroyed by the Self-knowledge, reveals the Supreme like the sun (reveals the beauty of objects of the world). (5.16)

They, whose mind and intellect are absorbed in the Self, who remain firmly attached with the Self, who have Self as their supreme goal, whose sins (or impurities) have been destroyed by the knowledge, do not take birth again. (5.17)

An enlightened person looks at a learned and humble Braahmana, an outcast, even a cow, an elephant, or a dog with an equal eye. (5.18)

Everything has been accomplished in this very life by those whose mind is set in equality. Such a person has realized Brahman because Brahman is flawless and impartial. (See also 18.55) (5.19)

One who neither rejoices on obtaining what is pleasant nor grieves on obtaining the unpleasant, who is undeluded, who has a steady mind, and who is a knower of Brahman; such a person abides in Brahman. (5.20)

A person whose mind is unattached to sensual pleasures, who discovers the joy of the Self, and whose mind is in union with Brahman through meditation, enjoys eternal bliss. (5.21)

Pleasures derived from the contact of senses with their objects (or the sensual pleasures) are verily the source of misery, and have a beginning and an end. The wise, O Arjuna, do not rejoice in sensual pleasures. (See also 18.38) (5.22)

One who is able to withstand the impulse of lust and anger before death is a yogi, and a happy person. (5.23)

One who finds happiness with the Self, who rejoices the Self within, and who is illuminated by the Self-knowledge; such a yogi becomes one with Brahman and attains supreme nirvana. (5.24)

Seers whose sins (or imperfections) are destroyed, whose doubts have been dispelled by knowledge, whose disciplined minds are attached with the Self, and who are engaged in the welfare of all beings attain Supreme Brahman. (5.25)

A Self-realized person who is free from lust and anger, and who has subdued the mind and senses easily attains nirvana. (5.26)

Renouncing sense enjoyments; fixing the eyes and mind at the midbrows; equalizing the breath moving through the nostrils (by Kriya techniques); (See also 4.29, 6.13 and 8.10) (5.27)

With senses, mind, and intellect under control; having liberation as the prime goal; free from lust, anger, and fear; such a sage is verily liberated. (5.28)

The one who knows Me as the enjoyer of sacrifices and austerities, as the great Lord of all the worlds, and as the friend of all beings, attains peace. (5.29)

Chapter 13: Creation and the Creator

The Supreme Lord said: O Arjuna, this body (the miniature universe) may be called the field or creation. One who knows the creation is called the creator by the seers of truth. (13.01)

Know Me to be the creator of all creation, O Arjuna. The true understanding of both the creator and the creation is considered by Me to be the transcendental or metaphysical knowledge. (13.02)

What the creation is, what it is like, what its transformations are, where the source is, who that creator is, and what His powers are, hear all these from Me in brief. (13.03)

The sages have described Him in many ways, in various Vedic hymns, and also in the conclusive and convincing verses of the Brahmasutra. (13.04)

The five basic elements, the "I" consciousness or ego, the intellect, the unmanifest Prakriti, the ten senses, the mind, and the five sense objects; (See also 7.04) (13.05)

Desire, hatred, pleasure, pain, the physical body, consciousness, and resolve. Thus the field (the creation or body) has been briefly described with its transformations. (13.06)

Humility, modesty, nonviolence, forbearance, honesty, service to guru, purity (of thought, word, and deed), steadfastness, self-control; and (13.07)

Aversion towards sense objects, absence of ego, constant reflection on the agony and suffering inherent in birth, old age, disease, and death. (13.08)

Detachment, non-fondness with son, wife, and home; unfailing equanimity upon attainment of the desirable and the undesirable; and (13.09)

Unswerving devotion to Me by the yoga of exclusivity, love for solitude, distaste for social gossips; and (13.10)

Steadfastness in knowledge of the Supreme Spirit, and the perception of (the omnipresent God as) the object of true knowledge is called knowledge; what is contrary to this is ignorance. (13.11)

I shall fully describe the object of knowledge, knowing which one attains immortality. The beginningless Supreme Brahman is said to be neither Sat nor Asat. (See also 9.19) (13.12)

Having hands and feet everywhere; having eyes, head, and face everywhere; having ears everywhere; the creator exists in the creation by pervading everything. (13.13)

He is the perceiver of all sense objects without the senses; unattached, yet the sustainer of all; devoid of the Gunas, yet the enjoyer of the Gunas. (13.14)

He is inside as well as outside all beings, animate and inanimate. He is incomprehensible because of His subtlety. He is very near as well as far away. (13.15)

Undivided, yet appears as if divided in beings; He, the object of knowledge, is the creator, sustainer, and destroyer of (all) beings. (13.16)

The light of all lights, He is said to be beyond darkness. He is the knowledge, the object of knowledge, and seated in the hearts of all beings, He is to be realized by the knowledge. (13.17)

Thus the creation as well as the knowledge and the object of knowledge have been briefly described. Understanding this, My devotee attains Me. (13.18)

Know that Prakriti and Purusha are both beginningless; and also know that all manifestations and Gunas arise from the Prakriti. (13.19)

The Prakriti is said to be the cause of production of physical body and organs (of perception and action). The Purusha (or the consciousness) is said to be the cause of experiencing pleasures and pains. (13.20)

The Purusha associating with Prakriti (or matter), enjoys the Gunas of Prakriti. Attachment to the Gunas (due to ignorance caused by previous Karma) is the cause of the birth of JeevaAtman in good and evil wombs. (13.21) (*JeevaAtman or Jeeva is defined as Atman accompanied by the subtle (or astral) body consisting of the six sensory faculties and vital forces; the living entity; the individual soul enshrined in the physical body.*)

The Supreme Spirit in the body is also called the witness, the guide, the supporter, the enjoyer, and the great Lord or ParamaAtman. (13.22)

They who truly understand Purusha and Prakriti with its Gunas are not born again regardless of their mode of life. (13.23)

Some perceive God in the heart by the intellect through meditation; others by the yoga of knowledge; and others by the yoga of work (or Karma-yoga). (13.24)

Some, however, do not understand Brahman, but having heard (of it) from others, take to worship. They also transcend death by their firm faith to what they have heard. (13.25)

Whatever is born, animate or inanimate, know them to be (born) from the union of the field (or Prakriti) and the field knower (or Purusha), O Arjuna. (See also 7.06) (13.26)

The one who sees the imperishable Supreme Lord dwelling equally within all perishable beings truly sees. (13.27)

Seeing the same Lord existing in everybeing, one does not injure the other self and thereupon attains the Supreme goal. (13.28)

Those who perceive that all works are done by the (Gunas of) Prakriti alone, and thus they are not the doer, they truly understand. (See also 3.27, 5.09, and 14.19) (13.29)

When one perceives diverse variety of beings resting in One and spreading out from That alone, then one attains Brahman. (13.30)

The imperishable Supreme Self, being beginningless and without Gunas, though dwelling in the body (as Atman) neither does anything nor gets tainted, O Arjuna. (13.31)

As the all-pervading ether is not tainted because of its subtlety, similarly the Self, seated in everybody, is not tainted. (13.32)

O Arjuna, just as one sun illuminates this entire world, similarly the creator illumines (or gives life to) the entire creation. (13.33)

They, who understand the difference between the creation (or the body) and the creator (or the Atman) and know the technique of liberation (of Jeeva) from the trap of Maya with the help of knowledge, attain the Supreme. (13.34)

Citation and Use

This reading was taken from the following source.

Levin, Noah, ed. "Self and Atman." In SOUTH AND EAST ASIAN PHILOSOPHY READIER, AN OPEN EDUCATIONAL RESOURCE, 105–15. NGE Far Press, 2019.

Notes

1. Dharma may be defined as the eternal law governing, upholding, and supporting the creation and the world order. It also means duty, righteousness, ideal conduct, moral principles, and truth. Adharma is an antonym to Dharma. Expert guidance should be sought during the moment of crisis.

2. Atma or Atmann means consciousness, spirit, soul, self, the source of life and the cosmic power behind the body-mind complex. Just as our body exists in space, similarly our thoughts, intellect, emotions, and psyche exist in Atman, the space of consciousness. Atman cannot be perceived by the senses, because, the senses abide in Atman.

SHIP OF THESEUS

Plutarch and Henry Imler

Classic Formulation as Recounted by Plutarch

The ship wherein Theseus and the youth of Athens returned had thirty oars, and was preserved by the Athenians down even to the time of Demetrius Phalereus, for they took away the old planks as they decayed, putting in new and stronger timber in their place, insomuch that this ship became a standing example among the philosophers, for the logical question of things that grow; one side holding that the ship remained the same, and the other contending that it was not the same.

Citation and Use

> Plutarch. "Theseus." Internet Classics Archive, n.d. http://classics.mit.edu/Plutarch/theseus.html.

Notes

1. This section was written by Henry Imler

Scavenger Variant[1]

Theseus leaves Athens on a 30-year journey in a brand new ship. During the course of this journey, parts of the ship wear out. As parts wear out, they are replaced with new parts. At the same time,

Theseus is dogged by a scavenger. She collects each of the discarded parts and begins to reassemble them in the same pattern.

By the time Theseus returns, every single part of the ship has been replaced. Theseus and the Scavenger arrive in Athens at the same time.

Which ship (scavenger's or Theses') is the ship that left Athens?

THE TEN OXHERDING PICTURES

Daisetz Suzuki and Kaku-an

Preliminary

The author of these "Ten Oxherding Pictures" is said to be a Zen master of the Sung Dynasty known as Kaku-an Shi-en (Kuo-an Shih-yuan) belonging to the Rinzai school.[1] He is also the author of the poems and introductory words attached to the pictures. He was not however the first who attempted to illustrate by means of pictures stages of Zen discipline, for in his general preface to the pictures he refers to another Zen master called Seikyo (Ching-chu), probably a contemporary of his, who made use of the ox to explain his Zen teaching. But in Seikyo's case the gradual development of the Zen life was indicated by a progressive whitening of the animal, ending in the disappearance of the whole being. There were in this only five pictures, instead of ten as by Kaku-an. Kaku-an thought this was somewhat misleading because of an empty circle being made the goal of Zen discipline. Some might take mere emptiness as all important and final. Hence his improvement resulting in the "Ten Oxherding Pictures" as we have them now.

According to a commentator of Kaku-an's Pictures, there is another series of the Oxherding Pictures by a Zen master called jitoku Ki (Tzu-te Hui), who apparently knew of the existence of the Five Pictures by Seikyo, for jitoku's are six in number. The last one, No. 6, goes beyond the stage of absolute emptiness where Seikyo's end: the poem reads:

> Even beyond the ultimate limits there extends a passageway,
> Whereby he comes back among the six realms of existence;
> Every worldly affair is a Buddhist work,
> And wherever he goes he finds his home air;
> Like a gem he stands out even in the mud,

The Ten Oxherding Pictures, I.

by Kaku-an

> Like pure gold he shines even in the furnace;
> Along the end-
> less road [of birth and death] he walks suffi-
> cient unto himself,
> In whatever associa-
> tions he is found he moves leisurely unattached.

Jitoku's ox grows whiter as Seikyo's, and in this particular respect both differ from Kaku-an's conception. In the latter there is no whitening process. In Japan Kaku-an's Ten Pictures gained a wide circulation, and at present all the oxherding books reproduce them. The earliest one belongs I think to the fifteenth century. In China however a different edition seems to have been in vogue, one belonging to the Seikyo and Jitoku series of pictures. The author is not known. The edition containing the preface by Chu-hung, 1585, has ten pictures, each of which is preceded by Pu-ming's poem. As to who this Pu-ming was, Chu-hung himself professes ignorance. In these pictures the ox's colouring changes together with the oxherd's management of him. The quaint original Chinese prints are reproduced below, and also Pu-ming's verses translated into English.

Thus as far as I can identify there are four varieties of the Oxherding Pictures:
1. by Kaku-an,
2. by Seikyo,
3. by Jitoku, and
4. by an unknown author.

Kaku-an's "Pictures" here reproduced are by Shubun, a Zen priest of the fifteenth century. The original pictures are preserved at Shokokuji, Kyoto. He was one of the greatest painters in black and white in the Ashikaga period.

I. Searching for the Ox

The beast has never gone astray, and what is the use of searching for him? The reason why the oxherd is not on intimate terms with him is because the oxherd himself has violated his own inmost nature. The beast is lost, for the oxherd has himself been led out of the way through his deluding senses. His home is receding farther away from him, and byways and crossways are ever confused. Desire for gain and fear of loss burn like fire; ideas of right and wrong shoot up like a phalanx.

Alone in the wilderness, lost in the jungle, the boy is searching, searching!
The swelling waters, the far-away mountains, and the unending path;
Exhausted and in despair, he knows not where to go,

Searching for the Ox

He only hears the evening cicadas singing in the maple-woods.

II. Seeing the Traces

By the aid of the sutras and by inquiring into the doctrines, he has come to understand something, he has found the traces. He now knows that vessels, however varied, are all of gold, and that the objective world is a reflection of the Self. Yet, he is unable to distinguish what is good from what is not, his mind is still confused as to truth and falsehood. As he has not yet entered the gate, he is provisionally said to have noticed the traces.

By the stream and under the trees, scattered are the traces of the lost;
The sweet-scented grasses are growing thick—did he find the way?
How-

Seeing the Traces

ever remote over the hills and far away the beast may wander,
His nose reaches the heavens and none can conceal it.

III. Seeing the Ox

The boy finds the way by the sound he hears; he sees thereby into the origin of things, and all his senses are in harmonious order. In all his activities, it is manifestly present. It is like the salt in water and the glue in color. [It is there though not distinguishable as an individual entity.] When the eye is properly directed, he will find that it is no other than himself.

On a yonder branch perches a nightingale cheerfully singing;
The sun is warm, and a sooth-
ing breeze blows, on the bank the willows are green;
The ox is there all by him-
self, nowhere is he to hide himself;
The splendid head deco-
rated with stately horns what painter can reproduce him?

Seeing the Ox

IV. Catching the Ox

Long lost in the wilderness, the boy has at last found the ox and his hands are on him. But, owing to the over-whelming pressure of the outside world, the ox is hard to keep under control. He constantly longs for the old sweet-scented field. The wild nature is still unruly, and altogether refuses to be broken. If the oxherd wishes to see the ox completely in harmony with himself, he has surely to use the whip freely.

Catching the Ox

With the energy of his whole being, the boy has at last taken hold of the ox:
But how wild his will, how ungovernable his power!
At times he struts up a plateau,
When lo! he is lost again in a misty unpenetrable mountain-pass.

V. Herding the Ox

When a thought moves, another follows, and then another-an endless train of thoughts is thus awakened. Through enlightenment all this turns into truth; but falsehood asserts itself when confusion prevails. Things oppress us not because of an objective world, but because of a self-deceiving mind. Do not let the nose-string loose, hold it tight, and allow no vacillation.

The boy is not to separate himself with his whip and tether,
Lest the animal should wan-
der away into a world of defilements;
When the ox is prop-
erly tended to, he will grow pure and docile;
Without a chain, nothing binding, he will by himself follow the oxherd.

Herding the Ox

VI. Coming Home on the Ox's Back

The struggle is over; the man is no more concerned with gain and loss. He hums a rustic tune of the wood-man, he sings simple songs of the village-boy. Saddling himself on the ox's back, his eyes are fixed on things not of the earth, earthy. Even if he is called, he will not turn his head; however enticed he will no more be kept back.

Riding on the ani-
mal, he leisurely wends his way home:
Enveloped in the evening mist, how tune-
fully the flute vanishes away!
Singing a ditty, beat-
ing time, his heart is filled with a joy indescribable!
That he is now one of those who know, need it be told?

Coming Home on the Ox's Back

VII. The Ox Forgotten, Leaving the Man Alone

The dharmas are one and the ox is symbolic. When you
know that what you need is not the snare or set-net but
the hare or fish, it is like gold separated from the dross,
it is like the moon rising out of the clouds. The one ray
of light serene and penetrating shines even before days
of creation.

Riding on the animal, he is at last back in his home,

The Ox Forgotten, Leaving the Man Alone

Where lo! the ox is no more; the man alone sits serenely.
Though the red sun is high up in the sky, he is still quietly dreaming,
Under a straw-thatched roof are his whip and rope idly lying.

VIII. The Ox and the Man Gone out of Sight

All confusion is set aside, and serenity alone prevails;
even the idea of holiness does not obtain. He does not
linger about where the Buddha is, and as to where there
is no Buddha he speedily passes by. When there exists
no form of dualism, even a thousand-eyed one fails to
detect a loop-hole. A holiness before which birds offer
flowers is but a farce.[2]

All is empty-the whip, the rope, the man, and the ox:
Who can ever survey the vastness of heaven?
Over the furnace burn-
ing ablaze, not a flake of snow can fall:
When this state of things obtains, mani-
fest is the spirit of the ancient master.

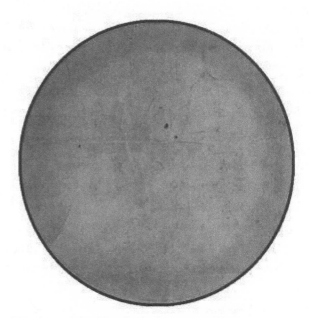

The Ox and the Man Both Gone out of Sight

IX. Returning to the Origin, Back to the Source

From the very beginning, pure and immaculate, the man has never been affected by defilement. He watches the growth of things, while himself abiding in the immovable serenity of nonassertion. He does not identify himself with the maya-like transformations [that are going on about him], nor has he any use of himself [which is artificiality]. The waters are blue, the mountains are green; sitting alone, he observes things undergoing changes.

To return to the Ori-
gin, to be back at the Source—already a false step this!
Far bet-
ter it is to stay at home, blind and deaf, and without much ado;
Sitting in the hut, he takes no cogni-
sance of things outside,
Behold the streams flowing-whither nobody knows; and the flowers vividly red-for whom are they?

Returning to the Origin, Back to the Source

X. Entering the City with Bliss-bestowing Hands

His thatched cottage gate is closed, and even the wisest know him not. No glimpses of his inner life are to be caught; for he goes on his own way without following the steps of the ancient sages. Carrying a gourd[3] he goes out into the market, leaning against a staff[4] he comes home. He is found in company with wine-bibbers and butchers, he and they are all converted into Buddhas.

Bare-chested and bare-
footed, he comes out into the market-place;
Daubed with mud and ashes, how broadly he smiles!
There is no need for the miraculous power of the gods,

Entering the City with Bliss-bestowing Hands

For he touches, and lo! the dead trees are in full bloom.

The Ten Oxherding Pictures, II.

1. Undisciplined

Undisciplined

With his horns fiercely projected in the air the beast snorts,
Madly running over the mountain paths, farther and farther he goes astray!
A dark cloud is spread across the entrance of the valley,
And who knows how much of the fine fresh herb is trampled under his wild hoofs!

2. Discipline Begun

Discipline Begun

I am in possession of a straw rope, and I pass it through his nose,
For once he makes a frantic attempt to run away, but he is severely whipped and whipped;

The beast resists the training with all the power there is in a nature wild and ungoverned,
But the rustic oxherd never relaxes his pulling tether and ever-ready whip.

3. In Harness

In Harness

Gradually getting into harness the beast is now content to be led by the nose,
Crossing the stream, walking along the mountain path, he follows every step of the leader;
The leader holds the rope tightly in his hand never letting it go,
All day long he is on the alert almost unconscious of what fatigue is.

4. Faced Round

Faced Round

After long days of training the result begins to tell and the beast is faced round,

A nature so wild and ungoverned is finally broken, he has become gentler;
But the tender has not yet given him his full confidence,
He still keeps his straw rope with which the ox is now tied to a tree.

5. Tamed

Tamed

Under the green willow tree and by the ancient mountain stream,
The ox is set at liberty to pursue his own pleasures;
At the eventide when a grey mist descends on the pasture,
The boy wends his homeward way with the animal quietly following.

6. Unimpeded

Unimpeded

On the verdant field the beast contentedly lies idling his time away,
No whip is needed now, nor any kind of restraint;
The boy too sits leisurely under the pine tree,
Playing a tune of peace, overflowing with joy.

7. Laissez Faire

Laissez Faire

The spring stream in the evening sun flows languidly along the willow-lined bank,
In the hazy atmosphere the meadow grass is seen growing thick;
When hungry he grazes, when thirsty he quaffs, as time sweetly slides,
While the boy on the rock dozes for hours not noticing anything that goes on about him.

8. All Forgotten

All Forgotten

The beast all in white now is surrounded by the white clouds,
The man is perfectly at his case and care-free, so is his companion;
The white clouds penetrated by the moon-light cast their white shadows below,
The white clouds and the bright moon-light-each following its course of movement.

9. The Solitary Moon

The Solitary Moon

Nowhere is the beast, and the oxherd is master of his time,
He is a solitary cloud wafting lightly along the mountain peaks;
Clapping his hands he sings joyfully in the moon-light,
But remember a last wall is still left barring his homeward walk.

10. Both Vanished

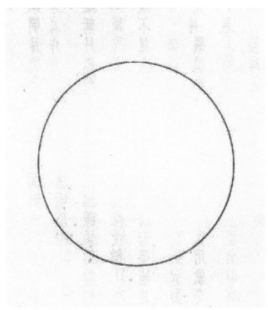

Both Vanished

Both the man and the animal have disappeared, no traces are left,
The bright moon-light is empty and shadowless with all the ten-thousand objects in it;
If anyone should ask the meaning of this,
Behold the lilies of the field and its fresh sweet-scented verdure.

Citation and Use

This reading was taken from the following work.

Suzuki, Daisetz Teitaro. "Ten Oxherding Pictures." In South and East Asian Philosophy Readier, an Open Educational Resource, edited by Noah Levin, 264–75. NGE Far Press, 2019.

Use of this work is governed by **CC-BY-SA-NC** license.

Notes

1. Daisetz Teitaro Suzuki. Manual of Zen Buddhism. 1934
2. It will be interesting to note what a mystic philosopher has to say about this: "A man shall become truly poor and as free from his creature will as he was when he was born. And I say to you, by the eternal truth, that as long as ye desire to fulfil the will of God, and have any desire after eternity and God; so long are ye not truly poor. He alone hath true spiritual poverty who wills nothing, knows nothing, desires nothing."—(From Eckhart as quoted by Inge in Light, Life, and Love.)]
3. Symbol of emptiness (sunyata).
4. No extra property he has, for he knows that the desire to possess is the curse of human life.

RIKERS

Henry Imler

This thought experiment is a mashup of the classic Star Trek episode, "Second Chances" and Daniel Parfitt's teletransportation problem.

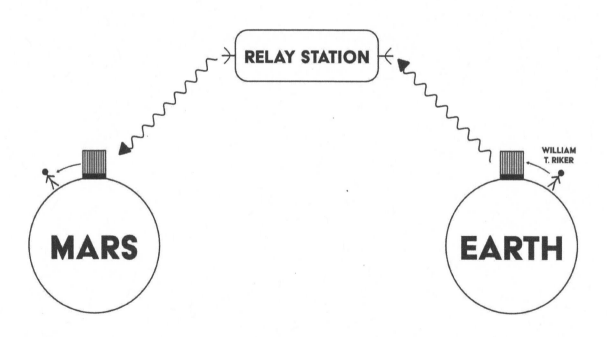

Diagram of the teleportation process. The physical and mental states of the person are recorded and sent as a "profile" from the teleporter to the relay station where they are then sent to the teleporter assembly on the other planet. It takes roughly 5 minutes for the profile to pass between the relay station and a planet.

We have invented a new method of transportation, a teleporter that records your body down to the quantum level of resolution, transmits that information to another teleporter pad that then transmutes that information into a exact physical copy of the being that stepped onto the other pad. Same memories, same scars, everything. The pattern is preserved, although different atoms, electrons et cetera constitute the being's matter.

Case 1

William T. Riker intends to travel from his home on Earth to the Mars colony via the teleporter. Because Mars is so far away, there is a relay station halfway between the planets. It collects information from the teleporter pad on Earth and beams it to Mars and vice versa.

When William T. Riker steps onto the pad, his five aggregates[1] are recorded and burned way in the process by the teleporter. His information profile is beamed to the relay station, a process which takes four minutes. After two minutes of processing, the profile is beamed to the teleporter on Mars, which takes four more minutes to arrive. At that point, a being steps off the pad who is identical to the being that stepped onto the pad on Earth.

Did William T. Riker survive the trip or did he die and a clone stepped off the pad on Mars?

Case 2

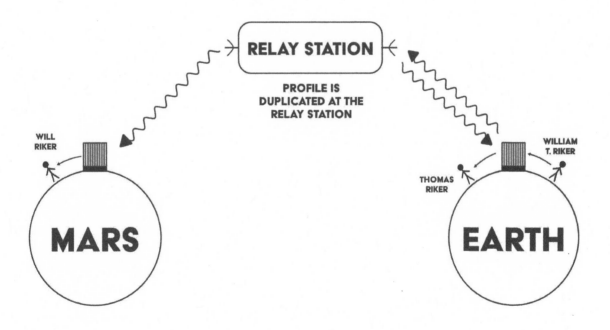

Diagram of of the duplicate profile information being sent to Mars and Earth.

Same situation as before. Only this time, there is a malfunction in the relay station and Riker's profile is duplicated on accident and the exact same profile is sent to Mars *and* back to Earth.

At the exact same moment beings step off of the pads on Earth and Mars, both of which are physically and mentally identical to William T. Riker. Let's call the being on Mars Will Riker and the being who stepped off the pad on Earth Thomas Riker. The second after they step off the pads, they start to have *new and divergent* memories, thoughts, et cetera.

What is the relationship between the being we named William T. Riker at Time 1 and the beings we called Thomas Riker and Will Riker at Time 1?

What is the relationship between Thomas and Will Riker? Are they the same person, clones, twins, brothers, two heads of the time-hydra that is William T. Riker?

Notes

1. The Buddha teaches in the Pali Canon the five aggregates as follows:
    1. **form**: material form of a being
    2. **Current sensations**: sensory experience of an object.
    3. **Current perceptions**: sensory and mental process
    4. **Mental formations**: all types of mental imprints and conditioning
    5. **Consciousness**: "discrimination" or "discernment". Awareness, that which discerns, a series of rapidly changing interconnected discrete acts of cognizance.

Bhagavad Gita

Chapter 3: Path of Karma Yoga

Arjuna said: If You consider that transcendental knowledge is better than work then why do You want me to engage in this horrible war, O Krishna? (3.01)

You seem to confuse my mind by apparently conflicting words. Tell me, decisively, one thing by which I may attain the Supreme. (3.02)

The Supreme Lord said: In this world, O Arjuna, a twofold path of Sadhana (or the spiritual practice) has been stated by Me in the past. The path of Self-knowledge (or Jnana-yoga) for the contemplative, and the path of unselfish work (or Karma-yoga) for the active. (3.03) [1]

One does not attain freedom from the bondage of Karma by merely abstaining from work. No one attains perfection by merely giving up work. (3.04)

Because no one can remain actionless even for a moment. Everyone is driven to action, helplessly indeed, by the Gunas of nature. (3.05)

The deluded ones, who restrain their organs of action but mentally dwell upon the sense enjoyment, are called hypocrites. (3.06)

The one who controls the senses by the (trained and purified) mind and intellect, and engages the organs of action to Nishkaama Karma-yoga, is superior, O Arjuna. (3.07)

Perform your obligatory duty, because action is indeed better than inaction. Even the maintenance of your body would not be possible by inaction. (3.08)

Human beings are bound by Karma (or works) other than those done as Yajna. Therefore, O Arjuna, do your duty efficiently as a service or Seva to Me, free from attachment to the fruits of work. (3.09) [2]

Brahmaa, the creator, in the beginning created human beings together with Yajna and said: By Yajna you shall prosper and Yajna shall fulfill all your desires. (3.10)

Nourish the Devas with Yajna, and the Devas will nourish you. Thus nourishing one another you shall attain the Supreme goal. (3.11) [3]

The Devas, nourished by Yajna, will give you the desired objects. One who enjoys the gift of the Devas without offering them (anything in return) is, indeed, a thief. (3.12)

The righteous who eat the remnants of the Yajna are freed from all sins, but the impious who cook food only for themselves (without sharing with others in charity) verily eat sin. (3.13)

The living beings are born from food, food is produced by rain, rain comes by performing Yajna. The Yajna is performed by doing Karma. (See also 4.32) (3.14)

The Karma or duty is prescribed in the Vedas. The Vedas come from Brahman. Thus the all-pervading Brahman is ever present in Yajna or service. (3.15)

The one who does not help to keep the wheel of creation in motion by sacrificial duty, and who rejoices in sense pleasures, that sinful person lives in vain, O Arjuna. (3.16)

The one who rejoices in the Self only, who is satisfied with the Self, who is content in the Self alone, for such a (Self-realized) person there is no duty. (3.17)

Such a person has no interest, whatsoever, in what is done or what is not done. A Self-realized person does not depend on anybody (except God) for anything. (3.18)

Therefore, always perform your duty efficiently and without attachment to the results, because by doing work without attachment one attains the Supreme. (3.19)

King Janaka and others attained perfection (or Self-realization) by Karma-yoga alone. You should perform your duty (with apathetic frame of mind) with a view to guide people and for the universal welfare (of the society). (3.20)

Because, whatever noble persons do, others follow. Whatever standard they set up, the world follows. (3.21)

O Arjuna, there is nothing in the three worlds (earth, heaven, and the upper regions) that should be done by Me, nor there is anything unobtained that I should obtain, yet I engage in action. (3.22)

Because, if I do not engage in action relentlessly, O Arjuna, people would follow My path in every way. (3.23)

These worlds would perish if I do not work, and I shall be the cause of confusion and destruction of all these people. (3.24)

As the ignorant work, O Arjuna, with attachment (to the fruits of work), so the wise should work without attachment, for the welfare of the society. (3.25)

The wise should not unsettle the mind of the ignorant who is attached to the fruits of work, but the enlightened one should inspire others by performing all works efficiently without attachment. (See also 3.29) (3.26)

All works are being done by the Gunas (or the energy and power) of nature, but due to delusion of ego people assume themselves to be the doer. (See also 5.09, 13.29, and 14.19) (3.27)

The one who knows the truth, O Arjuna, about the role of Guna and action does not get attached to the work, knowing that it is the Gunas that work with their instruments, the organs. (3.28)

Those who are deluded by the Gunas of nature get attached to the works of the Gunas. The wise should not disturb the mind of the ignorant whose knowledge is imperfect. (See also 3.26) (3.29)

Dedicating all works to Me in a spiritual frame of mind, free from desire, attachment, and mental grief, do your duty. (3.30)

Those who always practice this teaching of Mine, with faith and free from cavil, are freed from the bondage of Karma. (3.31)

But, those who carp at My teaching and do not practice it, consider them as ignorant of all knowledge, senseless, and lost. (3.32)

All beings follow their nature. Even the wise act according to their own nature. What, then, is the value of sense restraint? (3.33)

Raaga and Dwesha (or the attachments and aversions) for the sense objects remain in the senses. One should not come under the control of these two, because they are two stumbling blocks, indeed, on one's path of Self-realization. (3.34)

One's inferior natural work is better than superior unnatural work. Death in carrying out one's natural work is useful. Unnatural work produces too much stress. (See also 18.47) (3.35)

Arjuna said: O Krishna, what impels one to commit sin as if unwillingly and forced against one's will? (3.36)

The Supreme Lord said: It is Kaama and anger born of Rajo Guna. Kaama is insatiable and is a great devil. Know this as the enemy. (3.37)

Kaama, the passionate desire for all sensual and material pleasures, becomes anger if it is unfulfilled. As the fire is covered by smoke, as a mirror by dust, and as an embryo by the amnion, similarly the Self-knowledge gets obscured by Kaama. (3.38)

O Arjuna, Jnana gets covered by this insatiable fire of Kaama, the eternal enemy of Jnani. (3.39)

The senses, the mind, and the intellect are said to be the seat of Kaama. Kaama, with the help of the senses, deludes a person by veiling Jnana. (3.40)

Therefore, O Arjuna, by controlling the senses kill this devil (of material desire) that destroys knowledge and discrimination. (3.41)

The senses are said to be superior (to matter or the body), the mind is superior to the senses, the intellect is superior to the mind, and Atma is superior to the intellect. (3.42)

Thus, knowing the Atma to be superior to the intellect, and controlling the mind by the intellect (that is purified by Jnana), one must kill this mighty enemy, Kaama, O Arjuna. (3.43)

Chapter 4: Path of Renunciation with Knowledge

The Supreme Lord said: I taught this imperishable (science of right action, or) Karma-yoga to (King) Vivasvaan. Vivasvaan taught it to Manu. Manu taught it to Ikshavaaku. (4.01)

Thus handed down in succession the royal sages knew this (Karma-yoga). After a long time the science of Karma-yoga was lost from this earth. (4.02)

Today I have described the same ancient science to you, because you are my sincere devotee and friend. Karma-yoga is a supreme secret indeed. (4.03)

Arjuna said: You were born later, but Vivasvaan was born in ancient time. How am I to understand that You taught this yoga in the beginning (of the creation)? (4.04)

The Supreme Lord said: Both you and I have taken many births. I remember them all, O Arjuna, but you do not remember. (4.05)

Though I am eternal, imperishable, and the Lord of all beings; yet I (voluntarily) manifest by controlling My own material nature using My Yoga-Maya. [4](4.06) [5]

Whenever there is a decline of Dharma and the rise of Adharma, O Arjuna, then I manifest (or incarnate) Myself.

I incarnate from time to time for protecting the good, for transforming the wicked, and for establishing Dharma, the world order. (4.07-08)

The one who truly understands My transcendental birth and activities (of creation, maintenance, and dissolution), is not born again after leaving this body and attains My abode, O Arjuna. (4.09)

Freed from attachment, fear, and anger; fully absorbed in Me, taking refuge in Me, and purified by the fire of Self-knowledge, many have attained Me. (4.10)

With whatever motive people worship Me, I reward them (or fulfill their desires) accordingly. People worship (or approach) Me with different motives. (4.11)

Those who long for success in their work here (on the earth) worship the demigods (or Devas). Success in work comes quickly in this human world. (4.12)

The four Varna or divisions of human society, based on aptitude and vocation, were created by Me. Though I am the author of this system, one should know that I do nothing and I am eternal. (See also 18.41) (4.13)

Works do not bind Me, because I have no desire for the fruits of work. The one who understands this truth is (also) not bound by Karma. (4.14)

The ancient seekers of liberation also performed their duties with this understanding. Therefore, you should do your duty as the ancients did. (4.15)

Even the wise are confused about what is action and what is inaction. Therefore, I shall clearly explain what is action, knowing that one shall be liberated from the evil (of birth and death). (4.16)

The true nature of action is very difficult to understand. Therefore, one should know the nature of attached action, the nature of detached action, and also the nature of forbidden action. (4.17)

Attached action is selfish work that produces Karmic bondage, detached action is unselfish work or Seva that leads to nirvana, and forbidden action is harmful to society. The one who sees inaction in action, and action in inaction, is a wise person. Such a person is a yogi and has accomplished everything. (See also 3.05, 3.27, 5.08 and 13.29) (4.18)

A person whose all works are free from selfish desires and motives, and whose all Karma is burned up in the fire of Self-knowledge, is called a sage by the wise. (4.19)

Having abandoned attachment to the fruits of work, ever content, and dependent on no one (but God); though engaged in activity, one does nothing at all (and incurs no Karmic reaction). (4.20)

Free from desires, mind and senses under control, renounc-ing all proprietorship, doing mere bodily action, one does not incur sin (or Karmic reaction). (4.21)

Content with whatever gain comes naturally by His will, unaffected by dualities, free from envy, equanimous in success and failure; though engaged in work such a person is not bound (by Karma). (4.22)

Those who are devoid of attachment, whose mind is fixed in knowledge, who does work as a Seva to the Lord, all Karma of such liberated persons dissolves away. (4.23)

Brahman is the oblation. Brahman is the clarified butter. The oblation is poured by Brahman into the fire of Brahman. Brahman shall be realized by the one who considers everything as (a manifestation or) an act of Brahman. (Also see 9.16) (4.24)

Some yogis perform the Yajna of worship to Devas alone, while others offer Yajna itself as offering in the fire of Brahman by performing the Yajna (of Self-knowledge). (4.25)

Some offer their hearing and other senses (as sacrifice) in the fires of restraint, others offer sound and other objects of the senses (as sacrifice) in the fires of the senses. (4.26)

Others offer all the functions of the senses, and the functions of Prana (or the five bioimpulses) as sacrifice in the fire of the yoga of self-restraint that is kindled by knowledge. (4.27)

Others offer their wealth, their austerity, and their practice of yoga as sacrifice, while the ascetics with strict vows offer their study of scriptures and knowledge as sacrifice. (4.28)

Those who are engaged in yogic practice, reach the breathless state by offering inhalation into exhalation and exhalation into inhalation as sacrifice (by using short breathing Kriya techniques).[6] (4.29)

Others restrict their diet and offer their inhalations as sacrifice into their inhalations. All these are the knowers of sacrifice, and are purified by (theirs) sacrifice. (4.30)

Those who perform Yajna obtain the nectar (of knowledge) as a result of their sacrifice and attain eternal Brahman. O Arjuna, even this world is not (a happy place) for the non-sacrificer, how can the other world be?[7]. (4.31)

Thus many types of sacrifice are described in the Vedas. Know them all to be born from Karma or the action of body, mind, and senses. Knowing this, you shall attain nirvana. (See also 3.14) (4.32)

The knowledge sacrifice is superior to any material sacrifice, O Arjuna. Because, all actions in their entirety culminate in knowledge. (4.33)

Acquire this transcendental knowledge by humble reverence, by sincere inquiry, and by service (to a Self-realized guru). The wise who have realized the truth will teach you. (4.34)

Knowing that, O Arjuna, you shall not again get deluded like this. By this knowledge you shall behold the entire creation in your own Self/Lord, or in Brahman. (See also 6.29) (4.35)

Even if one is the most sinful of all sinners, yet one shall cross over the ocean of sin by the raft of knowledge alone. (4.36)

As the blazing fire reduces wood to ashes, similarly, the fire of Self-knowledge reduces all Karma to ashes, O Arjuna. (4.37)

Verily there is no purifier in this world like knowledge. One who becomes purified by Karma-yoga discovers this knowledge within (naturally) in course of time. (See also 4.31, and 5.06). (4.38)

The one who has faith, and is sincere, and has mastery over the senses, gains this knowledge. Having gained this, one at once attains the supreme peace. (4.39)

But the ignorant, who has no faith and is full of doubt (about the Self), perishes. There is neither this world nor the world beyond nor happiness for the one who doubts. (4.40)

Karma does not bind one who has renounced work (by renouncing the fruits of work) through Karma-yoga; whose doubt is completely destroyed by knowledge; and who is Self-realized, O Arjuna. (4.41)

Therefore, resort to Karma-yoga and cut the ignorance-born doubt abiding in your heart by the sword of Self-knowledge, and get up (to fight), O Arjuna. (4.42)

Chapter 10: Manifestation of the Absolute

The Supreme Lord said: O Arjuna, listen once again to My supreme word that I shall speak to you, who are dear, for your welfare. (10.01)

Neither the Devas nor the great sages know My origin, because I am the origin of all Devas and sages also. (10.02)

One who knows Me as the unborn, the beginningless, and the Supreme Lord of the universe, is considered wise among the mortals, and gets liberation from the bondage of Karma. (10.03)

Discrimination, knowledge, non-delusion, forgiveness, truthfulness, control over the mind and senses, pleasure, pain, birth, death, fear, fearlessness; (10.04).

Nonviolence, equanimity, contentment, austerity, charity, fame, and ill fame; all these diverse qualities in human beings arise from Me alone. (10.05)

The seven great sages and four ancient Manus, from whom all these creatures of the world were born, originated from My potential energy. (10.06)

One who truly understands My manifestations and yogic powers, is united with Me in unswerving devotion. There is no doubt about this. (10.07)

I am the origin of all. Everything emanates from Me. Understanding this, the wise ones worship Me with love and devotion. (10.08)

With their minds absorbed in Me, with their lives surrendered unto Me, always enlightening each other by talking about Me; they remain ever content and delighted. (10.09)

I give the knowledge, to those who are ever united with Me and lovingly adore Me, by which they come to Me. (10.10)

Out of compassion for them I, who dwell within their heart, destroy the darkness born of ignorance by the shining lamp of knowledge. (10.11)

Arjuna said: You are the Supreme Brahman, the supreme abode, the supreme purifier, the eternal divine spirit, the primal God, the unborn, and the omnipresent. (10.12)

All sages have thus acclaimed You. The divine sage Narada, Asita, Devala, Vyaasa, and You Yourself tell me. (10.13)

O Krishna, I believe all that You have told Me to be true. O Lord, neither the Devas nor the demons fully understand Your manifestations. (See also 4.06) (10.14)

O Creator and Lord of all beings, God of all gods, Supreme person and Lord of the universe, You alone know Yourself by Yourself. (10.15)

(Therefore), You alone are able to fully describe Your own divine glories, the manifestations, by which You exist pervading all the universe. (10.16)

How may I know You, O Lord, by constant contemplation? In what form (of manifestation) are You to be thought of by me, O Lord? (10.17)

O Lord, explain to me again in detail, Your yogic power and glory; because, I am not satiated by hearing Your nectar-like words. (10.18)

The Supreme Lord said: O Arjuna, now I shall explain to you My prominent divine manifestations, because My manifestations are endless. (10.19)

O Arjuna, I am the Atma abiding in the heart of all beings. I am also the beginning, the middle, and the end of all beings. (10.20)

I am Vishnu among the (twelve) sons of Aditi, I am the radiant sun among the luminaries, I am Marici among the gods of wind, I am the moon among the stars. (10.21)

I am the Sama Veda among the Vedas; I am Indra among the Devas; I am the mind among the senses; I am the consciousness in living beings. (10.22)

I am Shiva among the Rudras; (I am) Kubera among the

Yakshas and demons; I am the fire among the Vasus; and I am Meru among the mountain peaks. (10.23)

Among the priests, O Arjuna, know Me to be the chief, Brihaspati. Among the army generals, I am Skanda; I am the ocean among the bodies of water. (10.24)

I am Bhrigu among the great sages; I am the monosyllable OM among the words; I am Japa among the Yajna; and I am the Himalaya among the immovables. (10.25)

I am the Peepal tree among the trees, Narada among the sages, Chitraaratha among the Gandharvas, and sage Kapila among the Siddhas. (10.26)

Know Me as Uchchaihshrava, born at the time of churning the ocean for getting the nectar, among the horses; Airaavata among the elephants; and the King among men. (10.27)

I am thunderbolt among the weapons, Kaamadhenu among the cows, and the cupid among the procreators. Among the serpents, I am Vaasuki. (10.28)

I am Sheshanaaga among the Naagas, I am Varuna among the water gods, and Aryamaa among the manes. I am Yama among the controllers. (10.29)

I am Prahlaada among Diti's progeny, time or death among the healers, lion among the beasts, and the Garuda among birds. (10.30)

I am the wind among the purifiers, and Lord Rama among the warriors. I am the shark among the fishes, and the Ganges among the rivers. (10.31)

I am the beginning, the middle, and the end of the creation, O Arjuna. Among the knowledge I am knowledge of the supreme Self. I am logic of the logician. (10.32)

I am the letter "A" among the alphabets, among the compound words I am the dual compound, I am the endless time, I am the sustainer of all, and have faces on all sides (or I am omniscient). (10.33)

I am the all-devouring death, and also the origin of future beings. Among the feminine nouns I am fame, prosperity, speech, memory, intellect, resolve, and forgiveness. (10.34)

I am Brihatsaama among the hymns. I am Gaayatri among the mantras, I am Maargsirsha (November-December) among the months, I am the spring among the seasons. (10.35)

I am the fraud of the gambler; I am the splendor of the splendid; I am victory (of the victorious); I am resolution (of the resolute); I am the goodness of the good. (10.36)

I am Vaasudeva among the Vrishni, Arjuna among the Paandavas, Vyaasa among the sages, and Ushanaa among the poets. (10.37)

I am the power of rulers, the statesmanship of the seekers of victory, I am silence among the secrets, and the Self-knowledge of the knowledgeable. (10.38)

I am the origin or seed of all beings, O Arjuna. There is nothing, animate or inanimate, that can exist without Me. (See also 7.10 and 9.18) (10.39)

There is no end of My divine manifestations, O Arjuna. This is only a brief description by Me of the extent of My divine manifestations. (10.40)

Whatever is endowed with glory, brilliance, and power; know that to be a manifestation of a fraction of My splendor. (10.41)

What is the need for this detailed knowledge, O Arjuna? I continually support the entire universe by a small fraction of My energy. (10.42)

Chapter 11: Vision of the Cosmic Form

Arjuna said: My illusion is dispelled by Your profound words, that You spoke out of compassion towards me, about the supreme secret of the Self. (11.01)

O Krishna, I have heard from You in detail about the origin and dissolution of beings, and Your imperishable glory. (11.02)

O Lord, You are as You have said, yet I wish to see Your divine cosmic form, O Supreme Being. (11.03)

O Lord, if You think it is possible for me to see this, then O Lord of the yogis, show me Your imperishable Self. (11.04)

The Supreme Lord said: O Arjuna, behold My hundreds and thousands of multifarious divine forms of different colors and shapes. (11.05)

See the Adityas, the Vasus, the Rudras, the Ashvins, and the Maruts. Behold, O Arjuna, many wonders never seen before. (11.06)

O Arjuna, now behold the entire creation; animate, inanimate, and whatever else you like to see; all at one place in My body. (11.07)

But, you are not able to see Me with your physical eye; therefore, I give you the divine eye to see My majestic power and glory. (11.08)

Sanjaya said: O King, having said this; Lord Krishna, the great Lord of (the mystic power of) yoga, revealed His supreme majestic form to Arjuna. (11.09)

(Arjuna saw the Universal Form of the Lord) with many mouths and eyes, and many visions of marvel, with numerous divine ornaments, and holding divine weapons. (11.10)

Wearing divine garlands and apparel, anointed with celestial perfumes and ointments, full of all wonders, the limitless God with faces on all sides. (11.11)

If the splendor of thousands of suns were to blaze forth all at once in the sky, even that would not resemble the splendor of that exalted being. (11.12)

Arjuna saw the entire universe, divided in many ways, but standing as (all in) One (and One in all) in the body of Krishna, the God of gods. (11.13)

Then Arjuna, filled with wonder and his hairs standing on end, bowed his head to the Lord and prayed with folded hands. (11.14)

Arjuna said: O Lord, I see in Your body all the gods and multitude of beings, all sages, celestial serpents, Lord Shiva as well as Lord Brahmaa seated on the lotus. (11.15)

O Lord of the universe, I see You everywhere with infinite form, with many arms, stomachs, faces, and eyes. Neither do I see the beginning nor the middle nor the end of Your Universal Form. (11.16)

I see You with Your crown, club, discus; and a mass of radiance, difficult to behold, shining all around with immeasurable brilliance of the sun and the blazing fire. (11.17)

I believe You are the imperishable, the Supreme to be realized. You are the ultimate resort of the universe. You are the protector of eternal Dharma, and the imperishable primal spirit. (11.18)

I see You with infinite power, without beginning, middle, or end; with many arms, with the sun and the moon as Your eyes, with Your mouth as a blazing fire whose radiance is scorching all the universe. (11.19)

The entire space between heaven and earth is pervaded by You alone in all directions. Seeing Your marvelous and terrible form, the three worlds are trembling with fear, O Lord. (11.20)

These hosts of demigods enter into You. Some with folded hands sing Your names and glories in fear. A multitude of Maharishis and Siddhas hail and adore You with abundant praises. (11.21)

Rudras, Adityas, Vasus, Saadhyas, Vishwedevas, Ashvins, Maruts, Ushmapas, Gandharvas, Yakshas, Asuras, and Siddhas; they all amazingly gaze at You. (11.22)

Seeing your infinite form with many mouths, eyes, arms, thighs, feet, stomachs, and many fearful teeth; the worlds are trembling with fear and so do I, O mighty Lord. (11.23)

Seeing Your great effulgent and various-colored form touching the sky; Your mouth wide open and large shining eyes; I am frightened and find neither peace nor courage, O Krishna. (11.24)

Seeing Your mouths, with fearful teeth, glowing like fires of cosmic dissolution, I lose my sense of direction and find no comfort. Have mercy on me! O Lord of gods, refuge of the universe. (11.25)

The sons of Dhritaraashtra along with the hosts of kings; Bheeshma, Drona, and Karna together with chief warriors on our side are also quickly entering into Your fearful mouths having terrible teeth. Some are seen caught in between the teeth with their heads crushed. (11.26-27)

As many torrents of the rivers rush toward the ocean, similarly, those warriors of the mortal world are entering Your blazing mouths. (11.28)

As moths rush with great speed into the blazing flame for destruction, similarly all these people are rapidly rushing into Your mouths for destruction. (11.29)

You are licking up all the worlds with Your flaming mouths, swallowing them from all sides. Your powerful radiance is burning the entire universe, and filling it with splendor, O Krishna. (11.30)

Tell me who are You in such a fierce form? My salutations to You, O best of gods, be merciful! I wish to understand You, the primal Being, because I do not know Your mission. (11.31)

The Supreme Lord said: I am death, the mighty destroyer of the world, out to destroy. Even without your participation all the warriors standing arrayed in the opposing armies shall cease to exist. (11.32)

Therefore, you get up and attain glory. Conquer your enemies and enjoy a prosperous kingdom. All these (warriors) have already been destroyed by Me. You are only an instrument, O Arjuna. (11.33)

Kill Drona, Bheeshma, Jayadratha, Karna, and other great warriors who are already killed by Me. Do not fear. You will certainly conquer the enemies in the battle, therefore, fight! (11.34)

Sanjaya said: Having heard these words of Krishna; the crowned Arjuna, trembling with folded hands, prostrated with fear and spoke to Krishna in a choked voice. (11.35)

Arjuna said: Rightly, O Krishna, the world delights and rejoices in glorifying You. Terrified demons flee in all directions. The hosts of Siddhas bow to You in adoration. (11.36)

Why should they not, O great soul, bow to You, the original creator who is even greater than Brahmaa? O infinite Lord, O God of gods, O abode of the universe, You are both Sat and Asat, and the imperishable Brahman that is beyond both (Sat and Asat). (11.37)

You are the primal God, the most ancient Person. You are the ultimate resort of all the universe. You are the knower, the object of knowledge, and the supreme abode. The entire universe is pervaded by You, O Lord of the infinite form. (11.38)

You are Vaayu, Yama, Agni, Varuna, Shashaanka, and Brahmaa as well as the father of Brahmaa. Salutations to You a thousand times, and again and again salutations to You. (11.39)

My salutations to You from front and from behind. O Lord, my obeisances to You from all sides. You are infinite valor and the boundless might. You pervade everything, and therefore You are everywhere and in everything. (11.40)

Considering You merely as a friend, not knowing Your greatness, I have inadvertently addressed You as O Krishna, O Yadava, O friend; merely out of affection or carelessness. (11.41)

In whatever way I may have insulted You in jokes; while playing, reposing in bed, sitting, or at meals; when alone, or in front of others; O Krishna, I implore You for forgiveness. (11.42)

You are the father of this animate and inanimate world, and the greatest guru to be worshipped. No one is even equal to You in the three worlds; how can there be one greater than You? O Being of Incomparable Glory. (11.43)

Therefore, O adorable Lord, I seek Your grace by bowing down and prostrating my body before You. Bear with me as a father to his son, as a friend to a friend, and as a husband to his wife, O Lord. (11.44)

I am delighted by beholding that which has never been seen before, and yet my mind is tormented with fear. Show me that (four-armed) form. O God of gods, the refuge of the universe have mercy! (11.45)

I wish to see You with a crown, holding mace and discus in Your hand. O Lord with thousand arms and universal form, appear in the four-armed form. (11.46)

The Supreme Lord said: O Arjuna, being pleased with you I have shown you, through My own yogic powers, this supreme, shining, universal, infinite, and primal form of Mine that has never been seen before by anyone other than you. (11.47)

Neither by study of the Vedas, nor by Yajna, nor by charity, nor by rituals, nor by severe austerities, can I be seen in the cosmic form in this human world by anyone other than you, O Arjuna. (11.48)

Do not be perturbed and deluded by seeing such a terrible form of Mine as this. With fearless and cheerful mind, now behold My four-armed form. (11.49)

Sanjaya said: Lord Krishna, having thus spoken to Arjuna, revealed His four-armed form. Then assuming His gentle human form, Mahatma Krishna consoled Arjuna who was terrified. (11.50)

Arjuna said: O Krishna, seeing this gentle human form of Yours, I have now become composed and I am normal again. (11.51)

The Supreme Lord said: This (four-armed) form of Mine that you have seen is very difficult, indeed, to see. Even the gods are ever longing to see this form. (11.52)

Neither by study of the Vedas, nor by austerity, nor by charity, nor by ritual, can I be seen in this form as you have seen Me. (11.53)

However, through single-minded devotion alone, I can be seen in this form, can be known in essence, and also can be reached, O Arjuna. (11.54)

The one who does all works for Me, and to whom I am the supreme goal, who is my devotee, who has no attachment, and is free from enmity towards any being attains Me, O Arjuna. (See also 8.22) (11.55)

Chapter 15: Supreme Spirit

The Supreme Lord said: They (or the wise) speak of the eternal Ashvattha tree having its origin above (in unmanifest Brahman) and its branches below (in the cosmos) whose leaves are the (Vedic) hymns. One who understands this is a knower of the Vedas. (15.01)

The branches (of this world tree of Maya) spread below and above (or all over the cosmos). The tree is nourished by the Gunas; sense pleasures are its sprouts; and its roots (of ego and desires) stretch below in the human world causing Karmic bondage. (15.02)

Neither its (real) form nor its beginning, neither its end nor its existence is perceptible here on the earth. Having cut these firm roots of the Ashvattha tree by the mighty ax of (Jnana and) Vairaagya or detachment; (15.03)

The goal (of nirvana) should be sought reaching which one does not come back; thus thinking: In that very primal spirit I take refuge from which this primal manifestation comes forth. (15.04)

Those who are free from pride and delusion, who have conquered the evil of attachment, who are constantly dwelling in the Supreme Self with all Kaama completely stilled, who are free from the dualities known as pleasure and pain; such undeluded persons reach the eternal goal. (15.05)

The sun does not illumine there, nor the moon, nor the fire. That is My supreme abode. Having reached there they do not come back. (15.06)

Atma in the body is My eternal indivisible fragment indeed. Atma gets bound (or attached, and is called Jeevaatma) due to superimposition or association with the six sensory faculties, including the mind, of perception. (15.07)

As the air takes away the aroma from the source (or flower), similarly Atma takes the six sensory faculties from the physical body it casts off (during death) to the (new physical) body it acquires (in reincarnation by the power of Karma). (See also 2.13) (15.08)

The Jeevaatma enjoys sense pleasures with the help of six

sensory faculties: hearing, touch, sight, taste, smell, and mind. (15.09)

The ignorant do not perceive Jeeva departing from the body, or remaining in the body and enjoying sense pleasures by associating with the Gunas. Those with the eye of knowledge can see. (15.10)

The yogis striving (for perfection) behold Atma abiding in their heart; but the ignorant, whose intellect is not pure, do not perceive Him even though striving. (15.11)

The light that coming from the sun illumines the whole world; and which is in the moon, and in the fire; know that light to be Mine. (See also 13.17 and 15.06) (15.12).

Entering the earth I support all beings with My energy; becoming the sap-giving moon I nourish all the plants. (15.13)

Becoming the digestive fire, I remain in the body of all living beings; uniting with vital breaths, the Prana and Apana, I digest all four varieties of food; and (15.14)

I am seated in the hearts of all beings. The memory, knowledge, and the removal of doubts and wrong notions (about the Self) by reasoning or in Samadhi come from Me. I am verily that which is to be known by (the study of) all the Vedas. I am, indeed, the author of the Vedanta and the knower of the Vedas. (See also 6.39) (15.15)

There are two entities in this world: the perishable and the imperishable. (The bodies of) all beings are perishable, and the Atma is imperishable. (15.16)

There is another supreme spirit called Ishvara or Paramaatma, the indestructible Lord who pervades the three worlds and sustains them. (15.17)

I am beyond the perishable body, and higher than the imperishable Atma; therefore, I am known in this world and in the Vedas as Purushottama, or the Supreme Spirit. (15.18)

The wise one, who truly knows Me as the Purushottama, knows everything and worships (or surrenders unto) Me wholeheartedly, O Arjuna. (See also 7.14, 14.26, and 18.66) (15.19)

Thus this most secret science has been explained by Me, O sinless Arjuna. Having understood this, one becomes enlightened and one's all duties are accomplished. (15.20)

Citation and Use

This reading was taken from the following source.

Levin, Noah, ed. "Reality and Time." In SOUTH AND EAST ASIAN PHILOSOPHY READIER, AN OPEN EDUCATIONAL RESOURCE, 116–30. NGE Far Press, 2019.

Notes

1. Jnana-yoga is also called Saamkhya-yoga, Samnyasa-yoga, and yoga of knowledge. A Jnana-yogi does not consider oneself the doer of any action, but only an instrument in the hands of divine for His use. The word Jnana means metaphysical or transcendental knowledge.

2. Yajna means sacrifice, selfless service, unselfish work, Seva, meritorious deeds, giving away something to others, and a religious rite in which oblation is offered to gods through the mouth of fire.

3. Deva means a deity, a demigod, a celestial person, the agent of God, one who fulfills desires and protects.

4. See also 10.14

5. Yoga-Maya is same as Maya; the supernatural, extraordinary, and mystic power of Brahman. The word Maya means unreal, illusory, or deceptive image of the creation. Due to the power of Maya one consider the universe as existent and distinct from Brahman, the Supreme spirit. Brahman is invisible potential energy; Maya is kinetic energy, the force of action. They are inseparable like fire and heat. Maya is a metaphor used to explain the visible world or Jagat to common people.

6. Deep spiritual meaning and interpretation of the practical yogic verses (4.29, 4.30, 5.27, 6.13, 8.10, 8.12, 8.13, 8.24, and 8.25) should be acquired from a Self-realized master of Kriya-yoga.

7. See also 4.38, and 5.06

WE ARE OUR AWARENESS

John Locke

Another context in which the mind compares things [= 'considers things together'] is their very being: when we consider something as existing at a given time and place and compare it with itself existing at another time, we are led to form the ideas of identity and diversity. [In this context 'diversity' means 'nonidentity.' To say that x is diverse from y is to say only that x is not y.] When we see a thing—anything, of whatever sort—to be in a certain place at a certain time, we are sure that it is that very thing and not another thing existing at that time in some other place, however alike the two may be in all other respects. And in this consists identity, when the ideas to which it is attributed do not vary from what they were at the moment of their former existence that we are comparing with the present. We never find—and cannot even conceive of—two things of the same kind existing in the same place at the same time, so we rightly conclude that whatever exists in a certain place at a certain time excludes all others of the same kind, and is there itself alone. So, when we ask whether a thing is 'the same' or not, we are always referring to something that existed at a given time in a given place, a thing that at that instant was certainly the same as itself and not the same as anything else. From this it follows that

- one thing cannot have two beginnings of existence because it is impossible for one thing to be in different places at the same time and
- two things cannot have one beginning, because it is impossible for two things of the same kind to exist in the same instant at the very same place.

Thus, what had one beginning is the same thing; and what had a different beginning in time and place from that is not the same but diverse. The difficulties philosophers have had with this relation of identity have arisen from their not attending carefully to the precise notions of the things to which it is attributed.

We have ideas of only three sorts of substances: God, finite intelligences, and bodies.

1. **God** is without beginning, eternal, unalterable, and everywhere; and so there can be no doubt concerning his identity.
2. Each **finite spirit** had its determinate time and place

of beginning to exist, so its relation to that time and place will always determine its identity for as long as it exists.
3. The same holds for every particle of **matter**, which continues as the same as long as no matter is added to or removed from it. . . .

These three sorts of 'substances' (as we call them) don't exclude one another out of the same place, but we can't conceive any of them allowing another of the same kind into its place. If that were to happen, the notions and names of identity and diversity would be useless, and there would be no way of distinguishing substances or anything else from one another. For example: if two bodies could be in the same place at the same time, then those two portions of matter would be one and the same, whatever their size. Indeed, all bodies would be one and the same, because allowing two bodies to be in one place at one time allows for all bodies to do so. To suppose this to be possible is to obliterate the distinction between identity and diversity, the difference between one and more....

That all concerned the identity of substances. There remain modes and relations, but because they ultimately depend on substances [Locke says they are 'ultimately terminated in substances'], the identity and diversity of each particular one of them will be determined in the same way as the identity of particular substances. Questions of identity and diversity do not arise for things whose existence consists in a sequence of events such as the actions of finite beings, e.g. motion and thought. Because each of these events perishes the moment it begins, they cannot exist at different times or in different places, as enduring things can; and therefore, no motion or thought can be the same as any earlier motion or thought.

There has been much inquiry after the principle of individuation; but what I have said enables us easily to discover what that is: it is existence itself, which ties a being of a given sort to a particular time and place that cannot be shared by any other being of the same kind. This seems easier to conceive in simple substances or modes, but if we are careful we can just as easily apply it to compound ones. Consider an atom, i.e. a continued body under one unchanging surface, existing at a particular time and place: it is evident that at that instant it is the same as itself. For being at that instant what it is and nothing else, it is the same and so must continue as long as its existence is continued; for so long it will be the same and no other. [That sentence is Locke's.] Similarly, if two or more atoms are joined together into a single mass, every one of those atoms will be the same by the foregoing rule. And while they exist united together, the mass whose parts they are must be the same mass, or the same body, however much the parts have been re arranged. But if one atom is removed from the mass, or one new one added, it is no longer the same mass, or the same body. The identity of living creatures depends not on a mass of the same particles but on something else. For in them the variation of large amounts of matter does not alter the identity. An oak growing from a sapling to a great tree, and then lopped, is still the same oak; and a colt grown up to be a horse, sometimes fat, sometimes lean, is the same horse throughout all this. In neither case is there the same mass of matter, though there truly is the same oak, or horse. That is because in these two cases, a mass of matter and a living body, identity is not applied to the same thing.

How, then, does an oak differ from a mass of matter? The answer seems to me to be this: the mass is merely the cohesion of particles of matter anyhow united, whereas the oak is such a disposition of particles as constitutes the parts of an oak, and an organization of those parts that enables the whole to receive and distribute nourishment so as to continue and form the wood, bark, and leaves, etc. of an oak, in which consists the vegetable life. Thus, something is one plant if it has an organization of parts in one cohering body partaking of one common life, and it continues to be the same plant as long as it partakes of the same life, even if that life is passed along to new particles of matter vitally united to the living plant, in a similar continued organization suitable for that sort of plants. This organization is at any one instant in some one collection of matter, which distinguishes it from all others at that instant; and what has the identity that makes the same plant is that individual life, existing constantly from that moment forwards and backwards, in the same continuity of imperceptibly succeeding parts united to the living body of the plant. It also makes all the parts of it be parts of the same plant, for as long as they exist united in that continued organization that is fit to convey that common life to all the parts so united.

The identity of lower animals is sufficiently like that for anyone to be able to see, from what I have said, what makes one animal and continues it the same. It can be illustrated by something similar, namely the identity of machines. What is a watch? Clearly it is nothing, but a construction of parts organized to a certain end—an end that it can attain when sufficient force is applied to it. If we suppose this machine to be one continued body whose parts were repaired, added to, or subtracted from, by a constant addition or separation of imperceptible parts, with one common life, it would be very much like the body of an animal; with

the difference that in an animal the fitness of the organization and the motion wherein life consists begin together, because the motion comes from within; but in a machine the force can be seen to come from outside, and is often lacking even when the machine is in order and well fitted to receive it— for example, when a clock isn't wound up.

This also shows what the identity of the same man consists in, namely: a participation in the same continued life by constantly fleeting particles of matter that are successively vitally united to the same organized body. If you place the identity of man in anything but this, you will find it hard to make an embryo and an adult the same man, or a well man and a madman the same man.

Your only chance of doing this is by tying 'same man' to 'same soul,' but by that standard you will make it possible for Seth, Ismael, Socrates, Pilate, St. Augustine, and Cesare Borgia to be the same man. If identity of soul alone makes the same man, and nothing in the nature of matter rules out an individual spirit's being united to different bodies, it will be possible that those men with their different characters and living at widely different times, may have been the same man! That strange way of using the word 'man' is what one is led to by giving it a meaning from which body and shape are excluded. ...

So unity of substance does not constitute all sorts of identity. To conceive and judge correctly about identity, we must consider what idea the word it is applied to stands for: it is one thing to be the same substance, another the same man, and a third the same person, if 'person', 'man', and 'substance' are names for three different ideas; for such as is the idea belonging to that name, such must be the identity. If this had been more carefully attended to, it might have prevented a great deal of that confusion that often occurs regarding identity, and especially personal identity, to which I now turn after one more section on 'same man.'

An animal is a living organized body; and consequently, the same animal, as I have said, is the same continued life communicated to different particles of matter, as they are successively united to that organized living body. And whatever other definitions are propounded, there should be no doubt that the word 'man' as we use it stands for the idea of an animal of a certain form. The time hallowed definition of 'man' as 'rational animal' is wrong.

If we should see a creature of our own shape and physical constitution, though it had no more reason all its life than a cat or a parrot, we would still call him a man; and anyone who heard a cat or a parrot talk, reason, and philosophize would still think it to be a cat or a parrot and would describe it as such. One of these two is
- a dull, irrational man, the other
- a very intelligent rational parrot.

[Locke then quotes a tediously long traveler's tale about encountering a rational parrot. His point is that someone who believes this account will go thinking of this rational animal as a parrot, not as a man.]

With 'same man' in hand, let us turn to 'same person'. To find what personal identity consists in, we must consider what 'person' stands for.

I think it is a thinking intelligent being, that has reason and reflection, and can consider itself as itself, the same thinking thing at different times and places. What enables it to think of itself is its consciousness, which is inseparable from thinking and (it seems to me) essential to it.

It is impossible for anyone to perceive, without perceiving that he perceives. When we see, hear, smell, taste, feel, meditate, or will anything, we know that we do so. It is always like that with our present sensations and perceptions. And it is through this that everyone is to himself that which he calls 'self, not raising the question of whether the same self is continued in the same substance.

Consciousness always accompanies thinking, and makes everyone to be what he calls 'self' and thereby distinguishes himself from all other thinking things; in this alone consists personal identity, i.e. the sameness of a rational being; and as far as this consciousness can be extended backwards to any past action or thought, so far reaches the identity of that person; it is the same self now that it was then; and this present self that now reflects on it is the one by which that action was performed.

Given that it is the same person, is it the same identical substance? Most people would think that it is the same substance if these perceptions with their consciousness always remained present in the mind, making the same thinking thing always consciously present and (most people would think) evidently the same to itself. What seems to make the difficulty— that is, to make it at least questionable whether the same person must be the same substance— is the following fact.

Consciousness is often interrupted by forgetfulness, and at no moment of our lives do we have the whole sequence of all our past actions before our eyes in one view; even the best memories lose the sight of one part while they are viewing another.

Furthermore, for the greatest part of our lives we don't reflect on our past selves at all, because we are intent on our present thoughts or (in sound sleep) have no thoughts at all, or at least none with the consciousness that characterizes our waking thoughts. In all these cases our consciousness is interrupted, and we lose the sight of our past selves, and so doubts are raised as to whether or not we are the same thinking thing, i.e. the same substance.

That may be a reasonable question, but it has nothing to do with personal identity. For the latter, the question is about what makes the same person, and not whether the same identical substance always thinks in the same person. Different substances might all partake in a single consciousness and thereby be united into one person, just as different bodies can enter into the same life and thereby be united into one animal, whose identity is preserved throughout that change of substances by the unity of the single continued life. What makes a man be himself to himself is sameness of consciousness, so personal identity depends entirely on that—whether the consciousness is tied to one substance throughout or rather is continued in a series of different substances. For as far as any thinking being can repeat the idea of any past action with the same consciousness that he had of it at first, and with the same consciousness he has of his present actions, so far is he the same personal self. For it is by the consciousness he has of his present thoughts and actions that he is self to himself now, and so will be the same self as far as the same consciousness can extend to actions past or to come. Distance of time doesn't make him two or more persons, and nor does change of substance; any more than a man is made to be two men by having a long or short sleep or by changing his clothes.

Our own bodies give us some kind of evidence for this. All the particles of your body, while they are vitally united to a single thinking conscious self—so that you feel when they are touched, and are affected by and conscious of good or harm that happens to them—are a part of yourself, i.e. of your thinking conscious self. Thus, the limbs of his body are to everyone a part of himself; he feels for them and is concerned for them. Cut off a hand and thereby separate it from that consciousness the person had of its heat, cold, and other states, and it is then no longer a part of himself, any more than is the remotest material thing. Thus, we see the substance of which the personal self consisted at one time may be varied at another without change of personal identity; for there is no doubt that it is the same person, even though one of its limbs has been cut off.

But it is asked: Can it be the same person if the substance changes? and Can it be different persons if the same substance does the thinking throughout?

Before I address these questions in sections 13 and 14, there's a preliminary point I want to make. It is that neither question is alive for those who hold that thought is a property of a purely material animal constitution, with no immaterial substance being involved. Whether or not they are right about that, they obviously conceive personal identity as being preserved in something other than identity of substance; just as animal identity is preserved in identity of life, not of substance. This pair of questions does present a challenge to those who hold that only immaterial substances can think, and that sameness of person requires sameness of immaterial substance.

Before they can confront their materialist opponents, they have to show why personal identity can't be preserved through a change of immaterial substances, just as animal identity is preserved through a change of material substances. Unless they say that what makes the same life and thus the animal identity in lower animals is one immaterial spirit, just as (according to them) one immaterial spirit makes the same person in men—and Cartesians at least won't take that way out, for fear of making the lower animals thinking things too.

As to the first question, If the thinking substance is changed, can it be the same person? I answer that this can be settled only by those who know what kind of substances they are that think, and whether the consciousness of past actions can be transferred from one such substance to another.

Admittedly, if the same consciousness were the same individual action, it couldn't be transferred because in that case bringing a past headache (say) into one's consciousness would be bringing back that very headache, and that is tied to the substance to which it occurred. But a present consciousness of a past event isn't like that. Rather it is a present representation of a past action, and we have still to be shown why something can't be represented to the mind as having happened though really it did not. How far the consciousness of past actions is tied to one individual agent, so that another can't possibly have it, will be hard for us to determine until we know what kind of action it is that can't be done without a reflex act of perception accompanying it, and how such an action is done by thinking substances who can't think without being conscious of it. In our present state of knowledge, it is hard to see how it can be impossible, in the nature of things, for an intellectual substance to have represented to it as done by itself something that it never did, and was perhaps done by some other agent.... Until we have a clearer view of the nature of thinking substances, we had better assume that such changes of substance within a single person never do in fact happen, basing this on the goodness of God. Having a concern for the happiness or misery of his creatures, he won't transfer from one substance to another the consciousness that draws reward or punishment with it. ...

The second question, Can it be different persons if the same substance does the thinking throughout? seems to me to arise out of the question of whether the following is possible:

An immaterial being that has been conscious of the events in its past is wholly stripped of all that consciousness, losing it beyond the power of ever retrieving it again; so that now it (as it were) opens a new account, with a new starting date, having a consciousness that can't reach back beyond this new state.

Really, the question is whether if this happened it could be the same person who had first one consciousness and then another, with no possibility of communication between them. [Locke says that this must be regarded as possible by 'those who hold preexistence', that is, who believe in reincarnation. He attacks them, thereby attacking the separation of 'same person' from 'same consciousness', and proposes a thought experiment:] Reflect on yourself, and conclude that you have in yourself an immaterial spirit that is what thinks in you, keeps you the same throughout the constant change of your body, and is what you call 'myself'. Now try to suppose also that it is the same soul that was in Nestor or Thersites at the siege of Troy. This isn't obviously absurd; for souls, as far as we know anything of their nature, can go with any portion of matter as well as with

any other; so the soul or thinking substance that is now yourself may once really have been the soul of someone else, such as Thersites or Nestor. But you don't now have any consciousness of any of the actions either of those two; so can you conceive yourself as being the same person with either of them? Can their actions have anything to do with you? Can you attribute those actions to yourself, or think of them as yours more than the actions of any other men that ever existed? Of course you can't ....

So we can easily conceive of being the same person at the resurrection, though in a body with partly different parts or structure from what one has now, as long as the same consciousness stays with the soul that inhabits the body. But the soul alone, in the change of bodies, would not be accounted enough to make the same man—except by someone who identifies the soul with the man. If the soul of a prince, carrying with it the consciousness of the prince's past life, were to enter and inform the body of a cobbler who has been deserted by his own soul, everyone sees that he would be the same person as the prince, accountable only for the prince's actions; but who would say it was the same man? The body contributes to making the man, and in this case, I should think everyone would let the body settle the 'same man' question, not dissuaded from this by the soul, with all its princely thoughts. To everyone but himself he would be the same cobbler, the same man. I know that in common parlance 'same person' and 'same man' stand for the same thing; and of course everyone will always be free to speak as he pleases, giving words what meanings he thinks fit, and changing them as often as he likes. Still, when we want to explore what makes the same spirit, man, or person, we must fix the ideas of spirit, man, or person in our minds; and when we have become clear about what we mean by them, we shan't find it hard to settle, for each of them, when it is 'the same' and when not.

But although the same immaterial substance or soul does not by itself, in all circumstances, make the same man, it is clear that consciousness unites actions—whether from long ago or from the immediately preceding moment—into the same person. Whatever has the consciousness of present and past actions is the same person to whom they both belong. If my present consciousness that I am now writing were also a consciousness that I saw an overflowing of the Thames last winter and that I saw Noah's ark and the flood, I couldn't doubt that I who write this now am the same self that saw the Thames overflowed last winter and viewed the flood at the general deluge—place that self in what substance you please. I could no more doubt this than I can doubt that I who write this am the same myself now while I write as I was yesterday, whether or not I consist of all the same substance, material or immaterial. For sameness of substance is irrelevant to sameness of self: I am as much involved in—and as justly accountable for— an action that was done a thousand years ago and is appropriated to me now by this self-consciousness as I am for what I did a moment ago.

Self is that conscious thinking thing that feels or is conscious of pleasure and pain and capable of happiness or misery, and so is concerned for itself as far as that consciousness extends. (This holds true whatever substance the thinking thing is made up of; it doesn't matter whether it is spiritual or material, simple or compounded.) You must find that while your little finger is brought under your consciousness it is as much a part of yourself as is your head or your heart. If the finger were amputated and this consciousness went along with it, deserting the rest of the body, it is evident that the little finger would then be the person, the same person; and this self would then would have nothing to do with the rest of the body. As with spatial separation so also with temporal: something with which the consciousness of this present thinking thing can join itself makes the same person, and is one self with it, as everyone who reflects will perceive.

Personal identity is the basis for all the right and justice of reward and punishment. What everyone is concerned for, for himself, is happiness and misery—with no concern for what becomes of any substance that isn't connected with that consciousness. [Locke goes on to apply that to his 'finger' example, supposing that the finger takes the original consciousness with it, and that the rest of the body acquires a new consciousness.]

This illustrates my thesis that personal identity consists not in the identity of substance but in the identity of consciousness. If Socrates and the present mayor of Queenborough agree in that, they are the same person; if Socrates awake doesn't partake of the same consciousness as Socrates sleeping, they aren't the same person. And to punish Socrates awake for something done by sleeping Socrates without Socrates awake ever being conscious of it would be as unjust as to punish someone for an action of his twin brother's merely because their outsides were so alike that they couldn't be distinguished.

It may be objected: 'Suppose I wholly lose the memory of some parts of my life beyond any possibility of retrieving them, so that I shall never be conscious of them again; aren't I still the same person who did those actions, had those thoughts that I once was conscious of, even though I have now forgotten them?' To this I answer that we must be careful about what the word 'I' is applied to. This objector is thinking of sameness of the man, and calls it 'I' because he assumes that the same man is the same person. But the assumption isn't necessarily correct . If one man could have distinct disconnected consciousnesses at different times, that same man would certainly make different persons at different times. That this is what people in general think can be seen in the most solemn declaration of their opinions: human laws don't punish the madman for the sane man's actions, or the sane man for what the madman did, because they treat them as two persons. This is reflected in common speech when we say that someone is 'not himself or is 'beside himself'. Those phrases insinuate that the speaker thinks—or that those who coined the phrases thought—that the self was changed, the self-same person was no longer in that man.

'It is still hard to conceive that Socrates, the same individual man, might be two persons.' To help us with this we must consider what is meant by 'Socrates', or 'the same individual man'. There are three options . The same man might be any of these:
- the same individual, immaterial, thinking substance; in short, the numerically same soul and nothing else,
- the same animal, without any regard to an immaterial soul,
- the same immaterial spirit united to the same animal.

Help yourself! On any of these accounts of 'same man', it is impossible for personal identity to consist in anything but consciousness, or reach any further than that does. According to 1, a man born of different women, and in distant times, might still be the same man. Anyone who allows this must also allow that the same man could be two distinct persons. . . . According to 2 and 3, Socrates in this life cannot be the same man as anyone in the afterlife. The only way to do this— allowing for the possibility that Socrates in Athens and Socrates in Limbo are the same man— is through an appeal to sameness of consciousness; and that amounts to equating human identity— 'same man'— with personal identity. But that equation is problematic, because it makes it hard to see how the infant Socrates can be the same man as Socrates after the resurrection. There seems to be little agreement about what makes a man, and thus about what makes the same individual man; but whatever we think about that, if we are not to fall into great absurdities we must agree that sameness of person resides in consciousness.

You may want to object: 'But isn't a man drunk and sober the same person? Why else is he punished for what he does when drunk, even if he is never afterwards conscious of it? He is just as much a single person as a man who walks in his sleep and is answerable, while awake, for any harm he did in his sleep.' Here is my reply to that . Human laws punish both, with a justice suitable to the state of knowledge of those who administer the law: in these cases they can't distinguish for sure what is real from what is counterfeit; and so they don't allow the ignorance in drunkenness or sleep as a plea. Granted: punishment is tied to personhood, which is tied to consciousness, and the drunkard may not be conscious of what he did; but the courts justly punish him, because his bad actions are proved against him, and his lack of consciousness of them can't be proved for him. It may be reasonable to think that on the great day when the secrets of all hearts are laid open, nobody will be held accountable for actions of which he knows nothing; everybody will receive his sentence with his conscience agreeing with God's judgment by accusing or excusing him.

Nothing but consciousness can unite remote existences into the same person. The identity of substance won't do it. For whatever substance there is, and whatever it is like, without consciousness there is no person. A substance without consciousness can no more be a person that a carcass can.

[In the remainder of this section, and in section 24. Locke discusses possible cases: two persons who take turns in animating one animal body ('the night man and the day man'); and one person who alternately animates two different animal bodies. The central emphasis throughout is on the uselessness in these questions of the concept of the same immaterial substance.]

I agree that on the question of contingent fact the more probable opinion is that this consciousness is tied to, and is a state of, a single immaterial substance. Please yourself about that. However, every thinking being that can experience happiness or misery must grant that there is something, himself, that he is concerned for and wants to be happy; and that this self has existed continuously for a period of time and therefore may exist for months and years to come, with no set limit to its duration, and thus may be the same self, carried by consciousness into the future. It is through this consciousness that he finds himself to be the same self that acted thus and so some years ago and through which he is happy or miserable now. In all these thoughts we place sameness of self in sameness not of substance but of consciousness. Substances might come and go through the duration of such a consciousness; and for as long as a substance is in a vital union with the thing containing this consciousness it is a part of that same self. Thus, any part of my body, while vitally united to that which is conscious in me, is a part of myself (for example my little finger, while it relates to me in such a way that if it is damaged I feel pain); but when the vital union is broken, what was a part of myself a moment ago is now not so, any more than a part of another man's self is a part of me. [The rest of the section illustrates and repeats this line of thought.]

'Person', I take it, is the name for this self. Wherever you find what you call 'myself, anyone else may say there is 'the same person'. 'Person' is a forensic term [= 'a term designed for use in legal proceedings'], having to do with actions and their merit; and so it applies only to active thinking beings that are capable of a law, and of happiness and misery. It is only through consciousness that this personality [Locke's word] extends itself beyond present existence to what is past, becoming concerned and accountable; the person owns and attributes past actions to itself for the same reason that it does the present. All this is founded in a concern for happiness, which unavoidably accompanies consciousness— something that is conscious of pleasure and pain desires that the self that is conscious should be happy. As for past actions that the self cannot through consciousness square with or join to the present self—it can no more be concerned with them than if they had never been done. To receive pleasure or pain, i.e. reward or punishment, on account of any such action is all of a piece with being born happy or miserable, without any merit or demerit at all. Suppose a man were punished now for what

he had done in another life of which he cannot have any consciousness, how does that so-called punishment differ from simply being created miserable?

In treating this subject I have considered as perhaps possible some states of affairs— e.g. the one about the prince and the cobbler— that will look strange to some readers, and perhaps are strange. But I think they are permissible, given our ignorance about the nature of the thinking thing in us which we look on as ourselves. If we knew with regard to this thinking thing what it is, or how it is tied to a certain system of fleeting animal spirits [see note in viii.12], or whether or not it can perform its operations of thinking and memory outside of a body organized as ours is, and whether God has decided that every such spirit or thinking thing shall be united to only one such body, with its memory depending on the health of that body's organs, we might see the absurdity of some of the cases I considered. But as we are in the dark about these matters, we ordinarily think of the thinking thing or soul of a man as an immaterial substance, owing nothing to matter and compatible with any kind of matter; and on that basis there cannot from the nature of things be any absurdity in supposing that the same soul might at different times be united to different bodies, making one man with each of them for as long as they were united....

To conclude: any substance that begins to exist must during its existence necessarily be the same; any complex of substances that begins to exist must during the existence of its component parts be the same; any mode that begins to exist is throughout its existence the same. . . . It appears from this that the difficulty or obscurity that people have found in this matter has arisen from the poor use of words rather than from any obscurity in things themselves. For whatever makes the specific idea to which the name is applied, if we steadily keep to that idea it will be easy for us to distinguish same and different, with no doubts arising. I defend this in the next, final section .

Suppose we take a man to be a rational spirit, then it is easy to know what is the same man, namely the same spirit—whether or not it is embodied. Suppose our idea of a man is a rational spirit vitally united to a body with a certain structure; then such a rational spirit will be the same man as long as it is united to such a body, though it needn't be the same body throughout. If anyone's idea of a man is that of the vital union of parts in a certain shape [here = 'structure'], as long as that vital union and shape remain in a compound body, remaining the same except for a turnover in its constituent particles, it will be the same man. For the complex idea we use when classifying a thing as being of a certain kind also determines what it is for a thing of that kind to continue in existence.

Citation and Use

The text was taken from the following work.

Locke, John. AN ESSAY CONCERNING HUMANE UNDERSTANDING, VOLUME 2. Project Gutenberg, 1694. https://www.gutenberg.org/ebooks/10616.

ETHICS

THE RING OF GYGES

Plato

With these words I [Socrates] thought myself released from talking, but it seems it was only a prelude, since Glaukon,[1] who is always most brave about everything, did not accept Thrasymachos' withdrawal but said, "Socrates, do you want to seem to have persuaded us, or truly persuade us, that justice is better than injustice in every respect?"

"I would prefer truly," I said, "if it were in my power."

"Well you aren't doing what you want," he said. "Tell me, do you think there is the following kind of good, which we are pleased to possess not because we desire its consequences, but which we welcome for its own sake, such as pleasant experiences and pleasures that are harmless and give rise to nothing else subsequently besides the pleasure of having them?"

"I certainly do think there is this kind of good," I said.

"And what about a kind that we love both in its own right and for what comes from it, such as thinking and seeing and being healthy? We welcome such things for both reasons, I suppose."

"Yes," I said.

"And do you see some third kind of good," he said, "which includes exercise and medical treatment when sick and medical practice and other forms of money-making, since we say these things are laborious and yet beneficial for us, and we don't want to have them for their own sakes, but for the sake of the wages and various other things that come from them."

"There is indeed this third kind," I said. "But what of it?"

"Into which of these would you put justice?" he said.

"I think," I said, "into the most fine, the one that is loved, by the person who intends to be blessed, for itself and for what comes from it."

"That's not where most people put it," he said, "but in the laborious class, which must be practiced for the sake of

wages and the standing that comes from reputation, but which itself should be avoided because difficult."

"I know it's thought of this way," I said, "and Thrasymachos has been finding fault with it on such grounds for a long time, and praising injustice. It seems I am somewhat slow to learn."

"Come then," he said, "listen to me and see if it still seems so to you. For Thrasymachos appears to me to have been soothed by you, like a snake, earlier than he should. For me, the presentation on each of them was somewhat unsatisfactory and I still want to hear what each of them is and what effect each of them has, just by itself, on the soul, putting aside the wages and the things that come from them."

"So this is what I will do, if it seems okay to you. I will revive Thrasymachos' argument, first, by describing what kind of thing people say justice is and where it comes from, and second, how everyone who practices it does so unwilling, as a necessity rather than as a good, and, third, how they do so reasonably, since the life of the unjust man is far better than the life of the just man, or so they say."

"It doesn't seem this way to me at all, Socrates, but my ears have been drenched by listening to Thrasymachos and countless others and I am at a loss. I haven't quite heard from anyone concerning the account of justice, that it is better than injustice, to my satisfaction. I want to hear it celebrated just by itself, and I think I will hear that from you most of all. That's why I will speak positively, step by step, about the unjust life, showing you the way I want to hear you disparage injustice and praise justice. But see if what I propose is agreeable."

"More than anything," I said. "What else is there that an intelligent person would appreciate talking and hearing about more often?"

"Beautifully put," he said. "And so listen to what I said would be first, what justice is and where it comes from."

"They say that committing injustice is by nature good,

while suffering it is bad, but the greater evil of suffering it outstrips the benefit of doing it, so that when they commit and suffer injustice at each other's hands, and have experienced both, to those who are unable to escape the one and choose the other it seems profitable to promise one another to neither commit injustice or suffer it. And that's when they begin to make their laws and contracts between one another, and they name what is commanded by law "lawful" and "just"."

"This is the origin and nature of justice, midway between what's best—to do injustice without repaying with justice—and the worst—to be done injustice without the power to avenge it. Justice is in the middle of these both, endorsed not as something good but as worthwhile, due to the inability to commit injustice. And so the person who has the power to do this and is a truly a man would never make even a single agreement not to do injustice nor suffer it; he would be mad. And this, in sum, Socrates, is the nature of justice, and it is of this kind, and it naturally arises from these things, according to this account."

"That even those who practice it do so unwilling, from a lack of power to commit injustice, we can see especially if we imagine something like this: give each man, both the just and the unjust man, the freedom to do whatever he likes, and then follow them to see where the desire of each one will lead. We would catch the just man in the act, going after the same things as the unjust, due to the desire to get ahead, which every natural thing inherently pursues as good, though it is led astray by the force of law to the honor of equality."

"The freedom of which I speak would be illustrated especially if they were ever to acquire the power that they say befell the ancestor of Gyges the Lydian. He was working as a shepherd for the then-ruler of Lydia, when there was a great thunderstorm and an earthquake cracked open a part of the ground and a chasm opened up where he had been shepherding. He was amazed at the sight and went down into it and he saw, among many other marvelous objects from mythology, a bronze bull, hollow, with windows. And when he peeked inside he saw a corpse, which seemed of superhuman size, with nothing else on but a gold ring on its hand, which he removed, and he went out."

"The usual meeting of the shepherds was taking place, in order to make the monthly report to the king about the flocks, and he went, wearing the ring. Sitting there with the others, it so happened that he turned the socket for the gem towards him, into the palm of his hand, and when he did this, he became invisible to those sitting around him, and they spoke about him as though he had departed. He was amazed and feeling again for the ring he turned the socket to the outside, and when he did so he became visible. Taking note of this, he tested the ring to see if it had this power and in this way came to this conclusion, that, with the socket turned to the inside he became invisible, while turned to the outside he was visible."

"Perceiving this, he immediately managed to get himself appointed as one of the messengers to the king, and when he went he seduced his wife and with her help set upon the king and killed him. In this way he took possession of the throne."

"Now if there were two such rings and one was given to the just man and one to the unjust, we would see that there was no one who would be so strong of character to stick with justice and have the resolve to stay away from the goods of others and not take them, when he is able to take whatever he wants from the market without fear, and could enter any house and have sex with whomever he wanted, and could kill, or release from bonds, anyone he wants, and anything else, since among men he is equal to a god. Acting in this way, he would be no different from the other, and they would both go after the same things."

"This is strong evidence, someone might surely say, that no one is just willingly but by necessity. It's not something good for the individual, since whenever someone believes he will be able to do injustice, he does it. Every man thinks that injustice is much more profitable than justice, and rightly so, or so someone giving this account would say, since if someone possessed this kind of power and did not then want to commit injustice or to take the goods of others, those who were aware of it would think him extremely pitiful and stupid, though they would praise him as the opposite to one another, persuading one another for fear of suffering injustice. And that's how it is, on this matter."

"In deciding between the two lives we were talking about, we will be able to make a correct decision if we juxtapose the most just man with the most unjust, and only if we do this. What, then, is this juxtaposition? This: we must take away nothing of injustice from the unjust man and nothing of justice from the just man, but will make each of them perfect in his particular practice."

"First, then, let the unjust man act just like clever craftsmen, such as a top-class captain or doctor. He is well aware of what is impossible and what is possible in his craft, and attempts the latter and lets the former go. If he nonetheless stumbles in some way, he is sufficient to recover himself. In the same way, let the unjust man, attempting his unjust deeds, get away with them, since he must be exceedingly unjust. The person who is caught must be thought a poor specimen, since ultimate injustice is to appear just without being just. To the completely unjust man must be given the most perfect injustice. Nothing must be taken away, and it must be granted that he does the greatest injustices while having the greatest reputation for justice. And that, if he lets something slip, he corrects it, both by the force of his speech, which is sufficiently persuasive, if any of his unjust acts are revealed, and by force, wherever force is needed, since he is bold and strong and has friends and wealth."

"Having set up the first one like this, we must in turn, according to our argument, set up the just man beside him, a simple and noble man, who wants, as Aeschylos[2] says, not only to appear good but to be good. And yet the appearance must be taken away, because if he appears just, he will receive awards and gifts by appearing this way and so it would be unclear whether he was like this for the sake of justice or for the sake of the awards and gifts. He must be stripped bare of everything except justice and must be made the exact opposite of the previous character. Let him have the greatest reputation for injustice, even though he does no wrong, so that he proves his justice by not being weakened by ill-repute and what comes with it. Let him carry on like this without changing until death, appearing unjust throughout life but being just, so that, with both having arrived at the ultimate state, the one of justice, the other of injustice, we can judge which of the two is happier."

"Wow!" I said. "My dear Glaukon! How thoroughly you have scoured clean each of the men, like statues, for the judgment!"

"As much as I can," he said. "And with these two in this state, there'll be no further difficulty filling out the account with the kind of life that awaits each of them. So, allow me to tell it. And if I speak crudely, don't think that it is I who is speaking, Socrates, but those who praise injustice ahead of justice. They will say the following things: that in this condition the just man will be whipped, stretched on the rack, tied up in bonds, his eyes burnt out, and at the end, when he has undergone every evil, he will be impaled, and

will realize that he should want to appear just rather than be just."

"And the saying of Aeschylos is in reality much more applicable to the unjust man, for they say of the unjust man that he really does not wish to appear unjust but to be it, because he is devoted to deeds based on reality and does not live for appearances, "Reaping a deep furrow of the mind, From which wise plans shoot forth". First, he governs the city because he is thought to be just, and next, he marries from whatever class he wants and marries his children to whomever he wants, and makes contracts and partnerships with whomever he likes, and that he benefits from all of this, profiting because he is untroubled by acting unjustly. When he enters into contests, whether in private or public, he is successful and out-does those he hates, and by out-doing them he grows wealthy and does good things for his friends and harms his enemies. And he makes sacrifices and sets up offerings to the gods that are abundant and magnificent, and attends to the gods and to the humans he favors far better than the just man does, so that he is also more worthy to enjoy the favor of the gods more than the just man, in all probability."

"In this way, Socrates, they say that the unjust man is provided with a better life than the just man, both from the gods and from men."

Questions for Discussion

1. If you were to obtain the ring, what would you really do? Consider both the first week as well as 5 years from now.

2. Does this account by Glaucon explain why most people act justly? Is this true for you and those you know?

3. What are the merits and problems with the claim that the unjust should remain unjust and the just should remain just?

4. Can we speak of justice and injustice apart from society?

5. Is Glaucon's account of human nature and origins of society a helpful or unhelpful model?

Citation and Use

Woods, Cathal, Glaukon's Challenge (Republic 2) (August 19, 2010). Available at
   SSRN: https://ssrn.com/abstract=1661519 or http://dx.doi.org/10.2139/ssrn.1661519

Notes

1. Glaucon is another acceptable spelling of the name.
2. or Aeschylus

JEALOUSY: CAUSES AND A POSSIBLE CURE

Emma Goldman

No one at all capable of an intense conscious inner life need ever hope to escape mental anguish and suffering. Sorrow and often despair over the so-called eternal fitness of things are the most persistent companions of our life. But they do not come upon us from the outside, through the evil deeds of particularly evil people. They are conditioned in our very being; indeed, they are interwoven through a thousand tender and coarse threads with our existence.

It is absolutely necessary that we realize this fact, because people who never get away from the notion that their misfortune is due to the wickedness of their fellows never can outgrow the petty hatred and malice which constantly blames, condemns, and hounds others for something that is inevitable as part of themselves. Such people will not rise to the lofty heights of the true humanitarian to whom good and evil, moral and immoral, are but limited terms for the inner play of human emotions upon the human sea of life.

The "beyond good and evil" philosopher, Nietzsche, is at present denounced as the perpetrator of national hatred and machine gun destruction; but only bad readers and bad pupils interpret him so. "Beyond good and evil" means beyond prosecution, beyond judging, beyond killing, etc. *Beyond Good and Evil* opens before our eyes a vista the background of which is individual assertion combined with the understanding of all others who are unlike ourselves, who are different.

By that I do not mean the clumsy attempt of democracy to regular the complexities of human character by means of external equality. The vision of "beyond good and evil" points to the right to oneself, to one's personality. Such possibilities do not exclude pain over the chaos of life, but they do exclude the puritanic righteousness that sits in judgment on all others except oneself.

It is self-evident that the thoroughgoing radical — there are many half-baked ones, you know — must apply this deep, humane recognition to the sex and love relation. Sex emotions and love are among the most intimate, the most intense and sensitive, expressions of our being. They are so deeply related to individual physical and psychic traits as to stamp each love affair an independent affair, unlike any other love affair. In other words, each love is the result of the impressions and characteristics the two people involved give to it. Every love relation should by its very nature remain an absolutely private affair. Neither the State, the Church, morality, or people should meddle with it.

Unfortunately this is not the case. The most intimate relation is subject to proscriptions, regulations, and coercions, yet these external factors are absolutely alien to love, and as such lead to everlasting contradictions and conflict between love and law.

The result of it is that our love life is merged into corruption and degradation. "Pure love," so much hailed by the poets, is in the present matrimonial, divorce, and alienation wrangles, a rare specimen indeed. With money, social standing, and position as the criteria for love, prostitution is quite inevitable, even if it be covered with the mantle of legitimacy and morality.

The most prevalent evil of our mutilated love-life is jealousy, often described as the "green-eyed monster" who lies, cheats, betrays, and kills. The popular notion is that jealousy is inborn and therefore can never be eradicated from the human heart. This idea is a convenient excuse for those who lack ability and willingness to delve into cause and effect.

Anguish over a lost love, over the broken thread of love's continuity, is indeed inherent in our very beings. Emotional sorrow has inspired many sublime lyrics, much profound insight and poetic exultation of a Byron, Shelley, Heine, and their kind. But will anyone compare this grief with what commonly passes as jealousy? They are as unlike as wisdom and stupidity. As refinement and coarseness. As dignity and brutal coercion. Jealousy is the very reverse of understanding, of sympathy, and of generous feeling. Never has jealousy added to character, never does it make the individual big and fine. What it really does is to make him blind with fury, petty with suspicion, and harsh with envy.

Jealousy, the contortions of which we see in the matrimonial tragedies and comedies, is invariably a one-sided, bigoted accuser, convinced of his own righteousness and the meanness, cruelty, and guilt of his victim. Jealousy does not even attempt to understand. Its one desire is to punish, and to punish as severely as possible. This notion is embodied in the code of honor, as represented in dueling or the unwritten law. A code which will have it that the seduction of a woman must be atoned with the death of the seducer. Even where seduction has not taken place, where both have voluntarily yielded to the innermost urge, honor is restored only when blood has been shed, either that of the man or the woman.

Jealousy is obsessed by the sense of possession and vengeance. It is quite in accord with all other punitive laws upon the statutes which still adhere to the barbarous notion that an offence, often merely the result of social wrongs, must be adequately punished or revenged.

A very strong argument against jealousy is to be found in the data of historians like Morgan, Reclus, and others, as to the sex relations among primitive people. Anyone at all conversant with their works knows that monogamy is a much later sex from which came into being as a result of the domestication and ownership of women, and which created sex monopoly and the inevitable feeling of jealousy.

In the past, when men and women intermingled freely without interference of law and morality, there could be no jealousy, because the latter rests upon the assumption that a certain man has an exclusive sex monopoly over a certain woman and *vice-versa*. The moment anyone dates to trespass this sacred precept, jealousy is up in arms. Under such circumstances it is ridiculous to say that jealousy is perfectly natural. As a matter of fact, it is the artificial result of an artificial cause, nothing else.

Unfortunately, it is not only conservative marriages which are saturated with the notion of sex monopoly; the so-called free unions are also victims of it. The argument may be raised that this is one more proof that jealousy is an inborn trait. But it must be borne in mind that sex monopoly has been handed down from generation to generation as a sacred right and the basis of purity of the family and the home. And just as the Church and the State accepted sex monopoly as the only security to the marriage tie, so have both justified jealousy as the legitimate weapon of defense for the protection of the property right.

Now, while it is true that a great many people have outgrown the legality of sex monopoly, they have not outgrown its traditions and habits. Therefore they become as blinded by the "green-eyed monster" as their conservative neighbors the moment their possessions are at stake.

A man or woman free and big enough not to interfere or fuss over the outside attractions of the loved one is sure to be despised by his conservative, and ridiculed by his radical, friends. He will either be decried as a degenerate or a coward; often enough some petty material motives will be imputed to him. In any even, such men and women will be the target of coarse gossip or filthy jokes for no other reason than that they concede to wife, husband or lovers the right to their own bodies and their emotional expression, without making jealous scenes or wild threats to kill the intruder.

There are other factors in jealousy: the conceit of the male and the envy of the female. The male in matters sexual is an imposter, a braggart, who forever boasts of his exploits and success with women. He insists on playing the part of a conqueror, since he has been told that women want to be conquered, that they love to be seduced. Feeling himself the only cock in the barnyard, or the bull who must clash horns in order to win the cow, he feels mortally wounded in his conceit and arrogance the moment a rival appears on the scene — the scene, even among so-called refined men, continues to be woman's sex love, which must belong to only one master.

In other words, the endangered sex monopoly together with man's outraged vanity in ninety-nine cases out of a hundred are the antecedents of jealousy.

In the case of a woman, economic fear for herself and children and her petty envy of every other woman who gains grace in the eyes of her supporter invariably create jealousy. In justice to women be it said that for centuries past, physical attraction was her only stock in trade, therefore she must needs become envious of the charm and value of other women as threatening her hold upon her precious property.

The grotesque aspect of the whole matter is that men and women often grow violently jealous of those they really do not care much about. It is therefore not their outraged love, but their outraged conceit and envy which cry out against this "terrible wrong." Likely as not the woman never loved the man whom she now suspects and spies upon. Likely as not she never made an effort to keep his love. But the moment a competitor arrives, she begins to value her sex property for the defense of which no means are too despicable or cruel.

Obviously, then, jealousy is not the result of love. In fact, if it were possible to investigate most cases of jealousy, it would likely be found that the less people are imbued with a great love the more violent and contemptible is their jealousy. Two people bound by inner harmony and oneness are not afraid to impair their mutual confidence and security if one or the other has outside attractions, nor will their relations end in vile enmity, as is too often the case with many people. They many not be able, nor ought they to be expected, to receive the choice of the loved one into the intimacy of their lives, but that does not give either one the right to deny the necessity of the attraction.

As I shall discuss variety and monogamy two weeks from tonight, I will not dwell upon either here, except to say that to look upon people who can love more than one person as perverse or abnormal is to be very ignorant indeed. I have already discussed a number of causes for jealousy to which I must add the institution of marriage which the State and Church proclaim as "the bond until death doth part." This is accepted as the ethical mode of right living and right doing.

With love, in all its variability and changeability, fettered and cramped, it is small wonder if jealousy arises out of it. What else but pettiness, meanness, suspicion, and rancor can come when a man and wife are officially held together with the formula "from now on you are one in body and spirit." Just take any couple tied together in such a manner, dependent upon each other for every thought and feeling, without an outside interest or desire, and ask yourself whether such a relation must not become hateful and unbearable in time.

In some form or other the fetters are broken, and as the circumstances which bring this about are usually low and degrading, it is hardly surprising that they bring into play the shabbiest and meanest human traits and motives.

In other words, legal, religious, and moral interference are the parents of our present unnatural love and sex life, and out of it jealousy has grown. It is the lash which whips and tortures poor mortals because of their stupidity, ignorance, and prejudice.

But no one need attempt to justify himself on the ground of being a victim of these conditions. It is only too true that we all smart under the burdens of iniquitous social arrangements, under coercion and moral blindness. But are we not conscious individuals, whose aim it is to bring truth and justice into human affairs? The theory that man is a product of conditions has led only to indifference and to a sluggish acquiescence in these conditions. Yet everyone knows that adaptation to an unhealthy and unjust mode of life only strengthens both, while man, the so-called crown of all creation, equipped with a capacity to think and see and above all to employ his powers of initiative, grows ever weaker, more passive, more fatalistic.

There is nothing more terrible and fatal than to dig into the vitals of one's loved ones and oneself. It can only help to tear whatever slender threads of affection still inhere in the relation and finally bring us to the last ditch, which jealousy attempts to prevent, namely, the annihilation of love, friendship and respect.

Jealousy is indeed a poor medium to secure love, but it is a secure medium to destroy one's self-respect. For jealous people, like dope-fiends, stoop to the lowest level and in the end inspire only disgust and loathing.

Anguish over the loss of love or a nonreciprocated love among people who are capable of high and fine thoughts will never make a person coarse. Those who are sensitive and fine have only to ask themselves whether they can tolerate any obligatory relation, and an emphatic *no* would be the reply. But most people continue to live near each other although they have long ceased to live with each other — a life fertile enough for the operation of jealousy, whose methods go all the way from opening private correspondence to murder. Compared with such horrors, open adultery seems an act of courage and liberation.

A strong shield against the vulgarity of jealousy is that man and wife are not of one body and one spirit. They are two human beings, of different temperament, feelings, and emotions. Each is a small cosmos in himself, engrossed in his own thoughts and ideas. It is glorious and poetic if these two worlds meet in freedom and equality. Even if this lasts but a short time it is already worthwhile. But, the moment the two worlds are forced together all the beauty and fragrance ceases and nothing but dead leaves remain. Whoever grasps this truism will consider jealousy beneath him and will not permit it to hang as a sword of Damocles over him.

All lovers do well to leave the doors of their love wide open. When love can go and come without fear of meeting a watch-dog, jealousy will rarely take root because it will soon learn that where there are no locks and keys there is no place for suspicion and distrust, two elements upon which jealousy thrives and prospers.

Citation and Use

The reading was taken from the following work.

Emma Goldman. "TJealousy: Causes and a Possible Cure." The Anarchist Library, 2009. https://thean-
    archistlibrary.org/library/emma-goldman-jealousy-causes-and-a-possible-cure.

THE SIMPLE AND HAPPY LIFE

Epicurus

Epicurus to Menoeceus: Greetings.

Let no one delay to philosophize while he is young nor weary in philosophizing when he is old, for no one is either short of the age or past the age for enjoying health of the soul. And the man who says the time for philosophizing has not yet come or is already past may be compared to the man who says the time for happiness is not yet come or is already gone by. So both the young man and the old man should philosophize, the former that while growing old he may be young in blessings because of gratitude for what has been, the latter that he may be young and old at the same time because of the fearlessness with which he faces the future. Therefore the wise plan is to practice the things that make for happiness, since possessing happiness we have everything and not possessing it we do everything to have it.

THE GODS

Both practice and study the precepts which I continuously urged upon you, discerning these to be the A B C's of the good life. First of all, believing the divine being to be blessed and incorruptible, just as the universal idea of it is outlined in our minds, associate nothing with it that is incompatible with incorruption or alien to blessedness. And cultivate every thought concerning it that can preserve its blessedness along with incorruption. Because there are gods, for the knowledge of them is plain to see. They are not, however, such as many suppose them to be, for people do not keep their accounts of them consistent with their beliefs. And it is not the man who would abolish the gods of the multitude who is impious but the man who associates the beliefs of the multitude with the gods; for the pronouncements of the multitude concerning the gods are not innate ideas but false assumptions. According to their stories the greatest injuries and indignities are said to be inflicted upon evil men, and also benefits.

THE GODS INDIFFERENT TO WICKEDNESS

[These stories are false, because the gods], being exclusively devoted to virtues that become themselves, feel an affinity for those like themselves and regard all that is not of this kind as alien.

DEATH

Habituate yourself to the belief that death is nothing to us, because all good and evil lies in consciousness and death is the loss of consciousness. Hence a right understanding of the fact that death is nothing to us renders enjoyable the mortality of life, not by adding infinite time but by taking away the yearning for immortality, for there is nothing to be feared while living by the man who has genuinely grasped the idea that there is nothing to be feared when not living.

So the man is silly who says that he fears death, not because it will pain him when it comes, but because it pains him in prospect; for nothing that occasions no trouble when present has any right to pain us in anticipation. Therefore death, the most frightening of evils, is nothing to us, for the excellent reason that while we live it is not here and when it is here we are not living. So it is nothing either to the living or to the dead, because it is of no concern to the living and the dead are no longer.

THE INCONSISTENCY OF PEOPLE

But the multitude of men at one time shun death as the greatest of evils and at another choose death as an escape from the evils of life. The wise man, however, neither asks quarter of life nor has he any fear of not living, for he has no fault to find with life nor does he think it any evil to be out of it. Just as in the case of food, he does not always choose the largest portion but rather the most enjoyable; so with time, he does not pick the longest span of it but the most enjoyable.

And the one who bids the young man 'Live well' and the old man 'Die well' is simple-minded, not only because of the pleasure of being alive, but also for the reason that the art of living well and dying well is one and the same. And far worse is he who says: 'It were well never to have been born or having been born to have passed with all speed through the gates of Hades.' For if he is saying this out of conviction, why does he not take leave of life? Because this course is open to him if he has resolutely made up his mind to it. But if he is speaking in mockery, he is trifling in the case of things that do not countenance trifling.

THE FUTURE

As for the future, we must bear in mind that it is not quite beyond our control nor yet quite within our control, so that we must neither await it as going to be quite within our control nor despair of it as going to be quite beyond our control.

THE DESIRES

As for the desires, we should reflect that some are natural and some are imaginary; and of the natural desires some are necessary and some are natural only; and of the necessary desires some are necessary to happiness [he refers to friendship], and others to the comfort of the body [clothing and housing], and others to life itself [hunger and thirst].

Because a correct appraisal of the desires enables us to refer every decision to choose or to avoid to the test of the health of the body and the tranquility of the soul, for this is the objective of the happy life. For to this end we do everything, that we may feel neither pain nor fear. When once this boon is in our possession, every tumult of the soul is stilled, the creature having nothing to work forward to as something lacking or something additional to seek whereby the good of the soul and the body shall arrive at fullness. For only then have we need of pleasure when from the absence of pleasure we feel pain; and conversely, when we no longer feel pain we no longer feel need of pleasure.

THE BEGINNING AND THE END OF THE HAPPY LIFE

And for the following reason we say that pleasure is the beginning and the end of the happy life: because we recognize pleasure as the first good and connate with us and to this we have recourse as to a canon, judging every good by the reaction. And for the reason that pleasure is the first good and of one nature with us we do not choose every pleasure but at one time or another forgo many pleasures when a distress that will outweigh them follows in consequence of these pleasures; and many pains we believe to be preferable to pleasures when a pleasure that will outweigh them ensues for us after enduring those pains for a long time.

Therefore every pleasure is good because it is of one nature with us but every pleasure is not to be chosen; by the same reasoning every pain is an evil but every pain is not such as to be avoided at all times.

EXPEDIENCY: THE CALCULUS OF ADVANTAGE

The right procedure, however, is to weigh them against one another and to scrutinize the advantages and disadvantages; for we treat the good under certain circumstances as an evil and conversely the evil as a good.

SELF-SUFFICIENCY OR CONTENTMENT WITH LITTLE

And self-sufficiency we believe to be a great good, not that we may live on little under all circumstances but that we may be content with little when we do not have plenty, being genuinely convinced that they enjoy luxury most who feel the least need of it; that every natural appetite is easily gratified but the unnatural appetite difficult to gratify; and that plain foods bring a pleasure equal to that of a luxurious diet when all the pain originating in need has been removed; and that bread and water bring the most utter pleasure when one in need of them brings them to his lips.

Thus habituation to simple and inexpensive diets not only contributes to perfect health but also renders a man unshrinking in face of the inevitable emergencies of life; and it disposes us better toward the times of abundance that ensue after intervals of scarcity and renders us fearless in the face of Fortune. When therefore we say that pleasure is the end we do not mean the pleasures of profligates and those that consist in high living, as certain people think, either not understanding us and holding to different views or willfully misrepresenting us; but we mean freedom from pain in the body and turmoil in the soul. For it is not protracted drinking bouts and revels nor yet sexual pleasures with boys and women nor rare dishes of fish and the rest – all the delicacies that the luxurious table bears – that beget the happy life but rather sober calculation, which searches out the reasons for every choice and avoidance and expels the false opinions, the source of most of the turmoil that seizes upon the souls of men.

THE PRACTICAL REASON

Of all these virtues the source is the practical reason, the greatest good of all – and hence more precious than philosophy itself – teaching us the impossibility of living pleasurably without living according to reason, honor, and justice, and conversely, of living according to reason, honor, and justice without living pleasurably; for the virtues are of one nature with the pleasurable life and conversely, the pleasurable life is inseparable from the virtues.

DESCRIPTION OF THE HAPPY MAN

"Because who do you think is in better case than the man who holds pious beliefs concerning the gods and is invariably fearless of death; and has included in his reckoning the end of life as ordained by Nature; and concerning the utmost of things good discerns this to be easy to enjoy to the full and easy of procurement, while the utmost of things evil is either brief in duration or brief in suffering.

He has abolished the Necessity that is introduced by some thinkers as the mistress of all things, for it were better to subscribe to the myths concerning the gods than to be a slave to the Destiny of the physicists, because the former presumes a hope of mercy through worship but the latter assumes Necessity to be inexorable.

As for Fortune, he does not assume that she is a goddess, as the multitude believes, for nothing is done at random by a god; neither does he think her a fickle cause, for he does not suppose that either good or evil is dealt out to men by her to affect life's happiness; yet he does believe the starting points for great good or evil to originate with her, thinking it better to plan well and fail than to plan badly and succeed, for in the conduct of life it profits more for good judgment to miscarry than for misjudgment to prosper by chance.

THINK ON THESE THINGS

Meditate therefore by day and by night upon these precepts and upon the others that go with these, whether by yourself or in the company of another like yourself, and never will your soul be in turmoil either sleeping or waking but you will be living like a god among men, for in no wise does a man resemble a mortal creature who lives among immortal blessings.

Questions for Discussion

1. Why does Epicurus counsel his student to disregard the gods?

2. What is Epicurus' notion of true happiness? How does it differ from other notions of happiness from other philosophers, pop culture, your family or religion of origin, etc?

3. How should we confront the aspects of life we find unsavory?

4. What role does practical reason play in the good life for Epicurus?

5. If you were an Epicurean, how would your outlook and behaviors change?

Citation and Use

Epicurus, "Letter to Menoeceus," in Lives of Eminent Philosophers. Diogenes Laertius. R.D. Hicks. Cambridge. Harvard University Press. 1972 (First published 1925). 187–93, http://www.perseus.tufts.edu/hopper/text?doc=urn:cts:greekLit:tlg0004.tlg001.perseus-eng1:10.1.

The work is in the Public Domain.

A PIG, A FOOL, AND SOCRATES

John Stuart Mill

The creed which accepts as the foundation of morals, Utility, or the **Greatest Happiness Principle**, holds that actions are right in proportion as they tend to promote happiness, wrong as they tend to produce the reverse of happiness. By happiness is intended pleasure, and the absence of pain; by unhappiness, pain, and the privation of pleasure. To give a clear view of the moral standard set up by the theory, much more requires to be said; in particular, what things it includes in the ideas of pain and pleasure; and to what extent this is left an open question. But these supplementary explanations do not affect the theory of life on which this theory of morality is grounded namely, that pleasure, and freedom from pain, are the only things desirable as ends; and that all desirable things (which are as numerous in the utilitarian as in any other scheme) are desirable either for the pleasure inherent in themselves, or as means to the promotion of pleasure and the prevention of pain.

Now, such a theory of life excites in many minds, and among them in some of the most estimable in feeling and purpose, inveterate dislike. To suppose that life has (as they express it) no higher end than pleasure no better and nobler object of desire and pursuit they designate as utterly mean and grovelling; as a doctrine worthy only of swine, to whom the followers of Epicurus were, at a very early period, contemptuously likened; and modern holders of the doctrine are occasionally made the subject of equally polite comparisons by its German, French, and English assailants.

Higher and Lower Pleasures

When thus attacked, the Epicureans have always answered, that it is not they, but their accusers, who represent human nature in a degrading light; since the accusation supposes human beings to be capable of no pleasures except those of which swine are capable. If this supposition were true, the charge could not be gainsaid, but would then be no longer an imputation; for if the sources of pleasure were precisely the same to human beings and to swine, the rule of life which is good enough for the one would be good enough for the other. The comparison of the Epicurean life to that of beasts is felt as degrading, precisely because a beast's pleasures do not satisfy a human being's conceptions of happiness. Human beings have faculties more elevated than the animal appetites, and when once made conscious of them, do not regard anything as happiness which does not include their gratification. I do not, indeed, consider the Epicureans to have been by any means faultless in drawing out their scheme of consequences from the utilitarian principle. To do this in any sufficient manner, many Stoic, as well as Christian elements require to be included.

But there is no known Epicurean theory of life which does not assign to the pleasures of the intellect, of the feelings and imagination, and of the moral sentiments, a much higher value as pleasures than to those of mere sensation. It must be admitted, however, that utilitarian writers in general have placed the superiority of mental over bodily pleasures chiefly in the greater permanency, safety, uncostliness, etc., of the former that is, in their circumstantial advantages rather than in their intrinsic nature. And on all these points utilitarians have fully proved their case; but they might have taken the other, and, as it may be called, higher ground, with entire consistency. It is quite compatible with the principle of utility to recognize the fact, that some kinds of pleasure are more desirable and more valuable than others. It would be absurd that while, in estimating all other things, quality is considered as well as quantity, the estimation of pleasures should be supposed to depend on quantity alone.

If I am asked, what I mean by difference of quality in pleasures, or what makes one pleasure more valuable than another, merely as a pleasure, except its being greater in amount, there is but one possible answer. Of two pleasures, if there be one to which all or almost all who have experience of both give a decided preference, irrespective of any feeling of moral obligation to prefer it, that is the more desirable pleasure. If one of the two is, by those who are competently acquainted with both, placed so far above the other that they prefer it, even though knowing it to be attended with a greater amount of discontent, and would not resign it for any quantity of the other pleasure which their nature is capable of, we are justified in ascribing to the preferred enjoyment a superiority in quality, so far outweighing quantity as to render it, in comparison, of small account.

Now it is an unquestionable fact that those who are equally acquainted with, and equally capable of appreciating and enjoying, both, do give a most marked preference to the manner of existence which employs their higher faculties. Few human creatures would consent to be changed into any of the lower animals, for a promise of the fullest allowance of a beast's pleasures; no intelligent human being would consent to be a fool, no instructed person would be an ignoramus, no person of feeling and conscience would be selfish and base, even though they should be persuaded that the fool, the dunce, or the rascal is better satisfied with his lot than they are with theirs. They would not resign what they possess more than he for the most complete satisfaction of all the desires which they have in common with him. If they ever fancy they would, it is only in cases of unhappiness so extreme, that to escape from it they would exchange their lot for almost any other, however undesirable in their own eyes.

A being of higher faculties requires more to make him happy, is capable probably of more acute suffering, and certainly accessible to it at more points, than one of an inferior type; but in spite of these liabilities, he can never really wish to sink into what he feels to be a lower grade of existence. We may give what explanation we please of this unwillingness; we may attribute it to pride, a name which is given indiscriminately to some of the most and to some of the least estimable feelings of which mankind are capable: we may refer it to the love of liberty and personal independence, an appeal to which was with the Stoics one of the most effective means for the inculcation of it; to the love of power, or to the love of excitement, both of which do really enter into and contribute to it: but its most appropriate appellation is a sense of dignity, which all human beings possess in one form or other, and in some, though by no means in exact, proportion to their higher faculties, and which is so essential a part of the happiness of those in whom it is strong, that nothing which conflicts with it could be, otherwise than momentarily, an object of desire to them.

Whoever supposes that this preference takes place at a sacrifice of happiness that the superior being, in anything like equal circumstances, is not happier than the inferior confounds the two very different ideas, of happiness, and content. It is indisputable that the being whose capacities of enjoyment are low, has the greatest chance of having them fully satisfied; and a highly endowed being will always feel that any happiness which he can look for, as the world is constituted, is imperfect. But he can learn to bear its imperfections, if they are at all bearable; and they will not make him envy the being who is indeed unconscious of the imperfections, but only because he feels not at all the good which those imperfections qualify. It is better to be a human being dissatisfied than a pig satisfied; better to be Socrates dissatisfied than a fool satisfied. And if the fool, or the pig, are a different opinion, it is because they only know their own side of the question. The other party to the comparison knows both sides.

It may be objected, that many who are capable of the higher pleasures, occasionally, under the influence of temptation, postpone them to the lower. But this is quite compatible with a full appreciation of the intrinsic superiority of the higher. Men often, from infirmity of character, make their election for the nearer good, though they know it to be the less valuable; and this no less when the choice is between two bodily pleasures, than when it is between bodily and mental. They pursue sensual indulgences to the injury of health, though perfectly aware that health is the greater good.

It may be further objected, that many who begin with youthful enthusiasm for everything noble, as they advance in years sink into indolence and selfishness. But I do not believe that those who undergo this very common change, voluntarily choose the lower description of pleasures in preference to the higher. I believe that before they devote themselves exclusively to the one, they have already become incapable of the other. Capacity for the nobler feelings is in most natures a very tender plant, easily killed, not only by hostile influences, but by mere want of sustenance; and in the majority of young persons it speedily dies away if the occupations to which their position in life has devoted them, and the society into which it has thrown them, are not favorable to keeping that higher capacity in exercise.

Men lose their high aspirations as they lose their intellectual tastes, because they have not time or opportunity for indulging them; and they addict themselves to inferior pleasures, not because they deliberately prefer them, but because they are either the only ones to which they have access, or the only ones which they are any longer capable of enjoying. It may be questioned whether any one who has remained equally susceptible to both classes of pleasures, ever knowingly and calmly preferred the lower; though many, in all ages, have broken down in an ineffectual attempt to combine both.

From this verdict of the only competent judges, I apprehend there can be no appeal. On a question which is the best worth having of two pleasures, or which of two modes of existence is the most grateful to the feelings, apart from its moral attributes and from its consequences, the judgment of those who are qualified by knowledge of both, or, if they differ, that of the majority among them, must be admitted as final. And there needs be the less hesitation to accept this judgment respecting the quality of pleasures, since there is no other tribunal to be referred to even on the question of quantity.

What means are there of determining which is the acutest of two pains, or the intensest of two pleasurable sensations, except the general suffrage of those who are familiar with both? Neither pains nor pleasures are homogeneous, and pain is always heterogeneous with pleasure. What is there to decide whether a particular pleasure is worth purchasing at the cost of a particular pain, except the feelings and judgment of the experienced? When, therefore, those feelings and judgment declare the pleasures derived from the higher faculties to be preferable in kind, apart from the question of intensity, to those of which the animal nature, disjoined from the higher faculties, is suspectible, they are entitled on this subject to the same regard.

I have dwelt on this point, as being a necessary part of a perfectly just conception of Utility or Happiness, considered as the directive rule of human conduct. But it is by no means an indispensable condition to the acceptance of the utilitarian standard; for that standard is not the agent's own greatest happiness, but the greatest amount of happiness altogether; and if it may possibly be doubted whether a noble character is always the happier for its nobleness, there can be no doubt that it makes other people happier, and that the world in general is immensely a gainer by it. Utilitarianism, therefore, could only attain its end by the general cultivation of nobleness of character, even if each individual were only benefited by the nobleness of others, and his own, so far as happiness is concerned, were a sheer deduction from the benefit. But the bare enunciation of such an absurdity as this last, renders refutation superfluous.

Happiness as an Aim

According to the Greatest Happiness Principle, as above explained, the ultimate end, with reference to and for the sake of which all other things are desirable (whether we are considering our own good or that of other people), is an existence exempt as far as possible from pain, and as rich as possible in enjoyments, both in point of quantity and quality; the test of quality, and the rule for measuring it against quantity, being the preference felt by those who in their opportunities of experience, to which must be added their habits of self-consciousness and self-observation, are best furnished with the means of comparison. This, being, according to the utilitarian opinion, the end of human action, is necessarily also the standard of morality; which may accordingly be defined, the rules and precepts for human conduct, by the observance of which an existence such as has been described might be, to the greatest extent possible, secured to all mankind; and not to them only, but, so far as the nature of things admits, to the whole sentient creation.

[...]

A state of exalted pleasure lasts only moments, or in some cases, and with some intermissions, hours or days, and is the occasional brilliant flash of enjoyment, not its permanent and steady flame. Of this the philosophers who have taught that happiness is the end of life were as fully aware as those who taunt them. The happiness which they meant was not a life of rapture; but moments of such, in an existence made up of few and transitory pains, many and various pleasures, with a decided predominance of the active over the passive, and having as the foundation of the whole, not to expect more from life than it is capable of bestowing. A life thus composed, to those who have been fortunate enough to obtain it, has always appeared worthy of the name of happiness. And such an existence is even now the lot of many, during some considerable portion of their lives. The present wretched education, and wretched social arrangements, are the only real hindrance to its being attainable by almost all.

[...]

I must again repeat, what the assailants of utilitarianism seldom have the justice to acknowledge, that the happiness which forms the utilitarian standard of what is right in conduct, is not the agent's own happiness, but that of all concerned. As between his own happiness and that of others, utilitarianism requires him to be as strictly impartial as a disinterested and benevolent spectator. In the golden rule of Jesus of Nazareth, we read the complete spirit of the ethics of utility. To do as you would be done by, and to love your neighbor as yourself, constitute the ideal perfection of utilitarian morality.

As the means of making the nearest approach to this ideal, utility would enjoin, first, that laws and social arrangements should place the happiness, or (as speaking practically it may be called) the interest, of every individual, as nearly as possible in harmony with the interest of the whole; and secondly, that education and opinion, which have so vast a power over human character, should so use that power as to establish in the mind of every individual an indissoluble association between his own happiness and the good of the whole; especially between his own happiness and the practice of such modes of conduct, negative and positive, as regard for the universal happiness prescribes; so that not only he may be unable to conceive the possibility of happiness to himself, consistently with conduct opposed to the general good, but also that a direct impulse to promote the general good may be in every individual one of the habitual motives of action, and the sentiments connected therewith may fill a large and prominent place in every human being's sentient existence. If the, impugners of the utilitarian morality represented it to their own minds in this its, true character, I know not what recommendation possessed by any other morality they could possibly affirm to be wanting to it; what more beautiful or more exalted developments of human nature any other ethical system can be supposed to foster, or what springs of action, not accessible to the utilitarian, such systems rely on for giving effect to their mandates.

Questions for Discussion

1. What objections did Mill list and what was his reply to each?

2. In your informed judgement, does Mill do a good job answering each objection?

3. Is Mill's distinction between upper and lower pleasures a meaningful one? Should we take into account Mill's class and education when analyzing this?

4. How does Mill's account of happiness and general approach compare to Epicurus' account?

5. At first glance, Mill appears to make a lot of assumptions about other people. Does Mill allow for people choosing what makes them happy?

6. If a utilitarian does allow for different people preferring different pleasures, is Utilitarianism (as Mill discusses it) a universal or sujectivist / relativist theory?

Citation and Use

The text was taken from the following work.

John Stuart Mill, *Utilitarianism* (London: Parker, Son, and Bourn, West Strand, 1863).

The use of this work is governed by the Public Domain.

VIRTUE

Aristotle

Book I

vii

Presumably, however, to say that happiness is the chief good seems a platitude, and a clearer account of what it is still desired. This might perhaps be given, if we could first ascertain the function of man. For just as for a flute-player, a sculptor, or an artist, and, in general, for all things that have a function or activity, the good and the 'well' is thought to reside in the function, so would it seem to be for man, if he has a function. Have the carpenter, then, and the tanner certain functions or activities, and has man none? Is he born without a function? Or as eye, hand, foot, and in general each of the parts evidently has a function, may one lay it down that man similarly has a function apart from all these? What then can this be? Life seems to be common even to plants, but we are seeking what is peculiar to man. Let us exclude, therefore, the life of nutrition and growth. Next there would be a life of perception, but it also seems to be common even to the horse, the ox, and every animal. There remains, then, an active life of the element that has a rational principle; of this, one part has such a principle in the sense of being obedient to one, the other in the sense of possessing one and exercising thought. And, as 'life of the rational element' also has two meanings, we must state that life in the sense of activity is what we mean; for this seems to be the more proper sense of the term. Now if the function of man is an activity of soul which follows or implies a rational principle, and if we say 'so-and-so' and 'a good so-and-so' have a function which is the same in kind, e.g. a lyre, and a good lyre-player, and so without qualification in all cases, eminence in respect of goodness being idded to the name of the function (for the function of a lyre-player is to play the lyre, and that of a good lyre-player is to do so well): if this is the case, and we state the function of man to be a certain kind of life, and this to be an activity or actions of the soul implying a rational principle, and the function of a good man to be the good and noble performance of these, and if any action is well performed when it is performed in accordance with the appropriate excellence: if this is the case, human good turns out to be activity of soul in accordance with virtue, and if there

are more than one virtue, in accordance with the best and most complete.

But we must add 'in a complete life.' For one swallow does not make a summer, nor does one day; and so too one day, or a short time, does not make a man blessed and happy...

viii

We must consider it, however, in the light not only of our conclusion and our premises, but also of what is commonly said about it; for with a true view all the data harmonize, but with a false one the facts soon clash. Now goods have been divided into three classes, and some are described as external, others as relating to soul or to body; we call those that relate to soul most properly and truly goods, and psychical actions and activities we class as relating to soul. Therefore our account must be sound, at least according to this view, which is an old one and agreed on by philosophers. It is correct also in that we identify the end with certain actions and activities; for thus it falls among goods of the soul and not among external goods. Another belief which harmonizes with our account is that the happy man lives well and does well; for we have practically defined happiness as a sort of good life and good action. The characteristics that are looked for in happiness seem also, all of them, to belong to what we have defined happiness as being. For some identify happiness with virtue, some with practical wisdom, others with a kind of philosophic wisdom, others with these, or one of these, accompanied by pleasure or not without pleasure; while others include also external prosperity. Now some of these views have been held by many men and men of old, others by a few eminent persons; and it is not probable that either of these should be entirely mistaken, but rather that they should be right in at least some one respect or even in most respects.

With those who identify happiness with virtue or some one virtue our account is in harmony; for to virtue belongs virtuous activity. But it makes, perhaps, no small difference whether we place the chief good in possession or in use, in state of mind or in activity. For the state of mind may

140

exist without producing any good result, as in a man who is asleep or in some other way quite inactive, but the activity cannot; for one who has the activity will of necessity be acting, and acting well. And as in the Olympic Games it is not the most beautiful and the strongest that are crowned but those who compete (for it is some of these that are victorious), so those who act win, and rightly win, the noble and good things in life.

Their life is also in itself pleasant. For pleasure is a state of soul, and to each man that which he is said to be a lover of is pleasant; e.g. not only is a horse pleasant to the lover of horses, and a spectacle to the lover of sights, but also in the same way just acts are pleasant to the lover of justice and in general virtuous acts to the lover of virtue. Now for most men their pleasures are in conflict with one another because these are not by nature pleasant, but the lovers of what is noble find pleasant the things that are by nature pleasant; and virtuous actions are such, so that these are pleasant for such men as well as in their own nature. Their life, therefore, has no further need of pleasure as a sort of adventitious charm, but has its pleasure in itself. For, besides what we have said, the man who does not rejoice in noble actions is not even good; since no one would call a man just who did not enjoy acting justly, nor any man liberal who did not enjoy liberal actions; and similarly in all other cases. If this is so, virtuous actions must be in themselves pleasant. But they are also good and noble, and have each of these attributes in the highest degree, since the good man judges well about these attributes; his judgement is such as we have described. Happiness then is the best, noblest, and most pleasant thing in the world, and these attributes are not severed as in the inscription at Delos-

> Most noble is that which is justest, and best is health;
> But pleasantest is it to win what we love.

For all these properties belong to the best activities; and these, or one- the best- of these, we identify with happiness.

Yet evidently, as we said, it needs the external goods as well; for it is impossible, or not easy, to do noble acts without the proper equipment. In many actions we use friends and riches and political power as instruments; and there are some things the lack of which takes the lustre from happiness, as good birth, goodly children, beauty; for the man who is very ugly in appearance or ill-born or solitary and childless is not very likely to be happy, and perhaps a man would be still less likely if he had thoroughly bad children or friends or had lost good children or friends by death. As we said, then, happiness seems to need this sort of prosperity in addition; for which reason some identify happiness with good fortune, though others identify it with virtue...

x

...When then should we not say that he is happy who is active in accordance with complete virtue and is sufficiently equipped with external goods, not for some chance period but throughout a complete life? Or must we add 'and who is destined to live thus and die as befits his life'? Certainly the future is obscure to us, while happiness, we claim, is an end and something in every way final. If so, we shall call happy those among living men in whom these conditions are, and are to be, fulfilled- but happy men. So much for these questions....

Book II

i

Virtue, then, being of two kinds, intellectual and moral, intellectual virtue in the main owes both its birth and its growth to teaching (for which reason it requires experience and time), while moral virtue comes about as a result of habit, whence also its name (ethike) is one that is formed by a slight variation from the word ethos (habit). From this it is also plain that none of the moral virtues arises in us by nature; for nothing that exists by nature can form a habit contrary to its nature. For instance the stone which by nature moves downwards cannot be habituated to move upwards, not even if one tries to train it by throwing it up ten thousand times; nor can fire be habituated to move downwards, nor can anything else that by nature behaves in one way be trained to behave in another. Neither by nature, then, nor contrary to nature do the virtues arise in us; rather we are adapted by nature to receive them, and are made perfect by habit.

Again, of all the things that come to us by nature we first acquire the potentiality and later exhibit the activity (this is plain in the case of the senses; for it was not by often seeing or often hearing that we got these senses, but on the contrary we had them before we used them, and did not come to have them by using them); but the virtues we get by first exercising them, as also happens in the case of the arts as well. For the things we have to learn before we can do them, we learn by doing them, e.g. men become builders by building and lyreplayers by playing the lyre; so too we become just by doing just acts, temperate by doing temperate acts, brave by doing brave acts.

This is confirmed by what happens in states; for legislators make the citizens good by forming habits in them, and this is the wish of every legislator, and those who do not effect it miss their mark, and it is in this that a good constitution differs from a bad one.

Again, it is from the same causes and by the same means that every virtue is both produced and destroyed, and similarly every art; for it is from playing the lyre that both good and bad lyre-players are produced. And the corresponding statement is true of builders and of all the rest; men will be good or bad builders as a result of building well or badly. For if this were not so, there would have been no need of a teacher, but all men would have been born good or bad at their craft. This, then, is the case with the virtues also; by doing the acts that we do in our transactions with other men we become just or unjust, and by doing the acts that we do in the presence of danger, and being habituated to feel fear or confidence, we become brave or cowardly. The same is true of appetites and feelings of anger; some men become temperate and good-tempered, others self-indulgent and irascible, by behaving in one way or the other in the appropriate circumstances. Thus, in one word, states of character arise out of like activities. This is why the activities we exhibit must be of a certain kind; it is because the states of character correspond to the differences between these. It makes no small difference, then, whether we form habits of one kind or of another from our very youth; it makes a very great difference, or rather all the difference...

ii

...First, then, let us consider this, that it is the nature of such things to be destroyed by defect and excess, as we see in the case of strength and of health (for to gain light on things imperceptible we must use the evidence of sensible things); both excessive and defective exercise destroys the strength, and similarly drink or food which is above or below a certain amount destroys the health, while that which is proportionate both produces and increases and preserves it. So too is it, then, in the case of temperance and courage and the other virtues. For the man who flies from and fears everything and does not stand his ground against anything becomes a coward, and the man who fears nothing at all but goes to meet every danger becomes rash; and similarly the man who indulges in every pleasure and abstains from none becomes self-indulgent, while the man who shuns every pleasure, as boors do, becomes in a way insensible; temperance and courage, then, are destroyed by excess and defect, and preserved by the mean...

vi

...If it is thus, then, that every art does its work well- by looking to the intermediate and judgling its works by this standard (so that we often say of good works of art that it is not possible either to take away or to add anything, implying that excess and defect destroy the goodness of works of art, while the mean preserves it; and good artists, as we say, look to this in their work), and if, further, virtue is more exact and better than any art, as nature also is, then virtue must have the quality of aiming at the intermediate. I mean moral virtue; for it is this that is concerned with passions and actions, and in these there is excess, defect, and the intermediate. For instance, both fear and confidence and appetite and anger and pity and in general pleasure and pain may be felt both too much and too little, and in both cases not well; but to feel them at the right times, with reference to the right objects, towards the right people, with the right motive, and in the right way, is what is both intermediate and best, and this is characteristic of virtue. Similarly with regard to actions also there is excess, defect, and

the intermediate. Now virtue is concerned with passions and actions, in which excess is a form of failure, and so is defect, while the intermediate is praised and is a form of success; and being praised and being successful are both characteristics of virtue. Therefore virtue is a kind of mean, since, as we have seen, it aims at what is intermediate.

Again, it is possible to fail in many ways (for evil belongs to the class of the unlimited, as the Pythagoreans conjectured, and good to that of the limited), while to succeed is possible only in one way (for which reason also one is easy and the other difficult- to miss the mark easy, to hit it difficult); for these reasons also, then, excess and defect are characteristic of vice, and the mean of virtue;

> For men are good in but one way, but bad in many.

Virtue, then, is a state of character concerned with choice, lying in a mean, i.e. the mean relative to us, this being determined by a rational principle, and by that principle by which the man of practical wisdom would determine it. Now it is a mean between two vices, that which depends on excess and that which depends on defect; and again it is a mean because the vices respectively fall short of or exceed what is right in both passions and actions, while virtue both finds and chooses that which is intermediate. Hence in respect of its substance and the definition which states its essence virtue is a mean, with regard to what is best and right an extreme.

But not every action nor every passion admits of a mean; for some have names that already imply badness, e.g. spite, shamelessness, envy, and in the case of actions adultery, theft, murder; for all of these and suchlike things imply by their names that they are themselves bad, and not the excesses or deficiencies of them. It is not possible, then, ever to be right with regard to them; one must always be wrong. Nor does goodness or badness with regard to such things depend on committing adultery with the right woman, at the right time, and in the right way, but simply to do any of them is to go wrong. It would be equally absurd, then, to expect that in unjust, cowardly, and voluptuous action there should be a mean, an excess, and a deficiency; for at that rate there would be a mean of excess and of deficiency, an excess of excess, and a deficiency of deficiency. But as there is no excess and deficiency of temperance and courage because what is intermediate is in a sense an extreme, so too of the actions we have mentioned there is no mean nor any excess and deficiency, but however they are done they are wrong; for in general there is neither a mean of excess and deficiency, nor excess and deficiency of a mean.

For Review and Discussion:

1. What is the "golden mean" and why is it important for Aristotle's ethics?

2. What are some virtues that you think are important and why?

3. Can someone ever be *too* rational? Why or why not? What would Aristotle say?

Citation and Use

Aristotle. (1925). NICOMACHEAN ETHICS (W.D. Ross, Trans.). (Original work published circa 350 BCE).

HUMANIZATION IS LIBERATION

Paulo Freire

While the problem of **humanization** has always, from an axiological point of view, been humankind's central problem, it now takes on the character of an inescapable concern.[1] Concern for humanization leads at once to the recognition of **dehumanization**, not only as an ontological possibility but as an historical reality. And as an individual perceives the extent of dehumanization, he or she may ask if humanization is a viable possibility. Within history, in concrete, objective contexts, both humanization and dehumanization are possibilities for a person as an uncompleted being conscious of their incompletion.But while both humanization and dehumanization are real alternatives, only the first is the people's vocation. This vocation is constantly negated, yet it is affirmed by that very negation. It is thwarted by injustice, exploitation, oppression, and the violence of the oppressors; it is affirmed by the yearning of the oppressed for freedom and justice, and by their struggle to recover their lost humanity.

Dehumanization, which marks not only those whose humanity has been stolen, but also (though in a different way) those who have stolen it, is a *distortion* of the vocation of becoming more fully human. This distortion occurs within history; but it is not an historical vocation. Indeed, to admit of dehumanization as an historical vocation would lead either to cynicism or total despair. The struggle for humanization, for the emancipation of labor, for the overcoming of alienation, for the affirmation of men and women as persons would be meaningless. This struggle is possible only because dehumanization, although a concrete historical fact, is *not* a given destiny but the result of an unjust order that engenders violence in the oppressors, which in turn dehumanizes the oppressed.

Because it is a distortion of being more fully human, sooner or later being less human leads the oppressed to struggle against those who made them so. In order for this struggle to have meaning, the oppressed must not, in seeking to regain their humanity (which is a way to create it), become in turn oppressors of the oppressors, but rather restorers of the humanity of both.

This, then, is the great humanistic and historical task of the **oppressed**: to liberate themselves and their **oppressors** as well. The oppressors, who oppress, exploit, and rape by virtue of their power, cannot find in this power the strength to liberate either the oppressed or themselves. Only power that springs from the weakness of the oppressed will be sufficiently strong to free both. Any attempt to "soften" the power of the oppressor in deference to the weakness of the oppressed almost always manifests itself in the form of false generosity; indeed, the attempt never goes beyond this. In order to have the continued opportunity to express their "generosity," the oppressors must perpetuate injustice as well. An unjust social order is the permanent fount of this "generosity," which is nourished by death, despair, and poverty. That is why the dispensers of false generosity become desperate at the slightest threat to its source,

True generosity consists precisely in fighting to destroy the causes which nourish false charity. False charity constrains the fearful and subdued, the "rejects of life," to extend their trembling hands. True generosity lies in striving so that these hands—whether of individuals or entire peoples—need be extended less and less in supplication, so that more and more they become human hands which work and, working, transform the world.

This lesson and this apprenticeship must come, however, from the oppressed themselves and from those who are truly solidary with them. As individuals or as peoples, by fighting for the restoration of their humanity they will be attempting the restoration of true generosity.
- Who are better prepared than the oppressed to understand the terrible significance of an oppressive society?
- Who suffer the effects of oppression more than the oppressed?
- Who can better understand the necessity of liberation?

They will not gain this liberation by chance but through the praxis of their quest for it, through their recognition of the necessity to fight for it. And this fight, because of the purpose given it by the oppressed, will actually constitute an act of love opposing the lovelessness which lies at the heart of the oppressors' violence, lovelessness even when clothed in false generosity.

But almost always, during the initial stage of the struggle, the oppressed, instead of striving for liberation, tend themselves to become oppressors, or "sub-oppressors." The very structure of their thought has been conditioned by the contradictions of the concrete, existential situation by which they were shaped. Their ideal is to be men; but for them, to be men is to be oppressors. This is their model of humanity. This phenomenon derives from the fact that the oppressed, at a certain moment of their existential experience, adopt an attitude of "adhesion" to the oppressor. Under these circumstances they cannot "consider" him sufficiently clearly to objectivize him—to discover him "outside" themselves. This does not necessarily mean that the oppressed are unaware that they are downtrodden. But their perception of themselves as oppressed is impaired by their submersion in the reality of oppression. At this level, their perception of themselves as opposites of the oppressor does not yet signify engagement in a struggle to overcome the contradiction;[2] the one pole aspires not to liberation, but to identification with its opposite pole.

In this situation the oppressed do not see the "new man" as the person to be born from the resolution of this contradiction, as oppression gives way to liberation. For them, the new man or woman themselves become oppressors. Their vision of the new man or woman is individualistic; because of their identification with the oppressor, they have no consciousness of themselves as persons or as members of an oppressed class. It is not to become free that they want agrarian reform, but in order to acquire land and thus become landowners—or, more precisely, bosses over other workers. It is a rare peasant who, once "promoted" to overseer, does not become more of a tyrant towards his former comrades than the owner himself. This is because the context of the peasant's situation, that is, oppression, remains unchanged. In this example, the overseer, in order to make sure of his job, must be as tough as the owner—and more so. Thus is illustrated our previous assertion that during the initial stage of their struggle the oppressed find in the oppressor their model of "manhood."

Even revolution, which transforms a concrete situation of oppression by establishing the process of liberation, must confront this phenomenon. Many of the oppressed who directly or indirectly participate in revolution intend—conditioned by the myths of the old order—to make it their private revolution. The shadow of their former oppressor is still cast over them.

The "fear of freedom" which afflicts the oppressed,[3] a fear which may equally well lead them to desire the role of oppressor or bind them to the role of oppressed, should be examined. One of the basic elements of the relationship between oppressor and oppressed is *prescription*. Every prescription represents the imposition of one individual's choice upon another, transforming the consciousness of the person prescribed to into one that conforms with the prescriber's consciousness. Thus, the behavior of the oppressed is a prescribed behavior, following as it does the guidelines of the oppressor.

The oppressed, having internalized the image of the oppressor and adopted his guidelines, are fearful of freedom. Freedom would require them to eject this image and replace it with autonomy and responsibility. Freedom is acquired by conquest, not by gift. It must be pursued constantly and responsibly. Freedom is not an ideal located outside of man; nor is it an idea which becomes myth. It is rather the indispensable condition for the quest for human completion.

To surmount the situation of oppression, people must first critically recognize its causes, so that through transforming action they can create a new situation, one which makes possible the pursuit of a fuller humanity. But the struggle to be more fully human has already begun in the authentic struggle to transform the situation. Although the situation of oppression is a dehumanized and dehumanizing totality affecting both the oppressors and those whom they oppress, it is the latter who must, from their stifled humanity, wage for both the struggle for a fuller humanity; the oppressor, who is himself dehumanized because he dehumanizes others, is unable to lead this struggle.

However, the oppressed, who have adapted to the structure of domination in which they are immersed, and have become resigned to it, are inhibited from waging the struggle for freedom so long as they feel incapable of running the risks it requires. Moreover, their struggle for freedom threatens not only the oppressor, but also their own oppressed comrades who are fearful of still greater repression. When they discover within themselves the yearning to be free, they perceive that this yearning can be transformed into reality only when the same yearning is aroused in their comrades. But while dominated by the fear of freedom they refuse to appeal to others, or to listen to the appeals of others, or even to the appeals of their own conscience. They prefer gregariousness to authentic comradeship; they prefer the security of conformity with their state of unfreedom to the creative communion produced by freedom and even the very pursuit of freedom. [...]

The central problem is this: How can the oppressed, as divided, unauthentic beings, participate in developing the pedagogy of their liberation? Only as they discover themselves to be "hosts" of the oppressor can they contribute to the midwifery of their liberating pedagogy. As long as they live in the duality in which *to be* is *to be like*, and *to be like* is *to be like the oppressor*, this contribution is impossible. The pedagogy of the oppressed is an instrument for their critical discovery that both they and their oppressors are manifestations of dehumanization.

Liberation is thus a childbirth, and a painful one. The man or woman who emerges is a new person, viable only as the oppressor-oppressed contradiction is superseded by the humanization of all people. Or to put it another way, the solution of this contradiction is born in the labor which brings into the world this new being: no longer oppressor nor longer oppressed, but human in the process of achieving freedom.

This solution cannot be achieved in idealistic terms. In order for the oppressed to be able to wage the struggle for their liberation, they must perceive the reality of oppression not as a closed world from which there is no exit, but as a limiting situation which they can transform. This perception is a necessary but not a sufficient condition for liberation; it must become the motivating force for liberating action. Nor does the discovery by the oppressed that they exist in dialectical relationship to the oppressor, as his antithesis—that without them the oppressor could not exist[4]—in itself constitute liberation. The oppressed can overcome the contradiction in which they are caught only when this perception enlists them in the struggle to free themselves.

The same is true with respect to the individual oppressor as a person. Discovering himself to be an oppressor may cause considerable anguish, but it does not necessarily lead to solidarity with the oppressed. Rationalizing his guilt through paternalistic treatment of the oppressed, all the while holding them fast in a position of dependence, will not do. Solidarity requires that one enter into the situation of those with whom one is solidarity; it is a radical posture. If what characterizes the oppressed is their subordination to the consciousness of the master, as Hegel affirms,[5] true solidarity with the oppressed means fighting at their side to transform the objective reality which has made them these"beings for another." The oppressor is solidary with the oppressed only when he stops regarding the oppressed as an abstract category and sees them as persons who have been unjustly dealt with, deprived of their voice, cheated in the sale of their labor—when he stops making pious, sentimental, and individualistic gestures and risks an act of love. True solidarity is found only in the plenitude of this act of love, in its existentiality, in its praxis. To affirm that men and women are persons and as persons should be free, and yet to do nothing tangible to make this affirmation a reality, is a farce.

[...]

To deny the importance of subjectivity in the process of transforming the world and history is naïve and simplistic. It is to admit the impossible: a world without people. This objectivistic position is as ingenuous as that of subjectivism, which postulates people without a world. World and human beings do not exist apart from each other, they exist in constant interaction. Marx does not espouse such a dichotomy, nor does any other critical, realistic thinker. What Marx criticized and scientifically destroyed was not subjectivity, but subjectivism and psychologism. Just as objective social reality exists not by chance, but as the product of human action, so it is not transformed by chance. If humankind produce social reality (which in the "inversion of the praxis" turns back upon them and conditions them), then transforming that reality is an historical task, a task for humanity.

Reality which becomes oppressive results in the contradistinction of men as oppressors and oppressed. The latter, whose task it is to struggle for their liberation together with those who show true solidarity, must acquire a critical awareness of oppression through the praxis of this struggle. One of the gravest obstacles to the achievement of liberation is that oppressive reality absorbs those within it and thereby acts to submerge human beings' consciousness.[6] Functionally, oppression is domesticating. To no longer be prey to its force, one must emerge from it and turn upon it. This can be done only by means of the praxis: reflection and action upon the world in order to transform it.

[...]

In dialectical thought, world and action are intimately interdependent. But action is human only when it is not merely an occupation but also a preoccupation, that is, when it is not dichotomized from reflection. Reflection, which is essential to action, is implicit in Lukács' requirement of "explaining to the masses their own action," just as it is implicit in the purpose he attributes to this explanation: that of "consciously activating the subsequent development of experience."

For us, however, the requirement is seen not in terms of explaining to, but rather dialoguing with the people about their actions. In any event, no reality transforms itself,9 and the duty which Lukács ascribes to the revolutionary party of "explaining to the masses their own action" coincides with our affirmation of the need for the critical intervention of the people in reality through the praxis. The pedagogy of the oppressed, which is the pedagogy of people engaged in the fight for their own liberation, has its roots here. And those who recognize, or begin to recognize, themselves as oppressed must be among the developers of this pedagogy. No pedagogy which is truly liberating can remain distant from the oppressed by treating them as unfortunates and by presenting for their emulation models from among the oppressors. The oppressed must be their own example in the struggle for their redemption.

The pedagogy of the oppressed, animated by authentic, humanist (not humanitarian) generosity, presents itself as a pedagogy of humankind. Pedagogy which begins with the egoistic interests of the oppressors (an egoism cloaked in the false generosity of paternalism) and makes of the oppressed the objects of its humanitarianism, itself maintains and embodies oppression. It is an instrument of dehumanization. This is why, as we affirmed earlier, the pedagogy of the oppressed cannot be developed or practiced by the oppressors. It would be a contradiction in terms if the oppressors not only defended but actually implemented a liberating education.

[...]

The pedagogy of the oppressed, as a humanist and libertarian pedagogy, has two distinct stages. In the first, the oppressed unveil the world of oppression and through the praxis commit themselves to its transformation. In the second stage, in which the reality of oppression has already been transformed, this pedagogy ceases to belong to the oppressed and becomes a pedagogy of all people in the process of permanent liberation. In both stages, it is always through action in depth that the culture of domination is culturally confronted. In the first stage this confrontation occurs through the change in the way the oppressed perceive the world of oppression; in the second stage, through the expulsion of the myths created and developed in the old order, which like specters haunt the new structure emerging from the revolutionary transformation.

The pedagogy of the first stage must deal with the problem of the oppressed consciousness and the oppressor consciousness, the problem of men and women who oppress and men and women who suffer oppression. It must take into account their behavior, their view of the world, and their ethics. A particular problem is the duality of the oppressed: they are contradictory, divided beings, shaped by and existing in a concrete situation of oppression and violence.

Any situation in which "A" objectively exploits "B" or hinders his and her pursuit of self-affirmation as a responsible person is one of oppression. Such a situation in itself constitutes violence, even when sweetened by false generosity, because it interferes with the individual's ontological and historical vocation to be more fully human. With the establishment of a relationship of oppression, violence has *already* begun. Never in history has violence been initiated by the oppressed. How could they be the initiators, if they themselves are the result of violence? How could they be the sponsors of something whose objective inauguration called forth their existence as oppressed? There would be no oppressed had there been no prior situation of violence to establish their subjugation.

Violence is initiated by those who oppress, who exploit, who fail to recognize others as persons—not by those who are oppressed, exploited, and unrecognized. It is not the unloved who initiate disaffection, but those who cannot love because they love only themselves. It is not the helpless, subject to terror, who initiate terror, but the violent, who with their power create the concrete situation which begets the "rejects of life." It is not the tyrannized who initiate despotism, but the tyrants. It is not the despised who initiate hatred, but those who despise. It is not those whose humanity is denied them who negate humankind, but those who denied that humanity (thus negating their own as well). Force is used not by those who have become weak under the preponderance of the strong, but by the strong who have emasculated them.

For the oppressors, however, it is always the oppressed (whom they obviously never call "the oppressed" but—depending on whether they are fellow countrymen or not—"those people" or "the blind and envious masses" or "savages" or "natives" or "subversives") who are disaffected, who are "violent,""barbaric," "wicked," or "ferocious" when they react to the violence of the oppressors.

Yet it is—paradoxical though it may seem—precisely in the response of the oppressed to the violence of their oppressors that a gesture of love may be found. Consciously or unconsciously, the act of rebellion by the oppressed (an act which is always, or nearly always, as violent as the initial violence of the oppressors) can initiate love. Whereas the violence of the oppressors prevents the oppressed from being fully human, the response of the latter to this violence is grounded in the desire to pursue the right to be human. As the oppressors dehumanize others and violate their rights, they themselves also become dehumanized. As the oppressed, fighting to be human, take away the oppressors' power to dominate and suppress, they restore to the oppressors the humanity they had lost in the exercise of oppression.

It is only the oppressed who, by freeing themselves, can free their oppressors. The latter, as an oppressive class, can free neither others nor themselves. It is therefore essential that the oppressed wage the struggle to resolve the contradiction in which they are caught; and the contradiction will be resolved by the appearance of the new man: neither oppressor nor oppressed, but man in the process of liberation. If the goal of the oppressed is to become fully human, they will not achieve their goal by merely reversing the terms of the contradiction, by simply changing poles.

This may seem simplistic; it is not. Resolution of the oppressor-oppressed contradiction indeed implies the disappearance of the oppressors as a dominant class. However, the restraints imposed by the former oppressed on their oppressors, so that the latter cannot reassume their former position, do not constitute *oppression*. An act is oppressive only when it prevents people from being more fully human. Accordingly, these necessary restraints do not *in themselves* signify that yesterday's oppressed have become today's oppressors. Acts which prevent the restoration of the oppressive regime cannot be compared with those which create and maintain it, cannot be compared with those by which a few men and women deny the majority their right to be human.

However, the moment the new regime hardens into a dominating "bureaucracy"[7] the humanist dimension of the struggle is lost and it is no longer possible to speak of liberation. Hence our insistence that the authentic solution of the oppressor-oppressed contradiction does not lie in a mere reversal of position, in moving from one pole to the other. Nor does it lie in the replacement of the former oppressors with new ones who continue to subjugate the oppressed—all in the name of their liberation.

But even when the contradiction is resolved authentically by a new situation established by the liberated laborers, the former oppressors do not feel liberated. On the contrary, they genuinely consider themselves to be oppressed. Conditioned by the experience of oppressing others, any situation other than their former seems to them like oppression. Formerly, they could eat, dress, wear shoes, be educated, travel, and hear Beethoven; while millions did not eat, had no clothes or shoes, neither studied nor traveled, much less listened to Beethoven. Any restriction on this way of life, in the name of the rights of the community, appears to the former oppressors as a profound violation of their individual rights—although they had no respect for the millions who suffered and died of hunger, pain, sorrow, and despair. For the oppressors, "human beings" refers only to themselves; other people are "things." For the oppressors, there exists only one right: their right to live in peace, over against the right, not always even recognized, but simply conceded, of the oppressed to survival. And they make this concession only because the existence of the oppressed is necessary to their own existence.

This behavior, this way of understanding the world and people (which necessarily makes the oppressors resist the installation of a new regime) is explained by their experience as a dominant class. Once a situation of violence and oppression has been established, it engenders an entire way of life and behavior for those caught up in it—oppressors and oppressed alike. Both are submerged in this situation, and both bear the marks of oppression. Analysis of existential situations of oppression reveals that their inception lay in an act of violence—initiated by those with power. This violence, as a process, is perpetuated from generation to generation of oppressors, who become its heirs and are shaped in its climate. This climate creates in the oppressor a strongly possessive consciousness—possessive of the world and of men and women. Apart from direct, concrete, material possession of the world and of people, the oppressor consciousness could not understand itself—could not even exist. Fromm said of this consciousness that, without such possession, "it would lose contact with the world." The oppressor consciousness tends to transform everything surrounding it into an object of its domination. The earth, property, production, the creations of people, people themselves, time—everything is reduced to the status of objects at its disposal.

In their unrestrained eagerness to possess, the oppressors develop the conviction that it is possible for them to transform everything into objects of their purchasing power; hence their strictly materialistic concept of existence. Money is the measure of all things, and profit the primary goal. For the oppressors, what is worthwhile is to have more—always more—even at the cost of the oppressed having less or having nothing. For them, *to be is to have* and to be the class of the "haves."

As beneficiaries of a situation of oppression, the oppressors cannot perceive that if *having* is a condition of *being*, it is a necessary condition for all women and men. This is why their generosity is false. Humanity is a "thing," and they possess it as an exclusive right, as inherited property. To the oppressor consciousness, the humanization of the "others," of the people, appears not as the pursuit of full humanity, but as subversion.

The oppressors do not perceive their monopoly on *having more* as a privilege which dehumanizes others and themselves. They cannot see that, in the egoistic pursuit of *having* as a possessing class, they suffocate in their own possessions and no longer *are;* they merely *have.* For them, *having more* is an inalienable right, a right they acquired

through their own "effort," with their "courage to take risks." If others do not have more, it is because they are incompetent and lazy, and worst of all is their unjustifiable ingratitude towards the "generous gestures" of the dominant class. Precisely because they are "ungrateful" and "envious," the oppressed are regarded as potential enemies who must be watched.

It could not be otherwise. If the humanization of the oppressed signifies subversion, so also does their freedom; hence the necessity for constant control. And the more the oppressors control the oppressed, the more they change them into apparently inanimate "things." This tendency of the oppressor consciousness to "in-animate" everything and everyone it encounters, in its eagerness to possess, unquestionably corresponds with a tendency to sadism.

The pleasure in complete domination over another person (or other animate creature) is the very essence of the sadistic drive. Another way of formulating the same thought is to say that the aim of sadism is to transform a man into a thing, something animate into something inanimate, since by complete and absolute control the living loses one essential quality of life—freedom.[8]

[...]

On the other hand, at a certain point in their existential experience the oppressed feel an irresistible attraction towards the oppressors and their way of life. Sharing this way of life becomes an overpowering aspiration. In their alienation, the oppressed want at any cost to resemble the oppressors, to imitate them, to follow them. This phenomenon is especially prevalent in the middle-class oppressed, who yearn to be equal to the "eminent" men and women of the upper class. Albert Memmi, in an exceptional analysis of the "colonized mentality," refers to the contempt he felt towards the colonizer, mixed with "passionate" attraction towards him.

How could the colonizer look after his workers while periodically gunning down a crowd of colonized? How could the colonized deny himself so cruelly yet make such excessive demands? How could he hate the colonizers and yet admire them so passionately? (I too felt this admiration in spite of myself.)[9]

Self-depreciation is another characteristic of the oppressed, which derives from their internalization of the opinion the oppressors hold of them. So often do they hear that they are good for nothing, know nothing and are incapable of learning anything—that they are sick, lazy, and unproductive—that in the end they become convinced of their own unfitness.

The peasant feels inferior to the boss because the boss seems to be the only one who knows things and is able to run things.[10]

They call themselves ignorant and say the "professor" is the one who has knowledge and to whom they should listen. The criteria of knowledge imposed upon them are the conventional ones. "Why don't you," said a peasant participating in a culture circle, "explain the pictures first? That way it'll take less time and won't give us a headache."

Almost never do they realize that they, too, "know things" they have learned in their relations with the world and with other women and men. Given the circumstances which have produced their duality, it is only natural that they distrust themselves.

[...]

Critical and liberating dialogue, which presupposes action, must be carried on with the oppressed at whatever the stage of their struggle for liberation.[11] The content of that dialogue can and should vary in accordance with historical conditions and the level at which the oppressed perceive reality. But to substitute monologue, slogans, and communiqués for dialogue is to attempt to liberate the oppressed with the instruments of domestication. Attempting to liberate the oppressed without their reflective participation in the act of liberation is to treat them as objects which must be saved from a burning building; it is to lead them into the populist pitfall and transform them into masses which can be manipulated.

At all stages of their liberation, the oppressed must see themselves as women and men engaged in the ontological and historical vocation of becoming more fully human. Reflection and action become imperative when one does not erroneously attempt to dichotomize the content of humanity from its historical forms.

[...]

It is essential for the oppressed to realize that when they accept the struggle for humanization they also accept, from that moment, their total responsibility for the struggle. They must realize that they are fighting not merely for freedom from hunger, but for

> ... freedom to create and to construct, to wonder and to venture. Such freedom requires that the individual be active and responsible, not a slave or a well-fed cog in the machine. . . . It is not enough that men are not slaves; if social conditions further the existence of automatons, the result will not be love of life, but love of death.[12]

The oppressed, who have been shaped by the death-affirming climate of oppression, must find through their struggle the way to life-affirming humanization, which does not lie *simply* in having more to eat (although it does involve having more to eat and cannot fail to include this aspect). The oppressed have been destroyed precisely because their situation has reduced them to things. In order to regain their humanity they must cease to be things and fight as men and women. This is a radical requirement. They cannot enter the struggle as objects in order *later* to become human beings.

The struggle begins with men's recognition that they have been destroyed. Propaganda, management, manipulation—all arms of domination—cannot be the instruments of their rehumanization. The only effective instrument is a humanizing pedagogy in which the revolutionary leadership establishes a permanent relationship of dialogue with the oppressed. In a humanizing pedagogy the method ceases to be an instrument by which the teachers (in this instance, the revolutionary leadership) can manipulate the students (in this instance, the oppressed), because it expresses the consciousness of the students themselves.

The method is, in fact, the external form of consciousness manifest in acts, which takes on the fundamental property of consciousness—its intentionality. The essence of consciousness is being with the world, and this behavior is permanent and unavoidable. Accordingly, consciousness is in essence a 'way towards something apart from itself, outside itself, which surrounds it and which it apprehends by means of its ideational capacity. Consciousness is thus by definition a method, in the most general sense of the word.

A revolutionary leadership must accordingly practice *co-intentional* education. Teachers and students (leadership and people), co-intent on reality, are both Subjects, not only in the task of unveiling that reality, and thereby coming to know it critically, but in the task of re-creating that knowledge. As they attain this knowledge of reality through common reflection and action, they discover themselves as its permanent re-creators. In this way, the presence of the oppressed in the struggle for their liberation will be what it should be: not pseudo-participation, but committed involvement.

Questions for Discussion

1. "Oppression" as a term is on the verge of becoming an empty signifier, always referred to but never analyzed. How have you heard the term used in various discourses? How does Freire define the term (hint: look for him discussing when an "act is oppressive")?

2. What narratives have you heard that claim to better the world or otherwise foster a more just society? How do these narratives compare with what Freire sketches out there?

3. Freire mentions false and true generosity several times. What does he means by these terms?

What are contemporary examples of these? What's so bad about false generosity?

4. What are the processes that allow oppression to reproduce itself (even if the people and modes changes)? How can we short-circuit this and what processes might we replace them with?

5. What does it mean that a just society "must be forged *with,* not *for,* the oppressed"? Where have you seen both of these attempted?

Citation and Use

The text was taken from the following work.

Paulo Freire, "Chapter 1," in PEDAGOGY OF THE OPPRESSED: 30TH ANNIVERSARY EDITION, trans. Myra Bergman Ramos (New York, London, New Delhi, and Sydney: Bloomsbury, n.d.).

This use of this work is governed by the Fair Use doctrine. If you are the owner of the copyright to this work and wish to contest this, please begin that dialog with us by contacting the editor.

Notes

Notes

1. The current movements of rebellion, especially those of youth, while they necessarily reflect the peculiarities of their respective settings, manifest in their essence this preoccupation with people as beings in the world and with the world—preoccupation with what and how they are "being." As they place consumer civilization in judgment, denounce bureaucracies of all types, demand the transformation of the universities (changing the rigid nature of the teacher-student relationship and placing that relationship within the context of reality), propose the transformation of reality itself so that universities can be renewed, attack old orders and established institutions in the attempt to affirm human beings as the Subjects of decision, all these movements reflect the style of our age, which is more anthropological than anthropocentric.

2. As used throughout this book, the term "contradiction" denotes the dialectical conflict between opposing social forces.—Translator's note

3. This fear of freedom is also to be found in the oppressors though, obviously, in a different form. The oppressed are afraid to embrace freedom; the oppressors are afraid of losing the "freedom" to oppress.

4. See Hegel, op. cit., pp. 236-237.

5. Analyzing the dialectical relationship between the consciousness of the master and the consciousness of the oppressed, Hegel states: "The one is independent, and its essential nature is to be for itself; the other is dependent, and its essence is life or existence for another. The former is the Master, or Lord, the latter the Bondsman." Ibid., p. 234.

6. "Liberating action necessarily involves a moment of perception and volition. This action both precedes and follows that moment, to which it first acts as a prologue and which it subsequently serves to effect and continue within history. The action of domination, however, does not necessarily imply this dimension; for the structure of domination is maintained by its own mechanical and unconscious functionality." From an unpublished work by José Luiz Fiori, who has kindly granted permission to quote him.

7. This rigidity should not be identified with the restraints that must be imposed on the former oppressors so they cannot restore the oppressive order. Rather, it refers to the revolution which becomes stagnant and turns against the people, using the old repressive, bureaucratic State apparatus (which should have been drastically suppressed, as Marx so often emphasized).

8. Erich Fromm, The Heart of Man (New York, 1966), p. 32.

9. The Colonizer and the Colonized (Boston, 1967), p. x.

10. Words of a peasant during an interview with the author.

11. Not in the open, of course; that would only provoke the fury of the oppressor and lead to still greater repression.

12. Fromm, op. cit., pp. 52-53.

POLITICS

THE INDIVIDUAL, SOCIETY AND THE STATE

Emma Goldman

The minds of men are in confusion, for the very foundations of our civilization seem to be tottering. People are losing faith in the existing institutions, and the more intelligent realize that capitalist industrialism is defeating the very purpose it is supposed to serve.

The world is at a loss for a way out. Parliamentarism and democracy are on the decline. Salvation is being sought in Fascism and other forms of "strong" government.

The struggle of opposing ideas now going on in the world involves social problems urgently demanding a solution. The welfare of the individual and the fate of human society depend on the right answer to those questions. The crisis, unemployment, war, disarmament, international relations, etc., are among those problems.

The State, government with its functions and powers, is now the subject of vital interest to every thinking man. Political developments in all civilized countries have brought the questions home. Shall we have a strong government? Are democracy and parliamentary government to be preferred, or is Fascism of one kind or another, dictatorship — monarchical, bourgeois or proletarian — the solution of the ills and difficulties that beset society today?

In other words, shall we cure the evils of democracy by more democracy, or shall we cut the Gordian knot of popular government with the sword of dictatorship?

My answer is neither the one nor the other. I am against dictatorship and Fascism as I am opposed to parliamentary regimes and so-called political democracy.

Nazism has been justly called an attack on civilization. This characterization applies with equal force to every form of dictatorship; indeed, to every kind of suppression and coercive authority. For what is civilization in the true sense? All progress has been essentially an enlargement of the liberties of the individual with a corresponding decrease of the authority wielded over him by external forces. This holds good in the realm of physical as well as of political and economic existence. In the physical world man has progressed to the extent in which he has subdued the forces of nature and made them useful to himself. Primitive man made a step on the road to progress when he first produced fire and thus triumphed over darkness, when he chained the wind or harnessed water.

What role did authority or government play in human endeavor for betterment, in invention and discovery? None whatever, or at least none that was helpful. It has always been the individual that has accomplished every miracle in that sphere, usually in spite of the prohibition, persecution and interference by authority, human and divine.

Similarly, in the political sphere, the road of progress lay in getting away more and more from the authority of the tribal chief or of the clan, of prince and king, of government, of the State. Economically, progress has meant greater well-being of ever larger numbers. Culturally, it has signified the result of all the other achievements — greater independence, political, mental and psychic.

Regarded from this angle, the problems of man's relation to the State assumes an entirely different significance. It is no more a question of whether dictatorship is preferable to democracy, or Italian Fascism superior to Hitlerism. A larger and far more vital question poses itself: Is political government, is the State beneficial to mankind, and how does it affect the individual in the social scheme of things?

The individual is the true reality in life. A cosmos in himself, he does not exist for the State, nor for that abstraction called "society," or the "nation," which is only a collection of individuals. Man, the individual, has always been and, necessarily is the sole source and motive power of evolution and progress. Civilization has been a continuous struggle of the individual or of groups of individuals against the State and even against "society," that is, against the majority subdued and hypnotized by the State and State worship. Man's greatest battles have been waged against man-made obstacles and artificial handicaps imposed upon him to paralyze his growth and development. Human thought has always been falsified by tradition and custom, and perverted false education in the interests of those who held power and enjoyed privileges. In other words, by the State and the ruling classes. This constant incessant conflict has been the history of mankind.

Individuality may be described as the consciousness of the individual as to what he is and how he lives. It is inherent in every human being and is a thing of growth. The State and social institutions come and go, but individuality remains and persists. The very essence of individuality is expression; the sense of dignity and independence is the soil wherein it thrives. Individuality is not the impersonal and mechanistic thing that the State treats as an "individual". The individual is not merely the result of heredity and environment, of cause and effect. He is that and a great deal more, a great deal else. The living man cannot be defined; he is the fountain-head of all life and all values; he is not a part of this or of that; he is a whole, an individual whole, a growing, changing, yet always constant whole.

Individuality is not to be confused with the various ideas and concepts of Individualism; much less with that "rugged individualism" which is only a masked attempt to repress and defeat the individual and his individuality So-called Individualism is the social and economic *laissez faire*: the exploitation of the masses by the classes by means of legal trickery, spiritual debasement and systematic indoctrination of the servile spirit, which process is known as "education." That corrupt and perverse "individualism" is the strait-jacket of individuality. It has converted life into a degrading race for externals, for possession, for social prestige and supremacy. Its highest wisdom is "the devil take the hindmost."

This "rugged individualism" has inevitably resulted in the greatest modern slavery, the crassest class distinctions, driving millions to the breadline. "Rugged individualism" has meant all the "individualism" for the masters, while the people are regimented into a slave caste to serve a handful of self-seeking "supermen." America is perhaps the best representative of this kind of individualism, in whose name political tyranny and social oppression are defended and held up as virtues; while every aspiration and attempt of man to gain freedom and social opportunity to live is denounced as "unAmerican" and evil in the name of that same individualism.

There was a time when the State was unknown. In his natural condition man existed without any State or organized government. People lived as families in small communities; They tilled the soil and practiced the arts and crafts. The individual, and later the family, was the unit of social life where each was free and the equal of his neighbor. Human society then was not a State but an *association*; a *voluntary* association for mutual protection and benefit. The elders and more experienced members were the guides and advisers of the people. They helped to manage the affairs of life, not to rule and dominate the individual.

Political government and the State were a much later development, growing out of the desire of the stronger to take advantage of the weaker, of the few against the many. The State, ecclesiastical and secular, served to give an appear-

ance of legality and right to the wrong done by the few to the many. That appearance of right was necessary the easier to rule the people, because no government can exist without the consent of the people, consent open, tacit or assumed. Constitutionalism and democracy are the modern forms of that alleged consent; the consent being inoculated and indoctrinated by what is called "education," at home, in the church, and in every other phase of life.

That consent is the belief in authority, in the necessity for it. At its base is the doctrine that man is evil, vicious, and too incompetent to know what is good for him. On this all government and oppression is built. God and the State exist and are supported by this dogma.

Yet the State is nothing but a name. It is an abstraction. Like other similar conceptions — nation, race, humanity — it has no organic reality. To call the State an organism shows a diseased tendency to make a fetish of words.

The State is a term for the legislative and administrative machinery whereby certain business of the people is transacted, and badly so. There is nothing sacred, holy or mysterious about it. The State has no more conscience or moral mission than a commercial company for working a coal mine or running a railroad.

The State has no more existence than gods and devils have. They are equally the reflex and creation of man, for man, the individual, is the only reality. The State is but the shadow of man, the shadow of his opaqueness of his ignorance and fear.

Life begins and ends with man, the individual. Without him there is no race, no humanity, no State. No, not even "society" is possible without man. It is the individual who lives, breathes and suffers. His development, his advance, has been a continuous struggle against the fetishes of his own creation and particularly so against the "State."

In former days religious authority fashioned political life in the image of the Church. The authority of the State, the "rights" of rulers came from on high; power, like faith, was divine. Philosophers have written thick volumes to prove the sanctity of the State; some have even clad it with infallibility and with god-like attributes Some have talked themselves into the insane notion that the State is "superhuman," the supreme reality, "the absolute."

Enquiry was condemned as blasphemy. Servitude was the highest virtue. By such precepts and training certain things came to be regarded as self-evident, as sacred of their truth ,but [sic] because of constant and persistent repetition.

All progress has been essentially an unmasking of "divinity" and "mystery," of alleged sacred, eternal "truth"; it has been a gradual elimination of the abstract and the substitution in its place of the real, the concrete. In short, of facts against fancy, of knowledge against ignorance, of light against darkness.

That slow and arduous liberation of the individual was not

accomplished by the aid of the State. On the contrary, it was by continuous conflict, by a life-and death struggle with the State, that even the smallest vestige of independence and freedom has been won. It has cost mankind much time and blood to secure what little it has gained so far from kings, tsars and governments

The great heroic figure of that long Golgotha has been Man. It has always been the individual, often alone and singly, at other times in unity and co-operation with others of his kind, who has fought and bled in the age-long battle against suppression and oppression, against the powers that enslave and degrade him.

More than that and more significant: It was man, the individual, whose soul first rebelled against injustice and degradation; it was the individual who first conceived the idea of resistance to the conditions under which he chafed. In short, it is always the individual who is the parent of the liberating thought as well as of the deed.

This refers not only to political struggles, but to the entire gamut of human life and effort, in all ages and climes. It has always been the individual, the man of strong mind and will to liberty, who paved the way for every human advance, for every step toward a freer and better world; in science, philosophy and art, as well as in industry, whose genius rose to the heights, conceiving the "impossible," visualizing its realization and imbuing others with his enthusiasm to work and strive for it. Socially speaking, it was always the prophet, the seer, the idealist, who dreamed of a world more to his heart's desire and who served as the beacon light on the road to greater achievement.

The State, every government whatever its form, character or color — be it absolute or constitutional, monarchy or republic, Fascist, Nazi or Bolshevik — is by its very nature conservative, static, intolerant of change and opposed to it. Whatever changes it undergoes are always the result of pressure exerted upon it, pressure strong enough to compel the ruling powers to submit peaceably or otherwise, generally "otherwise" — that is, by revolution. Moreover, the inherent conservatism of government, of authority of any kind, unavoidably becomes reactionary. For two reasons: first, because it is in the nature of government not only to retain the power it has, but also to strengthen, widen and perpetuate it, nationally as well as internationally. The stronger authority grows, the greater the State and its power, the less it can tolerate a similar authority or political power along side of itself. The psychology of government demands that its influence and prestige constantly grow, at home and abroad, and it exploits every opportunity to increase it. This tendency is motivated by the financial and commercial interests back of the government, represented and served by it. The fundamental *raison d'etre* of every government to which, incidentally, historians of former days wilfully shut their eyes, has become too obvious now even for professors to ignore.

The other factor which impels governments to become even more conservative and reactionary is their inherent distrust of the individual and fear of individuality. Our political and social scheme cannot afford to tolerate the individual and his constant quest for innovation. In "self-defense" the State therefore suppresses, persecutes, punishes and even deprives the individual of life. It is aided in this by every institution that stands for the preservation of the existing order. It resorts to every form of violence and force, and its efforts are supported by the "moral indignation" of the majority against the heretic, the social dissenter and the political rebel — the majority for centuries drilled in State worship, trained in discipline and obedience and subdued by the awe of authority in the home, the school, the church and the press.

The strongest bulwark of authority is uniformity; the least divergence from it is the greatest crime. The wholesale mechanisation of modern life has increased uniformity a thousandfold. It is everywhere present, in habits, tastes, dress, thoughts and ideas. Its most concentrated dullness is "public opinion." Few have the courage to stand out against it. He who refuses to submit is at once labelled "queer," "different," and decried as a disturbing element in the comfortable stagnancy of modern life.

Perhaps even more than constituted authority, it is social uniformity and sameness that harass the individual most. His very "uniqueness," "separateness" and "differentiation" make him an alien, not only in his native place, but even in his own home. Often more so than the foreign born who generally falls in with the established.

In the true sense one's native land, with its back ground of tradition, early impressions, reminiscences and other things dear to one, is not enough to make sensitive human beings feel at home. A certain atmosphere of "belonging," the consciousness of being "at one" with the people and environment, is more essential to one's feeling of home. This holds good in relation to one's family, the smaller local circle, as well as the larger phase of the life and activities commonly called one's country. The individual whose vision encompasses the whole world often feels nowhere so hedged in and out of touch with his surroundings than in his native land.

In pre-war time the individual could at least escape national and family boredom. The whole world was open to his longings and his quests. Now the world has become a prison, and life continual solitary confinement. Especially is this true since the advent of dictatorship, right and left.

Friedrich Nietzsche called the State a cold monster. What would he have called the hideous beast in the garb of modern dictatorship? Not that government had ever allowed much scope to the individual; but the champions of the new State ideology do not grant even that much. "The individual is nothing," they declare, "it is the collectivity which counts." Nothing less than the complete surrender of the individual will satisfy the insatiable appetite of the new deity.

Strangely enough, the loudest advocates of this new gospel

are to be found among the British and American intelligentsia. Just now they are enamored with the "dictatorship of the proletariat." In theory only, to be sure. In practice, they still prefer the few liberties in their own respective countries. They go to Russia for a short visit or as salesmen of the "revolution," but they feel safer and more comfortable at home.

Perhaps it is not only lack of courage which keeps these good Britishers and Americans in their native lands rather than in the millennium come. Subconsciously there may lurk the feeling that individuality remains the most fundamental fact of all human association, suppressed and persecuted yet never defeated, and in the long run the victor.

The "genius of man," which is but another name for personality and individuality, bores its way through all the caverns of dogma, through the thick walls of tradition and custom, defying all taboos, setting authority at naught, facing contumely and the scaffold — ultimately to be blessed as prophet and martyr by succeeding generations. But for the "genius of man," that inherent, persistent quality of individuality, we would be still roaming the primeval forests.

Peter Kropotkin has shown what wonderful results this unique force of man's individuality has achieved when strengthened by *co-operation* with other individualities. The one-sided and entirely inadequate Darwinian theory of the struggle for existence received its biological and sociological completion from the great Anarchist scientist and thinker. In his profound work, *Mutual Aid* Kropotkin shows that in the animal kingdom, as well as in human society, co-operation — as opposed to internecine strife and struggle — has worked for the survival and evolution of the species. He demonstrated that only mutual aid and voluntary co-operation — not the omnipotent, all-devastating State — can create the basis for a free individual and associational life.

At present the individual is the pawn of the zealots of dictatorship and the equally obsessed zealots of "rugged individualism." The excuse of the former is its claim of a new objective. The latter does not even make a pretense of anything new. As a matter of fact "rugged individualism" has learned nothing and forgotten nothing. Under its guidance the brute struggle for physical existence is still kept up. Strange as it may seem, and utterly absurd as it is, the struggle for physical survival goes merrily on though the necessity for it has entirely disappeared. Indeed, the struggle is being continued apparently because there is no necessity for it. Does not so-called overproduction prove it? Is not the world-wide economic crisis an eloquent demonstration that the struggle for existence is being maintained by the blindness of "rugged individualism" at the risk of its own destruction?

One of the insane characteristics of this struggle is the complete negation of the relation of the producer to the things he produces. The average worker has no inner point of contact with the industry he is employed in, and he is a stranger to the process of production of which he is a mechanical part. Like any other cog of the machine, he is replaceable at any time by other similar depersonalized human beings.

The intellectual proletarian, though he foolishly thinks himself a free agent, is not much better off. He, too, has a little choice or self-direction, in his particular metier as his brother who works with his hands. Material considerations and desire for greater social prestige are usually the deciding factors in the vocation of the intellectual. Added to it is the tendency to follow in the footsteps of family tradition, and become doctors, lawyers, teachers, engineers, etc. The groove requires less effort and personality. In consequence nearly everybody is out of place in our present scheme of things. The masses plod on, partly because their senses have been dulled by the deadly routine of work and because they must eke out an existence. This applies with even greater force to the political fabric of today. There is no place in its texture for free choice of independent thought and activity. There is a place only for voting and tax-paying puppets.

The interests of the State and those of the individual differ fundamentally and are antagonistic. The State and the political and economic institutions it supports can exist only by fashioning the individual to their particular purpose; training him to respect "law and order;" teaching him obedience, submission and unquestioning faith in the wisdom and justice of government; above all, loyal service and complete self-sacrifice when the State commands it, as in war. The State puts itself and its interests even above the claims of religion and of God. It punishes religious or conscientious scruples against individuality because there is no individuality without liberty, and liberty is the greatest menace to authority.

The struggle of the individual against these tremendous odds is the more difficult — too often dangerous to life and limb — because it is not truth or falsehood which serves as the criterion of the opposition he meets. It is not the validity or usefulness of his thought or activity which rouses against him the forces of the State and of "public opinion." The persecution of the innovator and protestant has always been inspired by fear on the part of constituted authority of having its infallibility questioned and its power undermined.

Man's true liberation, individual and collective, lies in his emancipation from authority and from the belief in it. All human evolution has been a struggle in that direction and for that object. It is not invention and mechanics which constitute development. The ability to travel at the rate of 100 miles an hour is no evidence of being civilized. True civilization is to be measured by the individual, the unit of all social life; by his individuality and the extent to which it is free to have its being to grow and expand unhindered by invasive and coercive authority.

Socially speaking, the criterion of civilization and culture is the degree of liberty and economic opportunity which the individual enjoys; of social and international unity and co-operation unrestricted by man-made laws and other artificial obstacles; by the absence of privileged castes and by the reality of liberty and human dignity; in short, by the true emancipation of the individual.

Political absolutism has been abolished because men have realized in the course of time that absolute power is evil and destructive. But the same thing is true of all power, whether it be the power of privilege, of money, of the priest, of the politician or of so-called democracy. In its effect on individuality it matters little what the particular character of coercion is — whether it be as black as Fascism, as yellow as Nazism or as pretentiously red as Bolshevism. It is power that corrupts and degrades both master and slave and it makes no difference whether the power is wielded by an autocrat, by parliament or Soviets. More pernicious than the power of a dictator is that of a class; the most terrible — the tyranny of a majority.

The long process of history has taught man that division and strife mean death, and that unity and cooperation advance his cause, multiply his strength and further his welfare. The spirit of government has always worked against the social application of this vital lesson, except where it served the State and aided its own particular interests. It is this anti-progressive and anti-social spirit of the State and of the privileged castes back of it which has been responsible for the bitter struggle between man and man. The individual and ever larger groups of individuals are beginning to see beneath the surface of the established order of things. No longer are they so blinded as in the past by the glare and tinsel of the State idea, and of the "blessings" of "rugged individualism." Man is reaching out for the wider scope of human relations which liberty alone can give. For true liberty is not a mere scrap of paper called "constitution," "legal right" or "law." It is not an abstraction derived from the non-reality known as "the State." It is not the *negative* thing of being free *from* something, because with such freedom you may starve to death. Real freedom, true liberty is *positive*: it is freedom *to* something; it is the liberty to be, to do; in short, the liberty of actual and active opportunity.

That sort of liberty is not a gift: it is the natural right of man, of every human being. It cannot be given: it cannot be conferred by any law or government. The need of it, the longing for it, is inherent in the individual. Disobedience to every form of coercion is the instinctive expression of it. Rebellion and revolution are the more or less conscious attempt to achieve it. Those manifestations, individual and social, are fundamentally expressions of the values of man. That those values may be nurtured, the community must realize that its greatest and most lasting asset is the unit — the individual.

In religion, as in politics, people speak of abstractions and believe they are dealing with realities. But when it does come to the real and the concrete, most people seem to lose vital touch with it. It may well be because reality alone is too matter-of-fact, too cold to enthuse the human soul.

It can be aroused to enthusiasm only by things out of the commonplace, out of the ordinary. In other words, the Ideal is the spark that fires the imagination and hearts of men. Some ideal is needed to rouse man out of the inertia and humdrum of his existence and turn the abject slave into an heroic figure.

Right here, of course, comes the Marxist objector who has outmarxed Marx himself. To such a one, man is a mere puppet in the hands of that metaphysical Almighty called economic determinism or, more vulgarly, the class struggle. Man's will, individual and collective, his psychic life and mental orientation count for almost nothing with our Marxist and do not affect his conception of human history.

No intelligent student will deny the importance of the economic factor in the social growth and development of mankind. But only narrow and wilful dogmatism can persist in remaining blind to the important role played by an idea as conceived by the imagination and aspirations of the individual.

It were vain and unprofitable to attempt to balance one factor as against another in human experience. No one single factor in the complex of individual or social behavior can be designated as the factor of decisive quality. We know too little, and may never know enough, of human psychology to weigh and measure the relative values of this or that factor in determining man's conduct. To form such dogmas in their social connotation is nothing short of bigotry; yet, perhaps, it has its uses, for the very attempt to do so proved the persistence of the human will and confutes the Marxists.

Fortunately even some Marxists are beginning to see that all is not well with the Marxian creed. After all, Marx was but human — all too human — hence by no means infallible. The practical application of economic determinism in Russia is helping to clear the minds of the more intelligent Marxists. This can be seen in the transvaluation of Marxian values going on in Socialist and even Communist ranks in some European countries. They are slowly realising that their theory has overlooked the human element, *den Menschen*, as a Socialist paper put it. Important as the economic factor is, it is not enough. The rejuvenation of mankind needs the inspiration and energising force of an ideal.

Such an ideal I see in Anarchism. To be sure, not in the popular misrepresentations of Anarchism spread by the worshippers of the State and authority. I mean the philosophy of a new social order based on the released energies of the individual and the free association of liberated individuals.

Of all social theories Anarchism alone steadfastly proclaims that society exists for man, not man for society. The sole legitimate purpose of society is to serve the needs and advance the aspiration of the individual. Only by doing so can it justify its existence and be an aid to progress and culture.

The political parties and men savagely scrambling for power will scorn me as hopelessly out of tune with our time. I cheerfully admit the charge. I find comfort in the assurance that their hysteria lacks enduring quality. Their hosanna is but of the hour.

Man's yearning for liberation from all authority and power will never be soothed by their cracked song. Man's quest for freedom from every shackle is eternal. It must and will go on.

Citation and Use

The reading was taken from the following work.

Emma Goldman. "The Individual, Society and the State." The Anarchist Library, 2009. https://theanarchistlibrary.org/library/emma-goldman-the-individual-society-and-the-state.

WHENCE INEQUALITY?

Jean-Jacques Rousseau

Discourse on the Origin and Basis of Inequality Among Men

THE first man who, having enclosed a piece of ground, bethought himself of saying This is mine, and found people simple enough to believe him, was the real founder of civil society. From how many crimes, wars and murders, from how many horrors and misfortunes might not any one have saved mankind, by pulling up the stakes, or filling up the ditch, and crying to his fellows, "Beware of listening to this impostor; you are undone if you once forget that the fruits of the earth belong to us all, and the earth itself to nobody." But there is great probability that things had then already come to such a pitch, that they could no longer continue as they were; for the idea of property depends on many prior ideas, which could only be acquired successively, and cannot have been formed all at once in the human mind. Mankind must have made very considerable progress, and acquired considerable knowledge and industry which they must also have transmitted and increased from age to age, before they arrived at this last point of the state of nature. Let us then go farther back, and endeavour to unify under a single point of view that slow succession of events and discoveries in the most natural order.

Man's first feeling was that of his own existence, and his first care that of self-preservation. The produce of the earth furnished him with all he needed, and instinct told him how to use it. Hunger and other appetites made him at various times experience various modes of existence; and among these was one which urged him to propagate his species — a blind propensity that, having nothing to do with the heart, produced a merely animal act. The want once gratified, the two sexes knew each other no more; and even the offspring was nothing to its mother, as soon as it could do without her.

Such was the condition of infant man; the life of an animal limited at first to mere sensations, and hardly profiting by the gifts nature bestowed on him, much less capable of entertaining a thought of forcing anything from her. But difficulties soon presented themselves, and it became necessary to learn how to surmount them: the height of the trees, which prevented him from gathering their fruits, the competition of other animals desirous of the same fruits, and the ferocity of those who needed them for their own preservation, all obliged him to apply himself to bodily exercises. He had to be active, swift of foot, and vigorous in fight. Natural weapons, stones and sticks, were easily found: he learnt to surmount the obstacles of nature, to contend in case of necessity with other animals, and to dispute for the means of subsistence even with other men, or to indemnify himself for what he was forced to give up to a stronger.

In proportion as the human race grew more numerous, men's cares increased. The difference of soils, climates and seasons, must have introduced some differences into their manner of living. Barren years, long and sharp winters, scorching summers which parched the fruits of the earth, must have demanded a new industry. On the seashore and the banks of rivers, they invented the hook and line, and became fishermen and eaters of fish. In the forests they made bows and arrows, and became huntsmen and warriors. In cold countries they clothed themselves with the skins of the beasts they had slain. The lightning, a volcano, or some lucky chance acquainted them with fire, a new resource against the rigours of winter: they next learned how to preserve this element, then how to reproduce it, and finally how to prepare with it the flesh of animals which before they had eaten raw.

This repeated relevance of various beings to himself, and one to another, would naturally give rise in the human mind to the perceptions of certain relations between them. Thus the relations which we denote by the terms, great, small, strong, weak, swift, slow, fearful, bold, and the like, almost insensibly compared at need, must have at length produced in him a kind of reflection, or rather a mechanical prudence, which would indicate to him the precautions most necessary to his security.

The new intelligence which resulted from this development increased his superiority over other animals, by making him sensible of it. He would now endeavour, therefore, to ensnare them, would play them a thousand tricks, and though many of them might surpass him in swiftness or in strength, would in time become the master of some and the scourge of others. Thus, the first time he looked into himself, he felt the first emotion of pride; and, at a time when he scarce knew how to distinguish the different orders of beings, by looking upon his species as of the highest order, he prepared the way for assuming pre-eminence as an individual.

Other men, it is true, were not then to him what they now are to us, and he had no greater intercourse with them than with other animals; yet they were not neglected in his observations. The conformities, which he would in time discover between them, and between himself and his female, led him to judge of others which were not then perceptible; and finding that they all behaved as he himself would have done in like circumstances, he naturally inferred that their manner of thinking and acting was altogether in conformity with his own. This important truth, once deeply impressed on his mind, must have induced him, from an intuitive feeling more certain and much more rapid than any kind of reasoning, to pursue the rules of conduct, which he had best observe towards them, for his own security and advantage.

Taught by experience that the love of well-being is the sole motive of human actions, he found himself in a position to distinguish the few cases, in which mutual interest might justify him in relying upon the assistance of his fellows; and also the still fewer cases in which a conflict of interests might give cause to suspect them. In the former case, he joined in the same herd with them, or at most in some kind of loose association, that laid no restraint on its members, and lasted no longer than the transitory occasion that formed it. In the latter case, every one sought his own private advantage, either by open force, if he thought himself strong enough, or by address and cunning, if he felt himself the weaker.

In this manner, men may have insensibly acquired some gross ideas of mutual undertakings, and of the advantages of fulfilling them: that is, just so far as their present and apparent interest was concerned: for they were perfect strangers to foresight, and were so far from troubling themselves about the distant future, that they hardly thought of the morrow. If a deer was to be taken, every one saw that, in order to succeed, he must abide faithfully by his post: but if a hare happened to come within the reach of any one of them, it is not to be doubted that he pursued it without scruple, and, having seized his prey, cared very little, if by so doing he caused his companions to miss theirs.

It is easy to understand that such intercourse would not require a language much more refined than that of rooks or monkeys, who associate together for much the same purpose. Inarticulate cries, plenty of gestures and some imitative sounds, must have been for a long time the universal language; and by the addition, in every country, of some conventional articulate sounds (of which, as I have already intimated, the first institution is not too easy to explain) particular languages were produced; but these were rude

and imperfect, and nearly such as are now to be found among some savage nations.

Hurried on by the rapidity of time, by the abundance of things I have to say, and by the almost insensible progress of things in their beginnings, I pass over in an instant a multitude of ages; for the slower the events were in their succession, the more rapidly may they be described.

These first advances enabled men to make others with greater rapidity. In proportion as they grew enlightened, they grew industrious. They ceased to fall asleep under the first tree, or in the first cave that afforded them shelter; they invented several kinds of implements of hard and sharp stones, which they used to dig up the earth, and to cut wood; they then made huts out of branches, and afterwards learnt to plaster them over with mud and clay. This was the epoch of a first revolution, which established and distinguished families, and introduced a kind of property, in itself the source of a thousand quarrels and conflicts. As, however, the strongest were probably the first to build themselves huts which they felt themselves able to defend, it may be concluded that the weak found it much easier and safer to imitate, than to attempt to dislodge them: and of those who were once provided with huts, none could have any inducement to appropriate that of his neighbour; not indeed so much because it did not belong to him, as because it could be of no use, and he could not make himself master of it without exposing himself to a desperate battle with the family which occupied it.

The first expansions of the human heart were the effects of a novel situation, which united husbands and wives, fathers and children, under one roof. The habit of living together soon gave rise to the finest feelings known to humanity, conjugal love and paternal affection. Every family became a little society, the more united because liberty and reciprocal attachment were the only bonds of its union. The sexes, whose manner of life had been hitherto the same, began now to adopt different ways of living. The women became more sedentary, and accustomed themselves to mind the hut and their children, while the men went abroad in search of their common subsistence. From living a softer life, both sexes also began to lose something of their strength and ferocity: but, if individuals became to some extent less able to encounter wild beasts separately, they found it, on the other hand, easier to assemble and resist in common.

The simplicity and solitude of man's life in this new condition, the paucity of his wants, and the implements he had invented to satisfy them, left him a great deal of leisure, which he employed to furnish himself with many conveniences unknown to his fathers: and this was the first yoke he inadvertently imposed on himself, and the first source of the evils he prepared for his descendants. For, besides continuing thus to enervate both body and mind, these conveniences lost with use almost all their power to please, and even degenerated into real needs, till the want of them became far more disagreeable than the possession of them had been pleasant. Men would have been unhappy at the loss of them, though the possession did not make them happy.

We can here see a little better how the use of speech became established, and insensibly improved in each family, and we may form a conjecture also concerning the manner in which various causes may have extended and accelerated the progress of language, by making it more and more necessary. Floods or earthquakes surrounded inhabited districts with precipices or waters: revolutions of the globe tore off portions from the continent, and made them islands. It is readily seen that among men thus collected and compelled to live together, a common idiom must have arisen much more easily than among those who still wandered through the forests of the continent. Thus it is very possible that after their first essays in navigation the islanders brought over the use of speech to the continent: and it is at least very probable that communities and languages were first established in islands, and even came to perfection there before they were known on the mainland.

Everything now begins to change its aspect. Men, who have up to now been roving in the woods, by taking to a more settled manner of life, come gradually together, form separate bodies, and at length in every country arises a distinct nation, united in character and manners, not by regulations or laws, but by uniformity of life and food, and the common influence of climate. Permanent neighbourhood could not fail to produce, in time, some connection between different families. Among young people of opposite sexes, living in neighbouring huts, the transient commerce required by nature soon led, through mutual intercourse, to another kind not less agreeable, and more permanent. Men began now to take the difference between objects into account, and to make comparisons; they acquired imperceptibly the ideas of beauty and merit, which soon gave rise to feelings of preference. In consequence of seeing each other often, they could not do without seeing each other constantly. A tender and pleasant feeling insinuated itself into their souls, and the least opposition turned it into an impetuous fury: with love arose jealousy; discord triumphed, and human blood was sacrificed to the gentlest of all passions.

As ideas and feelings succeeded one another, and heart and head were brought into play, men continued to lay aside their original wildness; their private connections became every day more intimate as their limits extended. They accustomed themselves to assemble before their huts round a large tree; singing and dancing, the true offspring of love and leisure, became the amusement, or rather the occupation, of men and women thus assembled together with nothing else to do. Each one began to consider the rest, and to wish to be considered in turn; and thus a value came to be attached to public esteem. Whoever sang or danced best, whoever was the handsomest, the strongest, the most dexterous, or the most eloquent, came to be of most consideration; and this was the first step towards inequality, and at the same time towards vice. From these first distinctions arose on the one side vanity and contempt and on the other shame and envy: and the fermentation caused by these new leavens ended by producing combinations fatal to innocence and happiness.

As soon as men began to value one another, and the idea of consideration had got a footing in the mind, every one put in his claim to it, and it became impossible to refuse it to any with impunity. Hence arose the first obligations of civility even among savages; and every intended injury became an affront; because, besides the hurt which might result from it, the party injured was certain to find in it a contempt for his person, which was often more insupportable than the hurt itself.

Thus, as every man punished the contempt shown him by others, in proportion to his opinion of himself, revenge became terrible, and men bloody and cruel. This is precisely the state reached by most of the savage nations known to us: and it is for want of having made a proper distinction in our ideas, and see how very far they already are from the state of nature, that so many writers have hastily concluded that man is naturally cruel, and requires civil institutions to make him more mild; whereas nothing is more gentle than man in his primitive state, as he is placed by nature at an equal distance from the stupidity of brutes, and the fatal ingenuity of civilised man. Equally confined by instinct and reason to the sole care of guarding himself against the mischiefs which threaten him, he is restrained by natural compassion from doing any injury to others, and is not led to do such a thing even in return for injuries received. For, according to the axiom of the wise Locke, There can be no injury, where there is no property.

But it must be remarked that the society thus formed, and the relations thus established among men, required of them qualities different from those which they possessed from their primitive constitution. Morality began to appear in human actions, and every one, before the institution of law, was the only judge and avenger of the injuries done him, so that the goodness which was suitable in the pure state of nature was no longer proper in the new-born state of society. Punishments had to be made more severe, as opportunities of offending became more frequent, and the dread of vengeance had to take the place of the rigour of the law. Thus, though men had become less patient, and their natural compassion had already suffered some diminution, this period of expansion of the human faculties, keeping a just mean between the indolence of the primitive state and the petulant activity of our egoism, must have been the happiest and most stable of epochs. The more we reflect on it, the more we shall find that this state was the least subject to revolutions, and altogether the very best man could experience; so that he can have departed from it only through some fatal accident, which, for the public good, should never have happened. The example of savages, most of whom have been found in this state, seems to prove that men were meant to remain in it, that it is the real youth of the world, and that all subsequent advances have been apparently so many steps towards the perfection of the individual, but in reality towards the decrepitude of the species.

[...]

The cultivation of the earth necessarily brought about its distribution; and property, once recognised, gave rise to the first rules of justice; for, to secure each man his own, it had to be possible for each to have something. Besides, as men began to look forward to the future, and all had something to lose, every one had reason to apprehend that reprisals would follow any injury he might do to another. This origin is so much the more natural, as it is impossible to conceive how property can come from anything but manual labour: for what else can a man add to things which he does not originally create, so as to make them his own property? It is the husbandman's labour alone that, giving him a title to the produce of the ground he has tilled, gives him a claim also to the land itself, at least till harvest, and so, from year to year, a constant possession which is easily transformed into property. When the ancients, says Grotius, gave to Ceres the title of Legislatrix, and to a festival celebrated in her honour the name of Thesmophoria, they meant by that that the distribution of lands had produced a new kind of right: that is to say, the right of property, which is different from the right deducible from the law of nature.

In this state of affairs, equality might have been sustained, had the talents of individuals been equal, and had, for example, the use of iron and the consumption of commodities always exactly balanced each other; but, as there was nothing to preserve this balance, it was soon disturbed; the strongest did most work; the most skilful turned his labour to best account; the most ingenious devised methods of diminishing his labour: the husbandman wanted more iron, or the smith more corn, and, while both laboured equally, the one gained a great deal by his work, while the other could hardly support himself. Thus natural inequality unfolds itself insensibly with that of combination, and the difference between men, developed by their different circumstances, becomes more sensible and permanent in its effects, and begins to have an influence, in the same proportion, over the lot of individuals.

Matters once at this pitch, it is easy to imagine the rest. I shall not detain the reader with a description of the successive invention of other arts, the development of language, the trial and utilisation of talents, the inequality of fortunes, the use and abuse of riches, and all the details connected with them which the reader can easily supply for himself. I shall confine myself to a glance at mankind in this new situation.

Behold then all human faculties developed, memory and imagination in full play, egoism interested, reason active, and the mind almost at the highest point of its perfection. Behold all the natural qualities in action, the rank and condition of every man assigned him; not merely his share of property and his power to serve or injure others, but also his wit, beauty, strength or skill, merit or talents: and these being the only qualities capable of commanding respect, it soon became necessary to possess or to affect them.

It now became the interest of men to appear what they really were not. To be and to seem became two totally different things; and from this distinction sprang insolent pomp and cheating trickery, with all the numerous vices that go in their train. On the other hand, free and independent as men were before, they were now, in consequence of a multiplicity of new wants, brought into subjection, as it were, to all nature, and particularly to one another; and each became in some degree a slave even in becoming the master of other men: if rich, they stood in need of the services of others; if poor, of their assistance; and even a middle condition did not enable them to do without one another. Man must now, therefore, have been perpetually employed in getting others to interest themselves in his lot, and in making them, apparently at least, if not really, find their advantage in promoting his own. Thus he must have been sly and artful in his behaviour to some, and imperious and cruel to others; being under a kind of necessity to ill-use all the persons of whom he stood in need, when he could not frighten them into compliance, and did not judge it his interest to be useful to them. Insatiable ambition, the thirst of raising their respective fortunes, not so much from real want as from the desire to surpass others, inspired all men with a vile propensity to injure one another, and with a secret jealousy, which is the more dangerous, as it puts on the mask of benevolence, to carry its point with greater security. In a word, there arose rivalry and competition on the one hand, and conflicting interests on the other, together with a secret desire on both of profiting at the expense of others. All these evils were the first effects of property, and the inseparable attendants of growing inequality.

Before the invention of signs to represent riches, wealth could hardly consist in anything but lands and cattle, the only real possessions men can have. But, when inheritances so increased in number and extent as to occupy the whole of the land, and to border on one another, one man could aggrandise himself only at the expense of another; at the same time the supernumeraries, who had been too weak or too indolent to make such acquisitions, and had grown poor without sustaining any loss, because, while they saw everything change around them, they remained still the same, were obliged to receive their subsistence, or steal it, from the rich; and this soon bred, according to their different characters, dominion and slavery, or violence and rapine. The wealthy, on their part, had no sooner begun to taste the pleasure of command, than they disdained all others, and, using their old slaves to acquire new, thought of nothing but subduing and enslaving their neighbours; like ravenous wolves, which, having once tasted human flesh, despise every other food and thenceforth seek only men to devour.

Thus, as the most powerful or the most miserable considered their might or misery as a kind of right to the possessions of others, equivalent, in their opinion, to that of property, the destruction of equality was attended by the most terrible disorders.

Usurpations by the rich, robbery by the poor, and the unbridled passions of both, suppressed the cries of natural compassion and the still feeble voice of justice, and filled men with avarice, ambition and vice. Between the title of the strongest and that of the first occupier, there arose perpetual conflicts, which never ended but in battles and bloodshed. The new-born state of society thus gave rise to a horrible state of war; men thus harassed and depraved were no longer capable of retracing their steps or renouncing the fatal acquisitions they had made, but, labouring by the abuse of the faculties which do them honour, merely to their own confusion, brought themselves to the brink of ruin.

Citation and Use

The reading was taken from the following work.

Jean-Jacques Rousseau. "On Inequality." The Originals: Classic Readings in Western Philosophy, 2019. https://pressbooks.bccampus.ca/classicreadings/chapter/jean-jacques-rousseau-on-inequality/.

THE SOVEREIGN

Thomas Hobbes

Men naturally love liberty, and dominion over others; so what is the final cause or end or design they have in mind when they introduce the restraint upon themselves under which we see them live in commonwealths? It is the prospect of their own preservation and, through that, of a more contented life; i.e. of getting themselves out of the miserable condition of war which (as I have shown) necessarily flows from the natural passions of men when there is no visible power to keep them in awe and tie them by fear of punishment to keep their covenants and to obey the laws of nature set down in my chapters 14 and 15.

For the laws of nature—enjoining justice, fairness, modesty, mercy, and (in short) treating others as we want them to treat us—are in themselves contrary to our natural passions, unless some power frightens us into observing them. In the absence of such a power, our natural passions carry us to partiality, pride, revenge, and the like. And covenants without the sword are merely words, with no strength to secure a man at all. Every man has obeyed the laws of nature when he has wanted to, which is when he could do it safely; but if there is no power set up, or none that is strong enough for our security, no-one can safely abide by the laws; and in that case every man will and lawfully may rely on his own strength and skill to protect himself against all other men. In all places where men have lived in small families with no larger organized groupings, the trade of robber was so far from being regarded as against the law of nature that it was outright honored, so that the greater spoils someone gained by robbery, the greater was his honor. The only constraints on robbery came from the laws of honor, which enjoined robbers to abstain from cruelty and to let their victims keep their lives and their farm implements. These days cities and kingdoms (which are only greater families) do what small families used to do back then: for their own security they enlarge their dominions, on the basis of claims that they are in danger and in fear of invasion, or that assistance might be given to invaders by the country they are attacking. They try as hard as they can to subdue or weaken their neighbors, by open force and secret manoeuvres; and if they have no other means for their own security, they do this justly, and are honored for it in later years.

Nor can the joining together of a small number of men give them this security that everyone seeks; because when the numbers are small, a small addition on the one side or the other makes the advantage of strength so great that it suffices to carry the victory, and so it gives encouragement for an invasion. How many must we be, to be secure? That depends not on any particular number, but on comparison with the enemy we fear. We have enough if the enemy doesn't outnumber us by so much that that would settle the outcome of a war between us, which would encourage the enemy to start one.

And however great the number, if their actions are directed according to their individual wants and beliefs, they can't expect their actions to defend or protect them against a common enemy or against injuries from one another. For being drawn in different directions by their differing opinions concerning how best to use their strength, they hinder rather than help one another, and by quarreling among themselves they reduce their strength to nothing. When that happens they are easily subdued by a very few men who agree together; and when there's no common enemy they make war on each other for their particular interests. For if we could suppose a great multitude of men to agree in the observation of justice and other laws of nature, without a common power to keep them all in awe, we might as well suppose all mankind to do the same; and then there would not be—and would not need to be—any civil government or commonwealth at all, because there would be peace without subjection.

For the security that men desire to last throughout their lifetimes, it's not enough that they be governed and directed by one judgment for a limited time—e.g. for one battle, or one war. For in that case, even if they obtain a victory through their unanimous efforts against a foreign enemy, yet afterwards—when they have no common enemy, or when some of them regard as an enemy someone whom the others regard as a friend—the difference of their interests makes it certain that they will fall apart and once more come to be at war among themselves.

It's true that certain living creatures, such as bees and ants, live sociably with one another (which is why Aristotle counts them among the 'political' creatures [Greek *politike* = 'social']), although each of them is steered only by its particular judgments and appetites, and they don't have speech through which one might indicate to another what it thinks expedient for the common benefit. You may want to know why mankind can't do the same. My answer to that has six parts.

1. Men continually compete with one another for honor and dignity, which ants and bees do not; and that leads men, but not those other animals, to envy and hatred and finally war.

2. Among those lower creatures, the common good of all is the same as the private good of each; and being naturally inclined to their private benefit, in procuring that they also procure the common benefit. But a man's biggest pleasure in his own goods comes from their being greater than those of others!

3. Bees and ants etc. don't have the use of reason (as man does), and so they don't see—and don't think they see—any fault in how their common business is organized; whereas very many men think themselves wiser than the rest, and better equipped to govern the public. These men struggle to reform and innovate, one in this way and another in that, thereby bringing the commonwealth into distraction and civil war.

4. These creatures, though they have some use of voice in making known to one another their desires and other affections, don't have that skill with words through which some men represent good things to others in the guise of evil, and evil in the guise of good, and misrepresent how great various goods and evils are. These activities enable their practitioners to make men discontented, and to disturb their peace, whenever they feel like doing so.

5. Creatures that lack reason don't have the notion of being insulted or wronged as distinct from being physically damaged; so as long as they are at ease physically they are not offended with their fellows; whereas man is most troublesome when he is most at ease, for that is when he loves to show his wisdom and to control the actions of those who govern the commonwealth.

6. The agreement of these creatures is natural, whereas men's agreement is by covenant only, which is artificial; so it's no wonder if something besides the covenant is needed to make their agreement constant and lasting, namely a common power to keep them in awe and direct their actions to the common benefit.

The only way to establish a common power that can defend them from the invasion of foreigners and the injuries of one another, and thereby make them secure enough to be able to nourish themselves and live contentedly through their own labors and the fruits of the earth, is to confer all their power and strength on one man, or one assembly of men, so as to turn all their wills by a majority vote into a single will. That is to say:

- to appoint one man or assembly of men to bear their person; and everyone
- to own and acknowledge himself to be the author of every act that he who bears their person performs or

causes to be performed in matters concerning the common peace and safety, and all of them

- to submit their wills to his will, and
- their judgments to his judgment.

[Hobbes explains the key concepts of that sentence early in Chapter 16.] This is more than mere agreement or harmony; it is a real unity of them all. They are unified in that they constitute one single person, created through a covenant of every man with every other man, as though each man were to say to each of the others:

> I authorize and give up my right of governing myself to this man, or to this assembly of men, on condition that you surrender to him your right of governing yourself, and authorize all his actions in the same way.

[Rather than 'you' and 'your', Hobbes here uses 'thou' and 'thy'—the second-person singular, rare in *Leviathan*—emphasizing the one-on-one nature of the covenant.] When this is done, the multitude so united in one person is called a **Commonwealth**, in Latin *Civitas*. This is the method of creation of that great **Leviathan**, or rather (to speak more reverently) of that mortal god to which we owe, under the immortal God, our peace and defense. For by this authority that has been given to 'this man' by every individual man in the commonwealth, he has conferred on him the use of so much power and strength that people's fear of it enables him to harmonize and control the wills of them all, to the end of peace at home and mutual aid against their enemies abroad. He is the essence of the commonwealth, which can be defined thus:

> A commonwealth is one person of whose acts a great multitude of people have made themselves the authors (each of them an author), doing this by mutual covenants with one another, so that the commonwealth may use the strength and means of them all, as he shall think appropriate, for their peace and common defense.

He who carries this person is called SOVEREIGN, and said to have 'sovereign power', and all the others are his SUBJECTS.

Sovereign power can be attained in two ways. One is by natural force, as when a man makes his children submit themselves and their children to his government, by being able to destroy them if they refuse, or subdues his enemies to his will by war, sparing their lives on condition that they submit their wills to his government. The other is when men agree among themselves to submit to some one man or assembly of men, doing this voluntarily in the confidence that this man or assembly will protect them against all others. This latter, may be called a political commonwealth, or commonwealth by institution, and the former a commonwealth by acquisition. I shall speak first of a commonwealth by institution, turning to commonwealth by acquisition in chapter 20.

Chapter 18. The rights of sovereigns by

institution

A commonwealth is said to be 'instituted' when a multitude of men agree and covenant—each one with each other—that

> When some man or assembly of men is chosen by majority vote to present the person of them all (i.e. to be their representative), each of them will authorize all the actions and judgments of that man or assembly of men as though they were his own, doing this for the purpose of living peacefully among themselves and being protected against other men. This binds those who did not vote for this representative, as well as those who did. For unless the votes are all understood to be included in the majority of votes, they have come together in vain, and contrary to the end that each proposed for himself, namely the peace and protection of them all.

From the form of the institution are derived all the power and all the rights of the one having supreme power, as well as the duties of all the citizens. I shall discuss these rights, powers, and duties under twelve headings.

First, because the people make a covenant, it is to be understood they aren't obliged by any previous covenant to do anything conflicting with this new one. Consequently those who have already instituted a commonwealth, being thereby bound by a covenant to own the actions and judgments of one sovereign, cannot lawfully get together to make a new covenant to be obedient to someone else, in any respect at all, without their sovereign's permission. So those who are subject to a monarch can't without his leave throw off monarchy and return to the confusion of a disunited multitude, or transfer their person from him who now bears it to some other man or other assembly of men; for they are bound, each of them to each of the others, to own and be the proclaimed author of everything that their existing sovereign does and judges fit to be done; so that any one man dissenting, all the rest should break their covenant made to that man, which is injustice [from the semi-colon to the end, those words are Hobbes's]. And they have also—every man of them—given the sovereignty to him who bears their person; so if they depose him they take from him something that is his, and that again is injustice. Furthermore, if anyone who tries to depose his sovereign is killed or punished for this by the sovereign, he is an author of his own punishment, because the covenant makes him an author of everything his sovereign does; and since it is injustice for a man to do anything for which he may be punished by his own authority, his attempt to depose his sovereign is unjust for that reason also.

Some men have claimed to base their disobedience to their sovereign on a new covenant that they have made not with men but with God; and this also is unjust, for there's no covenant with God except through the mediation of somebody who represents God's person, and the only one who does that is God's lieutenant, who has the sovereignty under God. But this claim of a covenant with God is so obvi-ously a lie, even in the claimant's own consciences, that it is the act of a disposition that is not only unjust but also vile and unmanly.

Secondly, what gives the sovereign a right to bear the person of all his subjects is a covenant that they make with one another, and not a covenant between him and any of them; there can't be a breach of covenant on his part; and consequently none of his subjects can be freed from subjection by a claim that the sovereign has forfeited his right to govern by breaking his covenant with his subject(s). It is obvious that the sovereign makes no covenant with his subjects on the way to becoming sovereign. To see why this is true, suppose that it isn't, and for ease of exposition suppose that you are one of the subjects. In that case the sovereign must either make a covenant with the whole multitude as the other party, or make a separate covenant with each man, including one with you. But it can't be with the whole as one party, because at this point they are not one person; and if he makes as many separate covenants as there are men, those covenants become void after he becomes sovereign. Why? Because any act of the sovereign's that you (for example) can claim to be a breach of your covenant with him is an act of yours and of everyone else's, because it was done by the sovereign, and thus was done in the person, and by the right, of every individual subject including you.

Besides, if one or more of the subjects claims a breach of the covenant made by the sovereign in his becoming sovereign, and one or more other subjects contend that there was no such breach (or indeed if only the sovereign himself contends this), there's no judge to decide the controversy, so it returns to the sword again, and every man regains the right of protecting himself by his own strength, contrary to the design they had in the institution of the commonwealth. . . . The opinion that any monarch receives his power by covenant—i.e. on some condition—comes from a failure to grasp this easy truth:

> Because covenants are merely words and breath, they have no force to oblige, contain, constrain, or protect any man, except whatever force comes from the public sword—i.e. from the untied hands of that man or assembly of men that has the sovereignty, whose actions all the subjects take responsibility for, and are performed by the strength of them all, united in their sovereign.

When an assembly of men is made sovereign, nobody imagines this to have happened through any such covenant; for no man is so stupid as to say, for example, that the people of Rome made a covenant with the Romans to hold the sovereignty on such and such conditions, the nonperformance of which would entitle the Romans to depose the Roman people! Why don't men see that the basic principles of a monarchy are the same as those of a popular government? They are led away from seeing this by the ambition of people who are kinder to the government of an assembly than to that of a monarchy, because they can hope to participate in the former, but despair of enjoying the latter.

Thirdly, because the majority have by consenting voices declared a sovereign, someone who dissented must now go along with the others, i.e. be contented to accept all the actions the sovereign shall do; and if he doesn't, he may justly be destroyed by the others. For if he voluntarily entered into the congregation of those who came together to consider instituting a sovereign, he thereby sufficiently declared his willingness to accept what the majority should decide on (and therefore tacitly covenanted to do so); so if he then refuses to accept it, or protests against any of their decrees, he is acting contrary to his tacit covenant, and therefore unjustly. Furthermore: whether or not he enters into the congregation, and whether or not his consent is asked, he must either submit to the majority's decrees or be left in the condition of war he was in before, in which he can without injustice be destroyed by any man at all.

Fourthly, because every subject is by this institution of the commonwealth the author of all the actions and judgments of the sovereign, it follows that nothing the sovereign does can wrong any of his subjects, nor ought any of them to accuse him of injustice. For someone who acts by the authority of someone else can't in acting wrong the person by whose authority he acts; but according to this institution of a commonwealth, every individual man is an author of everything the sovereign does; so someone who complains of being wronged by his sovereign complains about something of which he himself is an author; so he oughtn't to accuse anyone but himself—and indeed he oughtn't even to accuse himself of wronging himself, because to wrong one's self is impossible. [Throughout this paragraph up to this point, 'wrong' replaces Hobbes's 'injury'.] It's true that those who have sovereign power may commit iniquity [= 'do wicked things'], but not injustice or injury in the proper meaning of that term.

Fifthly, following from the preceding point: no man who has sovereign power can justly be put to death or punished in any other way by his subjects. For seeing that every subject is an author of the actions of his sovereign, if he punishes the sovereign he punishes someone else for actions committed by himself.

And because the goal of this institution is the peace and defence of them all, and whoever has a right to the goal has a right to the means to it, the man or assembly that has the sovereignty has the right to be judge both of the means to peace and defence, and also of the hindrances and disturbances of peace and defence; and to do whatever he thinks is needed, both beforehand for preserving of peace and security by prevention of discord at home and hostility from abroad, and for the recovery of peace and security after they have been lost. And therefore,

Sixthly, it is for the sovereignty [= 'the man or assembly of men to whom the sovereignty has been given'] to be the judge
- of what opinions and doctrines are threats to peace and what ones tend to support it; and consequently of
- which men are to be trusted to speak to multitudes of people,
  - on what occasions, and
  - how far they should be allowed to go; and
- of who shall examine the doctrines of all books before they are published.

For the actions of men come from their opinions, and the way to govern men's actions in the interests of peace and harmony is to govern their opinions. When we are considering doctrines, nothing ought to be taken account of but truth; but this doesn't conflict with regulating doctrines on grounds having to do with peace. For a doctrine that is harmful to peace can't be true, any more than peace and harmony can be against the law of nature. It's true that in a commonwealth where the negligence or incompetence of governors and teachers has allowed false doctrines to become generally believed, the contrary truths may be generally found to be offensive. But even the most sudden and rough bustling in of a new truth never breaks the peace, but only sometimes awakens the war. I said 'awakens' the war, not 'starts' it. For men who are so slackly governed that they dare take up arms to defend or introduce an opinion are at war already; their state is not peace, but only a cessation of arms through mutual fear, and they live continually on the fringe of a battlefield, so to speak. So he who has the sovereign power must be the judge—or establish others as judges—of opinions and doctrines, this being necessary for peace and the avoidance of discord and civil war.

Seventhly, the sovereignty has the whole power of prescribing the rules that let every man know what goods he may enjoy, and what actions he may perform, without being troubled by any of his fellow-subjects; and this is what men call 'property' [Hobbes writes 'propriety']. Before the establishment of sovereign power (as I have already shown), all men had a right to all things, a state of affairs which necessarily causes war; and therefore this system of property, being necessary for peace and dependent on sovereign power, is one of the things done by sovereign power in the interests of public peace. These rules of property (or meum and tuum [Latin for 'mine' and 'yours']) and of good, bad, lawful, and unlawful in the actions of subjects, are the civil laws, i.e. the laws of each individual commonwealth. . . .

Eighthly, the sovereignty alone has the right of judging, i.e. of hearing and deciding any controversies that may arise concerning law (civil or natural) or concerning fact. For if controversies are not decided, one subject has no protection against being wronged by another, the laws concerning meum and tuum have no effect, and every man retains—because of the natural and inevitable desire for his own preservation—the right to protect himself by his own private strength, which is the condition of war, and is contrary to the purpose for which every commonwealth is instituted.

Ninthly, the sovereignty alone has the right to make war and peace with other nations, and commonwealths, i.e. the right to judge when war is for the public good, to decide what size of military forces are to be assembled for that purpose and armed and paid for, and to tax the subjects to get money to defray the expenses of those forces. For the power by which the people are to be defended consists in their armies, and the strength of an army consists in the union of the soldiers' strengths under one command; and it's the instituted sovereign who has that command. Indeed, having command of the military is enough to make someone sovereign, without his being instituted as such in any other way. So whoever is appointed as general of an army, it's always the sovereign power who is its supreme commander.

Tenthly, it is for the sovereignty to choose all counsellors, ministers, magistrates, and officers, in both peace and war. For seeing that the sovereign is charged with achieving the goal of the common peace and defence, he is understood to have the power to use whatever means he thinks most fit for this purpose.

Eleventhly, to the sovereign is committed [= 'entrusted'] the power of rewarding with riches or honour, and of punishing with corporal punishment or fines or public disgrace, every subject according to the law the sovereign has already made; or if no relevant law has been made, according to his (the sovereign's) judgment about what will conduce most to encouraging men to serve the commonwealth, or to deterring them from doing disservice to it.

Lastly, because of how highly men are naturally apt to value themselves, what respect they want from others, and how little they value other men—all of which continually gives rise to resentful envy, quarrels, side-taking, and eventually war, in which they destroy one another and lessen their strength against a common enemy—it's necessary to have laws of honour, and a public rate [= 'price-list'] stating the values of men who have deserved well of the commonwealth or may yet do so, and to put into someone's hands the power to put those laws in execution. But I have already shown that not only the whole military power of the commonwealth, but also the judging of all controversies, is assigned to the sovereignty. So it's the sovereign whose role it is to give titles of honour, and to appoint what order of place and dignity each man shall hold, and what signs of respect they shall give to one another in public or private meetings.

These are the rights that make the essence of sovereignty, and are the marks by which one can tell what man or assembly of men has the sovereign power. For these rights and powers can't be shared and can't be separated from one another. The sovereign may transfer to someone else the power to coin money, to dispose of the estate and persons of infant heirs, to have certain advantages in markets, or any other prerogative that is governed by particular laws, while still retaining the power to protect his subjects. But if he transfers the military it's no use his retaining the power of judging, because he will have no way of enforcing the laws; or if he gives away the power of raising money, the military is useless; or if he gives away the control of doctrines, men will be frightened into rebellion by the fear of spirits. So if we consider any one of the rights I have discussed, we shall immediately see that it is necessary,

because the holding of all the others without that one will have no effect on the conservation of peace and justice, the purpose for which all commonwealths are instituted. This division of powers that ought not to be divided was the topic when it was said that a kingdom divided in itself cannot stand (Mark 3:24); for a division into opposite armies can never happen unless this division of powers happens first. If a majority of people in England hadn't come to think that these powers were divided between the king, the Lords, and the House of Commons, the people would never have been divided and fallen into this civil war—first over disagreements in politics, and then over disagreements about freedom of religion—a war that has so instructed men in this matter of sovereign rights that most people in England do now see that these rights are inseparable. This will be generally acknowledged when peace next returns, and it will continue to be acknowledged for as long as people remember their miseries in the war (though it won't continue beyond that unless the common people come to be better taught than they have been until now!).

And because these rights are essential and inseparable, it necessarily follows that in whatever words any of them seem to be granted to someone other than the sovereign, the grant is void unless the sovereign power itself is explicitly renounced at the same time, and the title 'sovereign' is no longer given by the grantees to him who grants the rights in question; for when he has granted as much as he can, if we grant back or he retains the sovereignty itself, all the rights he has supposedly granted to someone else are restored to him, because they are inseparably attached to the sovereignty.

This great authority being indivisible, and inseparably assigned to the sovereignty, there is little basis for the opinion of those who say of sovereign kings that though they have greater power than every one of their subjects, they have less power than all their subjects together. For if by 'all together' they don't mean the collective body as one person, then 'all together' and 'every one' mean the same, and what these people say is absurd. But if by 'all together' they understand them as one person (which person the sovereign bears), then the power of 'all together' is the same as the sovereign's power, and so again what they say is absurd. They could see its absurdity well enough when the sovereign is an assembly of all the people, but they don't see it when the sovereign is a monarch; yet the power of sovereignty is the same, whoever has it.

Just as the power of the sovereign ought to be greater than that of any or all the subjects, so should the sovereign's honour. For the sovereignty is the fountain of honour. The dignities of lord, earl, duke, and prince are created by him. Just as servants in the presence of their master are equal, and without any honour at all, so are subjects in the presence of their sovereign. When they are out of his sight some may shine more than others, but in his presence they shine no more than do the stars in the presence of the sun.

But someone may object here that subjects are in a miserable situation because they are at the mercy of the lusts and other irregular passions of him who has (or of them who have) such unlimited power. Commonly those who live under a monarch think their troubles are the fault of monarchy, and those who live under the government of democracy or some other kind of sovereign assembly attribute all the inconvenience to that form of commonwealth (when really the sovereign power is the same in every form of commonwealth, as long as it is complete enough to protect the subjects). These complainers don't bear in mind that the human condition can never be without some inconvenience or other, or that the greatest trouble that can possibly come to the populace in any form of government is almost nothing when compared with the miseries and horrible calamities that accompany a civil war, or with the dissolute condition of ungoverned men who are not subject to laws and to a coercive power to hold them back from robbery and revenge. Nor do they bear in mind that the greatest burdens laid on subjects by sovereign governors does not come from any pleasure or profit they can expect from damaging or weakening their subjects (in whose vigour consists their own strength and glory), but from the stubbornness of the subjects themselves, who are unwilling to contribute to their own defence, and so make it necessary for their governors to get what they can from them in taxes in time of peace, so that they may have the means to resist their enemies, or to get an advantage over them, if an occasion for this should suddenly present itself. For all men are provided by nature with notable microscopes (that is their passions and self-love) through which every little payment appears as a great grievance, but don't have the telescopes (namely moral and political science) that would enable them to see far off the miseries that hang over them, which can't be avoided without such payments.

Citation and Use

The reading was taken from the following work.

Thomas Hobbes. "On The Social Contract – The Originals: Classic Readings in Western Philosophy." The Originals: Classic Readings in Western Philosophy, 2019. https://pressbooks.bccampus.ca/classicreadings/chapter/thomas-hobbes-on-the-social-contract/.

ORIGINAL ACQUISITION

John Locke

25. Whether we consider natural reason, which tells us, that men, being once born, have a right to their preservation, and consequently to meat and drink, and such other things as nature affords for their subsistence: or revelation, which gives us an account of those grants God made of the world to Adam, and to Noah, and his sons, it is very clear, that God, as king David says, Psal. cxv. 16. has given the earth to the children of men; given it to mankind in common. But this being supposed, it seems to some a very great difficulty, how any one should ever come to have a property in any thing: I will not content myself to answer, that if it be difficult to make out property, upon a supposition that God gave the world to Adam, and his posterity in common, it is impossible that any man, but one universal monarch, should have any property upon a supposition, that God gave the world to Adam, and his heirs in succession, exclusive of all the rest of his posterity. But I shall endeavor to show, how men might come to have a property in several parts of that which God gave to mankind in common, and that without any express compact of all the commoners.

26. God, who hath given the world to men in common, hath also given them reason to make use of it to the best advantage of life, and convenience. The earth, and all that is therein, is given to men for the support and comfort of their being. And tho' all the fruits it naturally produces, and beasts it feeds, belong to mankind in common, as they are produced by the spontaneous hand of nature; and no body has originally a private dominion, exclusive of the rest of mankind, in any of them, as they are thus in their natural state: yet being given for the use of men, there must of necessity be a means to appropriate them some way or other, before they can be of any use, or at all beneficial to any particular man. The fruit, or venison, which nourishes the wild Indian, who knows no enclosure, and is still a tenant in common, must be his, and so his, i.e. a part of him, that another can no longer have any right to it, before it can do him any good for the support of his life.

27. Though the earth, and all inferior creatures, be common to all men, yet every man has a property in his own person: this no body has any right to but himself. The labor of his body, and the work of his hands, we may say, are prop-erly his. Whatsoever then he removes out of the state that nature hath provided, and left it in, he hath mixed his labor with, and joined to it something that is his own, and thereby makes it his property. It being by him removed from the common state nature hath placed it in, it hath by this labor something annexed to it, that excludes the common right of other men: for this labor being the unquestionable property of the laborer, no man but he can have a right to what that is once joined to, at least where there is enough, and as good, left in common for others.

28. He that is nourished by the acorns he picked up under an oak, or the apples he gathered from the trees in the wood, has certainly appropriated them to himself. No body can deny but the nourishment is his. I ask then, when did they begin to be his? when he digested? or when he eat? or when he boiled? or when he brought them home? or when he picked them up? and it is plain, if the first gathering made them not his, nothing else could. That labor put a distinction between them and common: that added something to them more than nature, the common mother of all, had done; and so they became his private right. And will any one say, he had no right to those acorns or apples, he thus appropriated, because he had not the consent of all mankind to make them his? Was it a robbery thus to assume to himself what belonged to all in common? If such a consent as that was necessary, man had starved, notwithstanding the plenty God had given him. We see in commons, which remain so by compact, that it is the taking any part of what is common, and removing it out of the state nature leaves it in, which begins the property; without which the common is of no use. And the taking of this or that part, does not depend on the express consent of all the commoners. Thus the grass my horse has bit; the turfs my servant has cut; and the ore I have digged in any place, where I have a right to them in common with others, become my property, without the assignation or consent of any body. The labor that was mine, removing them out of that common state they were in, hath fixed my property in them.

29. By making an explicit consent of every commoner, necessary to any one's appropriating to himself any part of what is given in common, children or servants could not cut the meat, which their father or master had provided for them in common, without assigning to every one his peculiar part. Though the water running in the fountain be every one's, yet who can doubt, but that in the pitcher is his only who drew it out? His labor hath taken it out of the hands of nature, where it was common, and belonged equally to all her children, and hath thereby appropriated it to himself.

30. Thus this law of reason makes the deer that Indian's who hath killed it; it is allowed to be his goods, who hath bestowed his labor upon it, though before it was the common right of every one. And among those who are counted the civilized part of mankind, who have made and multiplied positive laws to determine property, this original law of nature, for the beginning of property, in what was before common, still takes place; and by virtue thereof, what fish any one catches in the ocean, that great and still remaining common of mankind; or what ambergris any one takes up here, is by the labor that removes it out of that common state nature left it in, made his property, who takes that pains about it. And even among us, the hare that any one is hunting, is thought his who pursues her during the chase: for being a beast that is still looked upon as common, and no man's private possession; whoever has employed so much labor about any of that kind, as to find and pursue her, has thereby removed her from the state of nature, wherein she was common, and hath begun a property.

31. It will perhaps be objected to this, that if gathering the acorns, or other fruits of the earth, &c. makes a right to them, then any one may engross as much as he will. To which I answer, Not so. The same law of nature, that does by this means give us property, does also bound that property too. God has given us all things richly, 1 Tim. vi. 12. is the voice of reason confirmed by inspiration. But how far has he given it us? To enjoy. As much as any one can make use of to any advantage of life before it spoils, so much he may by his labor fix a property in: whatever is beyond this, is more than his share, and belongs to others. Nothing was made by God for man to spoil or destroy. And thus, considering the plenty of natural provisions there was a long time in the world, and the few spenders; and to how small a part of that provision the industry of one man could extend itself, and engross it to the prejudice of others; especially keeping within the bounds, set by reason, of what might serve for his use; there could be then little room for quarrels or contentions about property so established.

32. But the chief matter of property being now not the fruits of the earth, and the beasts that subsist on it, but the earth itself; as that which takes in and carries with it all the rest; I think it is plain, that property in that too is acquired as the former. As much land as a man tills, plants, improves, cultivates, and can use the product of, so much is his property. He by his labor does, as it were, **enclose it from the common**. Nor will it invalidate his right, to say every body else has an equal title to it; and therefore he cannot appropriate, he cannot enclose, without the consent of all his fellow-commoners, all mankind. God, when he gave the world in common to all mankind, commanded man also to labor, and the penury of his condition required it of him. God and his reason commanded him to subdue the earth, i.e. improve it for the benefit of life, and therein lay out something upon it that was his own, his labor. He that in obedience to this command of God, subdued, tilled and sowed any part of it, thereby annexed to it something that was his property, which another had no title to, nor could without injury take from him.

33. Nor was this appropriation of any parcel of land, by improving it, any prejudice to any other man, since there was still enough, and as good left; and more than the yet unprovided could use. So that, in effect, there was never the less left for others because of his enclosure for himself: for he that leaves as much as another can make use of, does as good as take nothing at all. No body could think himself injured by the drinking of another man, though he took a good draught, who had a whole river of the same water left him to quench his thirst: and the case of land and water, where there is enough of both, is perfectly the same.

34. God gave the world to men in common; but since he gave it them for their benefit, and the greatest conveniences of life they were capable to draw from it, it cannot be supposed he meant it should always remain common and uncultivated. He gave it to the use of the industrious and rational, (and labor was to be his title to it;) not to the fancy or covetousness of the quarrelsome and contentious. He that had as good left for his improvement, as was already taken up, needed not complain, ought not to meddle with what was already improved by another's labor: if he did, it is plain he desired the benefit of another's pains, which he had no right to, and not the ground which God had given him in common with others to labor on, and whereof there was as good left, as that already possessed, and more than he knew what to do with, or his industry could reach to.

35. It is true, in land that is common in England, or any other country, where there is plenty of people under government, who have money and commerce, no one can enclose or appropriate any part, without the consent of all his fellow commoners; because this is left common by compact, i.e. by the law of the land, which is not to be violated. And though it be common, in respect of some men, it is not so to all mankind; but is the joint property of this country, or this parish. Besides, the remainder, after such enclosure, would not be as good to the rest of the commoners, as the whole was when they could all make use of the whole; whereas in the beginning and first peopling of the great common of the world, it was quite otherwise. The law man was under, was rather for appropriating. God commanded, and his wants forced him to labor. That was his property which could not be taken from him where-ever he had fixed it. And hence subduing or cultivating the earth, and having dominion, we see are joined together. The one gave title to the other. So that God, by commanding to subdue, gave authority so far to appropriate: and the condition of human life, which requires labor and materials to work on, necessarily introduces private possessions.

36. The measure of property nature has well set by the extent of men's labor and the conveniences of life: no man's labor could subdue, or appropriate all; nor could his enjoyment consume more than a small part; so that it was impossible for any man, this way, to entrench upon the right of another, or acquire to himself a property, to the prejudice of his neighbor, who would still have room for as good, and as large a possession (after the other had taken out his) as before it was appropriated. This measure did confine every man's possession to a very moderate proportion, and such as he might appropriate to himself, without injury to any body, in the first ages of the world, when men were more in danger to be lost, by wandering from their company, in the then vast wilderness of the earth, than to be straitened for want of room to plant in. And the same measure may be allowed still without prejudice to any body, as full as the world seems: for supposing a man, or family, in the state they were at first peopling of the world by the children of Adam, or Noah; let him plant in some inland, vacant places of America, we shall find that the possessions he could make himself, upon the measures we have given, would not be very large, nor, even to this day, prejudice the rest of mankind, or give them reason to complain, or think themselves injured by this man's encroachment, though the race of men have now spread themselves to all the corners of the world, and do infinitely exceed the small number was at the beginning. Nay, the extent of ground is of so little value, without labor, that I have heard it affirmed, that in Spain itself a man may be permitted to plough, sow and reap, without being disturbed, upon land he has no other title to, but only his making use of it. But, on the contrary, the inhabitants think themselves beholden to him, who, by his industry on neglected, and consequently waste land, has increased the stock of corn, which they wanted. But be this as it will, which I lay no stress on; this I dare boldly affirm, that the same rule of propriety, (viz.) that every man should have as much as he could make use of, would hold still in the world, without straitening any body; since there is land enough in the world to suffice double the inhabitants, had not the invention of money, and the tacit agreement of men to put a value on it, introduced (by consent) larger possessions, and a right to them; which, how it has done, I shall by and by shew more at large.

37. This is certain, that in the beginning, before the desire of having more than man needed had altered the intrinsic value of things, which depends only on their usefulness to the life of man; or had agreed, that a little piece of yellow metal, which would keep without wasting or decay, should be worth a great piece of flesh, or a whole heap of corn; though men had a right to appropriate, by their labor, each one of himself, as much of the things of nature, as he could use: yet this could not be much, nor to the prejudice of others, where the same plenty was still left to those who would use the same industry. To which let me add, that he who appropriates land to himself by his labor, does not lessen, but increase the common stock of mankind: for the provisions serving to the support of human life, produced by one acre of enclosed and cultivated land, are (to speak much within compass) ten times more than those which are yielded by an acre of land of an equal richness lying waste in common. And therefore he that encloses land, and has a greater plenty of the conveniences of life from ten acres, than he could have from an hundred left to nature, may truly be said to give ninety acres to mankind: for his labor now supplies him with provisions out of ten acres, which were but the product of an hundred lying in common. I have here rated the improved land very low, in making its product but as ten to one, when it is much nearer an hundred to one: for I ask, whether in the wild woods and uncultivated waste of America, left to nature, without any improvement, tillage or husbandry, a thousand acres yield the needy and wretched inhabitants as many conveniences of life, as ten acres of equally fertile land do in Devonshire, where they are well cultivated?

Before the appropriation of land, he who gathered as much of the wild fruit, killed, caught, or tamed, as many of the beasts, as he could; he that so employed his pains about any of the spontaneous products of nature, as any way to alter them from the state which nature put them in, by placing any of his labor on them, did thereby acquire a propriety in them: but if they perished, in his possession, without their due use; if the fruits rotted, or the venison putrefied, before he could spend it, he offended against the common law of nature, and was liable to be punished; he invaded his neighbor's share, for he had no right, farther than his use called for any of them, and they might serve to afford him conveniences of life.

38. The same measures governed the possession of land too: whatsoever he tilled and reaped, laid up and made use of, before it spoiled, that was his peculiar right; whatsoever he enclosed, and could feed, and make use of, the cattle and product was also his. But if either the grass of his enclosure rotted on the ground, or the fruit of his planting perished without gathering, and laying up, this part of the earth, notwithstanding his enclosure, was still to be looked on as waste, and might be the possession of any other. Thus, at the beginning, Cain might take as much ground as he could till, and make it his own land, and yet leave enough to Abel's sheep to feed on; a few acres would serve for both their possessions. But as families increased, and industry enlarged their stocks, their possessions enlarged with the need of them; but yet it was commonly without any fixed property in the ground they made use of, till they incorporated, settled themselves together, and built cities; and then, by consent, they came in time, to set out the bounds of their distinct territories, and agree on limits between them and their neighbors; and by laws within themselves, settled the properties of those of the same society: for we see, that in that part of the world which was first inhabited, and therefore like to be best peopled, even as low down as Abraham's time, they wandered with their flocks, and their herds, which was their substance, freely up and down; and this Abraham did, in a country where he was a stranger. Whence it is plain, that at least a great part of the land lay in common; that the inhabitants valued it not, nor claimed property in any more than they made use of. But when there was not room enough in the same place, for their herds to feed together, they by consent, as Abraham and Lot did, Gen. xiii. 5. separated and enlarged their pasture, where it best liked them. And for the same reason Esau went from his father, and his brother, and planted in Mount Seir, Gen. xxxvi. 6.

39. And thus, without supposing any private dominion, and property in Adam, over all the world, exclusive of all other men, which can no way be proved, nor any one's property be made out from it; but supposing the world given, as it was, to the children of men in common, we see how labor could make men distinct titles to several parcels of it, for their private uses; wherein there could be no doubt of right, no room for quarrel.

40. Nor is it so strange, as perhaps before consideration it may appear, that the property of labor should be able to over-balance the community of land: for it is labor indeed that puts the difference of value on every thing; and let any one consider what the difference is between an acre of land planted with tobacco or sugar, sown with wheat or barley, and an acre of the same land lying in common, without any husbandry upon it, and he will find, that the improvement of labor makes the far greater part of the value. I think it will be but a very modest computation to say, that of the products of the earth useful to the life of man nine tenths are the effects of labor: nay, if we will rightly estimate things as they come to our use, and cast up the several expenses about them, what in them is purely owing to nature, and what to labor, we shall find, that in most of them ninety-nine hundredths are wholly to be put on the account of labor.

41. There cannot be a clearer demonstration of any thing, than several nations of the Americans are of this, who are rich in land, and poor in all the comforts of life; whom nature having furnished as liberally as any other people, with the materials of plenty, i.e. a fruitful soil, apt to produce in abundance, what might serve for food, raiment, and delight; yet for want of improving it by labor, have not one hundredth part of the conveniences we enjoy: and a king of a large and fruitful territory there, feeds, lodges, and is clad worse than a day-laborer in England.

42. To make this a little clearer, let us but trace some of the ordinary provisions of life, through their several progresses, before they come to our use, and see how much they receive of their value from human industry. Bread, wine and cloth, are things of daily use, and great plenty; yet notwithstanding, acorns, water and leaves, or skins, must be our bread, drink and clothing, did not labor furnish us with these more useful commodities: for whatever bread is more worth than acorns, wine than water, and cloth or silk, than leaves, skins or moss, that is wholly owing to labor and industry; the one of these being the food and raiment which unassisted nature furnishes us with; the other, provisions which our industry and pains prepare for us, which how much they exceed the other in value, when any one hath computed, he will then see how much labor makes the far greatest part of the value of things we enjoy in this world: and the ground which produces the materials, is scarce to be reckoned in, as any, or at most, but a very small part of it; so little, that even among us, land that is left

wholly to nature, that hath no improvement of pasturage, tillage, or planting, is called, as indeed it is, waste; and we shall find the benefit of it amount to little more than nothing.

This shews how much numbers of men are to be preferred to largeness of dominions; and that the increase of lands, and the right employing of them, is the great art of government: and that prince, who shall be so wise and godlike, as by established laws of liberty to secure protection and encouragement to the honest industry of mankind, against the oppression of power and narrowness of party, will quickly be too hard for his neighbors: but this by the by. To return to the argument in hand,

43. An acre of land, that bears here twenty bushels of wheat, and another in America, which, with the same husbandry, would do the like, are, without doubt, of the same natural intrinsic value: but yet the benefit mankind receives from the one in a year, is worth 5l. and from the other possibly not worth a penny, if all the profit an Indian received from it were to be valued, and sold here; at least, I may truly say, not one thousandth. It is labor then which puts the greatest part of value upon land, without which it would scarcely be worth any thing: it is to that we owe the greatest part of all its useful products; for all that the straw, bran, bread, of that acre of wheat, is more worth than the product of an acre of as good land, which lies waste, is all the effect of labor: for it is not barely the plough-man's pains, the reaper's and thresher's toil, and the baker's sweat, is to be counted into the bread we eat; the labor of those who broke the oxen, who digged and wrought the iron and stones, who felled and framed the timber employed about the plough, mill, oven, or any other utensils, which are a vast number, requisite to this corn, from its being feed to be sown to its being made bread, must all be charged on the account of labor, and received as an effect of that: nature and the earth furnished only the almost worthless materials, as in themselves. It would be a strange catalog of things, that industry provided and made use of, about every loaf of bread, before it came to our use, if we could trace them; iron, wood, leather, bark, timber, stone, bricks, coals, lime, cloth, dying drugs, pitch, tar, masts, ropes, and all the materials made use of in the ship, that brought any of the commodities made use of by any of the workmen, to any part of the work; all which it would be almost impossible, at least too long, to reckon up.

44. From all which it is evident, that though the things of nature are given in common, yet man, by being master of himself, and proprietor of his own person, and the actions or labor of it, had still in himself the great foundation of property; and that, which made up the great part of what he applied to the support or comfort of his being, when invention and arts had improved the conveniences of life, was perfectly his own, and did not belong in common to others.

45. Thus labor, in the beginning, gave a right of property, wherever any one was pleased to employ it upon what was common, which remained a long while the far greater part, and is yet more than mankind makes use of. Men, at first, for the most part, contented themselves with what unassisted nature offered to their necessities: and though afterwards, in some parts of the world, (where the increase of people and stock, with the use of money, had made land scarce, and so of some value) the several communities settled the bounds of their distinct territories, and by laws within themselves regulated the properties of the private men of their society, and so, by compact and agreement, settled the property which labor and industry began; and the leagues that have been made between several states and kingdoms, either expressly or tacitly disowning all claim and right to the land in the others possession, have, by common consent, given up their pretenses to their natural common right, which originally they had to those countries, and so have, by positive agreement, settled a property among themselves, in distinct parts and parcels of the earth; yet there are still great tracts of ground to be found, which (the inhabitants thereof not having joined with the rest of mankind, in the consent of the use of their common money) lie waste, and are more than the people who dwell on it do, or can make use of, and so still lie in common; tho' this can scarce happen among that part of mankind that have consented to the use of money.

Money

46. The greatest part of things really useful to the life of man, and such as the necessity of subsisting made the first commoners of the world look after, as it does the Americans now, are generally things of short duration; such as, if they are not consumed by use, will decay and perish of themselves: gold, silver and diamonds, are things that fancy or agreement hath put the value on, more than real use, and the necessary support of life. Now of those good things which nature hath provided in common, every one had a right (as hath been said) to as much as he could use, and property in all that he could effect with his labor; all that his industry could extend to, to alter from the state nature had put it in, was his. He that gathered a hundred bushels of acorns or apples, had thereby a property in them, they were his goods as soon as gathered. He was only to look, that he used them before they spoiled, else he took more than his share, and robbed others. And indeed it was a foolish thing, as well as dishonest, to hoard up more than he could make use of. If he gave away a part to any body else, so that it perished not uselesly in his possession, these he also made use of. And if he also bartered away plums, that would have rotted in a week, for nuts that would last good for his eating a whole year, he did no injury; he wasted not the common stock; destroyed no part of the portion of goods that belonged to others, so long as nothing perished uselesly in his hands. Again, if he would give his nuts for a piece of metal, pleased with its colour; or exchange his sheep for shells, or wool for a sparkling pebble or a diamond, and keep those by him all his life he invaded not the right of others, he might heap up as much of these durable things as he pleased; the exceeding of the bounds of his just property not lying in the largeness of his possession, but the perishing of any thing uselesly in it.

47. And thus came in the use of money, some lasting thing that men might keep without spoiling, and that by mutual consent men would take in exchange for the truly useful, but perishable supports of life.

48. And as different degrees of industry were apt to give men possessions in different proportions, so this invention of money gave them the opportunity to continue and enlarge them: for supposing an island, separate from all possible commerce with the rest of the world, wherein there were but an hundred families, but there were sheep, horses and cows, with other useful animals, wholsome fruits, and land enough for corn for a hundred thousand times as many, but nothing in the island, either because of its commonness, or perishableness, fit to supply the place of money; what reason could any one have there to enlarge his possessions beyond the use of his family, and a plentiful supply to its consumption, either in what their own industry produced, or they could barter for like perishable, useful commodities, with others? Where there is not some thing, both lasting and scarce, and so valuable to be hoarded up, there men will not be apt to enlarge their possessions of land, were it never so rich, never so free for them to take: for I ask, what would a man value ten thousand, or an hundred thousand acres of excellent land, ready cultivated, and well stocked too with cattle, in the middle of the inland parts of America, where he had no hopes of commerce with other parts of the world, to draw money to him by the sale of the product? It would not be worth the enclosing, and we should see him give up again to the wild common of nature, whatever was more than would supply the conveniences of life to be had there for him and his family.

49. Thus in the beginning all the world was America, and more so than that is now; for no such thing as money was any where known. Find out something that hath the use and value of money among his neighbors, you shall see the same man will begin presently to enlarge his possessions.

50. But since gold and silver, being little useful to the life of man in proportion to food, raiment, and carriage, has its value only from the consent of men, whereof labor yet makes, in great part, the measure, it is plain, that men have agreed to a disproportionate and unequal possession of the earth, they having, by a tacit and voluntary consent, found out, a way how a man may fairly possess more land than he himself can use the product of, by receiving in exchange for the overplus gold and silver, which may be hoarded up without injury to any one; these metals not spoiling or decaying in the hands of the possessor. This partage of things in an inequality of private possessions, men have made practicable out of the bounds of society, and without compact, only by putting a value on gold and silver, and tacitly agreeing in the use of money: for in governments, the laws regulate the right of property, and the possession of land is determined by positive constitutions.

51. And thus, I think, it is very easy to conceive, without any difficulty, how labor could at first begin a title of property in the common things of nature, and how the spending it upon our uses bounded it. So that there could then be no reason of quarreling about title, nor any doubt about the largeness of possession it gave. Right and conveniency went together; for as a man had a right to all he could employ his labor upon, so he had no temptation to labor for more than he could make use of. This left no room for controversy about the title, nor for encroachment on the right of others; what portion a man carved to himself, was easily seen; and it was useless, as well as dishonest, to carve himself too much, or take more than he needed.

Citation and Use

The reading was taken from the following work.

Locke, John. "On Property and the Formation of Societies." Online Book. The Originals: Classic Readings in Western Philosophy, 2019. https://pressbooks.bccampus.ca/classicreadings/chapter/john-locke-on-property-and-the-formation-of-societies/.

GOVERNMENT IN THE FUTURE

Noam Chomsky

The following is a lecture given by Chomsky at the Poetry Center in New York on April 1970.

I think it is useful to set up as a framework for discussion four somewhat idealized positions with regard to the role of the state in an advanced industrial society. I want to call these positions:
1. classical liberal,
2. libertarian socialist,
3. state socialist, and
4. state capitalist;

and I want to consider each in turn. Also, I'd like to make clear my own point of view in advance, so that you can evaluate and judge what I am saying. I think that the libertarian socialist concepts, and by that I mean a range of thinking that extends from left-wing Marxism through to anarchism, I think that these are fundamentally correct and that they are the proper and natural extension of classical liberalism into the era of advanced industrial society.

In contrast, it seems to me that the ideology of state socialism, i.e. what has become of Bolshevism, and that of state capitalism, the modern welfare state, these of course are dominant in the industrial societies, but I believe that they are regressive and highly inadequate social theories, and a large number of our really fundamental problems stem from a kind of incompatibility and inappropriateness of these social forms to a modern industrial society.

Let me consider these four points of reference in sequence, beginning with the classical liberal point of view.

Classical Liberalism

Classical liberalism asserts as its major idea an opposition to all but the most restricted and minimal forms of state intervention in personal and social life. Well, this conclu-sion is quite familiar, however the reasoning that leads to it is less familiar and, I think, a good deal more important than the conclusion itself.

One of the earliest and most brilliant expositions of this position is in Wilhelm von Humboldt's "Limits of State Action" which was written in 1792, though not published for 60 or 70 years after that. In his view the state tends to, I quote,

> make man an instrument to serve its arbitrary ends, overlooking his individual purposes, and since man is in his essence a free, searching, self-perfecting being, it follows that the state is a profoundly anti-human institution.

I.e. its actions, its existence are ultimately incompatible with the full harmonious development of human potential in its richest diversity and, hence, incompatible with what Humboldt and in the following century Marx, Bakunin, Mill, and many others, what they see as the true end of man.

And, for the record, I think that this is an accurate description. The modern conservative tends to regard himself as the lineal descendant of the classical liberal in this sense, but I think that can be maintained only from an extremely superficial point of view, as one can see by studying more carefully the fundamental ideas of classical libertarian thought as expressed, in my opinion, in its most profound form by Humboldt.

I think the issues are of really quite considerable contemporary significance, and if you don't mind what may appear to be a somewhat antiquarian excursion, I'd like to expand on them.

For Humboldt as for Rousseau, and before him the Cartesians, man's central attribute is his freedom. Quote:

> To inquire and to create, these are the centers around which all human pursuits more or less directly revolve.

"But," he goes on to say,

all moral cultures spring solely and immediately from the inner life of the soul and can never be produced by external and artificial contrivances. The cultivation of the understanding, as of any of man's other faculties, is generally achieved by his own activity, his own ingenuity, or his own methods of using the discoveries of others.

From these assumptions quite obviously an educational theory follows, and he develops it but I won't pursue it. But also far more follows. Humboldt goes on to develop at least the rudiments of a theory of exploitation and of alienated labor that suggests in significant ways, I think, the early Marx. Humboldt in fact continues these comments that I quoted about the cultivation of the understanding through spontaneous action in the following way.

He says,

> Man never regards what he possesses as so much his own, as what he does, and the laborer who tends the garden is perhaps in a truer sense its owner than the listless voluptuary who enjoys its fruits. And since truly human action is that which flows from inner impulse, it seems as if all peasants and craftsmen might be elevated into artists, that is men who love their labor for its own sake, improve it by their own plastic genius and invented skill, and thereby cultivate their intellect, ennoble their character and exult and refine their pleasures, and so humanity would be ennobled by the very things which now, though beautiful in themselves, so often tend to be degraded.

> Freedom is undoubtedly the indispensable condition without which even the pursuits most congenial to individual human nature can never succeed in producing such salutary influences. Whatever does not spring from a man's free choice, or is only the result of instruction and guidance, does not enter into his very being but remains alien to his true nature. He does not perform it with truly human energies, but merely with mechanical exactness. And if a man acts in a mechanical way, reacting to external demands or instruction, rather than in ways determined by his own interests and energies and power, we may admire what he does, but we despise what he is.

For Humboldt then man

> is born to inquire and create, and when a man or a child chooses to inquire or create out of his own free choice then he becomes in his own terms an artist rather than a tool of production or a well trained parrot.

This is the essence of his concept of human nature. And I think that it is very revealing and interesting to compare it with Marx, with the early Marx manuscripts, and in particular his account of, quote

> the alienation of labor when work is external to the worker, not part of his nature, so that he does not fulfill

himself in his work but denies himself and is physically exhausted and mentally debased. This alienated labor that casts some of the workers back into a barbarous kind of work and turns others into machines, thus depriving man of his species character, of free conscious activity and productive life.

Recall also Marx's well known and often quoted reference to a higher form of society in which labor has become not only a means of life but also the highest want in life. And recall also his repeated criticism of the specialized labor which, I quote again,

> mutilates the worker into a fragment of a human being, degrades him to become a mere appurtenance of the machine, makes his work such a torment that its essential meaning is destroyed, estranges him from the intellectual potentialities of the labor process in very proportion to the extent to which science is incorporated into it as an independent power.

Robert Tucker, for one, has rightly emphasized that Marx sees the revolutionary more as a frustrated producer than as a dissatisfied consumer. And this far more radical critique of capitalist relations of production flows directly, often in the same words, from the libertarian thought of the enlightenment. For this reason, I think, one must say that classical liberal ideas in their essence, though not in the way they developed, are profoundly anti-capitalist. The essence of these ideas must be destroyed for them to serve as an ideology of modern industrial capitalism.

Writing in the 1780's and early 1790's, Humboldt had no conception of the forms that industrial capitalism would take. Consequently, in this classic of classical liberalism he stresses the problem of limiting state power, and he is not overly concerned with the dangers of private power. The reason is that he believes in and speaks of the essential equality of condition of private citizens. Of course, he has no idea, writing in 1790, of the ways in which the notion of a private person would come to be reinterpreted in the era of corporate capitalism.

He did not foresee, I now quote the anarchist historian Rudolf Rocker,

> "that democracy with its model of equality of all citizens before the law and liberalism with its right of man over his own person both would be wrecked on the realities of capitalist economy. Humboldt did not foresee that in a predatory capitalist economy state intervention would be an absolute necessity to preserve human existence, to prevent the destruction of the physical environment. I speak optimistically of course."

As Karl Polanyi, for one, has pointed out:

> The self-adjusting market could not exist for any length of time without annihilating the human and natural substance of society. It would have physically

destroyed man and transformed his surroundings into a wilderness.

I think that is correct. Humboldt also did not foresee the consequences of the commodity character of labor. The doctrine is, again in Polanyi's words,

> that it is not for the commodity to decide where it should be offered for sale, to what purpose it should be used, at what price it should be allowed to change hands, in what manner it should be consumed or destroyed.

But the commodity in this case is of course human life. And social protection was therefore a minimal necessity to constrain the irrational and destructive workings of the classical free market.

Nor did Humboldt understand in 1790 that capitalist economic relations perpetuated a form of bondage which long before that, in fact as early as 1767, Simon Linguet had declared to be even worse than slavery, writing

> it is the impossibility of earning a living by any other means that compels our farm laborers to till the soil whose fruits they will not eat and our masons to construct buildings in which they will not live. It is want that drags them to those markets where they await masters who will do them the kindness of buying them. It is want that compels them to go down on their knees to the rich man in order to get from him permission to enrich him. What effective gain has the suppression of slavery brought him? He is free, you say, that is his misfortune. These men, it is said, have no master. They have one, and the most terrible, the most imperious of masters: that is need. It is this that reduces them to the most cruel dependence.

And if there is something degrading to human nature in the idea of bondage – as every spokesman for the enlightenment would insist -, then it would follow that a new emancipation must be awaited, what Fourier referred to as the third and last emancipatory phase of history, the first having made serfs out of slaves, the second wage earners out of serfs, and the third, which will transform the proletariats to free men, by eliminating the commodity character of labor, ending wage slavery and bringing the commercial, industrial and financial institutions under democratic control.

These are all things that Humboldt in his classical liberal doctrine did not express and didn't see, but I think that he might have accepted these conclusions. He does, for example, agree that state intervention in social life is legitimate "if freedom would destroy the very conditions without which not only freedom but even existence itself would be inconceivable", which are precisely the circumstances that arise in an unconstrained capitalist economy. And he does, as in the remarks that I quoted, vigorously condemn the alienation of labor.

In any event, his criticism of bureaucracy and the autocratic state stands as a very eloquent forewarning of some of the most dismal aspects of modern history, and the important point is that the basis of his critique is applicable to a far broader range of coercive institutions than he imagined, in particular to the institutions of industrial capitalism.

Though he expresses a classical liberal doctrine, Humboldt is no primitive individualist, in the style of for example Rousseau. Rousseau extols the savage who lives within himself but Humboldt's vision is entirely different. He sums up his remarks as follows:

> The whole tenor of the ideas and arguments unfolded in this essay might fairly be reduced to this 'that while they would break all fetters in human society, they would attempt to find as many new social bonds as possible, the isolated man is no more able to develop than the one who is fettered.'

And he, in fact, looks forward to a community of free association, without coercion by the state or other authoritarian institutions, in which free men can create and inquire and achieve the highest development of their powers.

In fact, far ahead of his time, he presents an anarchist vision that is appropriate perhaps to the next stage of industrial society. We can perhaps look forward to a day when these various strands will be brought together within the framework of libertarian socialism, a social form that barely exists today, though its elements can perhaps be perceived. For example, in the guarantee of individual rights that has achieved so far its fullest realization, though still tragically flawed, in the western democracies or in the Israeli kibbutzim or in the experiments of workers' councils in Yugoslavia or in the effort to awaken popular consciousness and to create a new involvement in the social process which is a fundamental element in the third world revolutions coexisting uneasily with indefensible authoritarian practice.

Let me summarize the first point. The first concept of the state that I want to set up as a reference is classical liberal. Its doctrine is that the state functions should be drastically limited. But this familiar characterization is a very superficial one. More deeply, the classical liberal view develops from a certain concept of human nature, one that stresses the importance of diversity and free creation. Therefore, this view is in fundamental opposition to industrial capitalism with its wage slavery, its alienated labor and its hierarchic and authoritarian principles of social and economic organization.

At least in its ideal form, classical liberal thought is opposed as well to the concepts of possessive individualism that are intrinsic to capitalist ideology. It seeks to eliminate social fetters and to replace them by social bonds, not by competitive greed, not by predatory individualism, not of course by corporate empires, state or private. Classical libertarian thought seems to me, therefore, to lead directly to libertarian socialism or anarchism, if you like, when combined with an understanding of industrial capitalism.

Libertarian Socialism and Anarchism

The second point of reference that I want to discuss is the libertarian socialist vision of the state. A French writer, rather sympathetic to anarchism, once wrote that "anarchism has a broad back – like paper it endures anything." And there are many shades of anarchism. I am concerned here only with one, namely the anarchism of Bakunin who wrote in his anarchist manifesto of 1865 that to be an anarchist one must first be a socialist. I am concerned with the anarchism of Adolf Fisher, one of the martyrs of the Hay Market affair in 1886, who said that every anarchist is a socialist but not every socialist is necessarily an anarchist. A consistent anarchist must oppose private ownership of the means of production. Such property is indeed, as Proudhon in his famous remark asserted, a form of theft. But a consistent anarchist will also oppose the organization of production by government.

Quoting

> "it means state socialism, the command of the state officials over production and the command of managers, scientists, shop officials in the shop. The goal of the working class is liberation from exploitation, and this goal is not reached and cannot be reached by a new directing and governing class substituting itself for the bourgeoisie. It is only realized by the workers themselves, being master over production, by some form of workers' councils."

These remarks, it happens, are quoted from the left wing Marxist Anton Pannekoek, and in fact radical Marxism – what Lenin once called infantile ultra-leftism – merges with anarchist currents. This is an important point, I think, and let me give one further illustration of this convergence between left wing Marxism and socialist anarchism.

Consider the following characterization of revolutionary socialism:

> "The revolutionary socialist denies that state ownership can end in anything other than a bureaucratic despotism. We have seen why the state cannot democratically control industry. Industry can only be democratically owned and controlled by the workers electing directly from their own ranks industrial administrative committees. Socialism will fundamentally be an industrial system; its constituencies will be of an industrial character. Thus those carrying on the social activity and industries of society will be directly represented in the local and central councils of social administration. In this way the powers of such delegates will flow upwards from those carrying on the work and conversant with the needs of the community. When the central industrial administrative committee meets it will represent every phase of social activity. Hence the capitalist political or geographical state will be replaced by the industrial administrative committee of socialism. The transition from one social system to the other will be the social revolution. The political state throughout history has meant the government of men by ruling classes; the republic of socialism will be the government of industry administered on behalf of the whole community. The former meant the economic and political subjection of the many, the latter will mean the economic freedom of all. It will be, therefore, a true democracy."

These remarks are taken from a book called "The State: Its Origins and Function", written by William Paul in early 1917, just prior to Lenin's "State and Revolution", which is his most libertarian work.

William Paul was one of the founders of the British Communist Party, later the editor of the British Communist Party Journal. And it is interesting that his critique of state socialism resembles very closely, I think, the libertarian doctrine of the anarchists, in particular, in its principle that the state must disappear, to be replaced by the industrial organization of society in the course of the social revolution itself. Proudhon in 1851 wrote that what we put in place of the government is industrial organization, and many similar comments can be cited. That, in essence, is the fundamental idea of anarchist revolutionaries. What's more important than the fact that many such statements can be cited is that these ideas have been realized in spontaneous revolutionary action several times. For example, in Germany and Italy after the first World War, in Catalonia in 1936.

One might argue, or at least I would argue, that council communism in this sense, in the sense of the long quotation that I read is the natural form of revolutionary socialism in an industrial society. It reflects the intuitive understanding that democracy is largely a sham when the industrial system is controlled by any form of autocratic elite, whether of owners, managers, technocrats, a vanguard party, a state bureaucracy, or whatever. Under these conditions of authoritarian domination, the classical liberal ideals which are expressed also by Marx and Bakunin and all true revolutionaries cannot be realized.

Man will, in other words, not be free to inquire and create, to develop his own potentialities to their fullest. The worker will remain a fragment of a human being, degraded, a tool in the productive process directed from above. And the ideas of revolutionary libertarian socialism, in this sense, have been submerged in the industrial societies of the past half century. The dominant ideologies have been those of state socialism and state capitalism.

But there has been an interesting resurgence in the last couple of years. In fact, the theses that I quoted from Anton Pannekoek were taken from a recent pamphlet of a radical French workers group, and the quotation that I read from William Paul on revolutionary socialism was taken from a paper by Walter Kendall at the National Conference on Workers Control in Sheffield, England, last March.

Both of these groups represent something significant. The Workers Control Movement in England, in particular, has developed into, I think, a remarkably significant force in the last few years. It includes some of the largest trade unions, for example the Amalgamated Engineering Federation which, I think, is the second largest trade union in England and which has taken these principles as its fundamental ideas. It's had a series of successful conferences, putting out an interesting pamphlet literature, and on the continent there are parallel developments. May 1968 in France of course accelerated the growing interest in council communism and similar ideas and other forms of libertarian socialism in France and Germany, as it did in England.

Given the general conservative cast of our highly ideological society, it's not too surprising that the United States is relatively untouched by these currents. But that too may change. The erosion of the Cold War mythology at least makes it possible to discuss some of these questions, and if the present wave of repression can be beaten back, if the left can overcome its more suicidal tendencies and build on the achievements of the past decade, the problem of how to organize industrial society on truly democratic lines, with democratic control in the workplace as well as in the community, this should become the dominant intellectual issue for those who are alive to the problems of contemporary society. And as a mass movement for revolutionary libertarian socialism develops, as I hope it will, speculation should proceed to action.

It may seem quixotic to group left Marxism and anarchism under the same rubric, as I have done, given the antagonism throughout the past century between the Marxists and the anarchists, beginning with the antagonism between Marx and Engels on the one hand and, for example, Proudhon and Bakunin on the other. In the nineteenth century at least, their differences with regard to the question of the state was significant, but in a sense it was tactical. The anarchists were convinced that capitalism and the state must be destroyed together. But Engels, in a letter of 1883, expressed his opposition to this idea as follows:

> "The anarchists put the thing upside down. They declare that the proletarian revolution must begin by doing away with the political organization of the state. But to destroy it at such a moment would be to destroy the only organism by means of which the victorious proletariat can assert its newly conquered power, hold down its adversaries and carry out that economic revolution of society without which the whole victory must end in a new defeat and in a mass slaughter of the workers, similar to those after the Paris commune."

Now, the Paris commune, I think it is fair to say, did represent the ideas of libertarian socialism, of anarchism if you like, and Marx wrote about it with great enthusiasm. In fact, the experience of the commune led him to modify his concept of the role of the state and to take on something more of an anarchist perspective of the nature of social revolution, as you can see, for example, by looking at the introduction to the Communist Manifesto, the edition that was published in 1872. The commune was of course drowned in blood, as the anarchist communes of Spain were destroyed by Fascist and Communist armies. And it might be argued that more dictatorial structures would have defended the revolution against such forces. But I doubt this very much, at least in the case of Spain, it seems to me that a more consistent libertarian policy might have provided the only possible defense of the revolution.

Of course this can be contested and this is a long story that I don't want to go into here, but at the very least it is clear that one would have to be rather naive, after the events of the past half century, to fail to see the truth in Bakunin's repeated warnings that the red bureaucracy would prove to be the most violent and terrible lie of the century. "Take the most radical revolutionary and place him on the throne of all Russia", he said in 1870, "or give him dictatorial power, and before a year has passed he will become worse than the Czar himself."

I'm afraid, in this respect Bakunin was all too perceptive, and this kind of warning was repeatedly voiced from the left. For example, in the 1890's the anarchosyndicalist Fernand Pelloutier asked,

> "Must the transitional state to be endured necessarily or inevitably be the collectivist jail? Might it not consist of a free organization limited exclusively by the needs of production and consumption, all political institutions having disappeared?"

I don't pretend to know the answer to that question, but I think that it is tolerably clear that unless the answer is positive, the chances for a truly democratic revolution that will achieve the humanistic ideals of the left are perhaps rather slight. I think Martin Buber put the problem quite succinctly when he said: "One cannot in the nature of things expect a little tree that has been turned into a club to put forth leaves." For just this reason, it is essential that a powerful revolutionary movement exist in the United States, if there are to be any reasonable possibilities for democratic social change of a radical sort anywhere in the capitalist world. And comparable remarks, I think, undoubtedly hold for the Russian empire.

Lenin until the end of his life stressed the idea that

> it is an elementary truth of Marxism that the victory of socialism requires the joint effort of workers in a number of advanced countries. At the very least it requires that the great centers of world imperialism be impeded by domestic pressures from counter revolutionary intervention. Only such possibilities will permit any revolution to overthrow its own coercive state institutions as it tries to bring the economy under direct democratic control.

Let me summarize briefly again. I have mentioned so far two reference points for discussion of the state, classical liberalism and libertarian socialism. They are in agreement that the functions of the state are repressive and that state action must be limited. The libertarian socialist goes on to insist that the state power must be eliminated in favor of the democratic organization of the industrial society with direct popular control over all institutions by those who participate in as well as those who are directly affected by the workings of these institutions. So one might imagine a system of workers' councils, consumer councils, commune assemblies, regional federations, and so on, with the kind of representation that is direct and revocable, in the sense that representatives are directly answerable to and return directly to the well defined and integrated social group for which they speak in some higher order organization, something obviously very different than our system of representation.

Now it might very well be asked whether such a social structure is feasible in a complex, highly technological society. There are counter arguments, and I think they fall into two main categories. The first category is that such an organization is contrary to human nature, and the second category says roughly that it is incompatible with the demands of efficiency. I'd like to briefly consider each of these.

Consider the first, that a free society is contrary to human nature. It is often asked, do men really want freedom, do they want the responsibility that goes with it. Or would they prefer to be ruled by a benevolent master. Consistently, apologists for the existing distribution of power have held to one or another version of the idea of the happy slave. Two hundred years ago Rousseau denounced the sophistic politicians and intellectuals "who search for ways to obscure the fact," so he maintained,

> "that the essential and the defining property of man is his freedom. They attribute to man a natural inclination to servitude, without thinking that it is the same for freedom as for innocence and virtue. Their value is felt only as long as one enjoys them oneself, and the taste for them is lost as soon as one has lost them."

As proof of this doctrine he refers to the marvels done by all free peoples to guard themselves from oppression. "True" he says "those who have abandoned the life of a free man do nothing but boast incessantly of the peace, the repose they enjoy in their chains. But when I see the others sacrifice pleasures, repose, wealth, power and life itself for the preservation of this sole good which is so disdained by those who have lost it, when I see multitudes of entirely naked savages scorn European voluptuousness and endure hunger, fire, the sword and death to preserve only their independence, I feel it does not behoove slaves to reason about freedom." A comment to which we can perhaps give a contemporary interpretation.

Rather similar thoughts were expressed by Kant 40 years later. He cannot, he says,

> "accept the proposition that certain people are not right for freedom, for example, the serfs of some landlord. If one accepts this assumption, freedom will never be achieved. For one cannot arrive at the maturity for freedom without having already acquired it. One must be free to learn how to make use of ones powers freely and usefully. The first attempts will surely be brutal and will lead to a state of affairs more painful and dangerous than the former condition, under the dominance but also the protection of an external authority. However, one can achieve reason only through ones own experiences, and one must be free to be able to undertake them. To accept the principle that freedom is worthless for those under ones control and that one has the right to refuse it to them forever is an infringement on the right of God himself, who has created man to be free."

This particular remark is interesting because of its context as well. Kant on this occasion was defending the French revolution during the terror against those who claimed that it showed the masses to be unready for the privilege of freedom. And his remarks, too, I think, have obvious contemporary relevance. No rational person will approve of violence and terror, and in particular the terror of the post-revolutionary state that has fallen into the hands of a grim autocracy has more than once reached indescribable levels of savagery. At the same time, no person of understanding or humanity will too quickly condemn the violence that often occurs, when long subdued masses rise against their oppressors or take their first steps toward liberty and social reconstruction.

Humboldt, just a few years before Kant, had expressed a view that was very similar to that. He also said that freedom and variety are the preconditions for human self-realization.

> "Nothing promotes this rightness for freedom so much as freedom itself. This truth perhaps may not be acknowledged by those who have so often used this unrightness as an excuse for continuing repression, but it seems to me to follow unquestionably from the very nature of man. The incapacity for freedom can only arise from a want of moral and intellectual power. To heighten this power is the only way to supply the want, but to do so presupposes the freedom which awakens spontaneous activity. Those who do not comprehend this may justly be suspected of misunderstanding human nature, and wishing to make men into machines."

Rosa Luxemburg's fraternal sympathetic critique of Bolshevik ideology and practice was given in very similar terms.

> "Only the active participation of the masses in self-government and social reconstruction could bring about the complete spiritual transformation in the masses degraded by centuries of bourgeois class rule, just as only their creative experience and spontaneous action can solve the myriad problems of creating a libertarian socialist society."

She went on to say that historically the errors committed

by a truly revolutionary movement are infinitely more fruitful than the infallibility of the cleverest central committee, and I think that these remarks can be translated immediately for the somewhat parallel ideology of the soulful corporation which is now fairly popular among American academics. For example, Carl Kaysen writes:

> "No longer the agent of proprietorships seeking to maximize return on investment, management sees itself as responsible to stock holders, employees, customers, general public and perhaps most important the firm itself as an institution. There is no display of greed or graspingness, there is no attempt to push off on the workers and the community at least part of the social costs of the enterprise. The modern corporation is a soulful corporation."

Similarly, the vanguard party is a soulful party. In both cases those who urge that men submit to the rule of these benevolent autocracies may, I think, justly be accused of wishing to make men into machines. Now, the correctness of the view that is expressed by Rousseau and Kant and Humboldt and Luxemburg and innumerable others, I don't think that the correctness of this is for the moment susceptible to scientific proof. One can only evaluate it in terms of experience and intuition. But one can also point out the social consequences of adopting the view that men are born to be free, or that they are born to be ruled by benevolent autocrats.

What of the second question, the question of efficiency? Is democratic control of the industrial system, down to its smallest functional units, incompatible with efficiency? This is very frequently argued on several grounds. For example, some say that centralized management is a technological imperative, but I think the argument is exceedingly weak when one looks into it. The very same technology that brings relevant information to the board of managers can bring it at the time that it is needed to everyone in the work force. The technology that is now capable of eliminating the stupefying labor that turns men into specialized tools of production permits in principle the leisure and the educational opportunities that make them able to use this information in a rational way. Furthermore, even an economic elite which is dripping with soulfulness, to use Ralph Miliband's phrase, is constrained by the system in which it functions to organize production for certain ends: power, growth, profit, but not in the nature of the case human needs, needs that to an ever more critical degree can be expressed only in collective terms. It is surely conceivable and is perhaps even likely that decisions made by the collective itself, will reflect these needs and interests as well as those made by various soulful elites.

In any event, it is a bit difficult to take seriously arguments about efficiency in a society that devotes such enormous resources to waste and destruction. As everyone knows, the very concept of efficiency is dripping with ideology. Maximization of commodities is hardly the only measure of a decent existence. The point is familiar, and no elaboration is necessary.

State Socialism and State Capitalism

Let me turn to the two final points of reference: the Bolshevik or state socialist and the state capitalist. As I have tried to suggest, they have points in common, and in interesting respects they diverge from the classical liberal ideal or its later elaboration in libertarian socialism. Since I am concerned with our society, let me make a few rather elementary observations about the role of the state, its likely evolution and the ideological assumptions that accompany and sometimes disguise these phenomena.

To begin with, it is obvious that we can distinguish two systems of power, the political system and the economic system. The former consists in principle of elected representatives of the people who set public policy. The latter in principle is a system of private power, a system of private empires, that are free from public control, except in the remote and indirect ways in which even a feudal nobility or a totalitarian dictatorship must be responsive to the public will. There are several immediate consequences of this organization of society.

The first is that in a subtle way an authoritarian cast of mind is induced in a very large mass of the population which is subject to arbitrary decree from above. I think that this has a great effect on the general character of the culture. The effect is the belief that one must obey arbitrary dictates and accede to authority. And I think that in fact a remarkable and exciting fact about the youth movement in recent years is that it is challenging and beginning to break down some of these authoritarian patterns.

The second fact that is important is that the range of decisions that are in principle subject to public democratic control is quite narrow. For example, it excludes in law in principle the central institutions in any advanced industrial society, i.e. the entire commercial, industrial and financial system. And a third fact is that even within the narrow range of issues that are submitted in principle to democratic decision making, the centers of private power of course exert an inordinately heavy influence in perfectly obvious ways, through control of the media, through control of political organizations or in fact by the simple and direct means of supplying the top personnel for the parliamentary system itself, as they obviously do. Richard Barnet in his recent study of the top 400 decision makers in the postwar national security system reports that most have, I quote now, "come from executive suites and law offices within shouting distance of each other, in 15 city blocks in 5 major cities." And every other study shows the same thing.

In short, the democratic system at best functions within a narrow range in a capitalist democracy, and even within this narrow range its functioning is enormously biased by the concentrations of private power and by the authoritarian and passive modes of thinking that are induced by autocratic institutions such as industries, for example. It is a truism but one that must be constantly stressed that capitalism and democracy are ultimately quite incompatible. And a careful look at the matter merely strengthens this conclusion. There are perfectly obvious processes of centralization of control taking place in both the political and the industrial system. As far as the political system is concerned, in every parliamentary democracy, not only ours, the role of parliament in policy formation has been declining in the years since WWII, as everyone knows and political commentators repeatedly point out.

In other words, the executive becomes increasingly powerful as the planning functions of the state become more significant. The House Armed Services Committee a couple of years ago described the role of Congress as that of a sometimes querulous but essentially kindly uncle who complains while furiously puffing on his pipe but who finally, as everyone expects, gives in and hands over the allowance. And careful studies of civil military decisions since WWII show that this is quite an accurate perception.

Senator Vandenberg 20 years ago expressed his fear that the American chief executive would become the number one warlord of the earth, his phrase. That has since occurred. The clearest decision is the decision to escalate in Vietnam in February 1965, in cynical disregard of the expressed will of the electorate. This incident reveals, I think, with perfect clarity the role of the public in decisions about peace and war, the role of the public in decisions about the main lines about public policy in general. And it also suggests the irrelevance of electoral politics to major decisions of national policy.

Unfortunately, you can't vote the rascals out, because you never voted them in, in the first place. The corporate executives and the corporation lawyers and so on who overwhelmingly staff the executive, assisted increasingly by a university based mandarin class, remain in power no matter whom you elect.

Furthermore, it is interesting to note that this ruling elite is pretty clear about its social role. As an example take Robert McNamara, who is the person widely praised in liberal circles for his humanity, his technical brilliance and his campaign to control the military. His views of social organization, I think, are quite illuminating. He says that vital decision making in policy matters as well as in business must remain at the top. That is partly, though not completely, what the top is for. And he goes on to suggest that this is apparently a divine imperative. I quote:

> "God is clearly democratic, he distributes brain power universally, but he quite justifiably expects us to do something efficient and constructive with that priceless gift. That's what management is all about. Management in the end is the most creative of all the arts, for its medium is human talent itself. The real threat to democracy comes from under-management. The under-management of society is not the respect of liberty, it is simply to let some force other than reason shape reality. If it is not reason that rules man then man falls short of his potential."

So reason then is to be identified as the centralization of decision making at the top in the hands of management. Popular involvement in decision making is a threat to liberty, a violation of reason. Reason is embodied in autocratic, tightly managed institutions. Strengthening these institutions within which man can function most efficiently is, in his words,

> "the great human adventure of our times." All this has a faintly familiar ring to it. It is the authentic voice of the technical intelligentsia, the liberal intelligentsia of the technocratic corporate elite in a modern society.

There is a parallel process of centralization in economic life. A recent FTC report notes that the 200 largest manufacturing corporations now control about two thirds of all manufacturing assets. At the beginning of WWII the same amount of power was spread over a thousand corporations. The report says: "A small industrial elite of huge conglomerate companies is gobbling up American business and largely destroying competitive free enterprise." Furthermore it says: "These two hundred corporations are partially linked with each other and with other corporations in ways that may prevent or discourage independent behavior in market decisions." What is novel about such observations is only their source, the FTC. They are familiar, to the point of cliche, among left-liberal commentators on American society.

The centralization of power also has an international dimension. Quoting from Foreign Affairs, it has been pointed that

> "on the basis of the gross value of their output, US enterprises abroad in the aggregate comprise the third largest country in the world, with a gross product greater than that of any country except the United States and the Soviet Union. American firms control over half the automobile industry in England, almost 40% of petroleum in Germany, over 40% of the telegraphic, telephone and electronic and business equipment in France, 75% of the computers. Within a decade, given present trends, more than half of the British exports will be from American owned companies."

Furthermore, these are highly-concentrated investments: 40% of direct investment in Germany, France and Britain is by three firms, American firms.

George Ball has explained that the project of constructing an integrated world economy, dominated by American capital, an empire in other words, is no idealistic pipe dream, but a hard headed prediction. It is a role, he says, into which we are being pushed by the imperatives of our own economy, the major instrument being the multinational corporation which George Ball describes as follows:

> "In its modern form, the multinational corporation, or one with worldwide operations and markets, is a distinctly American development. Through such corporations it has become possible for the first time to use the

world's resources with maximum efficiency. But there must be greater unification of the world economy to give full play to the benefits of multinational corporations."

These multinational corporations are the beneficiary of the mobilization of resources by the federal government, and its world wide operations and markets are backed ultimately by American military force, now based in dozens of countries. It is not difficult to guess who will reap the benefits from the integrated world economy, which is the domain of operation of these American based international economic institutions.

At this stage in the discussion one has to mention the specter of communism. What is the threat of communism to this system? For a clear and cogent answer, one can turn to an extensive study of the Woodrow Wilson Foundation and National Planning Association called the Political Economy of American Foreign Policy, a very important book. It was compiled by a representative segment of the tiny elite that largely sets public policy for whoever is technically in office. In effect, it's as close as you can come to a manifesto of the American ruling class.

Here they define the primary threat of communism as

"the economic transformation of the communist powers in ways which reduce their willingness or ability to complement the industrial economies of the West."

That is the primary threat of communism. Communism, in short, reduces the willingness and ability of underdeveloped countries to function in the world capitalist economy in the manner of, for example, the Philippines which has developed a colonial economy of a classic type, after 75 years of American tutelage and domination. It is this doctrine which explains why British economist Joan Robinson describes the American crusade against communism as a crusade against development.

The cold war ideology and the international communist conspiracy function in an important way as essentially a propaganda device to mobilize support at a particular historical moment for this long time imperial enterprise. In fact, I believe that this is probably the main function of the cold war. It serves as a useful device for the managers of American society and their counterparts in the Soviet Union to control their own populations and their own respective imperial systems. I think that the persistence of the cold war can be in part explained by its utility for the managers of the two great world systems.

There is one final element that has to be added to this picture, namely the ongoing militarization of American society. How does this enter in? To see, one has to look back at WWII and to recall that prior to WWII, of course, we were deep in the depression. WWII taught an important economic lesson, it taught the lesson that government induced production in a carefully controlled economy – centrally controlled – could overcome the effects of a depression.

I think this is what Charles E. Wilson had in mind at the end of 1944 when he proposed that we have a permanent war economy in the postwar world. Of course, the trouble is that in a capitalist economy there are only a number of ways in which government intervention can take place. It can't be competitive with the private empires for example, which is to say that it can't be any useful production. In fact, it has to be the production of luxury goods, goods not capital, not useful commodities, which would be competitive. And unfortunately there is only one category of luxury goods that can be produced endlessly with rapid obsolescence, quickly wasting, and no limit on how many of them you can use. We all know what that is.

This whole matter is described pretty well by the business historian Alfred Chandler. He describes the economic lessons of WWII as follows:

"The government spent far more than the most enthusiastic New Dealer had ever proposed. Most of the output of the expenditures was destroyed or left on the battlefields of Europe or Asia but the resulting increased demand sent the nation into a period of prosperity, the likes of which had never before been seen. Moreover, the supplying of huge armies and navies fighting the most massive war of all time required a tight centralized control of the national economy. This effort brought corporate managers to Washington to carry out one of the most complex pieces of economic planning in history. That experience lessened the ideological fears over the government's role in stabilizing the economy."

This is a conservative commentator, I might point out. It may be added that the ensuing cold war carried further the depoliticization of the American society and created the kind of psychological environment in which the government is able to intervene in part through fiscal policies, in part through public work and public services, but very largely, of course, through defense spending.

In this way, to use Alfred Chandler's words, "the government acts as a coordinator of last resort when managers are unable to maintain a high level of aggregate demand." As another conservative business historian, Joseph Monsen, writes, "enlightened corporate managers, far from fearing government intervention in the economy, view the new economics as a technique for increasing corporate viability."

Of course, the most cynical use of these ideas is by the managers of the publicly subsidized war industries. There was a remarkable series in the Washington Post about a year ago, by Bernard Nossiter. For example, he quoted Samuel Downer, financial vice president of LTV Aerospace, one of the big new conglomerates, who explained why the postwar world must be bolstered by military orders. He said:

"Its selling appeal is the defense of the home. This is one of the greatest appeals the politicians have to adjusting the system. If you're the president and you need a control factor in the economy, and you need to sell this factor, you can't sell Harlem and Watts but you can sell self-preservation, a new environment. We are going to increase defense budgets as long as those bastards in Russia are ahead of us. The American people understand this."

Of course, those bastards aren't exactly ahead of us in this deadly and cynical game, but that is only a minor embarrassment to the thesis. In times of need, we can always follow Dean Rusk, Hubert Humphrey and other luminaries and appeal to the billion Chinese armed to the teeth and setting out on world conquest.

Again, I want to emphasize the role in this system of the cold war as a technique of domestic control, a technique for developing the climate of paranoia and psychosis in which the tax payer will be willing to provide an enormous endless subsidy to the technologically advanced sectors of American industry and the corporations that dominate this increasingly centralized system.

Of course, it is perfectly obvious that Russian imperialism is not an invention of American ideologists. It is real enough for the Hungarians and the Czechs, for example. What is an invention is the uses to which it is put, for example by Dean Acheson in 1950 or Walt Rostow a decade later, when they pretend that the Vietnam war is an example of Russian imperialism. Or by the Johnson administration in 1965 when it justifies the Dominican intervention with reference to the Sino-Soviet military bloc. Or by the Kennedy intellectuals, who as Townsend Hoopes put it in an article in the Washington Monthly in the last month, were deluded by the tensions of the cold war years, and could not perceive that the triumph of the national revolution in Vietnam would not be a triumph for Moscow and Peking. It was the most remarkable degree of delusion on the part of presumably literate men.
Or, for example, by Eugene Rostow who in a recent book that was very widely praised by liberal senators and academic intellectuals, outlined the series of challenges to world order in the modern era as follows: "Napoleon, Kaiser Wilhelm, Hitler," and continuing in the postwar world, "general strikes in France and Italy, the civil war in Greece, and the attack on South Vietnam where Russia has put us to severe tests in its efforts to spread communism by the sword."

This is a very interesting series of challenges to world order: Napoleon, Kaiser Wilhelm, Hitler, general strikes in France and Italy, the civil war in Greece and the Russian attack on South Vietnam. If one thinks it through, he can reach some pretty interesting conclusions about modern history.

One can continue with this indefinitely. I mean to suggest that the cold war is highly functional both to the American elite and its Soviet counterpart who in a perfectly similar way exploit Western imperialism, which they did not invent, as they send their armies into Czechoslovakia.

It is important in both cases in providing an ideology for empire and for the government subsidized system here of military capitalism. It is predictable then that the challenges to this ideology will be bitterly resisted, by force if necessary. In many ways, American society is indeed open and liberal values are preserved. However, as poor people and black people and other ethnic minorities know very well, the liberal veneer is pretty thin. Mark Twain once wrote that

> "it is by the goodness of God that in our country we have those three unspeakably precious things: freedom of speech, freedom of conscience, and the prudence never to practice either of them."

Those who lack the prudence may well pay the cost.

Roughly speaking, I think it is accurate to say that a corporate elite of managers and owners governs the economy and the political system as well, at least in very large measure. The people, so-called, do exercise an occasional choice among those who Marx once called the rival factions and adventurers of the ruling classes. Those who find this characterization too harsh may prefer the formulations of a modern democratic theorist like Joseph Schumpeter who describes modern political democracy, favorably, "as a system in which the deciding of issues by the electorate is secondary to the election of the men who are to do the deciding. The political party", he says accurately,

> "is a group whose members propose to act in concert in the competitive struggle for political power. If that were not so, it would be impossible for different parties to adopt exactly or almost exactly the same program."

That's all the advantages of political democracy, as he sees it.

This program that both parties adopt more or less exactly and the individuals who compete for power express a narrow conservative ideology, basically the interests of one or another element in the corporate elite, with some modifications. This is obviously no conspiracy. I think it is simply implicit in the system of corporate capitalism. These people and the institutions they represent are in effect in power, and their interests are the national interest. It is this interest that is served primarily and overwhelmingly by the overseas empire and the growing system of military state capitalism at home.

If we were to withdraw the consent of the governed, as I think we should, we are withdrawing our consent to have these men and the interests they represent, govern and manage American society and impose their concept of world order and their criteria for legitimate political and economic development in much of the world. Although an immense effort of propaganda and mystification is carried on to conceal these facts, nonetheless facts they remain.

We have today the technical and material resources to meet man's animal needs. We have not developed the cultural and moral resources or the democratic forms of social organization that make possible the humane and rational use of our material wealth and power. Conceivably, the classical liberal ideals, as expressed and developed in their libertarian socialist form, are achievable. But if so, only by a popular revolutionary movement, rooted in wide strata of the population, and committed to the elimination of repressive and authoritarian institutions, state and private. To create such a movement is the challenge we face and must meet if there is to be an escape from contemporary barbarism.

Discussion

1. Before coming into this reading, what came to mind when you heard the terms liberalism, socialism, capitalism, or democracy?

2. How do those impressions differ from the picture that Chomsky weaves for each?

3. How might state socialism differ from other forms of socialism (consider looking them up)?

4. Think of the culture, nation, or subculture in which you find yourself. How are these ways of organizing and reproducing society defined in those spaces?

5. What are the challenges you think we will face, as a society and as a species, in the next 10, 30, and 100 years? Did Chomsky adequately address those concerns?

Citation and Use

This text was taken from the following source.

Chomsky, Noam. "Government in the Future." Anarchist Archive. LibCom, April 1970. http://libcom.org/library/government-future-noam-chomsky.

ANARCHY

Pëtr Kropotkin

ANARCHISM (from the Gr. *an*, and *archos*, contrary to authority), the name given to a principle or theory of life and conduct under which society is conceived without government — harmony in such a society being obtained, not by submission to law, or by obedience to any authority, but by free agreements concluded between the various groups, territorial and professional, freely constituted for the sake of production and consumption, as also for the satisfaction of the infinite variety of needs and aspirations of a civilized being. In a society developed on these lines, the voluntary associations which already now begin to cover all the fields of human activity would take a still greater extension so as to substitute themselves for the state in all its functions. They would represent an interwoven network, composed of an infinite variety of groups and federations of all sizes and degrees, local, regional, national and international temporary or more or less permanent — for all possible purposes: production, consumption and exchange, communications, sanitary arrangements, education, mutual protection, defence of the territory, and so on; and, on the other side, for the satisfaction of an ever-increasing number of scientific, artistic, literary and sociable needs. Moreover, such a society would represent nothing immutable. On the contrary — as is seen in organic life at large — harmony would (it is contended) result from an ever-changing adjustment and readjustment of equilibrium between the multitudes of forces and influences, and this adjustment would be the easier to obtain as none of the forces would enjoy a special protection from the state.

If, it is contended, society were organized on these principles, man would not be limited in the free exercise of his powers in productive work by a capitalist monopoly, maintained by the state; nor would he be limited in the exercise of his will by a fear of punishment, or by obedience towards individuals or metaphysical entities, which both lead to depression of initiative and servility of mind. He would be guided in his actions by his own understanding, which necessarily would bear the impression of a free action and reaction between his own self and the ethical conceptions of his surroundings. Man would thus be enabled to obtain the full development of all his faculties, intellectual, artistic and moral, without being hampered by overwork for the

monopolists, or by the servility and inertia of mind of the great number. He would thus be able to reach full *individualization*, which is not possible either under the present system of *individualism*, or under any system of state socialism in the so-called *Volkstaat* (popular state).

The anarchist writers consider, moreover, that their conception is not a utopia, constructed on the *a priori* method, after a few desiderata have been taken as postulates. It is derived, they maintain, from an *analysis of tendencies* that are at work already, even though state socialism may find a temporary favour with the reformers. The progress of modern technics, which wonderfully simplifies the production of all the necessaries of life; the growing spirit of independence, and the rapid spread of free initiative and free understanding in all branches of activity — including those which formerly were considered as the proper attribution of church and state — are steadily reinforcing the no-government tendency.

As to their economical conceptions, the anarchists, in common with all socialists, of whom they constitute the left wing, maintain that the now prevailing system of private ownership in land, and our capitalist production for the sake of profits, represent a monopoly which runs against both the principles of justice and the dictates of utility. They are the main obstacle which prevents the successes of modern technics from being brought into the service of all, so as to produce general well-being. The anarchists consider the wage-system and capitalist production altogether as an obstacle to progress. But they point out also that the state was, and continues to be, the chief instrument for permitting the few to monopolize the land, and the capitalists to appropriate for themselves a quite disproportionate share of the yearly accumulated surplus of production. Consequently, while combating the present monopolization of land, and capitalism altogether, the anarchists combat with the same energy the state, as the main support of that system. Not this or that special form, but the state altogether, whether it be a monarchy or even a republic governed by means of the *referendum*.

The state organization, having always been, both in ancient

and modern history (Macedonian Empire, Roman Empire, modern European states grown up on the ruins of the autonomous cities), the instrument for establishing monopolies in favour of the ruling minorities, cannot be made to work for the destruction of these monopolies. The anarchists consider, therefore, that to hand over to the state all the main sources of economical life — the land, the mines, the railways, banking, insurance, and so on — as also the management of all the main branches of industry, in addition to all the functions already accumulated in its hands (education, state-supported religions, defence of the territory, etc.), would mean to create a new instrument of tyranny. State capitalism would only increase the powers of bureaucracy and capitalism. True progress lies in the direction of decentralization, both *territorial* and *functional*, in the development of the spirit of local and personal initiative, and of free federation from the simple to the compound, in lieu of the present hierarchy from the centre to the periphery.

In common with most socialists, the anarchists recognize that, like all evolution in nature, the slow evolution of society is followed from time to time by periods of accelerated evolution which are called revolutions; and they think that the era of revolutions is not yet closed. Periods of rapid changes will follow the periods of slow evolution, and these periods must be taken advantage of — not for increasing and widening the powers of the state, but for reducing them, through the organization in every township or commune of the local groups of producers and consumers, as also the regional, and eventually the international, federations of these groups.

In virtue of the above principles the anarchists refuse to be party to the present state organization and to support it by infusing fresh blood into it. They do not seek to constitute, and invite the working men not to constitute, political parties in the parliaments. Accordingly, since the foundation of the International Working Men's Association in 1864–1866, they have endeavoured to promote their ideas directly amongst the labour organizations and to induce those unions to a direct struggle against capital, without placing their faith in parliamentary legislation.

The historical development of anarchism

The conception of society just sketched, and the tendency which is its dynamic expression, have always existed in mankind, in opposition to the governing hierarchic conception and tendency — now the one and now the other taking the upper hand at different periods of history. To the former tendency we owe the evolution, by the masses themselves, of those institutions — the clan, the village community, the guild, the free medieval city — by means of which the masses resisted the encroachments of the conquerors and the power-seeking minorities. The same tendency asserted itself with great energy in the great religious movements of medieval times, especially in the early movements of the reform and its forerunners. At the same time it evidently found its expression in the writings of some thinkers, since the times of Lao-tsze, although, owing to its

non-scholastic and popular origin, it obviously found less sympathy among the scholars than the opposed tendency.

As has been pointed out by Prof. Adler in his *Geschichte des Sozialismus und Kommunismus*, Aristippus (430 BC), one of the founders of the Cyrenaic school, already taught that the wise must not give up their liberty to the state, and in reply to a question by Socrates he said that he did not desire to belong either to the governing or the governed class. Such an attitude, however, seems to have been dictated merely by an Epicurean attitude towards the life of the masses.

The best exponent of anarchist philosophy in ancient Greece was Zeno (342–267 or 270 BC), from Crete, the founder of the Stoic philosophy, who distinctly opposed his conception of a free community without government to the state-utopia of Plato. He repudiated the omnipotence of the state, its intervention and regimentation, and proclaimed the sovereignty of the moral law of the individual — remarking already that, while the necessary instinct of self-preservation leads man to egotism, nature has supplied a corrective to it by providing man with another instinct — that of sociability. When men are reasonable enough to follow their natural instincts, they will unite across the frontiers and constitute the cosmos. They will have no need of law-courts or police, will have no temples and no public worship, and use no money — free gifts taking the place of the exchanges. Unfortunately, the writings of Zeno have not reached us and are only known through fragmentary quotations. However, the fact that his very wording is similar to the wording now in use, shows how deeply is laid the tendency of human nature of which he was the mouthpiece.

In medieval times we find the same views on the state expressed by the illustrious bishop of Alba, Marco Girolamo Vida, in his first dialogue *De dignitate reipublicae* (Ferd. Cavalli, in *Mem. dell'Istituto Veneto*, xiii.; Dr E. Nys, *Researches in the History of Economics*). But it is especially in several early Christian movements, beginning with the ninth century in Armenia, and in the preachings of the early Hussites, particularly Chojecki, and the early Anabaptists, especially Hans Denk (cf. Keller, *Ein Apostel der Wiedertaufer*), that one finds the same ideas forcibly expressed — special stress being laid of course on their moral aspects.

Rabelais and Fenelon, in their utopias, have also expressed similar ideas, and they were also current in the eighteenth century amongst the French Encyclopaedists, as may be concluded from separate expressions occasionally met with in the writings of Rousseau, from Diderot's *Preface* to the *Voyage* of Bougainville, and so on. However, in all probability such ideas could not be developed then, owing to the rigorous censorship of the Roman Catholic Church.

These ideas found their expression later during the great French Revolution. While the Jacobins did all in their power to centralize everything in the hands of the government, it appears now, from recently published documents, that the masses of the people, in their municipalities and 'sections', accomplished a considerable constructive work. They appropriated for themselves the election of the judges, the organization of supplies and equipment for the army, as also for the large cities, work for the unemployed, the management of charities, and so on. They even tried to establish a direct correspondence between the 36,000 communes of France through the intermediary of a special board, outside the National Assembly (cf. Sigismund Lacroix, *Actes de la commune de Paris*).

It was Godwin, in his *Enquiry concerning Political Justice* (2 vols., 1793), who was the first to formulate the political and economical conceptions of anarchism, even though he did not give that name to the ideas developed in his remarkable work. Laws, he wrote, are not a product of the wisdom of our ancestors: they are the product of their passions, their timidity, their jealousies and their ambition. The remedy they offer is worse than the evils they pretend to cure. If and only if all laws and courts were abolished, and the decisions in the arising contests were left to reasonable men chosen for that purpose, real justice would gradually be evolved. As to the state, Godwin frankly claimed its abolition. A society, he wrote, can perfectly well exist without any government: only the communities should be small and perfectly autonomous. Speaking of property, he stated that the rights of every one 'to every substance capable of contributing to the benefit of a human being' must be regulated by justice alone: the substance must go 'to him who most wants it'. His conclusion was communism. Godwin, however, had not the courage to maintain his opinions. He entirely rewrote later on his chapter on property and mitigated his communist views in the second edition of *Political Justice* (8vo, 1796).

Proudhon was the first to use, in 1840 (*Qu'est-ce que la propriete?* first memoir), the name of anarchy with application to the no government state of society. The name of 'anarchists' had been freely applied during the French Revolution by the Girondists to those revolutionaries who did not consider that the task of the Revolution was accomplished with the overthrow of Louis XVI, and insisted upon a series of economical measures being taken (the abolition of feudal rights without redemption, the return to the village communities of the communal lands enclosed since 1669, the limitation of landed property to 120 acres, progressive income-tax, the national organization of exchanges on a just value basis, which already received a beginning of practical realization, and so on).

Now Proudhon advocated a society without government, and used the word anarchy to describe it. Proudhon repudiated, as is known, all schemes of communism, according to which mankind would be driven into communistic monasteries or barracks, as also all the schemes of state or state-aided socialism which were advocated by Louis Blanc and the collectivists. When he proclaimed in his first memoir on property that 'Property is theft', he meant only property in its present, Roman-law, sense of 'right of use and abuse'; in property-rights, on the other hand, understood in the limited sense of *possession*, he saw the best protection against the encroachments of the state. At the same time he did not want violently to dispossess the present owners of land, dwelling-houses, mines, factories and so on. He preferred to attain the same end by rendering capital incapable of earning interest; and this he proposed to obtain by means of a national bank, based on the mutual confidence of all those who are engaged in production, who would agree to exchange among themselves their produces at cost-value, by means of labour cheques representing the hours of labour required to produce every given commodity. Under such a system, which Proudhon described as 'Mutuellisme', all the exchanges of services would be strictly equivalent. Besides, such a bank would be enabled to lend money without interest, levying only something like I per cent, or even less, for covering the cost of administration. Everyone being thus enabled to borrow the money that would be required to buy a house, nobody would agree to pay any more a yearly rent for the use of it. A general 'social liquidation' would thus be rendered easy, without violent expropriation. The same applied to mines, railways, factories and so on.

In a society of this type the state would be useless. The chief relations between citizens would be based on free agreement and regulated by mere account keeping. The contests might be settled by arbitration. A penetrating criticism of the state and all possible forms of government, and a deep insight into all economic problems, were well-known characteristics of Proudhon's work.

It is worth noticing that French mutualism had its precursor in England, in William Thompson, who began by mutualism before he became a communist, and in his followers John Gray (*A Lecture on Human Happiness*, 1825; *The Social System*, 1831) and J. F. Bray (*Labour's Wrongs and Labour's Remedy*, 1839). It had also its precursor in America. Josiah Warren, who was born in 1798 (cf. W. Bailie, *Josiah Warren, the First American Anarchist*, Boston, 1900), and belonged to Owen's 'New Harmony', considered that the failure of this enterprise was chiefly due to the suppression of individuality and the lack of initiative and responsibility. These defects, he taught, were inherent to every scheme based upon authority and the community of goods. He advocated, therefore, complete individual liberty. In 1827 he opened in Cincinnati a little country store which was the first 'equity store', and which the people called 'time store', because it was based on labour being exchanged hour for hour in all sorts of produce. 'Cost — the limit of price', and consequently 'no interest', was the motto of his store, and later on of his 'equity village', near New York, which was still in existence in 1865. Mr Keith's 'House of Equity' at Boston, founded in 1855, is also worthy of notice.

While the economical, and especially the mutual-banking, ideas of Proudhon found supporters and even a practical application in the United States, his political conception of anarchy found but little echo in France, where the Christian socialism of Lamennais and the Fourierists, and the state socialism of Louis Blanc and the followers of Saint-Simon, were dominating. These ideas found, however, some temporary support among the left-wing Hegelians in Germany, Moses Hess in 1843, and Karl Grün in 1845, who advocated anarchism. Besides, the authoritarian communism of Wilhelm Weitling having given origin to opposition amongst the Swiss working men, Wilhelm Marr gave expression to it in the forties.

On the other side, individualist anarchism found, also in Germany, its fullest expression in Max Stirner (Kaspar Schmidt), whose remarkable works (*Der Einzige und sein Eigenthum* and articles contributed to the *Rheinische Zeitung*) remained quite overlooked until they were brought into prominence by John Henry Mackay.

Prof. V. Basch, in a very able introduction to his interesting book, *L'Individualisme anarchiste: Max Stirner* (1904), has shown how the development of the German philosophy from Kant to Hegel, and 'the absolute' of Schelling and the *Geist* of Hegel, necessarily provoked, when the anti-Hegelian revolt began, the preaching of the same 'absolute' in the camp of the rebels. This was done by Stirner, who advocated, not only a complete revolt against the state and against the servitude which authoritarian communism would impose upon men, but also the full liberation of the individual from all social and moral bonds — the rehabilitation of the 'I', the supremacy of the individual, complete 'amoralism', and the 'association of the egotists'. The final conclusion of that sort of individual anarchism has been indicated by Prof. Basch. It maintains that the aim of all superior civilization is, not to permit *all*members of the community to develop in a normal way, but to permit certain better endowed individuals 'fully to develop', even at the cost of the happiness and the very existence of the mass of mankind. It is thus a return towards the most common individual ism, advocated by all the would-be superior minorities, to which indeed man owes in his history precisely the state and the rest, which these individualists combat. Their individualism goes so far as to end in a negation of their own starting-point — to say nothing of the impossibility for the individual to attain a really full development in the conditions of oppression of the masses by the 'beautiful aristocracies'. His development would remain unilateral. This is why this direction of thought, notwithstanding its undoubtedly correct and useful advocacy of the full development of each individuality, finds a hearing only in limited artistic and literary circles.

Anarchism in the International Working Men's Association

A general depression in the propaganda of all fractions of socialism followed, as is known, after the defeat of the uprising of the Paris working men in June 1848 and the fall of the Republic. All the socialist press was gagged during the reaction period, which lasted fully twenty years. Nevertheless, even anarchist thought began to make some progress, namely in the writings of Bellegarrique (Caeurderoy), and especially Joseph Déjacque (*Les Lazareacute'ennes, L 'Humanisphère*, an anarchist-communist utopia, lately discovered and reprinted). The socialist movement revived only after 1864, when some French working men, all 'mutualists', meeting in London during the Universal Exhibition with English followers of Robert Owen, founded the International Working Men's Association. This association developed very rapidly and adopted a policy of direct economical struggle against capitalism, without interfering in the political parliamentary agitation, and this policy was followed until 1871. However, after the Franco-German War, when the International Association was prohibited in France after the uprising of the Commune, the German working men, who had received manhood suffrage for elections to the newly constituted imperial parliament, insisted upon modifying the tactics of the International, and began to build up a Social Democratic political party. This soon led to a division in the Working Men's Association, and the Latin federations, Spanish, Italian, Belgian and Jurassic (France could not be represented), constituted among themselves a Federal union which broke entirely with the Marxist general council of the International. Within these federations developed now what may be described as *modern anarchism*. After the names of 'Federalists' and 'Anti-authoritarians' had been used for some time by these federations the name of 'anarchists', which their adversaries insisted upon applying to them, prevailed, and finally it was revindicated.

Bakunin (q.v.) soon became the leading spirit among these Latin federations for the development of the principles of anarchism, which he did in a number of writings, pamphlets and letters. He demanded the complete abolition of the state, which — he wrote — is a product of religion, belongs to a lower state of civilization, represents the negation of liberty, and spoils even that which it undertakes to do for the sake of general well-being. The state was an historically necessary evil, but its complete extinction will be, sooner or later, equally necessary. Repudiating all legislation, even when issuing from universal suffrage, Bakunin claimed for each nation, each region and each commune, full autonomy, so long as it is not a menace to its neighbours, and full independence for the individual, adding that one becomes really free only when, and in proportion as, all others are free. Free federations of the communes would constitute free nations.

As to his economical conceptions, Bakunin described himself, in common with his Federalist comrades of the International (César De Paepe, James Guillaume, Schwitzguébel), a 'collectivist anarchist' — not in the sense of Vidal and Pecqueur in the 1840s, or of their modern Social Democratic followers, but to express a state of things in which all necessaries for production are owned in common by the labour groups and the free communes, while the ways of retribution of labour, communist or otherwise, would be settled by each group for itself. Social revolution, the near approach of which was foretold at that time by all socialists, would be the means of bringing into life the new conditions.

The Jurassic, the Spanish and the Italian federations and sections of the International Working Men's Association, as also the French, the German and the American anarchist groups, were for the next years the chief centres of anarchist thought and propaganda. They refrained from any participation in parliamentary politics, and always kept in close contact with the labour organizations. However, in the second half of the 'eighties and the early 'nineties of the nineteenth century, when the influence of the anarchists began to be felt in strikes, in the 1st of May demonstrations, where they promoted the idea of a general strike for an eight hours' day, and in the anti-militarist propaganda in the army, violent prosecutions were directed against them, especially in the Latin countries (including physical torture in the Barcelona Castle) and the United States (the execution of five Chicago anarchists in 1887). Against these prosecutions the anarchists retaliated by acts of violence which in their turn were followed by more executions from above, and new acts of revenge from below. This created in the general public the impression that violence is the substance of anarchism, a view repudiated by its supporters, who hold that in reality violence is resorted to by all parties in proportion as their open action is obstructed by repression, and exceptional laws render them outlaws. (Cf. *Anarchism and Outrage*, by C. M. Wilson, and *Report of the Spanish Atrocities Committee*, in 'Freedom Pamphlets'; *A Concise History of the Great Trial of the Chicago Anarchists*, by Dyer Lum (New York, 1886); *The Chicago Martyrs: Speeches*, etc.).

Anarchism continued to develop, partly in the direction of Proudhonian 'mutuellisme', but chiefly as communist-anarchism, to which a third direction, Christian-anarchism, was added by Leo Tolstoy, and a fourth, which might be ascribed as literary-anarchism, began amongst some prominent modern writers.

The ideas of Proudhon, especially as regards mutual banking, corresponding with those of Josiah Warren, found a considerable following in the United States, creating quite a school, of which the main writers are Stephen Pearl Andrews, William Grene, Lysander Spooner (who began to write in 1850, and whose unfinished work, *Natural Law*, was full of promise), and several others, whose names will be found in Dr Nettlau's *Bibliographie de l'anarchie*.

A prominent position among the individualist anarchists in America has been occupied by Benjamin R. Tucker, whose journal *Liberty* was started in 1881 and whose conceptions are a combination of those of Proudhon with those of Herbert Spencer. Starting from the statement that anarchists are egotists, strictly speaking, and that every group of individuals, be it a secret league of a few persons, or the Congress of the United States, has the right to oppress all mankind, provided it has the power to do so, that equal liberty for all and absolute equality ought to be the law, and 'mind every one your own business' is the unique moral law of anarchism, Tucker goes on to prove that a general and thorough application of these principles would be beneficial and would offer no danger, because the powers of every individual would be limited by the exercise of the equal rights of all others. He further indicated (following H. Spencer) the difference which exists between the encroachment on somebody's rights and resistance to such an encroachment; between domination and defence: the former being equally condemnable, whether it be encroachment of a criminal upon an individual, or the encroachment of one upon all others, or of all others upon one; while resistance to encroachment is defensible and necessary. For their self-defence, both the citizen and the group have the right to any violence, including capital punishment. Violence is also justified for enforcing the duty of keeping an agreement. Tucker thus follows Spencer, and, like him, opens (in the present writer's opinion) the way for reconstituting under the heading of 'defence' all the functions of the state. His criticism of the present state is very searching, and his defence of the rights of the individual very powerful. As regards his economical views B. R. Tucker follows Proudhon.

The individualist anarchism of the American Proudhonians finds, however, but little sympathy amongst the working masses. Those who profess it — they are chiefly 'intellectuals' — soon realize that the *individualization* they so highly praise is not attainable by individual efforts, and either abandon the ranks of the anarchists, and are driven into the liberal individualism of the classical economist or they retire into a sort of Epicurean amoralism, or superman theory, similar to that of Stirner and Nietzsche. The great bulk of the anarchist working men prefer the anarchist-communist ideas which have gradually evolved out of the anarchist collectivism of the International Working Men's Association. To this direction belong — to name only the better known exponents of anarchism Elisée Reclus, Jean Grave, Sebastien Faure, Emile Pouget in France; Errico Malatesta and Covelli in Italy; R. Mella, A. Lorenzo, and the mostly unknown authors of many excellent manifestos in Spain; John Most amongst the Germans; Spies, Parsons and their followers in the United States, and so on; while Domela Nieuwenhuis occupies an intermediate position in Holland. The chief anarchist papers which have been published since 1880 also belong to that direction; while a number of anarchists of this direction have joined the so-called syndicalist movement- the French name for the non-political labour movement, devoted to direct struggle with capitalism, which has lately become so prominent in Europe.

As one of the anarchist-communist direction, the present writer for many years endeavoured to develop the following ideas: to show the intimate, logical connection which exists between the modern philosophy of natural sciences and anarchism; to put anarchism on a scientific basis by the study of the tendencies that are apparent now in society and may indicate its further evolution; and to work out the basis of anarchist ethics. As regards the substance of anarchism itself, it was Kropotkin's aim to prove that communism at least partial — has more chances of being established than collectivism, especially in communes taking the lead, and that free, or anarchist-communism is the only form of communism that has any chance of being accepted in civilized societies; communism and anarchy are therefore two terms of evolution which complete each other, the one rendering the other possible and acceptable. He has tried, moreover, to indicate how, during a revolutionary period, a large city — if its inhabitants have accepted the idea could organize itself on the lines of free communism; the city guaranteeing to every inhabitant dwelling, food and clothing to an extent corresponding to the comfort now available to the middle classes only, in exchange for a half-day's, or five-hours' work; and how all those things which would be considered as luxuries might be obtained by everyone if he joins for the other half of the day all sorts of free associations pursuing all possible aims — educational, literary, scientific, artistic, sports and so on. In order to prove the first of these assertions he has analysed the possibilities of agriculture and industrial work, both being combined with brain work. And in order to elucidate the main factors of human evolution, he has analysed the part played in history by the popular constructive agencies of mutual aid and the historical role of the state.

Without naming himself an anarchist, Leo Tolstoy, like his predecessors in the popular religious movements of the fifteenth and sixteenth centuries, Chojecki, Denk and many others, took the anarchist position as regards the state and property rights, deducing his conclusions from the general spirit of the teachings of the Christ and from the necessary dictates of reason. With all the might of his talent he made (especially in *The Kingdom of God in Yourselves*) a powerful criticism of the church, the state and law altogether, and especially of the present property laws. He describes the state as the domination of the wicked ones, supported by brutal force. Robbers, he says, are far less dangerous than a well-organized government. He makes a searching criticism of the prejudices which are current now concerning the benefits conferred upon men by the church, the state and the existing distribution of property, and from the teachings of the Christ he deduces the rule of non-resistance and the absolute condemnation of all wars. His religious arguments are, however, so well combined with arguments borrowed from a dispassionate observation of the present evils, that the anarchist portions of his works appeal to the religious and the non-religious reader alike.

It would be impossible to represent here, in a short sketch, the penetration, on the one hand, of anarchist ideas into modern literature, and the influence, on the other hand, which the libertarian ideas of the best contemporary writers have exercised upon the development of anarchism. One ought to consult the ten big volumes of the *Supplément Littéraire* to the paper *La Révolte* and later the *Temps Nouveaux*, which contain reproductions from the works of hundreds of modern authors expressing anarchist ideas, in order to realize how closely anarchism is connected with all the intellectual movement of our own times. J. S. Mill's *Liberty*, Spencer's *Individual versus the State*, Marc Guyau's *Morality without Obligation or Sanction*, and Fouillée's *La Morale, l'art et la religion*, the works of Multatuli (E. Douwes Dekker), Richard Wagner's *Art and Revolution*, the works of Nietzsche, Emerson, W. Lloyd Garrison, Thoreau, Alexander Herzen, Edward Carpenter and so on; and in the domain of fiction, the dramas of Ibsen, the poetry of Walt Whitman, Tolstoy's *War and Peace*, Zola's *Paris* and *Le Travail*, the latest works of Merezhkovsky, and an infinity of works of less known authors, are full of ideas which show how closely anarchism is interwoven with the work that is going on in modern thought in the same direction of enfranchisement of man from the bonds of the state as well as from those of capitalism.

Citation and Use

The reading was taken from the following work.

Kropotkin, Pëtr. "Anarchism." The Anarchist Library, 1910. https://theanarchistlibrary.org/library/petr-kropotkin-anarchism-from-the-encyclopaedia-britannica.

JOHN RAWLS AND THE "VEIL OF IGNORANCE"

Ben Davies

Ben Davies is a Research Fellow at the Uehiro Centre for Practical Ethics at the University of Oxford. His work focuses mainly on health care justice, but he also has interests in human enhancement, animal ethics and well-being. Email benjamin.davies@philosophy.ac.uk.

John Rawls's Veil of Ignorance is probably one of the most influential philosophical ideas of the 20th century. The Veil of Ignorance is a way of working out the basic institutions and structures of a just society. According to Rawls, [1], working out what justice requires demands that we think as if we are building society from the ground up, in a way that everyone who is reasonable can accept. We therefore need to imagine ourselves in a situation *before* any particular society exists; Rawls calls this situation the Original Position. To be clear, Rawls does not think we can actually return to this original position, or even that it ever existed. It is a purely hypothetical idea: our job in thinking about justice is to imagine that we are designing a society from scratch. The idea is that social justice will be whatever reasonable people would agree to in such a situation. We can then start thinking about how to make our actual society look more like the ideal picture we have imagined.

Of course, if we were designing a society in the Original Position, people might try to ensure that it works in *their* favour. The process is thus vulnerable to biases, disagreements, and the potential for majority groups ganging up on minority groups. Rawls's solution to this problem comes in two parts. Firstly, he makes some assumptions about the people designing their own society. People in the Original Position are assumed to be free and equal, and to have certain motivations: they want to do well for themselves, but they are prepared to adhere to reasonable terms of cooperation, so long as others do too. Rawls also simplifies his discussion by imagining that people in the Original Position do not have total freedom to design society as they see fit. Rather, they must choose from a menu of views taken from traditional Western philosophy on what justice involves.

The second part of the solution is the Veil of Ignorance. This involves a further leap of imagination. When we are thinking about justice, Rawls suggests that we imagine that we do not know many of the facts – both about ourselves and the society we currently live in – that typically influence our thinking in biased ways. By intentionally ignoring these facts, Rawls hoped that we would be able to avoid the biases that might otherwise come into a group decision. For instance, if I were helping to design a society, I might be tempted to try to make sure that society is set up to benefit philosophers, or men, or people who love science fiction novels. But if I don't know any of those facts about myself, I can't be tempted. The Veil is meant to ensure that people's concern for their personal benefit could translate into a set of arrangements that were fair for everyone, assuming that they had to stick to those choices once the Veil of Ignorance 'lifts', and they are given full information again.

One set of facts hidden from you behind the Veil are what we might call 'demographic' facts. You do not know your gender, race, wealth, or facts about your personal strengths and weaknesses, such as their intelligence or physical prowess. Rawls thought these facts are morally arbitrary: individuals do not earn or deserve these features, but simply have them by luck. As such, they do not deserve any benefits or harms that come from them. By removing knowledge of the natural inequalities that give people unfair advantages, it becomes irrational to choose principles that discriminate against any particular group. The Veil also hides facts about society. You do not know anything other than general facts about human life, and in particular you do not how their society is organised. Finally, the Veil hides facts about your "view of the good": your values, preferences about how your own life should go, and specific moral and political beliefs. Rawls was a political liberal. That meant, among other things, that he thought the state should be neutral between different views about value. So, Rawls isn't afraid to make several significant assumptions about the people involved in making decisions behind the Veil. Some of his assumptions aim to turn the conflicts that arise between self-interested people into a fair decision procedure. As we'll see, however, others might be more fairly criticised as unreasonably narrowing the possible outcomes that people can reach behind the Veil.

I will outline Rawls's justification for the Veil of Ignorance, raise some potential challenges for the conclusions he thinks people will reach from behind it, and lastly consider three criticisms of the Veil of Ignorance as a theoretical device. While these criticisms differ in their substance, they are united by a common feature: their scepticism of the way the Veil *abstracts* from real life in order to reach conclusions about justice. I'll conclude that these criticisms have merit; the Veil of Ignorance, considered by itself, does lead us to ignore the real world too much. However, I'll suggest that, at least in their strongest versions, these criticisms miss an important benefit of the Veil: quite simply, the fact that our own personal concerns and values can bias our thinking about justice, and that we can make important progress by considering things from different points of view.

The principles of justice

Imagine that you find yourself behind the Veil of Ignorance. You might want to make sure that your life will go well. If you had to design a good life for yourself, you'd go for the specific things you care about. But behind the Veil you don't know those specifics; you only know things that generally make people's lives go well. Rawls calls these 'Primary Goods'. They include things like money and other resources; basic rights and freedoms; and finally, the "social bases of self-respect": the things you need to feel like an equal member of society.

In Rawls's view, a central challenge behind the Veil is the lack of probabilities available. If you knew that your society was 90% Catholic, you could set things up so that the rewards associated with being Catholic were much higher. That would be personally rational, since you are very likely to end up in the better off group. The Veil prevents this type of reasoning because it hides the information. In the complete absence of probabilities, Rawls thinks you should play it safe and *maximise the minimum* you could get (a policy he calls Maximin). Translated into a society, that means that we should ensure that the worst-off people in society do as well as possible.

Rawls suggests two principles will emerge from discussion behind the Veil:

First Principle: Each person has the same indefeasible

claim to a fully adequate scheme of *equal basic liberties*, compatible with the same liberties for all;

Second Principle: Social and economic inequalities must be:

1. Attached to offices and positions open to all under *fair equality of opportunity*;

2. To the greatest benefit of the least-advantaged members of society (the *difference principle*).

Rawls opts for equality of basic liberties in the First Principle because he thinks this is essential for seeing yourself as a *moral* equal in society. For other Primary Goods, though, equality is less important. By allowing some inequality, we could make life better for everyone. If we attach higher salaries to certain jobs, they may attract the hardest working people, producing greater economic benefits for everyone. The two parts of Rawls's second principle of justice set limits on when inequalities are allowed. Fair equality of opportunity says that positions which bring unequal payoffs must be open to people of equal talents and equal willingness to use them *on an equal basis*. If two people are just as capable of doing a job, and just as hardworking and willing to apply themselves, neither should have a greater chance of securing the position because they are wealthier, or because of their race or religion. Of course, we might wonder (and Rawls does not give a clear answer about this) when we are supposed to judge whether two people are equally hardworking and talented. The talents you choose to develop, and the amount of effort you put in, are heavily affected by education; so it might seem unfair to judge people if they have had very different educational experiences. Rawls's argument therefore seems to support ensuring broad equality of education, encouraging people to find and develop their talents to the fullest, even if this isn't a conclusion he explicitly draws.

Finally, the Difference Principle sets a further restriction on inequalities. Even if a particular inequality does not affect equality of opportunities, the Difference Principle tells us that it must be beneficial for the very worst off. For instance, it might be that by allowing inequalities, we motivate people to work harder, generating more Primary Goods overall. If these then benefit the worst off in society, making them better off than they would have been in a more equal distribution, the Difference Principle will allow that inequality.

Criticisms

As with any influential philosopher, Rawls has been the subject of much criticism and disagreement. In this final section, we consider three objections to Rawls's reasoning around the Veil of Ignorance.

Ownership and rights

We have already noted that Rawls explicitly makes several assumptions that shape the nature of the discussion behind the Veil of Ignorance, and the outcomes that are likely to come out of it. However, one might challenge Rawls by disputing the fairness or intuitiveness of one or more of his assumptions.

Probably the most famous example of this comes from Robert Nozick.[2] Recall that Rawls's principles establish rules to govern the institutions and principles that distribute goods. He thinks that if we work out what those institutions would look like in a perfectly just society, using the Veil of Ignorance, we can then start to move our current society in that direction. Nozick notes that in reality, most goods are already owned. Rawls's view establishes a pattern that looks fair; but Nozick argues that we also need to look at the history of how various goods came to be owned. In some cases, we find that the person who owns those goods worked for them. In other cases, the individual will have inherited those goods, but they will have come from an ancestor who worked for them. In both cases, we cannot simply redistribute these goods to fit our pattern, because people have rights.

In Nozick's view, once you have ownership *rights*, you can do pretty much what you want with it, so long as you do not violate anyone else's rights. The fact that taking money you earned would benefit someone else cannot be the basis for government forcibly taking your money. One possible basis for this is the idea of 'self-ownership'. Nozick thinks we will all agree that it would be wrong to force you to work if you didn't want to. The reason for this is that your body is owned by you and nobody else. That principle extends, Nozick says, to what you *do* with your body: your labour. If you make something, or work for money, that thing is yours and nobody else's. Just as the state has no right to force you to do things with your body that you don't want to do, it also has no right to force you to do things with your other property, like giving it away to the less fortunate. That might be a nice thing to do, but it isn't something others can force you to do.

One problem with this argument, to which Rawls might appeal, is that my *ability* to work (and therefore gain property) depends on many other things:
- my education,
- my health that was guaranteed by a public health system,
- a stable society that affords me opportunities for employment, or
- for employing others.

So it's not quite true that everything I produce comes from me alone.

Identity and 'Neutrality'

A second criticism also concerns the fact that, behind the Veil, various facts are hidden from you. Rather than worrying about the substantive conclusions Rawls reaches, as Nozick does, this criticism worries about the very coherence of reasoned discussion behind the Veil of Ignorance.

Rawls's Veil of Ignorance is an example of a theory of justice that has *universal* aspirations. Since one of the facts that is hidden by the veil is the nature of the society you live in, we may assume that the resulting principles are supposed to be applicable in all societies, though this is a view that Rawls attempted to reject in later work. In addition, people behind the Veil are supposed to come up with a view of how society should be structured while knowing almost nothing about themselves, and their lives.

One broad group who criticise these ideas are the so-called 'communitarian' philosophers, which includes Charles Taylor,[3] Michael Walzer[4], and Alasdair MacIntyre.[5] While their views differ, they tend to agree that what justice requires cannot be decided *abstractly*, but must instead be informed by local considerations and culture. Communitarians also suggest that Rawls's conception of the individuals behind the Veil of Ignorance is problematic because they have so few defining features. Even if Rawls is right that people behind the Veil would agree on his two principles, communitarians think that the hypothetical agreement ignores much that is important.

Individuals behind the Veil are assumed to be largely self-interested, and to have a strong interest in retaining the ability to abandon their current social roles and pursuits and take up new ones. According to the communitarians, however, we are born with existing social connections to particular people, cultures and social roles. Whereas Rawls emphasises our active engagement in shaping our own lives, communitarians want to remind us that our lives are unavoidably shaped by existing attachments that we do not choose. For instance, if you are born into a particular religious community, you can of course still renounce that religion. But your life will still be shaped by the fact that you are a member, or former member, of that community. It is worth noting, though, that this accusation is somewhat unfair on Rawls. While it is true that individuals behind the Veil do not know about their defining features, Rawls does not think that real people are like this. His interest is in trying to formulate a *neutral* way to decide between competing groups.

Certainly, it is a plausible worry that what justice requires may depend in part on the values of the society in question. As a liberal, Rawls is particularly worried about protecting individuals whose preferred lives go against the grain of the society in which they find themselves. Communitarians will object that the Veil of Ignorance goes beyond this protection, and rules out the possibility of different ideas of justice, informed by local values. Perhaps we should acknowledge that people behind the Veil of Ignorance would recognise the possibility that their society will turn' out to be strongly attached to a particular set of values. A rational person behind the Veil might want to try to find a way to give a special place to such values, while protecting dissenters.

Ideal justice?

Our final challenge also concerns the real-world applicability of Rawls's principles. In brief, the claim from scholars of race and of gender is that Rawls's abstract Veil of Ignorance ends up ignoring much that is relevant to justice.

The central criticism we consider here concerns the motivation of Rawls's overall project. Rawls's aim is to outline a theory of 'ideal' justice, or what a perfectly just society would look like. This ignores, purposefully, the many injustices that have happened and continue to happen, including the fact that most societies continue to exhibit racism, sexism and other forms of discrimination.[6] As critics argue, we then get at best an incomplete theory, which does not tell us how to *fix* existing injustice or, as it is sometimes called, 'non-ideal' justice (an issue that Rawls himself describes as a "pressing and urgent matter"). For instance, people disagree about the idea of 'reparations' for racial slavery that shaped the United States. Yet because this is an issue of non-ideal justice (how should we respond to the fact that the United States and many of its citizens failed to comply with the basic requirements of justice?), the idealisation of the Veil of Ignorance seems to give us no way to determine this important question.

This maps onto a more general question in political philosophy: if a theory of justice does not tell us how to act in our *actual* societies, does it have any value? While some[7] argue that Rawls's work can be used to draw concrete conclusions about issues such as racial profiling and affirmative action, critics who reject this view may also argue that a theory of justice that is concerned only with the ideal ignores the most pressing issues of the day. In Rawls's case, we may wonder whether we can accommodate such concerns by making small changes to his assumptions, or whether more radical changes (or even abandonment of the theory) are required.

Conclusion

The three criticisms outlined above all take issue, in different ways, with Rawls's *idealisation* away from the real world. Much of the value of Rawls's work will depend on whether it is useful to construct ideal views of justice before, or at the same time as, thinking about the messier real world. Even a pessimistic conclusion on this issue, though, should recognise the following insight from Rawls: that what seems just or fair or right to any person is influenced not just by our background but by our own selfish interests. Even if the details face problems, Rawls's Veil of Ignorance shows us that it can be valuable to imagine things from opposing points of view. While the criticisms from communitarians, scholars of race, and feminist scholars demonstrate the importance of considering the concrete features of our societies and lives, the basic idea of abstracting away from potential biases is an important one.

Nonetheless, this conclusion is consistent with recognising two mistakes in making use of the Veil of Ignorance. Firstly, recognising the importance of abstraction should not come at the cost of considering the real, concrete impact of policies we adopt, or of the social and historical context they are part of. Much political philosophy, at least in the USA and UK, can be criticised for neglecting these latter issues. Secondly, acknowledging the importance of the Veil of Ignorance does not mean that Rawls, and later philosophers, are right to have established an *order of priority*, where we first abstractly establish a view of ideal justice, and only then move on to non-ideal justice. It may be more productive to consider issues of justice from both the kind of abstracted view represented by the Veil of Ignorance, and from the more concrete view advocated by its critics.

For Review and Discussion:
1. The Difference Principle only allows inequalities if they benefit the worst off in society. Is this practical? Is it what people would agree to behind the Veil of Ignorance?
2. 'The Veil of Ignorance hides information that makes us who we are. Behind the Veil, we are not individuals, and so any decision we reach is meaningless.' Do you agree? Why/why not?
3. Since our talents and inclinations depend on what happens to us even before we are born, can we make sense of the idea of Rawls's idea of 'fair equality of opportunity'?

Citation and Use

This reading was taken from the following work.

Davies, Ben. "John Rawls and the 'Veil of Ignorance.'" In INTRODUCTION TO ETHICS: AN OPEN EDUCATIONAL RESOURCE, 92–97. Golden West College, Huntington Beach, CA: NGE Far Press, 2019.

Notes and Additional Readings

Notes

1. John Rawls (1999) A Theory of Justice: Revised Edition, Cambridge, MA: Harvard University Press

2. Robert Nozick (1974) Anarchy, State and Utopia Blackwell Publishing (Oxford) pp.149-232

3. Charles Taylor (1989) Sources of the Self: The Making of the Modern Identity Cambridge: CUP

4. Michael Walzer (1983) Spheres of Justice Oxford: Blackwell

5. Alasdair MacIntyre (1988) Whose Justice? Which Rationality? Notre Dame: University of Notre Dame Press.

6. Carol Pateman and Charles Mills (2007) Contract and Domination Cambridge: Polity Press

7. Tommie Shelby (2004) 'Race and Social Justice: Rawlsian Considerations' Fordham Law Review 72: pp.1697-1714.

COMMUNISM

Frederick Engels

What is Communism?

Communism is the doctrine of the conditions of the liberation of the proletariat.

What is the proletariat?

The proletariat is that class in society which lives entirely from the sale of its labor and does not draw profit from any kind of capital; whose weal and woe, whose life and death, whose sole existence depends on the demand for labor – hence, on the changing state of business, on the vagaries of unbridled competition. The proletariat, or the class of proletarians, is, in a word, the working class of the 19th century.[1]

Proletarians, then, have not always existed?

No. There have always been poor and working classes; and the working class have mostly been poor. But there have not always been workers and poor people living under conditions as they are today; in other words, there have not always been proletarians, any more than there has always been free unbridled competitions.

How did the proletariat originate?

The Proletariat originated in the industrial revolution, which took place in England in the last half of the last (18th) century, and which has since then been repeated in all the civilized countries of the world.

This industrial revolution was precipitated by the discovery of the steam engine, various spinning machines, the mechanical loom, and a whole series of other mechanical devices. These machines, which were very expensive and hence could be bought only by big capitalists, altered the whole mode of production and displaced the former workers, because the machines turned out cheaper and better commodities than the workers could produce with their inefficient spinning wheels and handlooms. The machines delivered industry wholly into the hands of the big capitalists and rendered entirely worthless the meagre property of the workers (tools, looms, etc.). The result was that the capitalists soon had everything in their hands and nothing remained to the workers. This marked the introduction of the factory system into the textile industry.

Once the impulse to the introduction of machinery and the factory system had been given, this system spread quickly to all other branches of industry, especially cloth- and book-printing, pottery, and the metal industries.

Labor was more and more divided among the individual workers so that the worker who previously had done a complete piece of work now did only a part of that piece. This division of labor made it possible to produce things faster and cheaper. It reduced the activity of the individual worker to simple, endlessly repeated mechanical motions which could be performed not only as well but much better by a machine. In this way, all these industries fell, one after another, under the dominance of steam, machinery, and the factory system, just as spinning and weaving had already done.

But at the same time, they also fell into the hands of big capitalists, and their workers were deprived of whatever independence remained to them. Gradually, not only genuine manufacture but also handicrafts came within the province of the factory system as big capitalists increasingly displaced the small master craftsmen by setting up huge workshops, which saved many expenses and permitted an elaborate division of labor.

This is how it has come about that in civilized countries at the present time nearly all kinds of labor are performed in factories – and, in nearly all branches of work, handicrafts and manufacture have been superseded. This process has, to an ever greater degree, ruined the old middle class, especially the small handicraftsmen; it has entirely transformed the condition of the workers; and two new classes have been created which are gradually swallowing up all the others. These are:

1. The **class of big capitalists**, who, in all civilized countries, are already in almost exclusive possession of all

the means of subsistance and of the instruments (machines, factories) and materials necessary for the production of the means of subsistence. This is the bourgeois class, or the bourgeoisie.

2. The **class of the wholly propertyless**, who are obliged to sell their labor to the bourgeoisie in order to get, in exchange, the means of subsistence for their support. This is called the class of proletarians, or the proletariat.

Under what conditions does this sale of the labor of the proletarians to the bourgeoisie take place?

Labor is a commodity, like any other, and its price is therefore determined by exactly the same laws that apply to other commodities. In a regime of big industry or of free competition – as we shall see, the two come to the same thing – the price of a commodity is, on the average, always equal to its cost of production. Hence, the price of labor is also equal to the cost of production of labor.

But, the costs of production of labor consist of precisely the quantity of means of subsistence necessary to enable the worker to continue working, and to prevent the working class from dying out. The worker will therefore get no more for his labor than is necessary for this purpose; the price of labor, or the wage, will, in other words, be the lowest, the minimum, required for the maintenance of life.

However, since business is sometimes better and sometimes worse, it follows that the worker sometimes gets more and sometimes gets less for his commodities. But, again, just as the industrialist, on the average of good times and bad, gets no more and no less for his commodities than what they cost, similarly on the average the worker gets no more and no less than his minimum.

This economic law of wages operates the more strictly the greater the degree to which big industry has taken possession of all branches of production.

What working classes were there before the industrial revolution?

The working classes have always, according to the different stages of development of society, lived in different circumstances and had different relations to the owning and ruling classes.

In antiquity, the workers were the slaves of the owners, just as they still are in many backward countries and even in the southern part of the United States.

In the Middle Ages, they were the serfs of the land-owning nobility, as they still are in Hungary, Poland, and Russia. In the Middle Ages, and indeed right up to the industrial revolution, there were also journeymen in the cities who worked in the service of petty bourgeois masters. Gradually, as manufacture developed, these journeymen became manufacturing workers who were even then employed by larger capitalists.

In what way do proletarians differ from slaves?

The slave is sold once and for all; the proletarian must sell himself daily and hourly.

The individual slave, property of one master, is assured an existence, however miserable it may be, because of the master's interest. The individual proletarian, property as it were of the entire bourgeois class which buys his labor only when someone has need of it, has no secure existence. This existence is assured only to the class as a whole.

The slave is outside competition; the proletarian is in it and experiences all its vagaries.

The slave counts as a thing, not as a member of society. Thus, the slave can have a better existence than the proletarian, while the proletarian belongs to a higher stage of social development and, himself, stands on a higher social level than the slave.

The slave frees himself when, of all the relations of private property, he abolishes only the relation of slavery and thereby becomes a proletarian; the proletarian can free himself only by abolishing private property in general.

In what way do proletarians differ from serfs?

The serf possesses and uses an instrument of production, a piece of land, in exchange for which he gives up a part of his product or part of the services of his labor.

The proletarian works with the instruments of production of another, for the account of this other, in exchange for a part of the product.

The serf gives up, the proletarian receives. The serf has an assured existence, the proletarian has not. The serf is outside competition, the proletarian is in it.

The serf liberates himself in one of three ways: either he runs away to the city and there becomes a handicraftsman; or, instead of products and services, he gives money to his lord and thereby becomes a free tenant; or he overthrows his feudal lord and himself becomes a property owner. In short, by one route or another, he gets into the owning class and enters into competition. The proletarian liberates himself by abolishing competition, private property, and all class differences.

In what way do proletarians differ from handicraftsmen?

In contrast to the proletarian, the so-called handicraftsman, as he still existed almost everywhere in the past (eighteenth) century and still exists here and there at present, is a proletarian at most temporarily. His goal is to acquire capital himself wherewith to exploit other workers. He can often achieve this goal where guilds still exist or where freedom from guild restrictions has not yet led to the introduction of factory-style methods into the crafts nor yet to fierce competition But as soon as the factory system has been introduced into the crafts and competition flourishes fully, this perspective dwindles away and the handicraftsman becomes more and more a proletarian. The handicraftsman therefore frees himself by becoming either bourgeois or entering the middle class in general, or becoming a proletarian because of competition (as is now more often the case). In which case he can free himself by joining the proletarian movement, i.e., the more or less communist movement. [2]

In what way do proletarians differ from manufacturing workers?

The manufacturing worker of the 16th to the 18th centuries still had, with but few exception, an instrument of production in his own possession – his loom, the family spinning wheel, a little plot of land which he cultivated in his spare time. The proletarian has none of these things.

The manufacturing worker almost always lives in the countryside and in a more or less patriarchal relation to his landlord or employer; the proletarian lives, for the most part, in the city and his relation to his employer is purely a cash relation.

The manufacturing worker is torn out of his patriarchal relation by big industry, loses whatever property he still has, and in this way becomes a proletarian.

What were the immediate consequences of the industrial revolution and of the division of society into bourgeoisie and proletariat?

First, the lower and lower prices of industrial products brought about by machine labor totally destroyed, in all countries of the world, the old system of manufacture or industry based upon hand labor.

In this way, all semi-barbarian countries, which had hitherto been more or less strangers to historical development, and whose industry had been based on manufacture, were violently forced out of their isolation. They bought the cheaper commodities of the English and allowed their own manufacturing workers to be ruined. Countries which had known no progress for thousands of years – for example, India – were thoroughly revolutionized, and even China is now on the way to a revolution.

We have come to the point where a new machine invented in England deprives millions of Chinese workers of their livelihood within a year's time.

In this way, big industry has brought all the people of the Earth into contact with each other, has merged all local markets into one world market, has spread civilization and progress everywhere and has thus ensured that whatever happens in civilized countries will have repercussions in all other countries.

It follows that if the workers in England or France now liberate themselves, this must set off revolution in all other countries – revolutions which, sooner or later, must accomplish the liberation of their respective working class.

Second, wherever big industries displaced manufacture, the bourgeoisie developed in wealth and power to the utmost and made itself the first class of the country. The result was that wherever this happened, the bourgeoisie took political power into its own hands and displaced the hitherto ruling classes, the aristocracy, the guildmasters, and their representative, the absolute monarchy.

The bourgeoisie annihilated the power of the aristocracy, the nobility, by abolishing the entailment of estates – in other words, by making landed property subject to purchase and sale, and by doing away with the special privileges of the nobility. It destroyed the power of the guildmasters by abolishing guilds and handicraft privileges. In their place, it put competition – that is, a state of society in which everyone has the right to enter into any branch of industry, the only obstacle being a lack of the necessary capital.

The introduction of free competition is thus public declaration that from now on the members of society are unequal only to the extent that their capitals are unequal, that capital is the decisive power, and that therefore the capitalists, the bourgeoisie, have become the first class in society.

Free competition is necessary for the establishment of big industry, because it is the only condition of society in which big industry can make its way.

Having destroyed the social power of the nobility and the guildmasters, the bourgeois also destroyed their political power. Having raised itself to the actual position of first class in society, it proclaims itself to be also the dominant political class. This it does through the introduction of the representative system which rests on bourgeois equality before the law and the recognition of free competition, and in European countries takes the form of constitutional monarchy. In these constitutional monarchies, only those who possess a certain capital are voters – that is to say, only members of the bourgeoisie. These bourgeois voters choose the deputies, and these bourgeois deputies, by using their right to refuse to vote taxes, choose a bourgeois government.

Third, everywhere the proletariat develops in step with the bourgeoisie. In proportion, as the bourgeoisie grows in wealth, the proletariat grows in numbers. For, since the proletarians can be employed only by capital, and since capital extends only through employing labor, it follows that the growth of the proletariat proceeds at precisely the same pace as the growth of capital.

Simultaneously, this process draws members of the bourgeoisie and proletarians together into the great cities where industry can be carried on most profitably, and by thus throwing great masses in one spot it gives to the proletarians a consciousness of their own strength.

Moreover, the further this process advances, the more new labor-saving machines are invented, the greater is the pressure exercised by big industry on wages, which, as we have seen, sink to their minimum and therewith render the condition of the proletariat increasingly unbearable. The growing dissatisfaction of the proletariat thus joins with its rising power to prepare a proletarian social revolution.

What were the further consequences of the industrial revolution?

Big industry created in the steam engine, and other machines, the means of endlessly expanding industrial production, speeding it up, and cutting its costs. With production thus facilitated, the free competition, which is necessarily bound up with big industry, assumed the most extreme forms; a multitude of capitalists invaded industry, and, in a short while, more was produced than was needed.

As a consequence, finished commodities could not be sold, and a so-called commercial crisis broke out. Factories had to be closed, their owners went bankrupt, and the workers were without bread. Deepest misery reigned everywhere.

After a time, the superfluous products were sold, the factories began to operate again, wages rose, and gradually business got better than ever.

But it was not long before too many commodities were again produced and a new crisis broke out, only to follow the same course as its predecessor.

Ever since the beginning of this (19th) century, the condition of industry has constantly fluctuated between periods of prosperity and periods of crisis; nearly every five to seven years, a fresh crisis has intervened, always with the greatest hardship for workers, and always accompanied by general revolutionary stirrings and the direct peril to the whole existing order of things.

What follows from these periodic commercial crises?

First:

That, though big industry in its earliest stage created free competition, it has now outgrown free competition;

that, for big industry, competition and generally the individualistic organization of production have become a fetter which it must and will shatter;

that, so long as big industry remains on its present footing, it can be maintained only at the cost of general chaos every seven years, each time threatening the whole of civilization and not only plunging the proletarians into misery but also ruining large sections of the bourgeoisie;

hence, either that big industry must itself be given up, which is an absolute impossibility, or that it makes unavoidably necessary an entirely new organization of society in which production is no longer directed by mutually competing individual industrialists but rather by the whole society operating according to a definite plan and taking account of the needs of all.

Second: That big industry, and the limitless expansion of production which it makes possible, bring within the range of feasibility a social order in which so much is produced that every member of society will be in a position to exercise and develop all his powers and faculties in complete freedom.

It thus appears that the very qualities of big industry which, in our present-day society, produce misery and crises are those which, in a different form of society, will abolish this misery and these catastrophic depressions.

We see with the greatest clarity:
1. That all these evils are from now on to be ascribed solely to a social order which no longer corresponds to the requirements of the real situation; and
2. That it is possible, through a new social order, to do away with these evils altogether.

What will this new social order have to be like?

Above all, it will have to take the control of industry and of all branches of production out of the hands of mutually competing individuals, and instead institute a system in which all these branches of production are operated by society as a whole – that is, for the common account, according to a common plan, and with the participation of all members of society.

It will, in other words, abolish competition and replace it with association.

Moreover, since the management of industry by individuals necessarily implies private property, and since competition is in reality merely the manner and form in which the control of industry by private property owners expresses itself, it follows that private property cannot be separated from competition and the individual management of industry. Private property must, therefore, be abolished and in its place must come the common utilization of all instruments of production and the distribution of all products according to common agreement – in a word, what is called the communal ownership of goods.

In fact, the abolition of private property is, doubtless, the shortest and most significant way to characterize the revolution in the whole social order which has been made necessary by the development of industry – and for this reason it is rightly advanced by communists as their main demand.

Was not the abolition of private property possible at an earlier time?

No. Every change in the social order, every revolution in property relations, is the necessary consequence of the creation of new forces of production which no longer fit into the old property relations.

Private property has not always existed.

When, towards the end of the Middle Ages, there arose a new mode of production which could not be carried on under the then existing feudal and guild forms of property, this manufacture, which had outgrown the old property relations, created a new property form, private property. And for manufacture and the earliest stage of development of big industry, private property was the only possible property form; the social order based on it was the only possible social order.

So long as it is not possible to produce so much that there is enough for all, with more left over for expanding the social capital and extending the forces of production – so long as this is not possible, there must always be a ruling class directing the use of society's productive forces, and a poor, oppressed class. How these classes are constituted depends on the stage of development.

The agrarian Middle Ages give us the baron and the serf; the cities of the later Middle Ages show us the guildmaster and the journeyman and the day laborer; the 17th century has its manufacturing workers; the 19th has big factory owners and proletarians.

It is clear that, up to now, the forces of production have never been developed to the point where enough could be developed for all, and that private property has become a fetter and a barrier in relation to the further development of the forces of production.

Now, however, the development of big industry has ushered in a new period. Capital and the forces of production have been expanded to an unprecedented extent, and the means are at hand to multiply them without limit in the near future. Moreover, the forces of production have been concentrated in the hands of a few bourgeois, while the great mass of the people are more and more falling into the proletariat, their situation becoming more wretched and intolerable in proportion to the increase of wealth of the bourgeoisie. And finally, these mighty and easily extended forces of production have so far outgrown private property and the bourgeoisie, that they threaten at any moment to unleash the most violent disturbances of the social order. Now, under these conditions, the abolition of private property has become not only possible but absolutely necessary.

Will the peaceful abolition of private property be possible?

It would be desirable if this could happen, and the communists would certainly be the last to oppose it. Communists know only too well that all conspiracies are not only useless, but even harmful. They know all too well that revolutions are not made intentionally and arbitrarily, but that, everywhere and always, they have been the necessary consequence of conditions which were wholly independent of the will and direction of individual parties and entire classes.

But they also see that the development of the proletariat in nearly all civilized countries has been violently suppressed, and that in this way the opponents of communism have been working toward a revolution with all their strength. If the oppressed proletariat is finally driven to revolution, then we communists will defend the interests of the proletarians with deeds as we now defend them with words.

Will it be possible for private property to be abolished at one stroke?

No, no more than existing forces of production can at one stroke be multiplied to the extent necessary for the creation of a communal society.

In all probability, the proletarian revolution will transform existing society gradually and will be able to abolish private property only when the means of production are available in sufficient quantity.

What will be the course of this revolution?

Above all, it will establish a democratic constitution, and through this, the direct or indirect dominance of the proletariat. Direct in England, where the proletarians are already a majority of the people. Indirect in France and Germany, where the majority of the people consists not only of proletarians, but also of small peasants and petty bourgeois who are in the process of falling into the proletariat, who are more and more dependent in all their political interests on the proletariat, and who must, therefore, soon adapt to the demands of the proletariat. Perhaps this will cost a second struggle, but the outcome can only be the victory of the proletariat.

Democracy would be wholly valueless to the proletariat if it were not immediately used as a means for putting through measures directed against private property and ensuring the livelihood of the proletariat. The main measures, emerging as the necessary result of existing relations, are the following:

1. Limitation of private property through progressive taxation, heavy inheritance taxes, abolition of inheritance through collateral lines (brothers, nephews, etc.) forced loans, etc.
2. Gradual expropriation of landowners, industrialists, railroad magnates and shipowners, partly through competition by state industry, partly directly through compensation in the form of bonds.
3. Confiscation of the possessions of all emigrants and rebels against the majority of the people.
4. Organization of labor or employment of proletarians

on publicly owned land, in factories and workshops, with competition among the workers being abolished and with the factory owners, in so far as they still exist, being obliged to pay the same high wages as those paid by the state.

5. An equal obligation on all members of society to work until such time as private property has been completely abolished. Formation of industrial armies, especially for agriculture.

6. Centralization of money and credit in the hands of the state through a national bank with state capital, and the suppression of all private banks and bankers.

7. Increase in the number of national factories, workshops, railroads, ships; bringing new lands into cultivation and improvement of land already under cultivation – all in proportion to the growth of the capital and labor force at the disposal of the nation.

8. Education of all children, from the moment they can leave their mother's care, in national establishments at national cost. Education and production together.

9. Construction, on public lands, of great palaces as communal dwellings for associated groups of citizens engaged in both industry and agriculture and combining in their way of life the advantages of urban and rural conditions while avoiding the one-sidedness and drawbacks of each.

10. Destruction of all unhealthy and jerry-built dwellings in urban districts.

11. Equal inheritance rights for children born in and out of wedlock.

12. Concentration of all means of transportation in the hands of the nation.

It is impossible, of course, to carry out all these measures at once. But one will always bring others in its wake. Once the first radical attack on private property has been launched, the proletariat will find itself forced to go ever further, to concentrate increasingly in the hands of the state all capital, all agriculture, all transport, all trade. All the foregoing measures are directed to this end; and they will become practicable and feasible, capable of producing their centralizing effects to precisely the degree that the proletariat, through its labor, multiplies the country's productive forces.

Finally, when all capital, all production, all exchange have been brought together in the hands of the nation, private property will disappear of its own accord, money will become superfluous, and production will so expand and man so change that society will be able to slough off whatever of its old economic habits may remain.

Will it be possible for this revolution to take place in one country alone?

No. By creating the world market, big industry has already brought all the peoples of the Earth, and especially the civilized peoples, into such close relation with one another that none is independent of what happens to the others.

Further, it has co-ordinated the social development of the civilized countries to such an extent that, in all of them, bourgeoisie and proletariat have become the decisive classes, and the struggle between them the great struggle of the day. It follows that the communist revolution will not merely be a national phenomenon but must take place simultaneously in all civilized countries – that is to say, at least in England, America, France, and Germany.

It will develop in each of these countries more or less rapidly, according as one country or the other has a more developed industry, greater wealth, a more significant mass of productive forces. Hence, it will go slowest and will meet most obstacles in Germany, most rapidly and with the fewest difficulties in England. It will have a powerful impact on the other countries of the world, and will radically alter the course of development which they have followed up to now, while greatly stepping up its pace.

It is a universal revolution and will, accordingly, have a universal range.

What will be the consequences of the ultimate disappearance of private property?

Society will take all forces of production and means of commerce, as well as the exchange and distribution of products, out of the hands of private capitalists and will manage them in accordance with a plan based on the availability of resources and the needs of the whole society. In this way, most important of all, the evil consequences which are now associated with the conduct of big industry will be abolished.

There will be no more crises; the expanded production, which for the present order of society is overproduction and hence a prevailing cause of misery, will then be insufficient and in need of being expanded much further. Instead of generating misery, overproduction will reach beyond the elementary requirements of society to assure the satisfaction of the needs of all; it will create new needs and, at the same time, the means of satisfying them. It will become the condition of, and the stimulus to, new progress, which will no longer throw the whole social order into confusion, as progress has always done in the past. Big industry, freed from the pressure of private property, will undergo such an expansion that what we now see will seem as petty in comparison as manufacture seems when put beside the big industry of our own day. This development of industry will make available to society a sufficient mass of products to satisfy the needs of everyone.

The same will be true of agriculture, which also suffers from the pressure of private property and is held back by the division of privately owned land into small parcels. Here, existing improvements and scientific procedures will be put into practice, with a resulting leap forward which will assure to society all the products it needs.

In this way, such an abundance of goods will be able to satisfy the needs of all its members.

The division of society into different, mutually hostile classes will then become unnecessary. Indeed, it will be not only unnecessary but intolerable in the new social order. The existence of classes originated in the division of labor, and the division of labor, as it has been known up to the present, will completely disappear. For mechanical and chemical processes are not enough to bring industrial and agricultural production up to the level we have described; the capacities of the men who make use of these processes must undergo a corresponding development.

Just as the peasants and manufacturing workers of the last century changed their whole way of life and became quite different people when they were drawn into big industry, in the same way, communal control over production by society as a whole, and the resulting new development, will both require an entirely different kind of human material.

People will no longer be, as they are today, subordinated to a single branch of production, bound to it, exploited by it; they will no longer develop *one* of their faculties at the expense of all others; they will no longer know only *one* branch, or one branch of a single branch, of production as a whole. Even industry as it is today is finding such people less and less useful.

Industry controlled by society as a whole, and operated according to a plan, presupposes well-rounded human beings, their faculties developed in balanced fashion, able to see the system of production in its entirety.

The form of the division of labor which makes one a peasant, another a cobbler, a third a factory worker, a fourth a stock-market operator, has already been undermined by machinery and will completely disappear. Education will enable young people quickly to familiarize themselves with the whole system of production and to pass from one branch of production to another in response to the needs of society or their own inclinations. It will, therefore, free them from the one-sided character which the present-day division of labor impresses upon every individual. Communist society will, in this way, make it possible for its members to put their comprehensively developed faculties to full use. But, when this happens, classes will necessarily disappear. It follows that society organized on a communist basis is incompatible with the existence of classes on the one hand, and that the very building of such a society provides the means of abolishing class differences on the other.

A corollary of this is that the difference between city and country is destined to disappear. The management of agriculture and industry by the same people rather than by two different classes of people is, if only for purely material reasons, a necessary condition of communist association. The dispersal of the agricultural population on the land, alongside the crowding of the industrial population into the great cities, is a condition which corresponds to an undeveloped state of both agriculture and industry and can already be felt as an obstacle to further development.

The general co-operation of all members of society for the purpose of planned exploitation of the forces of production, the expansion of production to the point where it will satisfy the needs of all, the abolition of a situation in which the needs of some are satisfied at the expense of the needs of others, the complete liquidation of classes and their conflicts, the rounded development of the capacities of all members of society through the elimination of the present division of labor, through industrial education, through engaging in varying activities, through the participation by all in the enjoyments produced by all, through the combination of city and country – these are the main consequences of the abolition of private property.

What will be the influence of communist society on the family?

It will transform the relations between the sexes into a purely private matter which concerns only the persons involved and into which society has no occasion to intervene. It can do this since it does away with private property and educates children on a communal basis, and in this way removes the two bases of traditional marriage – the dependence rooted in private property, of the women on the man, and of the children on the parents.

And here is the answer to the outcry of the highly moral philistines against the "community of women". Community of women is a condition which belongs entirely to bourgeois society and which today finds its complete expression in prostitution. But prostitution is based on private property and falls with it. Thus, communist society, instead of introducing community of women, in fact abolishes it.

What will be the attitude of communism to existing nationalities?

The nationalities of the peoples associating themselves in accordance with the principle of community will be compelled to mingle with each other as a result of this association and thereby to dissolve themselves, just as the various estate and class distinctions must disappear through the abolition of their basis, private property.[5]

What will be its attitude to existing religions?

All religions so far have been the expression of historical stages of development of individual peoples or groups of peoples. But communism is the stage of historical development which makes all existing religions superfluous and brings about their disappearance[4]

How do communists differ from socialists?

The so-called socialists are divided into three categories.

[Reactionary Socialists:]

The first category consists of adherents of a feudal and

patriarchal society which has already been destroyed, and is still daily being destroyed, by big industry and world trade and their creation, bourgeois society. This category concludes, from the evils of existing society, that feudal and patriarchal society must be restored because it was free of such evils. In one way or another, all their proposals are directed to this end.

This category of reactionary socialists, for all their seeming partisanship and their scalding tears for the misery of the proletariat, is nevertheless energetically opposed by the communists for the following reasons:

1. It strives for something which is entirely impossible.
2. It seeks to establish the rule of the aristocracy, the guildmasters, the small producers, and their retinue of absolute or feudal monarchs, officials, soldiers, and priests – a society which was, to be sure, free of the evils of present-day society but which brought it at least as many evils without even offering to the oppressed workers the prospect of liberation through a communist revolution.
3. As soon as the proletariat becomes revolutionary and communist, these reactionary socialists show their true colors by immediately making common cause with the bourgeoisie against the proletarians.

[Bourgeois Socialists:]

The second category consists of adherents of present-day society who have been frightened for its future by the evils to which it necessarily gives rise. What they want, therefore, is to maintain this society while getting rid of the evils which are an inherent part of it.

To this end, some propose mere welfare measures – while others come forward with grandiose systems of reform which, under the pretense of re-organizing society, are in fact intended to preserve the foundations, and hence the life, of existing society.

Communists must unremittingly struggle against these bourgeois socialists because they work for the enemies of communists and protect the society which communists aim to overthrow.

[Democratic Socialists:]

Finally, the third category consists of democratic socialists who favor some of the same measures the communists advocate, as described in Question 18, not as part of the transition to communism, however, but as measures which they believe will be sufficient to abolish the misery and evils of present-day society.

These democratic socialists are either proletarians who are not yet sufficiently clear about the conditions of the liberation of their class, or they are representatives of the petty bourgeoisie, a class which, prior to the achievement of democracy and the socialist measures to which it gives rise, has many interests in common with the proletariat.

It follows that, in moments of action, the communists will have to come to an understanding with these democratic socialists, and in general to follow as far as possible a common policy with them – provided that these socialists do not enter into the service of the ruling bourgeoisie and attack the communists.

It is clear that this form of co-operation in action does not exclude the discussion of differences.

Citation and Use

This reading was taken from the following source.

Engles, Frederick. "The Principles of Communism." Marxists Internet Archive, 1999.
    https://www.marxists.org/archive/marx/works/1847/11/prin-com.htm.

CAPITAL'S REVENGE

Lewis Powell Powell

Attack on American Free Enterprise System

CONFIDENTIAL MEMORANDUM

DATE: August 23, 1971

TO: Mr. Eugene B. Sydnor, Jr., Chairman, Education Committee, U.S. Chamber of Commerce

FROM: Lewis F. Powell, Jr.

This memorandum is submitted at your request as a basis for the discussion on August 24 with Mr. Booth (executive vice president) and others at the U.S. Chamber of Commerce. The purpose is to identify the problem, and suggest possible avenues of action for further consideration.

Dimensions of the Attack

No thoughtful person can question that the American economic system is under broad attack. This varies in scope, intensity, in the techniques employed, and in the level of visibility.

There always have been some who opposed the American system, and preferred socialism or some form of statism (communism or fascism). Also, there always have been critics of the system, whose criticism has been wholesome and constructive so long as the objective was to improve rather than to subvert or destroy.

But what now concerns us is quite new in the history of America. We are not dealing with sporadic or isolated attacks from a relatively few extremists or even from the minority socialist cadre. Rather, the assault on the enterprise system is broadly based and consistently pursued. It is gaining momentum and converts.

Sources of the Attack

The sources are varied and diffused. They include, not unexpectedly, the Communists, New Leftists and other revolutionaries who would destroy the entire system, both political and economic. These extremists of the left are far more numerous, better financed, and increasingly are more welcomed and encouraged by other elements of society, than ever before in our history. But they remain a small minority, and are not yet the principal cause for concern.

The most disquieting voices joining the chorus of criticism come from perfectly respectable elements of society: from the college campus, the pulpit, the media, the intellectual and literary journals, the arts and sciences, and from politicians. In most of these groups the movement against the system is participated in only by minorities. Yet, these often are the most articulate, the most vocal, the most prolific in their writing and speaking.

Moreover, much of the media — for varying motives and in varying degrees — either voluntarily accords unique publicity to these "attackers," or at least allows them to exploit the media for their purposes. This is especially true of television, which now plays such a predominant role in shaping the thinking, attitudes and emotions of our people.

One of the bewildering paradoxes of our time is the extent to which the enterprise system tolerates, if not participates in, its own destruction.

The campuses from which much of the criticism emanates are supported by
1. tax funds generated largely from American business, and
2. contributions from capital funds controlled or generated by American business.

The boards of trustees of our universities overwhelmingly are composed of men and women who are leaders in the system.

Most of the media, including the national TV systems, are owned and theoretically controlled by corporations which depend upon profits, and the enterprise system to survive.

Tone of the Attack

This memorandum is not the place to document in detail

the tone, character, or intensity of the attack. The following quotations will suffice to give one a general idea:

William Kunstler, warmly welcomed on campuses and listed in a recent student poll as the "American lawyer most admired," incites audiences as follows:

"You must learn to fight in the streets, to revolt, to shoot guns. We will learn to do all of the things that property owners fear." The New Leftists who heed Kunstler's advice increasingly are beginning to act — not just against military recruiting offices and manufacturers of munitions, but against a variety of businesses: "Since February, 1970, branches (of Bank of America) have been attacked 39 times, 22 times with explosive devices and 17 times with fire bombs or by arsonists." Although New Leftist spokesmen are succeeding in radicalizing thousands of the young, the greater cause for concern is the hostility of respectable liberals and social reformers. It is the sum total of their views and influence which could indeed fatally weaken or destroy the system.

A chilling description of what is being taught on many of our campuses was written by Stewart Alsop:

> Yale, like every other major college, is graduating scores of bright young men who are practitioners of 'the politics of despair.' These young men despise the American political and economic system . . . (their) minds seem to be wholly closed. They live, not by rational discussion, but by mindless slogans."A recent poll of students on 12 representative campuses reported that: "Almost half the students favored socialization of basic U.S. industries.

A visiting professor from England at Rockford College gave a series of lectures entitled "The Ideological War Against Western Society," in which he documents the extent to which members of the intellectual community are waging ideological warfare against the enterprise system and the values of western society. In a foreword to these lectures, famed Dr. Milton Friedman of Chicago warned: "It (is) crystal clear that the foundations of our free society are under wide-ranging and powerful attack — not by Communist or any other conspiracy but by misguided individuals parroting one another and unwittingly serving ends they would never intentionally promote."

Perhaps the single most effective antagonist of American business is Ralph Nader, who — thanks largely to the media — has become a legend in his own time and an idol of millions of Americans. A recent article in Fortune speaks of Nader as follows:

> The passion that rules in him — and he is a passionate man — is aimed at smashing utterly the target of his hatred, which is corporate power. He thinks, and says quite bluntly, that a great many corporate executives belong in prison — for defrauding the consumer with shoddy merchandise, poisoning the food supply with chemical additives, and willfully manufacturing unsafe

products that will maim or kill the buyer. He emphasizes that he is not talking just about 'fly-by-night hucksters' but the top management of blue chip business.

A frontal assault was made on our government, our system of justice, and the free enterprise system by Yale Professor Charles Reich in his widely publicized book: "The Greening of America," published last winter.

The foregoing references illustrate the broad, shotgun attack on the system itself. There are countless examples of rifle shots which undermine confidence and confuse the public. Favorite current targets are proposals for tax incentives through changes in depreciation rates and investment credits. These are usually described in the media as "tax breaks," "loop holes" or "tax benefits" for the benefit of business. * As viewed by a columnist in the Post, such tax measures would benefit "only the rich, the owners of big companies."

It is dismaying that many politicians make the same argument that tax measures of this kind benefit only "business," without benefit to "the poor." The fact that this is either political demagoguery or economic illiteracy is of slight comfort. This setting of the "rich" against the "poor," of business against the people, is the cheapest and most dangerous kind of politics.

The Apathy and Default of Business

What has been the response of business to this massive assault upon its fundamental economics, upon its philosophy, upon its right to continue to manage its own affairs, and indeed upon its integrity?

The painfully sad truth is that business, including the boards of directors' and the top executives of corporations great and small and business organizations at all levels, often have responded — if at all — by appeasement, ineptitude and ignoring the problem. There are, of course, many exceptions to this sweeping generalization. But the net effect of such response as has been made is scarcely visible.

In all fairness, it must be recognized that businessmen have not been trained or equipped to conduct guerrilla warfare with those who propagandize against the system, seeking insidiously and constantly to sabotage it. The traditional role of business executives has been to manage, to produce, to sell, to create jobs, to make profits, to improve the standard of living, to be community leaders, to serve on charitable and educational boards, and generally to be good citizens. They have performed these tasks very well indeed.

But they have shown little stomach for hard-nose contest with their critics, and little skill in effective intellectual and philosophical debate.

A column recently carried by the Wall Street Journal was entitled: "Memo to GM: Why Not Fight Back?" Although addressed to GM by name, the article was a warning to all American business. Columnist St. John said:

General Motors, like American business in general, is 'plainly in trouble' because intellectual bromides have been substituted for a sound intellectual exposition of its point of view." Mr. St. John then commented on the tendency of business leaders to compromise with and appease critics. He cited the concessions which Nader wins from management, and spoke of "the fallacious view many businessmen take toward their critics." He drew a parallel to the mistaken tactics of many college administrators: "College administrators learned too late that such appeasement serves to destroy free speech, academic freedom and genuine scholarship. One campus radical demand was conceded by university heads only to be followed by a fresh crop which soon escalated to what amounted to a demand for outright surrender.

One need not agree entirely with Mr. St. John's analysis. But most observers of the American scene will agree that the essence of his message is sound. American business "plainly in trouble"; the response to the wide range of critics has been ineffective, and has included appeasement; the time has come — indeed, it is long overdue — for the wisdom, ingenuity and resources of American business to be marshalled against those who would destroy it.

Responsibility of Business Executives

What specifically should be done? The first essential — a prerequisite to any effective action — is for businessmen to confront this problem as a primary responsibility of corporate management.

The overriding first need is for businessmen to recognize that the ultimate issue may be survival — survival of what we call the free enterprise system, and all that this means for the strength and prosperity of America and the freedom of our people.

The day is long past when the chief executive officer of a major corporation discharges his responsibility by maintaining a satisfactory growth of profits, with due regard to the corporation's public and social responsibilities. If our system is to survive, top management must be equally concerned with protecting and preserving the system itself. This involves far more than an increased emphasis on "public relations" or "governmental affairs" — two areas in which corporations long have invested substantial sums.

A significant first step by individual corporations could well be the designation of an executive vice president (ranking with other executive VP's) whose responsibility is to counter-on the broadest front-the attack on the enterprise system. The public relations department could be one of the foundations assigned to this executive, but his responsibilities should encompass some of the types of activities referred to subsequently in this memorandum. His budget and staff should be adequate to the task.

Possible Role of the Chamber of Commerce

But independent and uncoordinated activity by individual corporations, as important as this is, will not be sufficient. Strength lies in organization, in careful long-range planning and implementation, in consistency of action over an indefinite period of years, in the scale of financing available only through joint effort, and in the political power available only through united action and national organizations.

Moreover, there is the quite understandable reluctance on the part of any one corporation to get too far out in front and to make itself too visible a target.

The role of the National Chamber of Commerce is therefore vital. Other national organizations (especially those of various industrial and commercial groups) should join in the effort, but no other organizations appear to be as well situated as the Chamber. It enjoys a strategic position, with a fine reputation and a broad base of support. Also — and this is of immeasurable merit — there are hundreds of local Chambers of Commerce which can play a vital supportive role.

It hardly need be said that before embarking upon any program, the Chamber should study and analyze possible courses of action and activities, weighing risks against probable effectiveness and feasibility of each. Considerations of cost, the assurance of financial and other support from members, adequacy of staffing and similar problems will all require the most thoughtful consideration.

The Campus

The assault on the enterprise system was not mounted in a few months. It has gradually evolved over the past two decades, barely perceptible in its origins and benefiting (sic) from a gradualism that provoked little awareness much less any real reaction.

Although origins, sources and causes are complex and interrelated, and obviously difficult to identify without careful qualification, there is reason to believe that the campus is the single most dynamic source. The social science faculties usually include members who are unsympathetic to the enterprise system. They may range from a Herbert Marcuse, Marxist faculty member at the University of California at San Diego, and convinced socialists, to the ambivalent liberal critic who finds more to condemn than to commend. Such faculty members need not be in a majority. They are often personally attractive and magnetic; they are stimulating teachers, and their controversy attracts student following; they are prolific writers and lecturers; they author many of the textbooks, and they exert enormous influence — far out of proportion to their numbers — on their colleagues and in the academic world.

Social science faculties (the political scientist, economist, sociologist and many of the historians) tend to be liberally oriented, even when leftists are not present. This is not a criticism per se, as the need for liberal thought is essential to a balanced viewpoint. The difficulty is that "balance" is conspicuous by its absence on many campuses, with relatively few members being of conservatives or moderate persuasion and even the relatively few often being less articulate and aggressive than their crusading colleagues.

This situation extending back many years and with the imbalance gradually worsening, has had an enormous impact on millions of young American students. In an article in Barron's Weekly, seeking an answer to why so many young people are disaffected even to the point of being revolutionaries, it was said: "Because they were taught that way." Or, as noted by columnist Stewart Alsop, writing about his alma mater: "Yale, like every other major college, is graduating scores' of bright young men ... who despise the American political and economic system."

As these "bright young men," from campuses across the country, seek opportunities to change a system which they have been taught to distrust — if not, indeed "despise" — they seek employment in the centers of the real power and influence in our country, namely: (i) with the news media, especially television; (ii) in government, as "staffers" and consultants at various levels; (iii) in elective politics; (iv) as lecturers and writers, and (v) on the faculties at various levels of education.

Many do enter the enterprise system — in business and the professions — and for the most part they quickly discover the fallacies of what they have been taught. But those who eschew the mainstream of the system often remain in key positions of influence where they mold public opinion and often shape governmental action. In many instances, these "intellectuals" end up in regulatory agencies or governmental departments with large authority over the business system they do not believe in.

If the foregoing analysis is approximately sound, a priority task of business — and organizations such as the Chamber — is to address the campus origin of this hostility. Few things are more sanctified in American life than academic freedom. It would be fatal to attack this as a principle. But if academic freedom is to retain the qualities of "openness," "fairness" and "balance" — which are essential to its intellectual significance — there is a great opportunity for constructive action. The thrust of such action must be to restore the qualities just mentioned to the academic communities.

What Can Be Done About the Campus

The ultimate responsibility for intellectual integrity on the campus must remain on the administrations and faculties of our colleges and universities. But organizations such as the Chamber can assist and activate constructive change in many ways, including the following:

Staff of Scholars

The Chamber should consider establishing a staff of highly qualified scholars in the social sciences who do believe in the system. It should include several of national reputation whose authorship would be widely respected — even when disagreed with.

Staff of Speakers

There also should be a staff of speakers of the highest competency. These might include the scholars, and certainly those who speak for the Chamber would have to articulate the product of the scholars.

Speaker's Bureau

In addition to full-time staff personnel, the Chamber should have a Speaker's Bureau which should include the ablest and most effective advocates from the top echelons of American business.

Evaluation of Textbooks

The staff of scholars (or preferably a panel of independent scholars) should evaluate social science textbooks, especially in economics, political science and sociology. This should be a continuing program.

The objective of such evaluation should be oriented toward restoring the balance essential to genuine academic freedom. This would include assurance of fair and factual treatment of our system of government and our enterprise system, its accomplishments, its basic relationship to individual rights and freedoms, and comparisons with the systems of socialism, fascism and communism. Most of the existing textbooks have some sort of comparisons, but many are superficial, biased and unfair.

We have seen the civil rights movement insist on re-writing many of the textbooks in our universities and schools. The labor unions likewise insist that textbooks be fair to the viewpoints of organized labor. Other interested citizens groups have not hesitated to review, analyze and criticize textbooks and teaching materials. In a democratic society, this can be a constructive process and should be regarded as an aid to genuine academic freedom and not as an intrusion upon it.

If the authors, publishers and users of textbooks know that they will be subjected — honestly, fairly and thoroughly — to review and critique by eminent scholars who believe in the American system, a return to a more rational balance can be expected.

Equal Time on the Campus

The Chamber should insist upon equal time on the college speaking circuit. The FBI publishes each year a list of speeches made on college campuses by avowed Communists. The number in 1970 exceeded 100. There were, of course, many hundreds of appearances by leftists and ultra liberals who urge the types of viewpoints indicated earlier in this memorandum. There was no corresponding representation of American business, or indeed by individuals or organizations who appeared in support of the American system of government and business.

Every campus has its formal and informal groups which invite speakers. Each law school does the same thing. Many universities and colleges officially sponsor lecture and speaking programs. We all know the inadequacy of the representation of business in the programs.

It will be said that few invitations would be extended to Chamber speakers. This undoubtedly would be true unless the Chamber aggressively insisted upon the right to be heard — in effect, insisted upon "equal time." University administrators and the great majority of student groups and committees would not welcome being put in the position publicly of refusing a forum to diverse views, indeed, this is the classic excuse for allowing Communists to speak.

The two essential ingredients are (i) to have attractive, articulate and well-informed speakers; and (ii) to exert whatever degree of pressure — publicly and privately — may be necessary to assure opportunities to speak. The objective always must be to inform and enlighten, and not merely to propagandize.

Balancing of Faculties

Perhaps the most fundamental problem is the imbalance of many faculties. Correcting this is indeed a long-range and difficult project. Yet, it should be undertaken as a part of an overall program. This would mean the urging of the need for faculty balance upon university administrators and boards of trustees.

The methods to be employed require careful thought, and the obvious pitfalls must be avoided. Improper pressure would be counterproductive. But the basic concepts of balance, fairness and truth are difficult to resist, if properly presented to boards of trustees, by writing and speaking, and by appeals to alumni associations and groups.

This is a long road and not one for the fainthearted. But if pursued with integrity and conviction it could lead to a strengthening of both academic freedom on the campus and of the values which have made America the most productive of all societies.

Graduate Schools of Business

The Chamber should enjoy a particular rapport with the increasingly influential graduate schools of business. Much that has been suggested above applies to such schools.

Should not the Chamber also request specific courses in such schools dealing with the entire scope of the problem addressed by this memorandum? This is now essential training for the executives of the future.

Secondary Education

While the first priority should be at the college level, the trends mentioned above are increasingly evidenced in the high schools. Action programs, tailored to the high schools and similar to those mentioned, should be considered. The implementation thereof could become a major program for local chambers of commerce, although the control and direction — especially the quality control — should be retained by the National Chamber.

What Can Be Done About the Public?

Reaching the campus and the secondary schools is vital for the long-term. Reaching the public generally may be more important for the shorter term. The first essential is to establish the staffs of eminent scholars, writers and speakers, who will do the thinking, the analysis, the writing and the speaking. It will also be essential to have staff personnel who are thoroughly familiar with the media, and how most effectively to communicate with the public. Among the more obvious means are the following:

Television

The national television networks should be monitored in the same way that textbooks should be kept under constant surveillance. This applies not merely to so-called educational programs (such as "Selling of the Pentagon"), but to the daily "news analysis" which so often includes the most insidious type of criticism of the enterprise system. Whether this criticism results from hostility or economic ignorance, the result is the gradual erosion of confidence in "business" and free enterprise.

This monitoring, to be effective, would require constant examination of the texts of adequate samples of programs. Complaints — to the media and to the Federal Communications Commission — should be made promptly and strongly when programs are unfair or inaccurate.

Equal time should be demanded when appropriate. Effort should be made to see that the forum-type programs (the Today Show, Meet the Press, etc.) afford at least as much opportunity for supporters of the American system to participate as these programs do for those who attack it.

Other Media

Radio and the press are also important, and every available means should be employed to challenge and refute unfair attacks, as well as to present the affirmative case through these media.

The Scholarly Journals

It is especially important for the Chamber's "faculty of scholars" to publish. One of the keys to the success of the liberal and leftist faculty members has been their passion for "publication" and "lecturing." A similar passion must exist among the Chamber's scholars.

Incentives might be devised to induce more "publishing" by independent scholars who do believe in the system.

There should be a fairly steady flow of scholarly articles presented to a broad spectrum of magazines and periodicals — ranging from the popular magazines (Life, Look, Reader's Digest, etc.) to the more intellectual ones (Atlantic, Harper's, Saturday Review, New York, etc.) and to the various professional journals.

Books, Paperbacks and Pamphlets

The news stands — at airports, drugstores, and elsewhere — are filled with paperbacks and pamphlets advocating everything from revolution to erotic free love. One finds almost no attractive, well-written paperbacks or pamphlets on "our side." It will be difficult to compete with an Eldridge Cleaver or even a Charles Reich for reader attention, but unless the effort is made — on a large enough scale and with appropriate imagination to assure some success — this opportunity for educating the public will be irretrievably lost.

Paid Advertisements

Business pays hundreds of millions of dollars to the media for advertisements. Most of this supports specific products; much of it supports institutional image making; and some fraction of it does support the system. But the latter has been more or less tangential, and rarely part of a sustained, major effort to inform and enlighten the American people.

If American business devoted only 10% of its total annual advertising budget to this overall purpose, it would be a statesman-like expenditure.

The Neglected Political Arena

In the final analysis, the payoff — short-of revolution — is what government does. Business has been the favorite whipping-boy of many politicians for many years. But the measure of how far this has gone is perhaps best found in the anti-business views now being expressed by several leading candidates for President of the United States.

It is still Marxist doctrine that the "capitalist" countries are controlled by big business. This doctrine, consistently a part of leftist propaganda all over the world, has a wide public following among Americans.

Yet, as every business executive knows, few elements of American society today have as little influence in government as the American businessman, the corporation, or even the millions of corporate stockholders. If one doubts this, let him undertake the role of "lobbyist" for the business point of view before Congressional committees. The same situation obtains in the legislative halls of most states and major cities. One does not exaggerate to say that, in terms of political influence with respect to the course of legislation and government action, the American business executive is truly the "forgotten man."

Current examples of the impotency of business, and of the near-contempt with which businessmen's views are held, are the stampedes by politicians to support almost any legislation related to "consumerism" or to the "environment."

Politicians reflect what they believe to be majority views of their constituents. It is thus evident that most politicians are making the judgment that the public has little sympathy for the businessman or his viewpoint.

The educational programs suggested above would be designed to enlighten public thinking — not so much about the businessman and his individual role as about the system which he administers, and which provides the goods, services and jobs on which our country depends.

But one should not postpone more direct political action, while awaiting the gradual change in public opinion to be effected through education and information. Business must learn the lesson, long ago learned by labor and other self-interest groups. This is the lesson that political power is necessary; that such power must be assiduously (sic) cultivated; and that when necessary, it must be used aggressively and with determination — without embarrassment and without the reluctance which has been so characteristic of American business.

As unwelcome as it may be to the Chamber, it should consider assuming a broader and more vigorous role in the political arena.

Neglected Opportunity in the Courts

American business and the enterprise system have been affected as much by the courts as by the executive and legislative branches of government. Under our constitutional system, especially with an activist-minded Supreme Court, the judiciary may be the most important instrument for social, economic and political change.

Other organizations and groups, recognizing this, have been far more astute in exploiting judicial action than American business. Perhaps the most active exploiters of the judicial system have been groups ranging in political orientation from "liberal" to the far left.

The American Civil Liberties Union is one example. It initiates or intervenes in scores of cases each year, and it files briefs amicus curiae in the Supreme Court in a number of cases during each term of that court. Labor unions, civil rights groups and now the public interest law firms are extremely active in the judicial arena. Their success, often at business' expense, has not been inconsequential.

This is a vast area of opportunity for the Chamber, if it is willing to undertake the role of spokesman for American business and if, in turn, business is willing to provide the funds.

As with respect to scholars and speakers, the Chamber would need a highly competent staff of lawyers. In special situations it should be authorized to engage, to appear as counsel amicus in the Supreme Court, lawyers of national standing and reputation. The greatest care should be exercised in selecting the cases in which to participate, or the suits to institute. But the opportunity merits the necessary effort.

Neglected Stockholder Power

The average member of the public thinks of "business" as an impersonal corporate entity, owned by the very rich and managed by over-paid executives. There is an almost total failure to appreciate that "business" actually embraces — in one way or another — most Americans. Those for whom business provides jobs, constitute a fairly obvious class. But the 20 million stockholders — most of whom are of modest means — are the real owners, the real entrepreneurs, the real capitalists under our system. They provide the capital which fuels the economic system which has produced the highest standard of living in all history. Yet, stockholders have been as ineffectual as business executives in promoting a genuine understanding of our system or in exercising political influence.

The question which merits the most thorough examination is how can the weight and influence of stockholders — 20 million voters — be mobilized to support (i) an educational program and (ii) a political action program.

Individual corporations are now required to make numerous reports to shareholders. Many corporations also have expensive "news" magazines which go to employees and stockholders. These opportunities to communicate can be used far more effectively as educational media.

The corporation itself must exercise restraint in undertaking political action and must, of course, comply with applicable laws. But is it not feasible — through an affiliate of the Chamber or otherwise — to establish a national organization of American stockholders and give it enough muscle to be influential?

A More Aggressive Attitude

Business interests — especially big business and their national trade organizations — have tried to maintain low profiles, especially with respect to political action.

As suggested in the Wall Street Journal article, it has been fairly characteristic of the average business executive to be tolerant — at least in public — of those who attack his corporation and the system. Very few businessmen or business organizations respond in kind. There has been a disposition to appease; to regard the opposition as willing to compromise, or as likely to fade away in due time.

Business has shunted confrontation politics. Business, quite understandably, has been repelled by the multiplicity of non-negotiable "demands" made constantly by self-interest groups of all kinds.

While neither responsible business interests, nor the

United States Chamber of Commerce, would engage in the irresponsible tactics of some pressure groups, it is essential that spokesmen for the enterprise system — at all levels and at every opportunity — be far more aggressive than in the past.

There should be no hesitation to attack the Naders, the Marcuses and others who openly seek destruction of the system. There should not be the slightest hesitation to press vigorously in all political arenas for support of the enterprise system. Nor should there be reluctance to penalize politically those who oppose it.

Lessons can be learned from organized labor in this respect. The head of the AFL-CIO may not appeal to businessmen as the most endearing or public-minded of citizens. Yet, over many years the heads of national labor organizations have done what they were paid to do very effectively. They may not have been beloved, but they have been respected — where it counts the most — by politicians, on the campus, and among the media.

It is time for American business — which has demonstrated the greatest capacity in all history to produce and to influence consumer decisions — to apply their great talents vigorously to the preservation of the system itself.

The Cost

The type of program described above (which includes a broadly based combination of education and political action), if undertaken long term and adequately staffed, would require far more generous financial support from American corporations than the Chamber has ever received in the past. High level management participation in Chamber affairs also would be required.

The staff of the Chamber would have to be significantly increased, with the highest quality established and maintained. Salaries would have to be at levels fully comparable to those paid key business executives and the most prestigious faculty members. Professionals of the great skill in advertising and in working with the media, speakers, lawyers and other specialists would have to be recruited.

It is possible that the organization of the Chamber itself would benefit from restructuring. For example, as suggested by union experience, the office of President of the Chamber might well be a full-time career position. To assure maximum effectiveness and continuity, the chief executive officer of the Chamber should not be changed each year. The functions now largely performed by the President could be transferred to a Chairman of the Board, annually elected by the membership. The Board, of course, would continue to exercise policy control.

Quality Control is Essential

Essential ingredients of the entire program must be responsibility and "quality control." The publications, the articles, the speeches, the media programs, the advertising, the briefs filed in courts, and the appearances before legislative committees — all must meet the most exacting standards of accuracy and professional excellence. They must merit respect for their level of public responsibility and scholarship, whether one agrees with the viewpoints expressed or not.

Relationship to Freedom

The threat to the enterprise system is not merely a matter of economics. It also is a threat to individual freedom.

It is this great truth — now so submerged by the rhetoric of the New Left and of many liberals — that must be reaffirmed if this program is to be meaningful.

There seems to be little awareness that the only alternatives to free enterprise are varying degrees of bureaucratic regulation of individual freedom — ranging from that under moderate socialism to the iron heel of the leftist or rightist dictatorship.

We in America already have moved very far indeed toward some aspects of state socialism, as the needs and complexities of a vast urban society require types of regulation and control that were quite unnecessary in earlier times. In some areas, such regulation and control already have seriously impaired the freedom of both business and labor, and indeed of the public generally. But most of the essential freedoms remain: private ownership, private profit, labor unions, collective bargaining, consumer choice, and a market economy in which competition largely determines price, quality and variety of the goods and services provided the consumer.

In addition to the ideological attack on the system itself (discussed in this memorandum), its essentials also are threatened by inequitable taxation, and — more recently — by an inflation which has seemed uncontrollable. But whatever the causes of diminishing economic freedom may be, the truth is that freedom as a concept is indivisible. As the experience of the socialist and totalitarian states demonstrates, the contraction and denial of economic freedom is followed inevitably by governmental restrictions on other cherished rights. It is this message, above all others, that must be carried home to the American people.

Conclusion

It hardly need be said that the views expressed above are tentative and suggestive. The first step should be a thorough study. But this would be an exercise in futility unless the Board of Directors of the Chamber accepts the fundamental premise of this paper, namely, that business and the enterprise system are in deep trouble, and the hour is late.

Citation and Use

The reading was taken from the following source.

Powell, Lewis. "Memorandum: Attack On American Free Enterprise System." Powell Papers at the Washington and Lee University School of Law, 1971. https://scholarlycommons.law.wlu.edu/powellmemo/.

TO PRICE A THING IS TO KNOW A THING

Friedrich Hayek

I

What is the problem we wish to solve when we try to construct a rational economic order? On certain familiar assumptions the answer is simple enough.

- *If* we possess all the relevant information,
- *if* we can start out from a given system of preferences, and
- *if* we command complete knowledge of available means,

the problem which remains is purely one of logic.

That is, the answer to the question of what is the best use of the available means is implicit in our assumptions. The conditions which the solution of this optimum problem must satisfy have been fully worked out and can be stated best in mathematical form: put at their briefest, they are that the marginal rates of substitution between any two commodities or factors must be the same in all their different uses.

This, however, is emphatically *not* the economic problem which society faces. And the economic calculus which we have developed to solve this logical problem, though an important step toward the solution of the economic problem of society, does not yet provide an answer to it. The reason for this is that the "data" from which the economic calculus starts are never for the whole society "given" to a single mind which could work out the implications and can never be so given.

The peculiar character of the problem of a rational economic order is determined precisely by the fact that the knowledge of the circumstances of which we must make use never exists in concentrated or integrated form but solely as the dispersed bits of incomplete and frequently contradictory knowledge which all the separate individuals possess. The economic problem of society is thus not merely a problem of how to allocate "given" resources—if "given" is taken to mean given to a single mind which deliberately solves the problem set by these "data." It is rather a problem of how to secure the best use of resources known to any

of the members of society, for ends whose relative importance only these individuals know. Or, to put it briefly, it is a problem of the utilization of knowledge which is not given to anyone in its totality.

This character of the fundamental problem has, I am afraid, been obscured rather than illuminated by many of the recent refinements of economic theory, particularly by many of the uses made of mathematics. Though the problem with which I want primarily to deal in this paper is the problem of a rational economic organization, I shall in its course be led again and again to point to its close connections with certain methodological questions. Many of the points I wish to make are indeed conclusions toward which diverse paths of reasoning have unexpectedly converged. But, as I now see these problems, this is no accident. It seems to me that many of the current disputes with regard to both economic theory and economic policy have their common origin in a misconception about the nature of the economic problem of society. This misconception in turn is due to an erroneous transfer to social phenomena of the habits of thought we have developed in dealing with the phenomena of nature.

II

In ordinary language we describe by the word "planning" the complex of interrelated decisions about the allocation of our available resources. All economic activity is in this sense planning; and in any society in which many people collaborate, this planning, whoever does it, will in some measure have to be based on knowledge which, in the first instance, is not given to the planner but to somebody else, which somehow will have to be conveyed to the planner. The various ways in which the knowledge on which people base their plans is communicated to them is the crucial problem for any theory explaining the economic process, and the problem of what is the best way of utilizing knowledge initially dispersed among all the people is at least one of the main problems of economic policy—or of designing an efficient economic system.

The answer to this question is closely connected with that

other question which arises here, that of *who* is to do the planning. It is about this question that all the dispute about "economic planning" centers. This is not a dispute about whether planning is to be done or not. It is a dispute as to whether planning is to be done centrally, by one authority for the whole economic system, or is to be divided among many individuals. Planning in the specific sense in which the term is used in contemporary controversy necessarily means central planning—direction of the whole economic system according to one unified plan. Competition, on the other hand, means decentralized planning by many separate persons. The halfway house between the two, about which many people talk but which few like when they see it, is the delegation of planning to organized industries, or, in other words, monopoly.

Which of these systems is likely to be more efficient depends mainly on the question under which of them we can expect that fuller use will be made of the existing knowledge. And this, in turn, depends on whether we are more likely to succeed in putting at the disposal of a single central authority all the knowledge which ought to be used but which is initially dispersed among many different individuals, or in conveying to the individuals such additional knowledge as they need in order to enable them to fit their plans with those of others.

III

It will at once be evident that on this point the position will be different with respect to different kinds of knowledge; and the answer to our question will therefore largely turn on the relative importance of the different kinds of knowledge; those more likely to be at the disposal of particular individuals and those which we should with greater confidence expect to find in the possession of an authority made up of suitably chosen experts. If it is today so widely assumed that the latter will be in a better position, this is because one kind of knowledge, namely, scientific knowledge, occupies now so prominent a place in public imagination that we tend to forget that it is not the only kind that is relevant. It may be admitted that, as far as scientific knowledge is concerned, a body of suitably chosen experts may be in the best position to command all the best knowledge available—though this is of course merely shifting the difficulty to the problem of selecting the experts. What I wish to point out is that, even assuming that this problem can be readily solved, it is only a small part of the wider problem.

Today it is almost heresy to suggest that scientific knowledge is not the sum of all knowledge. But a little reflection will show that there is beyond question a body of very important but unorganized knowledge which cannot possibly be called scientific in the sense of knowledge of general rules: the knowledge of the particular circumstances of time and place. It is with respect to this that practically every individual has some advantage over all others because he possesses unique information of which beneficial use might be made, but of which use can be made only if the decisions depending on it are left to him or are made with his active coöperation. We need to remember only how much we have to learn in any occupation after we have completed our theoretical training, how big a part of our working life we spend learning particular jobs, and how valuable an asset in all walks of life is knowledge of people, of local conditions, and of special circumstances. To know of and put to use a machine not fully employed, or somebody's skill which could be better utilized, or to be aware of a surplus stock which can be drawn upon during an interruption of supplies, is socially quite as useful as the knowledge of better alternative techniques. And the shipper who earns his living from using otherwise empty or half-filled journeys of tramp-steamers, or the estate agent whose whole knowledge is almost exclusively one of temporary opportunities, or the *arbitrageur* who gains from local differences of commodity prices, are all performing eminently useful functions based on special knowledge of circumstances of the fleeting moment not known to others.

It is a curious fact that this sort of knowledge should today be generally regarded with a kind of contempt and that anyone who by such knowledge gains an advantage over somebody better equipped with theoretical or technical knowledge is thought to have acted almost disreputably. To gain an advantage from better knowledge of facilities of communication or transport is sometimes regarded as almost dishonest, although it is quite as important that society make use of the best opportunities in this respect as in using the latest scientific discoveries. This prejudice has in a considerable measure affected the attitude toward commerce in general compared with that toward production. Even economists who regard themselves as definitely immune to the crude materialist fallacies of the past constantly commit the same mistake where activities directed toward the acquisition of such practical knowledge are concerned—apparently because in their scheme of things all such knowledge is supposed to be "given." The common idea now seems to be that all such knowledge should as a matter of course be readily at the command of everybody, and the reproach of irrationality leveled against the existing economic order is frequently based on the fact that it is not so available. This view disregards the fact that the method by which such knowledge can be made as widely available as possible is precisely the problem to which we have to find an answer.

IV

If it is fashionable today to minimize the importance of the knowledge of the particular circumstances of time and place, this is closely connected with the smaller importance which is now attached to change as such. Indeed, there are few points on which the assumptions made (usually only implicitly) by the "planners" differ from those of their opponents as much as with regard to the significance and frequency of changes which will make substantial alterations of production plans necessary. Of course, if detailed economic plans could be laid down for fairly long periods in advance and then closely adhered to, so that no further economic decisions of importance would be required, the task of drawing up a comprehensive plan governing all economic activity would be much less formidable.

It is, perhaps, worth stressing that economic problems arise always and only in consequence of change. So long as things continue as before, or at least as they were expected to, there arise no new problems requiring a decision, no need to form a new plan. The belief that changes, or at least day-to-day adjustments, have become less important in modern times implies the contention that economic problems also have become less important. This belief in the decreasing importance of change is, for that reason, usually held by the same people who argue that the importance of economic considerations has been driven into the background by the growing importance of technological knowledge.

Is it true that, with the elaborate apparatus of modern production, economic decisions are required only at long intervals, as when a new factory is to be erected or a new process to be introduced? Is it true that, once a plant has been built, the rest is all more or less mechanical, determined by the character of the plant, and leaving little to be changed in adapting to the ever-changing circumstances of the moment?

The fairly widespread belief in the affirmative is not, as far as I can ascertain, borne out by the practical experience of the businessman. In a competitive industry at any rate—and such an industry alone can serve as a test—the task of keeping cost from rising requires constant struggle, absorbing a great part of the energy of the manager. How easy it is for an inefficient manager to dissipate the differentials on which profitability rests, and that it is possible, with the same technical facilities, to produce with a great variety of costs, are among the commonplaces of business experience which do not seem to be equally familiar in the study of the economist. The very strength of the desire, constantly voiced by producers and engineers, to be allowed to proceed untrammeled by considerations of money costs, is eloquent testimony to the extent to which these factors enter into their daily work.

One reason why economists are increasingly apt to forget about the constant small changes which make up the whole economic picture is probably their growing preoccupation with statistical aggregates, which show a very much greater stability than the movements of the detail. The comparative stability of the aggregates cannot, however, be accounted for—as the statisticians occasionally seem to be inclined to do—by the "law of large numbers" or the mutual compensation of random changes. The number of elements with which we have to deal is not large enough for such accidental forces to produce stability. The continuous flow of goods and services is maintained by constant deliberate adjustments, by new dispositions made every day in the light of circumstances not known the day before, by B stepping in at once when A fails to deliver. Even the large and highly mechanized plant keeps going largely because of an environment upon which it can draw for all sorts of unexpected needs; tiles for its roof, stationery for its forms, and all the thousand and one kinds of equipment in which it cannot be self-contained and which the plans for the operation of the plant require to be readily available in the market.

This is, perhaps, also the point where I should briefly mention the fact that the sort of knowledge with which I have been concerned is knowledge of the kind which by its nature cannot enter into statistics and therefore cannot be conveyed to any central authority in statistical form. The statistics which such a central authority would have to use would have to be arrived at precisely by abstracting from minor differences between the things, by lumping together, as resources of one kind, items which differ as regards location, quality, and other particulars, in a way which may be very significant for the specific decision. It follows from this that central planning based on statistical information by its nature cannot take direct account of these circumstances of time and place and that the central planner will have to find some way or other in which the decisions depending on them can be left to the "man on the spot."

V

If we can agree that the economic problem of society is mainly one of rapid adaptation to changes in the particular circumstances of time and place, it would seem to follow that the ultimate decisions must be left to the people who are familiar with these circumstances, who know directly of the relevant changes and of the resources immediately available to meet them. We cannot expect that this problem will be solved by first communicating all this knowledge to a central board which, after integrating *all* knowledge, issues its orders. We must solve it by some form of decentralization. But this answers only part of our problem. We need decentralization because only thus can we insure that the knowledge of the particular circumstances of time and place will be promptly used. But the "man on the spot" cannot decide solely on the basis of his limited but intimate knowledge of the facts of his immediate surroundings. There still remains the problem of communicating to him such further information as he needs to fit his decisions into the whole pattern of changes of the larger economic system.

How much knowledge does he need to do so successfully? Which of the events which happen beyond the horizon of his immediate knowledge are of relevance to his immediate decision, and how much of them need he know?

There is hardly anything that happens anywhere in the world that *might* not have an effect on the decision he ought to make. But he need not know of these events as such, nor of *all* their effects. It does not matter for him

- *why* at the particular moment more screws of one size than of another are wanted,
- *why* paper bags are more readily available than canvas bags, or
- *why* skilled labor, or particular machine tools, have for the moment become more difficult to obtain.

All that is significant for him is *how much more or less* difficult to procure they have become compared with other things with which he is also concerned, or how much more or less urgently wanted are the alternative things he produces or uses. It is always a question of the relative importance of the particular things with which he is concerned, and the causes which alter their relative importance are of no interest to him beyond the effect on those concrete things of his own environment.

It is in this connection that what I have called the "economic calculus" proper helps us, at least by analogy, to see how this problem can be solved, and in fact is being solved, by the price system. Even the single controlling mind, in possession of all the data for some small, self-contained economic system, would not—every time some small adjustment in the allocation of resources had to be made—go explicitly through all the relations between ends and means which might possibly be affected. It is indeed the great contribution of the pure logic of choice that it has demonstrated conclusively that even such a single mind could solve this kind of problem only by constructing and constantly using rates of equivalence (or "values," or "marginal rates of substitution"), *i.e.,* by attaching to each kind of scarce resource a numerical index which cannot be derived from any property possessed by that particular thing, but which reflects, or in which is condensed, its significance in view of the whole means-end structure. In any small change he will have to consider only these quantitative indices (or "values") in which all the relevant information is concentrated; and, by adjusting the quantities one by one, he can appropriately rearrange his dispositions without having to solve the whole puzzle *ab initio* or without needing at any stage to survey it at once in all its ramifications.

Fundamentally, in a system in which the knowledge of the relevant facts is dispersed among many people, prices can act to coördinate the separate actions of different people in the same way as subjective values help the individual to coördinate the parts of his plan. It is worth contemplating for a moment a very simple and commonplace instance of the action of the price system to see what precisely it accomplishes. Assume that somewhere in the world a new opportunity for the use of some raw material, say, tin, has arisen, or that one of the sources of supply of tin has been eliminated. It does not matter for our purpose—and it is very significant that it does not matter—which of these two causes has made tin more scarce. All that the users of tin need to know is that some of the tin they used to consume is now more profitably employed elsewhere and that, in consequence, they must economize tin. There is no need for the great majority of them even to know where the more urgent need has arisen, or in favor of what other needs they ought to husband the supply. If only some of them know directly of the new demand, and switch resources over to it, and if the people who are aware of the new gap thus created in turn fill it from still other sources, the effect will rapidly spread throughout the whole economic system and influence not only all the uses of tin but also those of its substitutes and the substitutes of these substitutes, the supply of all the things made of tin, and their substitutes, and so on; and all his without the great majority of those instrumental in bringing about these substitutions knowing anything at all about the original cause of these changes. The whole acts as one market, not because any of its members survey the whole field, but because their limited individual fields of vision sufficiently overlap so that through many intermediaries the relevant information is communicated to all. The mere fact that there is one price for any commodity—or rather that local prices are connected in a manner determined by the cost of transport, etc.—brings about the solution which (it is just conceptually possible) might have been arrived at by one single mind possessing all the information which is in fact dispersed among all the people involved in the process.

VI

We must look at the price system as such a mechanism for communicating information if we want to understand its real function—a function which, of course, it fulfils less perfectly as prices grow more rigid. (Even when quoted prices have become quite rigid, however, the forces which would operate through changes in price still operate to a considerable extent through changes in the other terms of the contract.) The most significant fact about this system is the economy of knowledge with which it operates, or how little the individual participants need to know in order to be able to take the right action. In abbreviated form, by a kind of symbol, only the most essential information is passed on and passed on only to those concerned. It is more than a metaphor to describe the price system as a kind of machinery for registering change, or a system of telecommunications which enables individual producers to watch merely the movement of a few pointers, as an engineer might watch the hands of a few dials, in order to adjust their activities to changes of which they may never know more than is reflected in the price movement.

Of course, these adjustments are probably never "perfect" in the sense in which the economist conceives of them in his equilibrium analysis. But I fear that our theoretical habits of approaching the problem with the assumption of more or less perfect knowledge on the part of almost everyone has made us somewhat blind to the true function of the price mechanism and led us to apply rather misleading standards in judging its efficiency. The marvel is that in a case like that of a scarcity of one raw material, without an order being issued, without more than perhaps a handful of people knowing the cause, tens of thousands of people whose identity could not be ascertained by months of investigation, are made to use the material or its products more sparingly; *i.e.,* they move in the right direction. This is enough of a marvel even if, in a constantly changing world, not all will hit it off so perfectly that their profit rates will always be maintained at the same constant or "normal" level.

I have deliberately used the word "marvel" to shock the reader out of the complacency with which we often take the working of this mechanism for granted. I am convinced that if it were the result of deliberate human design, and if the people guided by the price changes understood that their decisions have significance far beyond their immediate aim, this mechanism would have been acclaimed as one of the greatest triumphs of the human mind. Its misfortune is the double one that it is not the product of human design and that the people guided by it usually do not know why they are made to do what they do. But those who clamor for "conscious direction"—and who cannot believe that anything which has evolved without design (and even without our understanding it) should solve problems which we should not be able to solve consciously—should remember this: The problem is precisely how to extend the span of out utilization of resources beyond the span of the control of any one mind; and therefore, how to dispense with the need of conscious control, and how to provide inducements which will make the individuals do the desirable things without anyone having to tell them what to do.

The problem which we meet here is by no means peculiar to economics but arises in connection with nearly all truly social phenomena, with language and with most of our cultural inheritance, and constitutes really the central theoretical problem of all social science. As Alfred Whitehead has said in another connection, "It is a profoundly erroneous truism, repeated by all copy-books and by eminent people when they are making speeches, that we should cultivate the habit of thinking what we are doing. The precise opposite is the case. Civilization advances by extending the number of important operations which we can perform without thinking about them." This is of profound significance in the social field. We make constant use of formulas, symbols, and rules whose meaning we do not understand and through the use of which we avail ourselves of the assistance of knowledge which individually we do not possess. We have developed these practices and institutions by building upon habits and institutions which have proved successful in their own sphere and which have in turn become the foundation of the civilization we have built up.

The price system is just one of those formations which man has learned to use (though he is still very far from having learned to make the best use of it) after he had stumbled upon it without understanding it. Through it not only a division of labor but also a coördinated utilization of resources based on an equally divided knowledge has become possible. The people who like to deride any suggestion that this may be so usually distort the argument by insinuating that it asserts that by some miracle just that sort of system has spontaneously grown up which is best suited to modern civilization. It is the other way round: man has been able to develop that division of labor on which our civilization is based because he happened to stumble upon a method which made it possible. Had he not done so, he might still have developed some other, altogether different, type of civilization, something like the "state" of the termite ants, or some other altogether unimaginable type. All that we can say is that nobody has yet succeeded in designing an alternative system in which certain features of the existing one can be preserved which are dear even to those who most violently assail it—such as

particularly the extent to which the individual can choose his pursuits and consequently freely use his own knowledge and skill.

VII

It is in many ways fortunate that the dispute about the indispensability of the price system for any rational calculation in a complex society is now no longer conducted entirely between camps holding different political views. The thesis that without the price system we could not preserve a society based on such extensive division of labor as ours was greeted with a howl of derision when it was first advanced by von Mises twenty-five years ago. Today the difficulties which some still find in accepting it are no longer mainly political, and this makes for an atmosphere much more conducive to reasonable discussion. When we find Leon Trotsky arguing that "economic accounting is unthinkable without market relations"; when Professor Oscar Lange promises Professor von Mises a statue in the marble halls of the future Central Planning Board; and when Professor Abba P. Lerner rediscovers Adam Smith and emphasizes that the essential utility of the price system consists in inducing the individual, while seeking his own interest, to do what is in the general interest, the differences can indeed no longer be ascribed to political prejudice. The remaining dissent seems clearly to be due to purely intellectual, and more particularly methodological, differences.

A recent statement by Professor Joseph Schumpeter in his *Capitalism, Socialism, and Democracy* provides a clear illustration of one of the methodological differences which I have in mind. Its author is pre-eminent among those economists who approach economic phenomena in the light of a certain branch of positivism. To him these phenomena accordingly appear as objectively given quantities of commodities impinging directly upon each other, almost, it would seem, without any intervention of human minds. Only against this background can I account for the following (to me startling) pronouncement. Professor Schumpeter argues that the possibility of a rational calculation in the absence of markets for the factors of production follows for the theorist "from the elementary proposition that consumers in evaluating ('demanding') consumers' goods *ipso facto* also evaluate the means of production which enter into the production of these goods."[1]
[1]

Taken literally, this statement is simply untrue. The consumers do nothing of the kind. What Professor Schumpeter's *"ipso facto"* presumably means is that the valuation of the factors of production is implied in, or follows necessarily from, the valuation of consumers' goods. But this, too, is not correct. Implication is a logical relationship which can be meaningfully asserted only of propositions simultaneously present to one and the same mind. It is evident, however, that the values of the factors of production do not depend solely on the valuation of the consumers' goods but also on the conditions of supply of the various factors of production. Only to a mind to which all these facts were simultaneously known would the answer necessarily follow from the facts given to it. The practical problem, however, arises precisely because these facts are never so given to a single mind, and because, in consequence, it is necessary that in the solution of the problem knowledge should be used that is dispersed among many people.

The problem is thus in no way solved if we can show that all the facts, *if* they were known to a single mind (as we hypothetically assume them to be given to the observing economist), would uniquely determine the solution; instead we must show how a solution is produced by the interactions of people each of whom possesses only partial knowledge. To assume all the knowledge to be given to a single mind in the same manner in which we assume it to be given to us as the explaining economists is to assume the problem away and to disregard everything that is important and significant in the real world.

That an economist of Professor Schumpeter's standing should thus have fallen into a trap which the ambiguity of the term "datum" sets to the unwary can hardly be explained as a simple error. It suggests rather that there is something fundamentally wrong with an approach which habitually disregards an essential part of the phenomena with which we have to deal: the unavoidable imperfection of man's knowledge and the consequent need for a process by which knowledge is constantly communicated and acquired. Any approach, such as that of much of mathematical economics with its simultaneous equations, which in effect starts from the assumption that people's *knowledge* corresponds with the objective *facts* of the situation, systematically leaves out what is our main task to explain. I am far from denying that in our system equilibrium analysis has a useful function to perform. But when it comes to the point where it misleads some of our leading thinkers into believing that the situation which it describes has direct relevance to the solution of practical problems, it is high time that we remember that it does not deal with the social process at all and that it is no more than a useful preliminary to the study of the main problem.

Citation and Use

The reading was taken from the following work.

Friedrich August von Hayek, "The Use of Knowledge in Society," American Economic Review, XXXV, No. 4; September, 1945, pp. 519–30. 7/26/2019. https://oll.libertyfund.org/titles/92

Notes

1. J. Schumpeter, Capitalism, Socialism, and Democracy (New York; Harper, 1942), p. 175. Professor Schumpeter is, I believe, also the original author of the myth that Pareto and Barone have "solved" the problem of socialist calculation. What they, and many others, did was merely to state the conditions which a rational allocation of resources would have to satisfy and to point out that these were essentially the same as the conditions of equilibrium of a competitive market. This is something altogether different from knowing how the allocation of resources satisfying these conditions can be found in practice. Pareto himself (from whom Barone has taken practically everything he has to say), far from claiming to have solved the practical problem, in fact explicitly denies that it can be solved without the help of the market. See his Manuel d'économie pure (2d ed., 1927), pp. 233-34. The relevant passage is quoted in an English translation at the beginning of my article on "Socialist Calculation: The Competitive 'Solution,' " in Economica, New Series, Vol. VIII, No. 26 (May, 1940), p. 125.

SOCIAL CONTRACTS OF EXPLOITATION

Charles Mills

I will start with an overview of the Racial Contract, highlighting its differences from, as well as its similarities to, the classical and contemporary social contract. The Racial Contract is political, moral, and epistemological; the Racial Contract is real; and economically, in determining who gets what, the Racial Contract is an exploitation contract.

The Racial Contract is political, moral, and epistemological.

The "social contract" is actually several contracts in one. Contemporary contractarians usually distinguish, to begin with, between the political contract and the moral contract, before going on to make (subsidiary) distinctions within both. I contend, however, that the orthodox social contract also tacitly presupposes an "epistemological" contract, and that for the Racial Contract it is crucial to make this explicit.

The political contract is an account of the origins of government and our political obligations to it. The subsidiary distinction sometimes made in the political contract is between the contract to establish society (thereby taking "natural," presocial individuals out of the state of nature and reconstructing and constituting them as members of a collective body) and the contract to establish the state (thereby transferring outright or delegating in a relationship of trust the rights and powers we have in the state of nature to a sovereign governing entity).[1] The moral contract, on the other hand, is the foundation of the moral code established for the society, by which the citizens are supposed to regulate their behavior. The subsidiary distinction here is between two interpretations (to be discussed) of the relationship between the moral contract and state-of-nature morality. In modern versions of the contract, most notably Rawls's of course, the political contract largely vanishes, modern anthropology having long superseded the naive social origin histories of the classic contractarians. The focus is then almost exclusively on the moral contract. This is not conceived of as an actual historical event that took place on leaving the state of nature. Rather, the state of nature survives only in the attenuated form of what Rawls calls the "original position," and the

"contract" is a purely hypothetical exercise (a thought experiment) in establishing what a just "basic structure" would be, with a schedule of rights, duties, and liberties that shapes citizens' moral psychology, conceptions of the right, notions of self-respect, etc.[2]

Now the Racial Contract—and the "Racial Contract" as a theory, that is, the distanced, critical examination of the Racial Contract—follows the classical model in being both sociopolitical and moral. It explains how society was created or crucially transformed, how the individuals in that society were reconstituted, how the state was established, and how a particular moral code and a certain moral psychology were brought into existence. (As I have emphasized, the "Racial Contract" seeks to account for the way things are and how they came to be that way—the descriptive—as well as the way they should be—the normative—since indeed one of its complaints about white political philosophy is precisely its otherworldiness, its ignoring of basic political realities.) But the Racial Contract, as we will see, is also epistemological, prescribing norms for cognition to which its signatories must adhere. A preliminary characterization would run something like this:

The Racial Contract is that set of formal or informal agreements or meta-agreements (higher-level contracts about contracts, which set the limits of the contracts' validity) between the members of one subset of humans, henceforth designated by (shifting) "racial" (phenotypical/genealogical/cultural) criteria C1, C2, C3 . . . as "white," and coextensive (making due allowance for gender differentiation) with the class of full persons, to categorize the remaining subset of humans as "nonwhite" and of a different and inferior moral status, subpersons, so that they have a subordinate civil standing in the white or white-ruled polities the whites either already inhabit or establish or in transactions as aliens with these polities, and the moral and juridical rules normally regulating the behavior of whites in their dealings with one another either do not apply at all in dealings with nonwhites or apply only in a qualified form (depending in part on changing historical circumstances and what particular variety of nonwhite is involved), but in any case the general purpose of the Contract is always the differential privileging of the whites as a group with respect to the nonwhites as a group, the exploitation of their bodies, land, and resources, and the denial of equal socioeconomic opportunities to them. All whites are beneficiaries of the Contract, though some whites are not signatories to it.[3]

It will be obvious, therefore, that the Racial Contract is not a contract to which the nonwhite subset of humans can be a genuinely consenting party (though, depending again on the circumstances, it may sometimes be politic to pretend that this is the case). Rather, it is a contract between those categorized as white over the nonwhites, who are thus the objects rather than the subjects of the agreement.

The logic of the classic social contract, political, moral, and epistemological, then undergoes a corresponding refraction, with shifts, accordingly, in the key terms and principles.

Politically, the contract to establish society and the government, thereby transforming abstract raceless "men" from denizens of the state of nature into social creatures who are politically obligated to a neutral state, becomes the founding of a racial polity, whether white settler states (where preexisting populations already are or can be made sparse) or what are sometimes called "sojourner colonies," the establishment of a white presence and colonial rule over existing societies (which are somewhat more populous, or whose inhabitants are more resistant to being made sparse). In addition, the colonizing mother country is also changed by its relation to these new polities, so that its own citizens are altered.

In the social contract, the crucial human metamorphosis is from "natural" man to "civil/political" man, from the resident of the state of nature to the citizen of the created society. This change can be more or less extreme, depending on the theorist involved. For Rousseau it is a dramatic transformation, by which animal like creatures of appetite and instinct become citizens bound by justice and self-prescribed laws. For Hobbes it is a somewhat more laid-back affair by which people who look out primarily for themselves learn to constrain their self-interest for their own good.[4] But in all cases the original "state of nature" supposedly indicates the condition of all men, and the social metamorphosis affects them all in the same way.

In the Racial Contract, by contrast, the crucial metamorphosis is the preliminary conceptual partitioning and corresponding transformation of human populations into "white" and "nonwhite" men. The role played by the "state of nature" then becomes radically different. In the white settler state, its role is not primarily to demarcate the (temporarily) pre-political state of "all" men (who are really white men), but rather the permanently pre-political state or, perhaps better, nonpolitical state (insofar as "pre-" suggests eventual internal movement toward) of nonwhite men. The establishment of society thus implies the denial that a society already existed; the creation of society requires the intervention of white men, who are thereby

positioned as already sociopolitical beings. White men who are (definitionally) already part of society encounter nonwhites who are not, who are "savage" residents of a state of nature characterized in terms of wilderness, jungle, wasteland. These the white men bring partially into society as subordinate citizens or exclude on reservations or deny the existence of or exterminate. In the colonial case, admittedly preexisting but (for one reason or another) deficient societies (decadent, stagnant, corrupt) are taken over and run for the "benefit" of the nonwhite natives, who are deemed childlike, incapable of self-rule and handling their own affairs, and thus appropriately wards of the state. Here the natives are usually characterized as "barbarians" rather than "savages," their state of nature being somewhat farther away (though not, of course, as remote and lost in the past—if it ever existed in the first place—as the Europeans' state of nature). But in times of crisis the conceptual distance between the two, barbarian and savage, tends to shrink or collapse, for this technical distinction within the nonwhite population is vastly less important than the central distinction between whites and nonwhites.

In both cases, then, though in different ways, the Racial Contract establishes a racial polity, a racial state, and a racial juridical system, where the status of whites and nonwhites is clearly demarcated, whether by law or custom. And the purpose of this state, by contrast with the neutral state of classic contractarianism, is, inter alia, specifically to maintain and reproduce this racial order, securing the privileges and advantages of the full white citizens and maintaining the subordination of nonwhites. Correspondingly, the "consent" expected of the white citizens is in part conceptualized as a consent, whether explicit or tacit, to the racial order, to white supremacy, what could be called Whiteness. To the extent that those phenotypically/genealogically/culturally categorized as white fail to live up to the civic and political responsibilities of Whiteness, they are in dereliction of their duties as citizens. From the inception, then, race is in no way an "afterthought," a "deviation" from ostensibly raceless Western ideals, but rather a central shaping constituent of those ideals.

In the social contract tradition, there are two main possible relations between the moral contract and the political contract.

1. On the first view, the moral contract represents preexisting objectivist morality (theological or secular) and thus constrains the terms of the political contract. This is the view found in Locke and Kant. In other words, there is an objective moral code in the state of nature itself, even if there are no policemen and judges to enforce it. So any society, government, and legal system that are established should be based on that moral code.

2. On the second view, the political contract creates morality as a conventionalist set of rules. So there is no independent objective moral criterion for judging one moral code to be superior to another or for indicting a society's established morality as unjust. On this conception, which is famously attributed to Hobbes, morality is just a set of rules for expediting the rational

pursuit and coordination of our own interests without conflict with those other people who are doing the same thing.[5]

The Racial Contract can accommodate both versions, but as it is the former version (the contract as described in Locke and Kant) rather than the latter version (the contract as described in Hobbes) which represents the mainstream of the contract tradition, I focus on that one.[6] Here, the good polity is taken to rest on a preexisting moral foundation. Obviously, this is a far more attractive conception of a political system than Hobbes's view. The ideal of an objectively just polis to which we should aspire in our political activism goes back in the Western tradition all the way to Plato. In the medieval Christian worldview which continued to influence contractarianism well into the modern period, there is a "natural law" immanent in the structure of the universe which is supposed to direct us morally in striving for this ideal.[7] (For the later, secular versions of contractarianism, the idea would simply be that people have rights and duties even in the state of nature because of their nature as human beings.) So it is wrong to steal, rape, kill in the state of nature even if there are no human laws written down saying it is wrong. These moral principles must constrain the human laws that are made and the civil rights that are assigned once the polity is established. In part, then, the political contract simply codifies a morality that already exists, writing it down and filling in the details, so we don't have to rely on a divinely implanted moral sense, or conscience, whose perceptions may on occasion be distorted by self-interest. What is right and wrong, just and unjust, in society will largely be determined by what is right and wrong, just and unjust, in the state of nature.

The character of this objective moral foundation is therefore obviously crucial. For the mainstream of the contractarian tradition, it is the freedom and equality of all men in the state of nature. As Locke writes in the Second Treatise, "To understand Political Power right, and derive it from its Original, we must consider what State all Men are naturally in, and that is, a State of perfect Freedom to order their Actions.... A State also of Equality, wherein all the Power and Jurisdiction is reciprocal, no one having more than another."[8] For Kant, similarly, it is our equal moral personhood.[9] Contractarianism is (supposedly) committed to moral egalitarianism, the moral equality of all men, the notion that the interests of all men matter equally and all men must have equal rights. Thus, contractarianism is also committed to a principled and foundational opposition to the traditionalist hierarchical ideology of the old feudal order, the ideology of inherent ascribed status and natural subordination. It is this language of equality which echoes in the American and French Revolutions, the Declaration of Independence, and the Declaration of the Rights of Man. And it is this moral egalitarianism that must be retained in the allocation of rights and liberties in civil society. When in a modern Western society people insist on their rights and freedoms and express their outrage at not being treated equally, it is to these classic ideas that, whether they know it or not, they are appealing.

But as we will see in greater detail later on, the color-coded morality of the Racial Contract restricts the possession of this natural freedom and equality to white men. By virtue of their complete nonrecognition, or at best inadequate, myopic recognition, of the duties of natural law, nonwhites are appropriately relegated to a lower rung on the moral ladder (the Great Chain of Being).[10] They are designated as born unfree and unequal. A partitioned social ontology is therefore created, a universe divided between persons and racial subpersons, Untermenschen, who may variously be black, red, brown, yellow—slaves, aborigines, colonial populations—but who are collectively appropriately known as "subject races." And these subpersons—niggers, injuns, chinks, wogs, greasers, blackfellows, kaffirs, coolies, abos, dinks, googoos, gooks—are biologically destined never to penetrate the normative rights ceiling established for them below white persons. Henceforth, then, whether openly admitted or not, it is taken for granted that the grand ethical theories propounded in the development of Western moral and political thought are of restricted scope, explicitly or implicitly intended by their proponents to be restricted to persons, whites. The terms of the Racial Contract set the parameters for white morality as a whole, so that competing Lockean and Kantian contractarian theories of natural rights and duties, or later anticontractarian theories such as nineteenth-century utilitarianism, are all limited by its stipulations.

Finally, the Racial Contract requires its own peculiar moral and empirical epistemology, its norms and procedures for determining what counts as moral and factual knowledge of the world. In the standard accounts of contractarianism it is not usual to speak of there being an "epistemological" contract, but there is an epistemology associated with contractarianism, in the form of natural law. This provides us with a moral compass, whether in the traditional version of Locke—the light of reason implanted in us by God so we can discern objective right and wrong—or in the revisionist version of Hobbes—the ability to assess the objectively optimal prudential course of action and what it requires of us for self-interested cooperation with others. So through our natural faculties we come to know reality in both its factual and valuational aspects, the way things objectively are and what is objectively good or bad about them. I suggest we can think of this as an idealized consensus about cognitive norms and, in this respect, an agreement or "contract" of sorts. There is an understanding about what counts as a correct, objective interpretation of the world, and for agreeing to this view, one is ("contractually") granted full cognitive standing in the polity, the official epistemic community.[11]

But for the Racial Contract things are necessarily more complicated. The requirements of "objective" cognition, factual and moral, in a racial polity are in a sense more demanding in that officially sanctioned reality is divergent from actual reality. So here, it could be said, one has an agreement to misinterpret the world. One has to learn to see the world wrongly, but with the assurance that this set of mistaken perceptions will be validated by white epistemic authority, whether religious or secular.

Thus in effect, on matters related to race, the Racial Contract prescribes for its signatories an inverted epistemology, an epistemology of ignorance, a particular pattern of localized and global cognitive dysfunctions (which are psychologically and socially functional), producing the ironic outcome that whites will in general be unable to understand the world they themselves have made. Part of what it means to be constructed as "white" (the metamorphosis of the sociopolitical contract), part of what it requires to achieve Whiteness, successfully to become a white person (one imagines a ceremony with certificates attending the successful rite of passage: "Congratulations, you're now an official white person!"), is a cognitive model that precludes self-transparency and genuine understanding of social realities. To a significant extent, then, white signatories will live in an invented delusional world, a racial fantasyland, a "consensual hallucination," to quote William Gibson's famous characterization of cyberspace, though this particular hallucination is located in real space.[12] There will be white mythologies, invented Orients, invented Africas, invented Americas, with a correspondingly fabricated population, countries that never were, inhabited by people who never were—Calibans and Tontos, Man Fridays and Sambos—but who attain a virtual reality through their existence in travelers' tales, folk myth, popular and highbrow fiction, colonial reports, scholarly theory, Hollywood cinema, living in the white imagination and determinedly imposed on their alarmed real-life counterparts.[13] One could say then, as a general rule, that white misunderstanding, misrepresentation, evasion, and self-deception on matters related to race are among the most pervasive mental phenomena of the past few hundred years, a cognitive and moral economy psychically required for conquest, colonization, and enslavement. And these phenomena are in no way accidental, but prescribed by the terms of the Racial Contract, which requires a certain schedule of structured blindnesses and opacities in order to establish and maintain the white polity.

The Racial Contract is a historical actuality.

The social contract in its modern version has long since given up any pretensions to be able to explain the historical origins of society and the state. Whereas the classic contractarians were engaged in a project both descriptive and prescriptive, the modern Rawls-inspired contract is purely a prescriptive thought experiment. And even Pateman's Sexual Contract, though its focus is the real rather than the ideal, is not meant as a literal account of what men in 4004 B.C. decided to do on the plains of Mesopotamia. Whatever accounts for what Frederick Engels once called "the world historical defeat of the female sex"[14] —whether the development of an economic surplus, as he theorized, or the male discovery of the capacity to rape and the female disadvantage of being the childbearing half of the species, as radical feminists have argued—it is clearly lost in antiquity.

By contrast, ironically, the Racial Contract, never so far as I know explored as such, has the best claim to being an actual historical fact. Far from being lost in the mists of the ages, it is clearly historically locatable in the series of events marking the creation of the modern world by European colonialism and the voyages of "discovery" now increasingly and more appropriately called expeditions of conquest. The Columbian quincentenary a few years ago, with its accompanying debates, polemics, controversies, counterdemonstrations, and outpourings of revisionist literature, confronted many whites with the uncomfortable fact, hardly discussed in mainstream moral and political theory, that we live in a world which has been foundationally shaped for the past five hundred years by the realities of European domination and the gradual consolidation of global white supremacy. Thus not only is the Racial Contract "real," but—whereas the social contract is characteristically taken to be establishing the legitimacy of the nation-state, and codifying morality and law within its boundaries—the Racial Contract is global, involving a tectonic shift of the ethicojuridical basis of the planet as a whole, the division of the world, as Jean-Paul Sartre put it long ago, between "men" and "natives."[15]

Europeans thereby emerge as "the lords of human kind," the "lords of all the world," with the increasing power to determine the standing of the non-Europeans who are their subjects.[16] Although no single act literally corresponds to the drawing up and signing of a contract, there is a series of acts—papal bulls and other theological pronouncements; European discussions about colonialism, "discovery," and international law; pacts, treaties, and legal decisions; academic and popular debates about the humanity of nonwhites; the establishment of formalized legal structures of differential treatment; and the routinization of informal illegal or quasi-legal practices effectively sanctioned by the complicity of silence and government failure to intervene and punish perpetrators—which collectively can be seen, not just metaphorically but close to literally, as its conceptual, juridical, and normative equivalent.

Anthony Pagden suggests that a division of the European empires into their main temporal periods should recognize "two distinct, but interdependent histories": the colonization of the Americas, 1492 to the 1830s, and the occupation of Asia, Africa, and the Pacific, 1730s to the period after World War II.[17] In the first period, it was, to begin with, the nature and moral status of the Native Americans that primarily had to be determined, and then that of the imported African slaves whose labor was required to build this "New World." In the second period, culminating in formal European colonial rule over most of the world by the early twentieth century, it was the character of colonial peoples that became crucial. But in all cases "race" is the common conceptual denominator that gradually came to signify the respective global statuses of superiority and inferiority, privilege and subordination. There is an opposition of us against them with multiple overlapping dimensions: Europeans versus non-Europeans (geography), civilized versus wild/savage/barbarians (culture), Christians versus heathens (religion). But they all eventually coalesced into the basic opposition of white versus nonwhite.

A Lumbee Indian legal scholar, Robert Williams, has traced

the evolution of the Western legal position on the rights of native peoples from its medieval antecedents to the beginnings of the modern period, showing how it is consistently based on the assumption of "the rightness and necessity of subjugating and assimilating other peoples to [the European] worldview."[18] Initially the intellectual framework was a theological one, with normative inclusion and exclusion manifesting itself as the demarcation between Christians and heathens. The pope's powers over the **Societas Christiana**, the universal Christian commonwealth, were seen as "extending not only over all Christians within the universal commonwealth, but over unregenerated heathens and infidels as well," and this policy would subsequently underwrite not merely the Crusades against Islam but the later voyages to the Americas. Sometimes papal pronouncements did grant rights and rationality to nonbelievers. As a result of dealing with the Mongols in the thirteenth century, for example, Pope Innocent IV" conceded that infidels and heathens possessed the natural law right to elect their own secular leaders," and Pope Paul III's famous **Sublimis Deus** (1537) stated that Native Americans were rational beings, not to be treated as "dumb brutes created for our service" but "as truly men . . . capable of understanding the Catholic faith."[19] But as Williams points out, the latter qualification was always crucial. A Eurocentrically normed conception of rationality made it coextensive with acceptance of the Christian message, so that rejection was proof of bestial irrationality.

Even more remarkably, in the case of Native Americans this acceptance was to be signaled by their agreement to the **Requerimiento**, a long statement read aloud to them in, of course, a language they did not understand, failing which assent a just war could lawfully be waged against them.[20] One author writes:

> The requerimiento is the prototypical example of text justifying conquest. Informing the Indians that their lands were entrusted by Christ to the pope and thence to the kings of Spain, the document offers freedom from slavery for tho e Indians who accept Spanish rule. Even though it was entirely incomprehensible to a non-Spanish speaker, reading the document provided sufficient justification for dispossession of land and immediate enslavement of the indigenous people. [Bartolomé de] Las Casas's famous comment on the requerimiento was that one does not know "whether to laugh or cry at the absurdity of it." . . . While appearing to respect "rights" the requerimiento, in fact, takes them away.[21]

In effect, then, the Catholic Church's declarations either formally legitimated conquest or could be easily circumvented where a weak prima facie moral barrier was erected.

The growth of the Enlightenment and the rise of secularism did not challenge this strategic dichotomization (Christian/infidel) so much as translate it into other forms. Philip Curtin refers to the characteristic "exceptionalism in European thought about the non-West," "a conception of the world largely based on self-identification—and identification of 'the other people.'"[22] Similarly, Pierre van den Berghe describes the "Enlightenment dichotomization" of the normative theories of the period.[23] "Race" gradually became the formal marker of this differentiated status, replacing the religious divide (whose disadvantage, after all, was that it could always be overcome through conversion). Thus a category crystallized over time in European thought to represent entities who are humanoid but not fully human ("savages," "barbarians") and who are identified as such by being members of the general set of nonwhite races. Influenced by the ancient Roman distinction between the civilized within and the barbarians outside the empire, the distinction between full and question-mark humans, Europeans set up a two-tiered moral code with one set of rules for whites and another for nonwhites.[24]

Types of Contracts that makeup the Racial Contract

Correspondingly, various moral and legal doctrines were propounded which can be seen as specific manifestations and instantiations, appropriately adjusted to circumstances, of the overarching Racial Contract. These were specific subsidiary contracts designed for different modes of exploiting the resources and peoples of the rest of the world for Europe:

1. the expropriation contract,
2. the slavery contract,
3. the colonial contract.

The Expropriation Contract

The **"Doctrine of Discovery,"** for example, what Williams identifies as the "paradigmatic tenet informing and determining contemporary European legal discourse respecting relations with Western tribal societies," was central to the expropriation contract.[25] The American Justice Joseph Story glossed it as granting Europeans

> an absolute dominion over the whole territories afterwards occupied by them, not in virtue of any conquest of, or cession by, the Indian natives, but as a right acquired by discovery.... The title of the Indians was not treated as a right of property and dominion, but as a mere right of occupancy. As infidels, heathens, and savages, they were not allowed to possess the prerogatives belonging to absolute, sovereign, and independent nations. The territory over which they wandered, and which they used for their temporary and fugitive purposes, was, in respect to Christians, deemed as if it were inhabited only by brute animals.[26]

The Slavery Contract

Similarly, the slavery contract gave Europeans the right to enslave Native Americans and Africans at a time when slavery was dead or dying out in Europe, based on doctrines of the inherent inferiority of these peoples. A classic statement of the slavery contract is the **1857 Dred Scott v. Sanford** U.S. Supreme Court decision of Chief Justice Roger Taney, which stated that blacks had for more than a century before been regarded as beings of an inferior order, and altogether unfit to associate with the white race, either in social or political relations; and so far inferior, that they had no rights which the white man was bound to respect; and that the negro might justly and lawfully be reduced to slavery for his benefit.... This opinion was at that time fixed and universal in the civilized portion of the white race. It was regarded as an axiom in morals as well as in politics, which no one thought of disputing, or supposed to be open to dispute.[27]

The Colonial Contract

Finally, there is the colonial contract, which legitimated European rule over the nations in Asia, Africa, and the Pacific. Consider, for instance, this wonderful example, almost literally "contractarian" in character, from the French imperial theorist Jules Harmand (1845–1921), who devised the notion of association:

> Expansion by conquest, however necessary, seems especially unjust and disturbing to the conscience of democracies.... But to transpose democratic institutions into such a setting is aberrant nonsense. The subject people are not and cannot become citizens in the democratic sense of the term.... It is necessary, then, to accept as a principle and point of departure the fact that there is a hierarchy of races and civilizations, and that we belong to the superior race and civilization.... The basic legitimation of conquest over native peoples is the conviction of our superiority, not merely our mechanical, economic, and military superiority, but our moral superiority. Our dignity rests on that quality, and it underlies our right to direct the rest of humanity.

What is therefore necessary is a "'**Contract' of Association**":

> Without falling into Rousseauan reveries, it is worth noting that association implies a contract, and this idea, though nothing more than an illustration, is more appropriately applied to the coexistence of two profoundly different societies thrown sharply and artificially into contact than it is to the single society formed by natural processes which Rousseau envisaged. This is how the terms of this implicit agreement can be conceived. The European conqueror brings order, foresight, and security to a human society which, though ardently aspiring for these fundamental values without which no community can make progress, still lacks the aptitude to achieve them from within itself.... With these mental and material instruments, which it lacked and now receives, it gains the idea and ambition for a better existence, and the means of achieving it. We will obey you, say the subjects, if you begin by proving yourself worthy. We will obey you if you can succeed in convincing us of the superiority of that civilization of which you talk so much.[28]

Indian laws, slave codes, and colonial native acts formally codified the subordinate status of nonwhites and (ostensibly) regulated their treatment, creating a juridical space for nonEuropeans as a separate category of beings. So even if there was sometimes an attempt to prevent "abuses" (and these codes were honored far more often in the breach than the observance), the point is that "abuse" as a concept presupposes as a norm the legitimacy of the subordination. Slavery and colonialism are not conceived as wrong in their denial of autonomy to persons; what is wrong is the improper administration of these regimes.

It would be a fundamental error, then—a point to which I will return—to see racism as anomalous, a mysterious deviation from European Enlightenment humanism. Rather, it needs to be realized that, in keeping with the Roman precedent, European humanism usually meant that only Europeans were human. European moral and political theory, like European thought in general, developed within the framework of the Racial Contract and, as a rule, took it for granted. As Edward Said points out in Culture and Imperialism, we must not see culture as "antiseptically quarantined from its worldly affiliations." But this occupational blindness has in fact infected most "professional humanists" (and certainly most philosophers), so that "as a result [they are] unable to make the connection between the prolonged and sordid cruelty of practices such as slavery, colonialist and racial oppression, and imperial subjection on the one hand, and the poetry, fiction, philosophy of the society that engages in these practices on the other."[29] By the nineteenth century, conventional white opinion casually assumed the uncontroversial validity of a hierarchy of "higher" and "lower," "master" and "subject" races, for whom, it is obvious, different rules must apply.

The modern world was thus expressly created as a racially hierarchical polity, globally dominated by Europeans. A 1969 Foreign Affairs article worth rereading today reminds us that as late as the 1940s the world "was still by and large a Western white-dominated world. The long-established patterns of white power and nonwhite non-power were still the generally accepted order of things. All the accompanying assumptions and mythologies about race and color were still mostly taken for granted.... [W]hite supremacy was a generally assumed and accepted state of affairs in the United States as well as in Europe's empires."[30] But statements of such frankness are rare or nonexistent in mainstream white opinion today, which generally seeks to rewrite the past so as to deny or minimize the obvious fact of global white domination.

Yet the United States itself, of course, is a white settler state on territory expropriated from its aboriginal inhabitants through a combination of military force, disease, and a "century of dishonor" of broken treaties.[31] The expropriation involved literal genocide (a word now unfortunately devalued by hyperbolic overuse) of a kind that some recent revisionist historians have argued needs to be seen as comparable to the Third Reich's.[32] Washington, Father of the Nation, was, understandably, known somewhat differently to the Senecas as "Town Destroyer."[33] In the Declaration of

Independence, Jefferson characterized Native Americans as "merciless Indian Savages," and in the Constitution, blacks, of course, appear only obliquely, through the famous "60 percent solution." Thus, as Richard Drinnon concludes: "The Framers manifestly established a government under which non-Europeans were not men created equal—in the white polity . . . they were nonpeoples."[34]Though on a smaller scale and not always so ruthlessly (or, in the case of New Zealand, because of more successful indigenous resistance), what are standardly classified as the other white settler states—for example, Canada, Australia, New Zealand, Rhodesia, and South Africa—were all founded on similar policies: the extermination, displacement, and/or herding onto reservations of the aboriginal population. Pierre van den Berghe has coined the illuminating phrase "Herrenvolk democracies" to describe these polities, which captures perfectly the dichotomization of the Racial Contract.[35] Their subsequent evolution has been somewhat different, but defenders of South Africa's system of apartheid often argued that U.S. criticism was hypocritical in light of its own history of **Jim Crow**, especially since de facto segregation remains sufficiently entrenched that even today, forty years after Brown v. Board of Education, two American sociologists can title their study American Apartheid.[36] The racist record of preliberation Rhodesia (now Zimbabwe) and South Africa is well known; not so familiar may be the fact that the United States, Canada, and Australia all maintained "white" immigration policies until a few decades ago, and native peoples in all three countries suffer high poverty, infant mortality, and suicide rates.

Elsewhere, in Latin America, Asia, and Africa, large parts of the world were colonized, that is, formally brought under the rule of one or another of the European powers (or, later, the United States): the early Spanish and Portuguese empires in the Americas, the Philippines, and south Asia; the jealous competition from Britain, France, and Holland; the British conquest of India; the French expansion into Algeria and Indochina; the Dutch advance into Indonesia; the Opium Wars against China; the late nineteenth-century "**scramble for Africa**"; the U.S. war against Spain, seizure of Cuba, Puerto Rico, and the Philippines, and annexation of Hawaii.[37] The pace of change this century has been so dramatic that it is easy to forget that less than a hundred years ago, in 1914, "Europe held a grand total of roughly 85 percent of the earth as colonies, protectorates, dependencies, dominions, and commonwealths. No other associated set of colonies in history was as large, none so totally dominated, none so unequal in power to the Western metropolis."[38] One could say that the Racial Contract creates a transnational white polity, a virtual community of people linked by their citizenship in Europe at home and abroad (Europe proper, the colonial greater Europe, and the "fragments" of Euro-America, Euro-Australia, etc.), and constituted in opposition to their indigenous subjects. In most of Africa and Asia, where colonial rule ended only after World War II, rigid "color bars" maintained the separation between Europeans and indigenes. As European, as white, one knew oneself to be a member of the superior race, one's skin being one's passport: "Whatever a white man

did must in some grotesque fashion be 'civilized.'"[39] So though there were local variations in the Racial Contract, depending on circumstances and the particular mode of exploitation—for example, a bipolar racial system in the (Anglo) United States, as against a subtler color hierarchy in (Iberian) Latin America—it remains the case that the white tribe, as the global representative of civilization and modernity, is generally on top of the social pyramid.[40]

We live, then, in a world built on the Racial Contract. That we do is simultaneously quite obvious if you think about it (the dates and details of colonial conquest, the constitutions of these states and their exclusionary juridical mechanisms, the histories of official racist ideologies, the battles against slavery and colonialism, the formal and informal structures of discrimination, are all within recent historical memory and, of course, massively documented in other disciplines) and nonobvious, since most whites don't think about it or don't think about it as the outcome of a history of political oppression but rather as just "the way things are." ("You say we're all over the world because we conquered the world? Why would you put it that way?") In the **Treaty of Tordesillas** (1494) which divided the world between Spain and Portugal, the **Valladolid (Spain) Conference** (1550–1551) to decide whether Native Americans were really human, the later debates over African slavery and abolitionism, the Berlin Conference (1884–1885) to partition Africa, the various inter-European pacts, treaties, and informal arrangements on policing their colonies, the post-World War I discussions in Versailles after a war to make the world safe for democracy—we see (or should see) with complete clarity a world being governed by white people. So though there is also internal conflict—disagreements, battles, even world wars—the dominant movers and shapers will be Europeans at home and abroad, with non-Europeans lining up to fight under their respective banners, and the system of white domination itself rarely being challenged. (The exception, of course, is Japan, which escaped colonization, and so for most of the twentieth century has had a shifting and ambivalent relationship with the global white polity.) The legacy of this world is, of course, still with us today, in the economic, political, and cultural domination of the planet by Europeans and their descendants. The fact that this racial structure, clearly political in character, and the struggle against it, equally so, have not for the most part been deemed appropriate subject matter for mainstream Anglo-American political philosophy and the fact that the very concepts hegemonic in the discipline are refractory to an understanding of these realities, reveal at best, a disturbing provincialism and an ahistoricity profoundly at odds with the radically foundational questioning on which philosophy prides itself and, at worst, a complicity with the terms of the Racial Contract itself.

The Racial Contract is an exploitation contract that creates global European economic domination and national white racial privilege.

The classic social contract, as I have detailed, is primarily moral/political in nature. But it is also economic in the background sense that the point of leaving the state of nature is in part to secure a stable environment for the industrious appropriation of the world. (After all, one famous definition of politics is that it is about who gets what and why.) Thus even in Locke's moralized state of nature, where people generally do obey natural law, he is concerned about the safety of private property, indeed proclaiming that "the great and chief end therefore, of Mens uniting into Commonwealths, and putting themselves under Government, is the Preservation of their Property."[41] And in Hobbes's famously amoral and unsafe state of nature, we are told that "there is no place for Industry; because the fruit thereof is uncertain; and consequently no Culture of the Earth."[42] So part of the point of bringing society into existence, with its laws and enforcers of the law, is to protect what you have accumulated.

What, then, is the nature of the economic system of the new society? The general contract does not itself prescribe a particular model or particular schedule of property rights, requiring only that the "equality" in the prepolitical state be somehow preserved. This provision may be variously interpreted as a self-interested surrender to an absolutist Hobbesian government that itself determines property rights, or a Lockean insistence that private property accumulated in the moralized state of nature be respected by the constitutionalist government. Or more radical political theorists, such as socialists and feminists, might argue that state-of-nature equality actually mandates class or gender economic egalitarianism in society. So, different political interpretations of the initial moral egalitarianism can be advanced, but the general background idea is that the equality of human beings in the state of nature is somehow (whether as equality of opportunity or as equality of outcome) supposed to carry over into the economy of the created sociopolitical order, leading to a system of voluntary human intercourse and exchange in which exploitation is precluded.

By contrast, the economic dimension of the Racial Contract is the most salient, foreground rather than background, since the Racial Contract is calculatedly aimed at economic exploitation. The whole point of establishing a moral hierarchy and juridically partitioning the polity according to race is to secure and legitimate the privileging of those individuals designated as white/persons and the exploitation of those individuals designated as nonwhite/subpersons. There are other benefits accruing from the Racial Contract—far greater political influence, cultural hegemony, the psychic payoff that comes from knowing one is a member of the Herrenvolk (what W. E. B. Du Bois once called "the wages of whiteness")[43]—but the bottom line is material advantage. Globally, the Racial Contract creates Europe as the continent that dominates the world; locally, within Europe and the other continents, it designates Europeans as the privileged race.

The challenge of explaining what has been called "**the European miracle**"—the rise of Europe to global domination—has long exercised both academic and lay opinion.[44] How is it that a formerly peripheral region on the outskirts of the Asian land mass, at the far edge of the trade routes, remote from the great civilizations of Islam and the East, was able in a century or two to achieve global political and economic dominance? The explanations historically given by Europeans themselves have varied tremendously, from the straightforwardly racist and geographically determinist to the more subtly environmentalist and culturalist. But what they have all had in common, even those influenced by Marxism, is their tendency to depict this development as essentially autochthonous, their tendency to privilege some set of internal variables and correspondingly downplay or ignore altogether the role of colonial conquest and African slavery. Europe made it on its own, it is said, because of the peculiar characteristics of Europe and Europeans.

Thus whereas no reputable historian today would espouse the frankly biologistic theories of the past, which made Europeans (in both pre- and post-Darwinian accounts) inherently the most advanced race, as contrasted with the backward/less evolved races elsewhere, the thesis of European specialness and exceptionalism is still presupposed. It is still assumed that rationalism and science, innovativeness and inventiveness found their special home here, as against the intellectual stagnation and traditionalism of the rest of the world, so that Europe was therefore destined in advance to occupy the special position in global history it has. James Blaut calls this the theory, or "super-theory" (an umbrella covering many different versions: theological, cultural, biologistic, geographical, technological, etc.), of "Eurocentric diffusionism," according to which European progress is seen as "natural" and asymmetrically determinant of the fate of non-Europe.[45] Similarly, Sandra Harding, in her anthology on the "racial" economy of science, cites "the assumption that Europe functions autonomously from other parts of the world; that Europe is its own origin, final end, and agent; and that Europe and people of European descent in the Americas and elsewhere owe nothing to the rest of the world."[46]

Unsurprisingly, black and Third World theorists have traditionally dissented from this notion of happy divine or natural European dispensation. They have claimed, quite to the contrary, that there is a crucial causal connection between European advance and the unhappy fate of the rest of the world. One classic example of such scholarship from a half century ago was the Caribbean historian Eric Williams's *Capitalism and Slavery*, which argued that the profits from African slavery helped to make the industrial revolution possible, so that internalist accounts were fundamentally mistaken.[47] And in recent years, with decolonization, the rise of the New Left in the United States, and the entry of more alternative voices into the academy, this challenge has deepened and broadened. There are variations in the authors' positions—for example, Walter Rodney, Samir Amin, André Gunder Frank, Immanuel Wallerstein[48]—but the basic theme is that the exploitation of the empire (the bullion from the great gold and silver mines in Mexico and Peru, the profits from plantation slavery, the fortunes made by the colonial companies, the general social and economic stimulus provided by the opening up of the "New World") was to a greater or lesser extent crucial in enabling and then consolidating the takeoff of what had previously been an economic backwater. It was far from the case that Europe was specially destined to assume economic hegemony; there were a number of centers in Asia and Africa of a comparable level of development which could potentially have evolved in the same way. But the European ascent closed off this development path for others because it forcibly inserted them into a colonial network whose exploitative relations and extractive mechanisms prevented autonomous growth.

Overall, then, **colonialism "lies at the heart" of the rise of Europe.**[49] The economic unit of analysis needs to be Europe as a whole, since it is not always the case that the colonizing nations directly involved always benefited in the long term. Imperial Spain, for example, still feudal in character, suffered massive inflation from its bullion imports. But through trade and financial exchange, others launched on the capitalist path, such as Holland, profited. Internal national rivalries continued, of course, but this common identity based on the transcontinental exploitation of the non-European world would in many cases be politically crucial, generating a sense of Europe as a cosmopolitan entity engaged in a common enterprise, underwritten by race. As Victor Kiernan puts it, "All countries within the European orbit benefited however, as Adam Smith pointed out, from colonial contributions to a common stock of wealth, bitterly as they might wrangle over ownership of one territory or another.... [T]here was a sense in which all Europeans shared in a heightened sense of power engendered by the successes of any of them, as well as in the pool of material wealth . . . that the colonies produced."[50]

Today, correspondingly, though formal decolonization has taken place and in Africa and Asia black, brown, and yellow natives are in office, ruling independent nations, the global economy is essentially dominated by the former colonial powers, their offshoots (Euro-United States, Euro-Canada), and their international financial institutions, lending agencies, and corporations. (As previously observed, the notable exception, whose history confirms rather than challenges the rule, is Japan, which escaped colonization and, after the Meiji Restoration, successfully embarked on its own industrialization.) Thus one could say that the world i s essentially dominated by white capital. Global figures on income and property ownership are, of course, broken down nationally rather than racially, but if a transnational racial disaggregation were to be done, it would reveal that whites control a percentage of the world's wealth grossly disproportionate to their numbers. Since there is no reason to think that the chasm between First and Third Worlds (which largely coincides with this racial division) is going to be bridged—vide the abject failure of various United Nations plans from the "development decade" of the 1960s onward—it seems undeniable that for years to come, the planet will be white dominated. With the collapse of communism and the defeat of Third World attempts to seek alternative paths, the West reigns supreme, as celebrated in a London Financial Times headline: "The fall of the Soviet bloc has left the IMF and G7 to rule the world and create

a new imperial age."[51] Economic structures have been set in place, causal processes established, whose outcome is to pump wealth from one side of the globe to another, and which will continue to work largely independently of the ill will/good will, racist/antiracist feelings of particular individuals. This globally color-coded distribution of wealth and poverty has been produced by the Racial Contract and in turn reinforces adherence to it in its signatories and beneficiaries.

Moreover, it is not merely that Europe and the former white settler states are globally dominant but that within them, where there is a significant nonwhite presence (indigenous peoples, descendants of imported slaves, voluntary nonwhite immigration), whites continue to be privileged vis-à-vis nonwhites. The old structures of formal, de jure exclusion have largely been dismantled, the old explicitly biologistic ideologies largely abandoned[52]—the Racial Contract, as will be discussed later, is continually being rewritten—but opportunities for nonwhites, though they have expanded, remain below those for whites. The claim is not, of course, that all whites are better off than all nonwhites, but that, as a statistical generalization, the objective life chances of whites are significantly better.

As an example, consider the United States. A series of books has recently documented the decline of the integrationist hopes raised by the 1960s and the growing intransigence and hostility of whites who think they have "done enough," despite the fact that the country continues to be massively segregated, median black family incomes have begun falling by comparison to white family incomes after some earlier closing of the gap, the so-called "black underclass" has basically been written off, and reparations for slavery and post-Emancipation discrimination have never been paid, or, indeed, even seriously considered.[53] Recent work on racial inequality by Melvin Oliver and Thomas Shapiro suggests that wealth is more important than income in determining the likelihood of future racial equalization, since it has a cumulative effect that is passed down through intergenerational transfer, affecting life chances and opportunities for one's children. Whereas in 1988 black households earned sixty-two cents for every dollar earned by white households, the comparative differential with regard to wealth is much greater and, arguably, provides a more realistically negative picture of the prospects for closing the racial gap: "Whites possess nearly twelve times as much median net worth as blacks, or $43,800 versus $ 3,700. In an even starker contrast, perhaps, the average white household controls $6,999 in net financial assets while the average black household retains no NFA nest egg whatsoever." Moreover, the analytic focus on wealth rather than income exposes how illusory the much-trumpeted rise of a "black middle class" is: "Middle-class blacks, for example, earn seventy cents for every dollar earned by middle-class whites but they possess only fifteen cents for every dollar of wealth held by middleclass whites." This huge disparity in white and black wealth is not remotely contingent, accidental, fortuitous; it is the direct outcome of American state policy and the collusion with it of the white citizenry. In effect, "materially, whites and blacks constitute two nations,"[54] the white nation being constituted by the American Racial Contract in a relationship of structured racial exploitation with the black (and, of course, historically also the red) nation.

A collection of papers from panels organized in the 1980s by the National Economic Association, the professional organization of black economists, provides some insight into the mechanics and the magnitude of such exploitative transfers and denials of opportunity to accumulate material and human capital. It takes as its title *The Wealth of Races*—an ironic tribute to Adam Smith's famous book *The Wealth of Nations*—and analyzes the different varieties of discrimination to which blacks have been subjected: slavery, employment discrimination, wage discrimination, promotion discrimination, white monopoly power discrimination against black capital, racial price discrimination in consumer goods, housing, services, insurance, etc.[55] Many of these, by their very nature, are difficult to quantify; moreover, there are costs in anguish and suffering that can never really be compensated. Nonetheless, those that do lend themselves to calculation offer some remarkable figures. (The figures are unfortunately dated; readers should multiply by a factor that takes fifteen years of inflation into account.) If one were to do a calculation of the cumulative benefits (through compound interest) from labor market discrimination over the forty-year period from 1929 to 1969 and adjust for inflation, then in 1983 dollars, the figure would be over $1.6 trillion.[56] An estimate for the total of "diverted income" from slavery, 1790 to 1860, compounded and translated into 1983 dollars, would yield the sum of $2.1 trillion to $4.7 trillion.[57] And if one were to try to work out the cumulative value, with compound interest, of unpaid slave labor before 1863, underpayment since 1863, and denial of opportunity to acquire land and natural resources available to white settlers, then the total amount required to compensate blacks "could take more than the entire wealth of the United States."[58]

So this gives an idea of the centrality of racial exploitation to the U.S. economy and the dimensions of the payoff for its white beneficiaries from one nation's Racial Contract. But this very centrality, these very dimensions render the topic taboo, virtually undiscussed in the debates on justice of most white political theory. If there is such a backlash against affirmative action, what would the response be to the demand for the interest on the unpaid forty acres and a mule? These issues cannot be raised because they go to the heart of the real nature of the polity and its structuring by the Racial Contract. White moral theory's debates on justice in the state must therefore inevitably have a somewhat farcical air, since they ignore the central injustice on which the state rests. (No wonder a hypothetical contractarianism that evades the actual circumstances of the polity's founding is preferred!)

Both globally and within particular nations, then, white people, Europeans and their descendants, continue to benefit from the Racial Contract, which creates a world in their cultural image, political states differentially favoring their interests, an economy structured around the racial exploitation of others, and a moral psychology (not just in whites but sometimes in nonwhites also) skewed consciously or unconsciously toward privileging them, taking the status quo of differential racial entitlement as normatively legitimate, and not to be investigated further.

Questions for Discussion

1. What were the specific legal and political arrangements that formalized aspects of The Racial Contract? How did each contribute to the Racial Contract and, by extension, the material basis of The Racial Contract?

2. What does it mean that one can be a beneficiary to a contract without being a signatory to that contract? How does this interface with other ideas we've talked about in the class? How does it interface with you as a being in the historical, material, and philosophic continuum of relations you find yourself in?

3. If I steal something from you and I turn around and sell it before I'm caught, should the property I stole be returned to you once the authorities find out about all of this even though the property has changed hands? How does your answer here relate with the realization of the sheer amount of stolen wages (this does not include lost property, lost opportunities, slaying of leaders, burning of businesses, etc) as a result of America's slaving past?

4. Survey your society and present moment. What legal arrangements and discourse humanize the other and what arrangements and discourse dehumanize the other?

Citation and Use

The reading was taken from the following work:

Charles W. Mills, "Overview," in *The Racial Contract* (Cornell University Press, 1997).

This use of this work is governed by the Fair Use doctrine.

Notes

1. Otto Gierke termed these respectively the Gesellschaftsvertrag and the Herrschaftsvertrag. For a discussion, see, for example, Barker*, Introduction, Social Contract*; and Lessnoff, *Social Contract*, chap. 3.

2. Rawls, *Theory of Justice*, pt. 1.

3. In speaking generally of "whites," I am not, of course, denying that there are gender relations of domination and subordination or, for that matter, class relations of domination and subordination within the white population. I am not claiming that race is the only axis of social oppression. But race is what I want to focus on; so in the absence of that chimerical entity, a unifying theory of race, class, and gender oppression, it seems to me that one has to make generalizations that it would be stylistically cumbersome to qualify at every point. So these should just be taken as read. Nevertheless, I do want to insist that my overall picture is roughly accurate, i.e., that whites do in general benefit from white supremacy (though gender and class differentiation mean, of course, that they do not benefit equally) and that historically white racial solidarity has overridden class and gender solidarity. Women, subordinate classes, and nonwhites may be oppressed in common, but it is not a common oppression: the structuring is so different that it has not led to any common front between them. Neither white women nor white workers have as a group (as against principled individuals) historically made common cause with nonwhites against colonialism, white settlement, slavery, imperialism, Jim Crow, apartheid. We all have multiple identities, and, to this extent, most of us are both privileged and disadvantaged by different systems of domination. But white racial identity has generally triumphed over all others; it is race that (transgender, transclass) has generally determined the social world and loyalties, the lifeworld, of whites—whether as citizens of the colonizing mother country, settlers, nonslaves, or beneficiaries of the "color bar" and the "color line. There has been no comparable, spontaneously crystallizing transracial "workers'" world or transracial "female" world: race is the identity around which whites have usually closed ranks. Nevertheless, as a concession, a semantic signal of this admitted gender privileging within the white population, by which white women's personhood is originally virtual, dependent on their having the appropriate relation (daughter, sister, wife) to the white male, I will sometimes deliberately use the non-gender-neutral "men." For some recent literature on these problematic intersections of identity, see, for example, Ruth Frankenberg, *White Women, Race Matters: The Social Construction of Whiteness* (Minneapolis: University of Minnesota Press, 1993); Nupur Chaudhuri and Margaret Strobel, eds., *Western Women and Imperialism : Complicity and Resistance* (Bloomington: Indiana University Press, 1992); David Roediger, T*he Wages of Whiteness: Race and the Making of the American Working Class* (London: Verso, 1991).

4. Rousseau, Social Contract; Hobbes, Leviathan.

5. For a discussion of the two versions, see Kymlicka, "The Social Contract Tradition."

6. Hobbes's judgment that "INJUSTICE, is no other than the not Performance of Covenant," Leviathan, p. 100, has standardly been taken as a statement of moral conventionalism. Hobbes's egalitarian social morality is based not on the moral equality of humans, but on the fact of a rough parity of physical power and mental ability in the state of nature (chap. 13). Within this framework, the Racial Contract would then be the natural outcome of a systematic disparity in power—of weaponry rather than individual strength—between expansionist Europe and the rest of the world. This could be said to be neatly summed up in Hilaire Belloc's famous little ditty: "Whatever happens, we have got / The Maxim Gun, and they have not." Hilaire Belloc, "The Modern Traveller," quoted in John Ellis, The Social History of the Machine Gun (1975; rpt. Baltimore: Johns Hopkins Paperbacks, 1986), p. 94. Or at an earlier stage, in the conquest of the Americas, the musket and the steel sword.

7. See, for example, A. P. d'Entreves, Natural Law: An Introduction to Legal Philosophy, 2d rev. ed. (1951; rpt. London: Hutchinson, 1970).

8. Locke, Second Treatise of Two Treatises of Government, p. 269.

9. Kant, Metaphysics of Morals, pp. 230–32.

10. See Aithur O. Lovejoy, The Great Chain of Being: A Study of the History of an Idea (Cambridge: Harvard University Press, 1948).

11. For the notion of "epistemological communities," see recent work in feminist theory—for example, Linda Alcoff and Elizabeth Potter, eds., Feminist Epistemologies (New York: Routledge, 1993).

12. Thus Ward Churchill, a Native American, speaks sardonically of "fantasies of the master race." Ward Churchill, Fantasies of the Master Race: Literature, Cinema, and the Colonization of American Indians, ed. M. Annette Jaimes (Monroe, Maine: Common Courage Press, 1992); William Gibson, Neuromancer (New York: Ace Science Fiction Books, 1984).

13. Robert Young, White Mythologies: Writing History and the West (London: Routledge, 1990); Edward W. Said, Orientalism (1978; rpt. New York: Vintage Books, 1979); V. Y. Mudimbe, The Invention of Africa: Gnosis, Philosophy, and the Order of Knowledge (Bloomington: Indiana University Press, 1988); Enrique Dussel, The Invention of the Americas: Eclipse of "the Other" and the Myth of Modernity, trans. Michael D. Barber (1992; rpt. New York: Continuum, 1995); Robert Berkhofer Jr., The White Man's Indian: Images of the American Indian from Columbus to the Present (New York: Knopf, 1978); Gretchen M. Bataille and Charles L. P. Silet, eds., The Pretend Indians: Images of Native Americans in the Movies (Ames: Iowa State University Press, 1980); George M. Fredrickson, The Black Image in the White Mind: The Debate on Afro-American Character and Destiny, 1817–1914 (1971; rpt. Hanover, N.H.: Wesleyan University Press, 1987); Roberto Fernández Retamar, Caliban and Other Essays, trans. Edward Baker (Minneapolis: University of Minnesota Press, 1989); Peter Hulme, Colonial Encounters: Europe and the Native Caribbean, 1492–1797 (1986; rpt. London: Routledge, 1992).

14. Frederick Engels, The Origin of the Family, Private Property, and the State (New York: International, 1972), p. 120.

15. Jean-Paul Sartre, Preface to Frantz Fanon, The Wretched of the Earth, trans. Constance Farrington (1961; rpt. New York: Grove Weidenfeld, 1991).

16. V. G. Kiernan, The Lords of Human Kind: Black Man, Yellow Man, and White Man in an Age of Empire (1969; rpt. New York: Columbia University Press, 1986); Anthony Pagden, Lords of All World: Ideologies of Empire in Spain, Britain, and France, c. 1500–c. 1800 (New Haven: Yale University Press, 1995).

17. Pagden, Lord pp. 1–2.

18. Robert A. Williams Jr., "The Algebra of Federal Indian Law: The Hard Trail of Decolonizing and Americanizing the White Man's Indian Jurisprudence," Wisconsin Law Review 1986 (1986): 229. See also Robert A. Williams Jr., The American Indian in Western Legal Though t: The Discourses of Conquest (New York: Oxford University Press, 1 90).

19. Williams, "Algebra, " pp. 230–31, 233. See also Lewis Hanke, Aristotle and the American Indians: A Study in Race Prejudice in the Modern World (Bloomington: Indiana University Press, 1959), p. 19.

20. Williams, "Algebra"; Hanke, Aristotle.

21. Allen Carey-Webb, "Other-Fashioning: The Discourse of Empire and Nation in Lope de Vega's El Nuevo mundo descubierto por Cristobal Colon," in Amerindian Images and the Legacy of Columbus, ed. René Jara and Nicholas Spadaccini, Hispanic Issues, 9 (Minneapolis: University of Minnesota Press, 1992), pp. 433–34.

22. Philip D. Curtin, Introduction, to Imperialism, ed. Curtin (New York: Walker, 1971), p. xiii.

23. Pierre L. van den Berghe, Race and Racism: A Comparative Perspective, 2d ed. (New York: Wiley, 1978).

24. Pagden, Lords, chap. 1.

25. Williams, "Algebra," p. 253.

26. Justice Joseph Story, quoted in Williams, "Algebra," p. 256.

27. Dred Scott v. Sanford, 1857, in Race, Class, and Gender in the United States: An Integrated Study, ed. Paula S. Rothenberg, 3d ed. (New York: St. Martin's Press, 1995), p. 323.

28. Excerpt from Jules Harmand, Domination et colonisation (1910), in Curtin, Imperialism, pp. 294–98.

29. Edward W. Said, Culture and Imperialism (New York: Knopf, 1993), pp. xiv, xiii.

30. . Harold R. Isaacs, "Color in World Affairs," Foreign Affairs 47 (1969): 235, 246. See also Benjamin P. Bowser, ed.,

Racism and Anti-Racism in World Perspective (Thousand Oaks, Calif: Sage, 1995).

31. Helen Jackson, A Century of Dishonor: A Sketch of the United States Government's Dealings with Some of the Indian Tribes (1881; rpt. New York: Indian Head Books, 1993). In her classic expose, Jackson concludes (pp. 337–38): "It makes little difference . . . where one opens the record of the history of the Indians; every page and every year has its dark stain. The story of one tribe is the story of all, varied only by differences of time and place.... [T]he United States Government breaks promises now [1880] as deftly as then [1795], and with an added ingenuity from long practice." Jackson herself, it should be noted, saw Native Americans as having a "lesser right," since there was no question about the "fairness of holding that ultimate sovereignty belonged to the civilized discoverer, as against the savage barbarian." To think otherwise would merely be "feeble sentimentalism" (pp. 10-11). But she did at least want this lesser right recognized.

32. See, for example, David E. Stannard, American Holocaust: Columbus and the Conquest of the New World (New York: Oxford University Press, 1992).

33. Richard Drinnon, Facing West: The Metaphysics of IndianHating and Empire-Building (New York: Meridian, 1980), p. 332.

34. Ibid., p. 102. See also Reginald Horsman, Race and Manifest Destiny: The Origins of American Racial Anglo-Saxonism (Cambridge: Harvard University Press, 1981); and Ronald Takaki, Iron Cages: Race and Culture in 19th-Century America (1979; rpt. New York: Oxford University Press, 1990).

35. Van den Berghe, Race, p. 18.

36. C. Vann Woodward, The Strange Career of Tim Crow, 3d ed. (1955; rpt. New York: Oxford University Press, 1974); George M. Fredrickson, White Supremacy: A Comparative Study in American and South African History (New York: Oxford University Press, 1981); Douglas S. Massey and Nancy A. Denton, American Apartheid: Segregation and the Making of the Underclass (Cambridge: Harvard University Press, 1993).

37. See, for example, Kiernan, Lords; V. G. Kiernan, Imperialism and its Contradictions, ed. Harvey J. Kaye (New York: Routledge, 1995); D. K. Fieldhouse, The Colonial Empires: A Comparative Survey from the Eighteenth Century (1966; rpt. London: Macmillan, 1982); Pagden, Lords; Chinweizu, The West and the Rest of Us: White Predators, Black Slavers, and the African Elite (New York: Vintage Books, 1975); Henri Brunschwig, French Colonialism, 1871–1914: Myths and Realities, trans. William Granville Brown (1964; rpt. New York: Praeger, 1966); David Healy, U. S. Expansionism: The Imperialist Urge in the 1890s (Madison: University of Wisconsin Press, 1970).

38. Said, Culture, p. 8.

39. Kiernan, Lords, p. 24.

40. Linda Alcoff outlines an attractive, distinctively Latin American ideal of hybrid racial identity in her "Mestizo Identity," in American Mixed Race: The Culture of Microdiversity, ed. Naomi Zack (Lanham, Md.: Rowman and Littlefield, 1995), pp. 257–78. Unfortunately, however, this ideal has yet to be realized. For an exposure of the Latin American myths of "racial democracy" and a race-transcendent mestizaje, and an account of the reality of the ideal of blanqueamiento (whitening) and the continuing subordination of blacks and the darker-skinned throughout the region, see, for example, Minority Rights Group, ed., No Longer Invisible: Afro-Latin Americans Today (London: Minority Rights, 1995); and Bowser, Racism and Anti-Racism.

41. Locke, Second Treatise, pp. 350–51. Since Locke also uses "property" to mean rights, this is not quite as one-dimensional a vision of government as it sounds.

42. Hobbes, Leviathan, p. 89.

43. W. E. B. Du Bois, Black Reconstruction in America, 1860–1880 (1935; rpt. New York: Atheneum, 1992).

44. See Eric Jones, The European Miracle (Cambridge: Cambridge University Press, 1981). My discussion here follows J. M. Blaut et al., 1492: The Debate on Colonialism, Eurocentrism, and History (Trenton, N.J.: Africa World Press, 1992); and J. M. Blaut, The Colonizer's Model of the World: Geographical Diffusionism and Eurocentric History (New York: Guilford Press, 1993).

45. Blaut, 1492; Blaut, Colonizer's Model.

46. Sandra Harding, Introduction, to Harding, ed., The "Racial" Economy of Science: Toward a Democratic Future (Bloomington: Indiana University Press, 1993), p. 2.

47. Eric Williams, Capitalism and Slavery (1944; rpt. New York: Capricorn Books, 1966).

48. Walter Rodney, How Europe Underdeveloped Africa (1972; rpt. Washington, D.C.: Howard University Press,

1974); Samir Amin, Eurocentrism, trans. Russell Moore (1988: rpt. New York: Monthly Review Press, 1989); André Gunder Frank, World Accumulation, 1492–1789 (New York: Monthly Review Press, 1978); Immanuel Wallerstein, The Modern World System, 3 vols. (New York: Academic Press, 1974–1988).

49. Blaut, 1492, p. 3.

50. Kiernan, Imperialism, pp. 98, 149.

51. . Quoted in Noam Chomsky, Year 501: The Conquest Continues (Boston: South End Press, 1993), p. 61.

52. But see Richard J. Herrnstein and Charles Murray's bestseller The Bell Curve: Intelligence and Class Structure in American Life (New York: Free Press, 1994), as a sign that the older, straightforwardly racist theories may be making a comeback.

53. See, for example: Andrew Hacker, Two Nations: Black and White, Separate, Hostile, Unequal (New York: Scribner's, 1992); Derrick Bell, Faces at the Bottom of the Well: The Permanence of Racism (New York: BasicBooks, 1992); Massey and Denton, American Apartheid; Stephen Steinberg, Turning Back: The Retreat from Racial Justice in American Thought and Policy (Boston: Beacon Press, 1995); Donald R. Kinder and Lynn M. Sanders, Divided by Color: Racial Politics and Democratic Ideals (Chicago: University of Chicago Press, 1996); Tom Wicker, Tragic Failure: Racial Integration in America (New York: William Morrow, 1996).

54. Melvin L. Oliver and Thomas M. Shapiro, Black Wealth/White Wealth: A New Perspective on Racial Inequality (New York: Routledge 1995), pp. 86, 7.

55. Richard F. America, ed., The Wealth of Races: The Present Value of Benefits from Past Injustices (New York: Greenwood Press, 1990). For another ironic tribute, whose subject is the international distribution of wealth, see Malcolm Caldwell, The Wealth of Some Nations (London: Zed Press, 1977).

56. David H. Swinton, "Racial Inequality and Reparations," in America, Wealth of Races, p. 156.

57. James Marketti, "Estimated Present Value of Income Diverted during Slavery, " in America, Wealth of Races, p. 107.

58. Robert S. Browne, "Achieving Parity through Reparations," in America, Wealth of Races, p. 204; Swinton, "Racial Inequality, " p. 156.

ON MARXISM AND VALUE

Rasmin Canon

What it Means to be Marxist

It's unfortunate that there isn't a better word for "Marxism." Marx himself famously once said that he himself was "not a Marxist" if certain askew interpretations of his theories of historical materialism and capitalism were "Marxist." Part of the problem is that the theories and processes that Marx helped create are too big to fall under a single -ism; Marx was a philosopher (and sort of historian) of *political economy*, that is, the study of production and trade in relationship to laws, customs, and human systems, whose theories helped inform numerous other disciplines and practices: economics, sociology, history, literature and practical politics, among others.

The closest analogy that I can think of is to what we would today call "Darwinism," the theories of nineteenth century biologist Charles Darwin. Darwin didn't invent biology, paleontology, genetics, or any of the numerous disciplines and practices that are informed by "Darwinism." And in fact, there are many aspects of classical "Darwinism"—the theories and conclusions arrived at by Darwin and his immediate disciples—that have been outright revised or rejected by people who today would *still* consider themselves "Darwinists." Since Darwin published *On the Origin of Species* and *The Descent of Man*, hundreds if not thousands of scientists and philosophers have expanded on and improved on Darwin's theories (the so-called "modern synthesis")—obviously a necessity since during Darwin's lifetime there was no deep concept of molecular genetics.

It's useful to think of Marxism the same way. Marxism is not a detailed plan for how to create socialism. Marxism isn't a moral philosophy, in the way that the Enlightenment philosophers and their progeny—like John Rawls—tried to build up moral systems from first principles to determine what is the most "fair." It does not instruct us to engage in violent insurrection.

Marx, through his analysis of human society, gave us an understanding of the laws governing how society develops and how we can understand the process of history. His theories of alienation and class struggle inform us as to the causes of human misery and the obstacles to human flourishing. This is the "historical materialism" that is the strongest single thread of his work. Historical materialism is, simply stated, the theory that human societies develop according to how the "forces of production" are ordered, and that the features of a society will, ultimately, relate back to the ordering of the forces of production. People will "relate" to the system of production as a class. Therefore, the core conflict in society has been between classes on opposing sides of the systems of production—this is the *dialectical* part of his theory.

Just as Darwin was not the first "evolutionist," Marx was not by any means the first socialist. And as with Darwin and the word "evolution," "socialism" meant something fairly different before Marx came along. Socialism was basically a moral system, sometimes rooted in Christian values, utopian in character and justified based on what was "fair" or "just." Marx and Engels spent much of their active years differentiating their theories from prior theories of "utopian" socialism built on moral persuasion—Engels going as far as to publish a book-length pamphlet on it.

Darwin revolutionized existing theories of "evolution" by introducing the concept of *natural selection over geologic time*—he should better be remembered for the theory of natural selection than evolution; the early title of his book *Origin of Species* was *Natural Selection*. In the same way, Karl Marx took existing historical and philosophical analysis of human society and political economy and applied an *objective* approach, from which he developed the theory of historical materialism/dialectical materialism.

What Marxism teaches us is simply to approach questions of society from a material basis: how does human life persist? Through production of the goods and services needed to live. How are these things produced under capitalist society? Through exploitation of the labor of the working class, that is, by requiring one class of people to sell their labor as a commodity to another class to produce values. What is the result of this system? That workers are "alienated" from their labor, meaning from much of their waking life, constantly required to produce more and more with an ever-precarious access to the means of subsistence.

If we want to engage in political competition and analysis of what Marx would have called "political economy," there isn't an alternative to Marxism that has anything near its explanatory power or guidance. That said, I understand the caution many socialists or social democrats may have to subscribing to "Marxism": Marx's focus on class "struggle," the "overthrow" of the capitalist class, and the "dictatorship of the proletariat," all of which may strike modern American ears as prescriptions for violence and authoritarianism.

It's important to understand what Marx meant by these things.

The class struggle doesn't necessarily mean barricades in the streets and summary execution of plutocrats. That these things *can* result from struggle is a historical fact; but the "struggle" Marx is talking about is the social and political competition between classes, which is always present: whether in the form of wage demands, petitions, law changes, strikes, non-compliance, all the way up to armed revolt. In the *Manifesto*, Marx describes how sometimes, the capitalists will cave in to demands made via demonstrations and strikes; other times, they will resist until concessions are forcibly extracted. Only the relative strength of the sides determines the nature of the struggle. The whole point of Marx's method is to understand that the struggle is inherent to the capitalist system; it is *objective*. How socialists choose strategically to win the struggle depends on many factors, including the avenues available to them to win changes to the system—this is *subjective*. Whether we like it or not, the way commodities are produced under capitalism will always require struggle between the classes; workers want more, capitalists want them to have less and less.

As for "overthrow," Marx looks at how previous systems of production were ended and changed into new forms: from hunter-gatherer to militarized, to slave chiefdoms and kingdoms, to feudalism, and then to capitalism. It is true that these transitions were generally marked by periods of violent competition; but (just like with Darwinism) historical study has showed that the violent outbursts were not the chief or only means of change. In fact, decades, sometimes centuries, of smaller changes accumulated over time to put stress on existing systems and bring about major changes. This is especially true of capitalism, which arose in Europe not all at once after the French beheaded enough nobles, but took place over an extended period beginning as far back as the Fourteenth Century. The growth of state-like kingdoms, "free" trading cities, incremental changes in technology, improvements in communications and logistics, and changes in legal systems eroded the basis of feudalism; the French Revolution was one part of a much longer and broader process of change.

Perhaps most misunderstood is the idea of the "dictatorship of the proletariat," which comes from the *Manifesto*

and a work called *Critique of the Gotha Program*, but is often interpreted according to the later theories of Vladimir Lenin. The dictatorship of the proletariat does not mean revolutionary terror against class enemies and the death of freedom. It means something very simple: look around you. Do you see how in "free market" democracies, political power is monopolized (or nearly monopolized) by the ownership class? The "dictatorship" of the proletariat just flips this. For Marxists, the dictatorship of the proletariat simply means a period where political power is held *in common* for the sole benefit of the *working class*. Getting to this point requires the working class to realize it is in fact a single class, and acting in its own interests. That this be accompanied by violent revolution isn't necessary.

Dictatorship is bad. We live under a form of dictatorship today: a dictatorship on behalf of the capitalist class. This doesn't mean working class people have zero freedoms; it means that the states we live in are specifically organized to protect *the capitalist system of social relations*. Some people can own the means of production and the rest of us have to sell our labor to survive. The dictatorship of the proletariat just inverts this: it organizes the state to preserve the *common ownership of the means of production*.

Marx and Engels were critical of moral and "fairness" arguments for socialism because they were ahistorical; they lacked a truly rational basis, and were therefore just formed by ruling class ideology. This isn't unique to Marx, either: a contemporary philosopher, Bernard Williams (no socialist himself) is among the definitive moral philosophers who rejects the idea that we can reason our way to morality. Historically, the forces of production—the thing that determines human flourishing—had never been reordered through moral argument; it had required engaging in struggle—in political competition. Marx was not trying to provoke people into violence. He was merely exposing and acknowledging that the forces of production create a class struggle, which *will resolve in a change to the forces of production*.

As socialists post-Marx, as with biologists post-Darwin, we merely accept the material reality of the system we live in. The forces of production rest on exploitation to extract "surplus value" and requires commodifying labor, which alienates workers. Struggle is inherent to the capitalist system. Only when workers become conscious of themselves as a class and act on their own behalf will they act to affirmatively end the system. There isn't really a deep question of morality here; this isn't about fairness. It is about the struggle between those who control their own destiny and are not alienated from their means of subsistence (capitalists) and those who want this condition for themselves, but are kept from it (the working class).

A word about violence. Like most people, I abhor violence. Violence degrades its perpetrators as it harms its victims. Marx does not prescribe violence, although he does treat it as an obviously common outcome of periods of dramatic change in the forces of production—that is, in periods of "overthrow." We need to ask ourselves whether major social change has ever avoided violence, and where that violence came from. Consider the U.S. civil rights movement, treated in historical memory as the best example of change from "non-violence." But wasn't there violence? The fact is that the state, and individuals, reacted to the demands of Black Americans with violence. There *was* violence during the civil rights movement; it just wasn't meted out on a large scale *by those demanding their rights*. And once those demands were won, there was "violence" of another sort—when the state prosecuted and rounded up hate groups, like the Klan for example, that was a sort of state "violence" we would consider appropriate. Not to mention that attacks on freedom fighters, whether they were freedom riders, civil rights lawyers, or a person protecting their home from a lynch mob, always entailed violence.

And what about the labor movement? From private guards to local police to the federal army, violence was regularly called down on those engaging in struggle to win rights in the workplace. The U.S. labor movement, in fact, was *particularly* marked by violence, even over its European counterparts, especially in the mountain west where mining and energy concerns regularly called down armed forces to break strikes. Struggle for the workers were strikes and non-compliance; the *reaction* was violence.

In historical struggle, those clinging to the system under attack are the first to resort to violence. To be a Marxist doesn't require belief in an armed uprising to bring about a new world, in violent change or authoritarianism. It just means acknowledging as a fact something that already exists: the class struggle. The tactics and strategies workers employ to achieve class consciousness and act to end the exploitative system are ours to determine.

Why contemporary socialism is entwined with Marxism is this understanding of how history moves and how it will move, based not on the moral arguments we make, but on the *objective conditions* we live in. Workers will not struggle against abstract principles but against living human beings with material interests. In his *Eighteenth Brumaire of Louis Napoleon*, Marx wrote that "men make their own history, but they do not make it as they please." We can only change the world if we truly understand the actual forces around us. If we want to change the world, we need to be in it, to build from it; to truly be in it, we need to understand it. That makes us Marxists.

Value

Why does a tree catch fire so easily? Every tree holds in its cells the energy it has absorbed from the sun. We don't think of trees as energetic, but in fact, to grow like they do, trees have to absorb and store an immense amount of energy. When touched by fire, that energy is released—the captured energy from the sun, stored in the cells, is released. A tree is a tree, a fixed thing in the world we can climb or sleep under or chop down for wood or sell. A tree is also a process, a relationship between different processes—the interaction of soil, water, energy, air, and animal life.

Soil is formed by the deposit and interaction of minerals, water, and organic matter, being churned up by rain, worms, ants and other animals, and wind. The seed of a tree falls into the soil and is fed by the soil's nutrients and sunlight. The sunlight itself is part of a process—the thermonuclear reactions of the sun, the travel of the rays of sunlight to the Earth. Rain, too, is part of atmospheric and meteorological processes. All these processes interact to bring the seed into a sapling and the sapling into a tree. The tree itself contains bits of all of these process in its own process of growing.

A tree isn't just a tree: it is a physical expression of *and contains* these processes, most of which we never see. What we see is what we get out of the tree. Wood, relief from the sun, comfort from the rain. What goes into making the tree, what we enjoy the tree for, and what we can get *for* a tree we might all think of separately, but they're knotted together in a way that can't be unravelled. Still, we understand these different parts of "tree-ness" pretty instinctively.

So it goes for Marx's theory of value. Value is one of the most complicated concepts in Marx's work, so we'll go easy for this one. But there are three big categories of "value" that are important for us to understand in radical work: the labor value, use value and exchange value.

The stuff we buy and sell, the stuff of life—commodities—contains and expresses these three kinds of value: labor, use, and exchange values.

The labor value is the "socially-necessary labor time" (SNLT) necessary to make the commodity. In a capitalist economy, for example, a house is a commodity we buy and sell, and it has value based on the *socially-necessary* labor time to make it. By "socially necessary" Marx meant the "average" time the worker or workers would have to spend, using the average productivity and average tools in use at the time the house was built. All of the different bits needed to build that house also had to be produced themselves—the gypsum for the drywall, the wood for the frame, the concrete for the foundation, the architect's time. There is labor time in these, too. The final house has a certain amount of "embodied labor" in it. With automation (labor-saving equipment), the SNLT goes down; but rarely do workers end up working *less*; to the contrary, the time-savings results in ever more production of commodities. Why? Well, because commodities have "use-values."

The use value is more or less what it sounds like: it is what human beings get out of a commodity. In the case of the house, it has many use-values: a house gives us shelter, storage for our stuff, a sense of place; but it can also give us access to schools, and amenities by its proximity to cultural or natural centers. We get the use-value of a thing when we use it. We can assign a thing a use-value separately from its "labor value," and our trusty tree helps us understand why: a typical forest tree required no human labor to come into being, but we would certainly value it for the shade or wood it would provide us. So "use-value" isn't really tied to the "embodied labor" value—it isn't built into the thing itself.

It is a "relation" of the thing to the individuals who have a want for it. But there's no doubt that commodities, the stuff of life, have a use-value.

In capitalist economies, commodities will also have an "exchange-value," which, mercifully, is also what it sounds like: the worth of a thing in an exchange for another thing or things. This isn't the same as its *price* (which is an important difference we'll see in a minute). The exchange value is the value one commodity or quantity of commodities will get for another or other commodities. In capitalism, exchange-value gets reduced to *price*, but they are not the same thing.

The reason is that our work and ideas are commodities that we sell. The "socially-necessary labor time" that goes into a commodity is sold and paid for; we "commodify" our labor. The house has all that "embodied labor" in it; and when we sell the house, that embodied labor is being purchased. We look at the house and see shelter, and storage, and a school district; we look at the tree and see shade, and shelter, and wood; but running through those things are processes invisible to us. The house, like the tree, contains the energy spent to bring it into being. This is the labor running through it.

People want the house for the use-value, but cannot acquire it without exchange. The exchange value is related to—but not exclusively made up of—the socially-necessary labor-time, the "embodied labor" in the house. In the modern economy, this is expressed by the "price." Although exchange value and price are not the same thing, in modern market economies, price is the basic way we see exchange value.

In fact, price is the thing that "hides" the embodied labor. Again, this is something we get instinctively. A rare comic book has a limited use value to a limited number of people, and its price won't reflect the embodied labor in it. Similarly, a ratty house that happens to be in a good school district will have an exchange value-through-price higher than the embodied labor. Marx called this "commodity fetishism," and it is a reason why we don't "see" the labor value of commodities; it's why an iPhone 7 that costs $220 to make (including all labor, marketing, taxes, etc.) can sell for $650.

If this all seems pretty technical and not very relevant for radical work, it certainly can be; and there is a lot of debate about how relevant Marx's concepts of "value" are given modern advances in economic thought. But at their very basic levels, there is something very important to take away from the theories of value.

That is how commodities—not just things, but labor and ideas—have a *use value* that is distinct from its exchange value and/or price. Think of how in cities with thousands of people suffering homelessness, there are foreclosed homes boarded up, or second homes kept empty by absentee owners for short-term vacation rentals. The use-value of these commodities for people without them is intensely important, but it's the exchange values that determine how they're distributed.

In fact, it's the wild-eyed chase for higher and higher exchange values (as "prices"), instead of the reasonable distribution of use-values, that leaves so many people with so little and so few people with so much. Those who own much can't afford to let the use-values slip from their grasp, because it drives down the price. In fact, as with the case of boarded up homes, *they'd rather destroy the use-values than make them available to those in need.* Housing is an obvious example, but there are many others. The United States, and the West in general, produces use-values from clothing to food to housing to transportation, in surplus abundance, but finds ways to restrict them to only those who can afford the exchange value. This is the "artificial scarcity" that keeps us at each others' throats.

Understanding value types helps us understand why our society doesn't have to work this way. When we see cases of water held behind armed guard during a hurricane, we can point to that and say, we know what the social cost of producing that is; we know its value in *use* to people who don't have it; why isn't it being distributed rationally? Why is the entire distribution system of use-values built on the merciless drive for ever-higher exchange values?

When we understand the processes that went into making a tree and appreciate its uses, we're a step closer to seeing the world as it really is.

Citation and Use

The reading was taken from the following sources.

Canon, Ramsin. "Primer Red (Part 4): Value." Midwest Socialist (blog), October 24, 2017. http://midwestsocialist.com/2017/10/24/primer-red-part-4-value/.

———. "What It Means to Be a Marxist." Midwest Socialist (blog), November 29, 2018. http://midwestsocialist.com/2018/11/29/what-it-means-to-be-a-marxist/.

PUBLIC LUXURY AND PRIVATE SUFFICIENCY

George Monboit

Several people have asked whether the rich world will accept the "drastic cuts in living standards" required to prevent environmental breakdown. I understand the question, and it is true that no one ever rioted for austerity. But I think there's a different way of looking at it.

We have been induced to believe that our living standards are secured through private luxury. We have been encouraged, by advertising, marketing, the media and politics, to seek ever more for ourselves: bigger houses, bigger cars, more stuff to fill them with. But there is neither the physical nor ecological space for everyone to enjoy private luxury. If all the people of London got their own swimming pool and tennis court, London would cover all of England. We are quickly discovering the ecological limits of everyone seeking a mountain of stuff, as this pursuit sends us crashing through planetary boundaries. The reality is that one person's private luxury is another person's deprivation: the rich, under this system, intrude into the physical and ecological space needed by others.

However, there is enough physical and ecological space for everyone to enjoy public luxury: magnificent public parks and swimming pools, excellent mass transit systems (electric trams, trains, monorail etc), a rich cultural life that fills the void consumerism seeks – and fails – to fill. We can have a great quality of life and remain within ecological limits, but we have to give up the notion that we will achieve it on our own, through private accumulation. We can achieve it together, through the pooling of wealth. I've sought to boil this philosophy down to one phrase:

Private Sufficiency, Public Luxury

Citation and Use

The reading was taken from the following source.

Monbiot, George. "Author Comment, The Earth Is in a Death Spiral. It Will Take Radical Action to Save Us." News. The Guardian, November 2018. https://www.theguardian.com/commentisfree/2018/nov/14/earth-death-spiral-radical-action-climate-breakdown#comment-122502985.